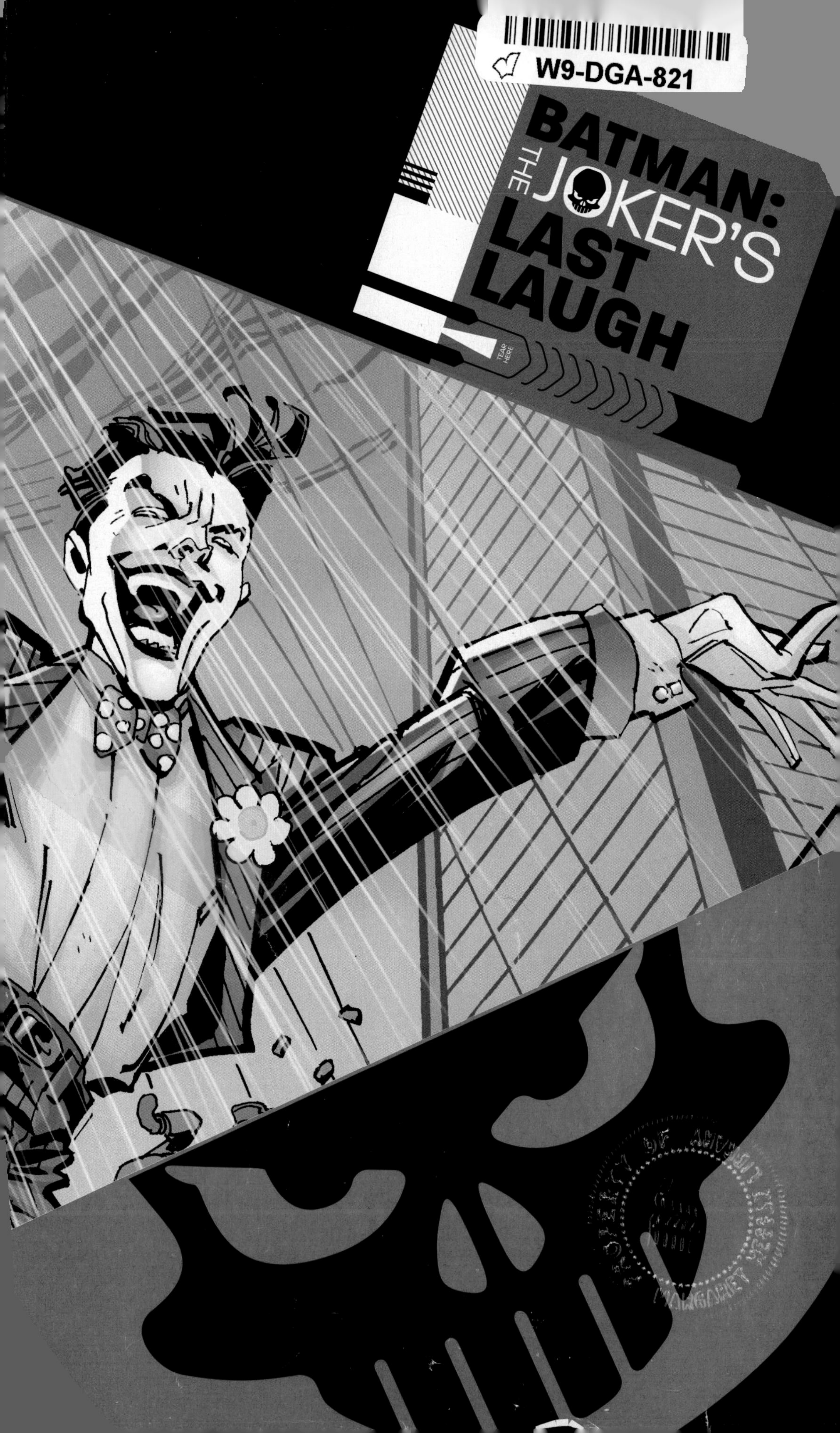
BATMAN:
THE JOKER'S
LAST
LAUGH
TEAR HERE

# BATMAN: THE JOKER'S LAST LAUGH

TEAR HERE

Written by
**Chick Dixon** and **Scott Beatty**

Pencilled by
**Pete Woods, Marcos Martin,
Walter McDaniel, Andy Kuhn,
Ron Randall, Rick Burchett**

Inked by
**Andrew Pepoy, Mark Farmer, Alvaro Lopez,
Walter McDaniel, Andy Kuhn, Ron Randall,
Mark Lipka, Dan Davis**

Colored by
**Tom McCraw, Gina Going**

Lettered by
**Willie Schubert**

Original series covers by
**Brian Bolland** (#1, #6)
**Scott McDaniel** and **Klaus Janson** (#2-5)

**Batman created by Bob Kane**

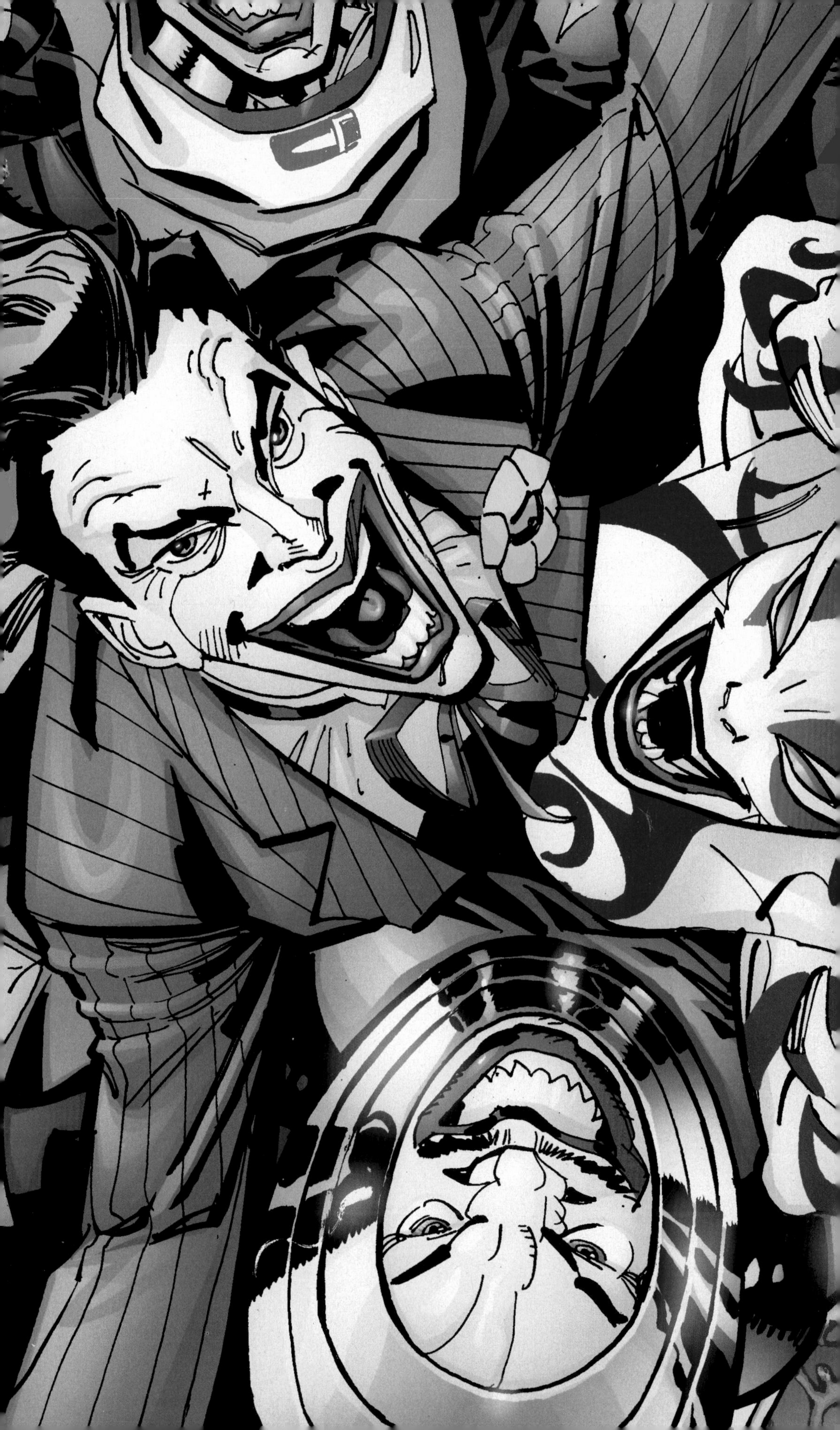

Dan DiDio   Senior VP-Executive Editor
Matt Idelson   Editor-original series
Nachie Castro   Assistant Editor-original series
Scott Nybakken   Editor-collected edition
Robbin Brosterman   Senior Art Director
Louis Prandi   Art Director
Paul Levitz   President & Publisher
Georg Brewer   VP-Design & DC Direct Creative
Richard Bruning   Senior VP-Creative Director
Patrick Caldon   Executive VP-Finance & Operations
Chris Caramalis   VP-Finance
John Cunningham   VP-Marketing
Terri Cunningham   VP-Managing Editor
Alison Gill   VP-Manufacturing
David Hyde   VP-Publicity
Hank Kanalz   VP-General Manager, WildStorm
Jim Lee   Editorial Director-WildStorm
Paula Lowitt   Senior VP-Business & Legal Affairs
MaryEllen McLaughlin   VP-Advertising & Custom Publishing
John Nee   Senior VP-Business Development
Gregory Noveck   Senior VP-Creative Affairs
Sue Pohja   VP-Book Trade Sales
Steve Rotterdam   Senior VP-Sales & Marketing
Cheryl Rubin   Senior VP-Brand Management
Jeff Trojan   VP-Business Development, DC Direct
Bob Wayne   VP-Sales

Cover illustrations by Brian Bolland.

**BATMAN: THE JOKER'S LAST LAUGH**

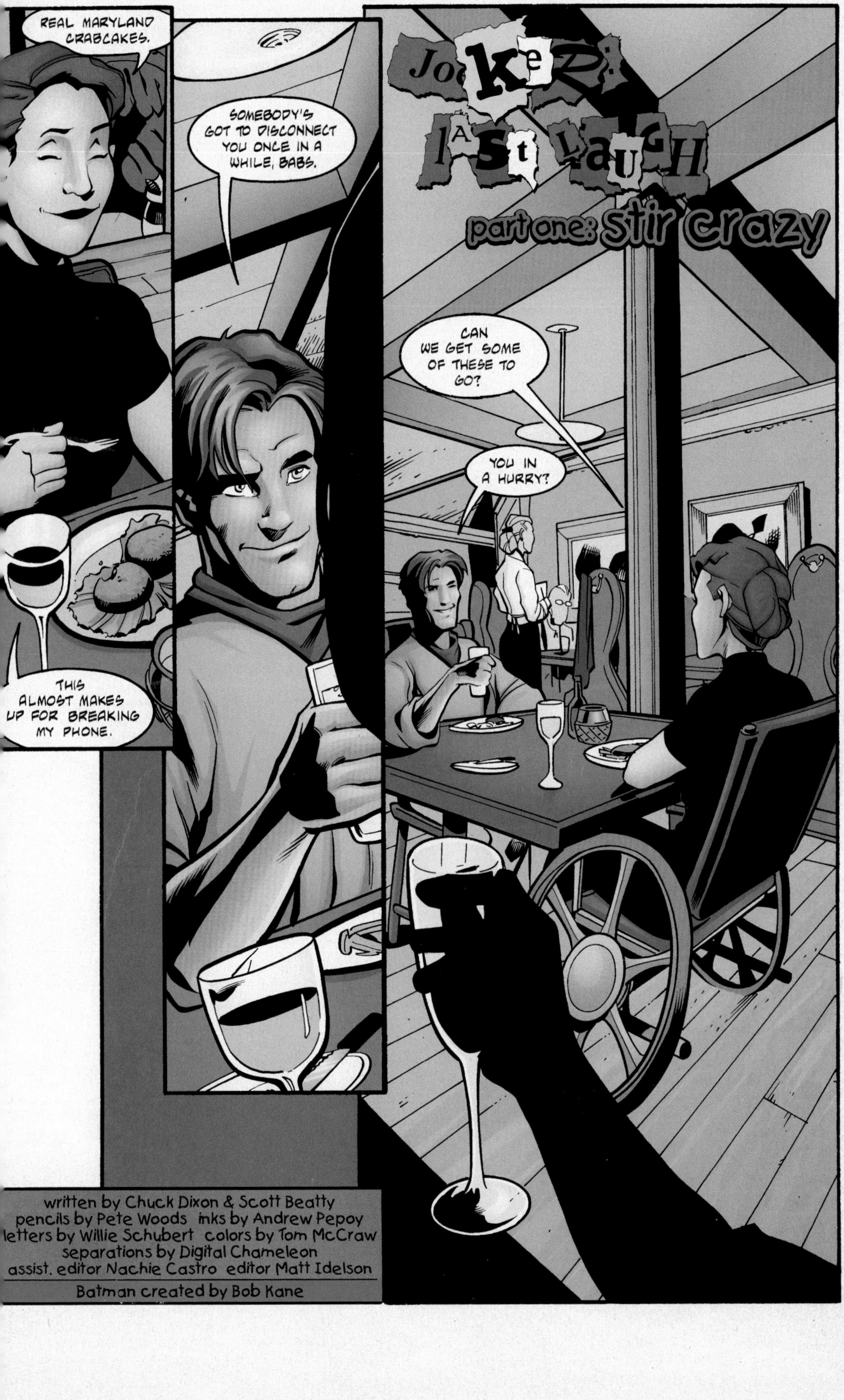
REAL MARYLAND CRABCAKES.
THIS ALMOST MAKES UP FOR BREAKING MY PHONE.
SOMEBODY'S GOT TO DISCONNECT YOU ONCE IN A WHILE, BABS.
JOKER: LAST LAUGH
part one: Stir Crazy
CAN WE GET SOME OF THESE TO GO?
YOU IN A HURRY?
written by Chuck Dixon & Scott Beatty
pencils by Pete Woods inks by Andrew Pepoy
letters by Willie Schubert colors by Tom McCraw
separations by Digital Chameleon
assist. editor Nachie Castro editor Matt Idelson
Batman created by Bob Kane

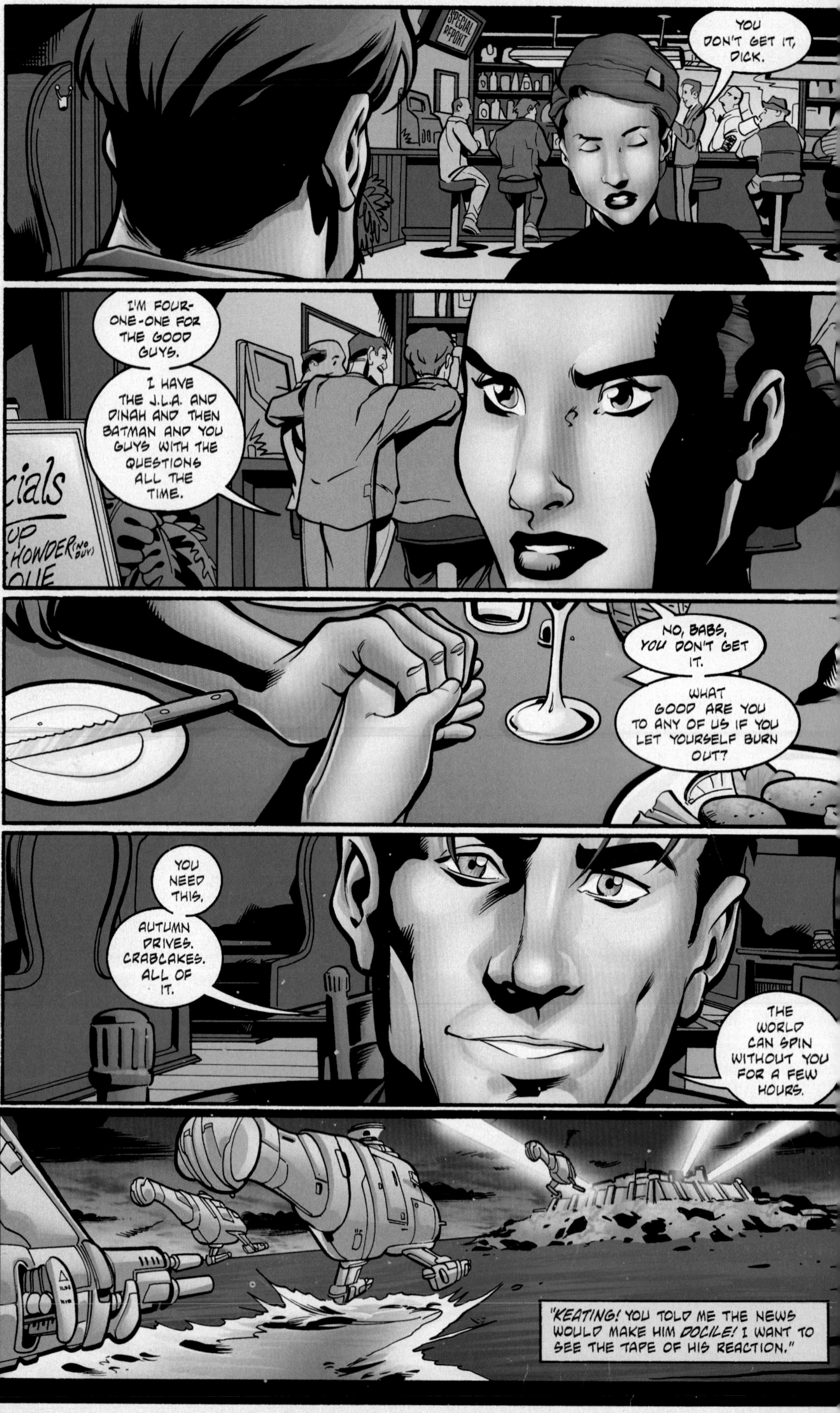
SPECIAL REPORT
YOU DON'T GET IT, DICK.
I'M FOUR-ONE-ONE FOR THE GOOD GUYS.
I HAVE THE J.L.A. AND DINAH AND THEN BATMAN AND YOU GUYS WITH THE QUESTIONS ALL THE TIME.
NO, BABS, YOU DON'T GET IT.
WHAT GOOD ARE YOU TO ANY OF US IF YOU LET YOURSELF BURN OUT?
YOU NEED THIS.
AUTUMN DRIVES. CRABCAKES. ALL OF IT.
THE WORLD CAN SPIN WITHOUT YOU FOR A FEW HOURS.
"*KEATING!* YOU TOLD ME THE NEWS WOULD MAKE HIM *DOCILE!* I WANT TO SEE THE TAPE OF HIS REACTION."

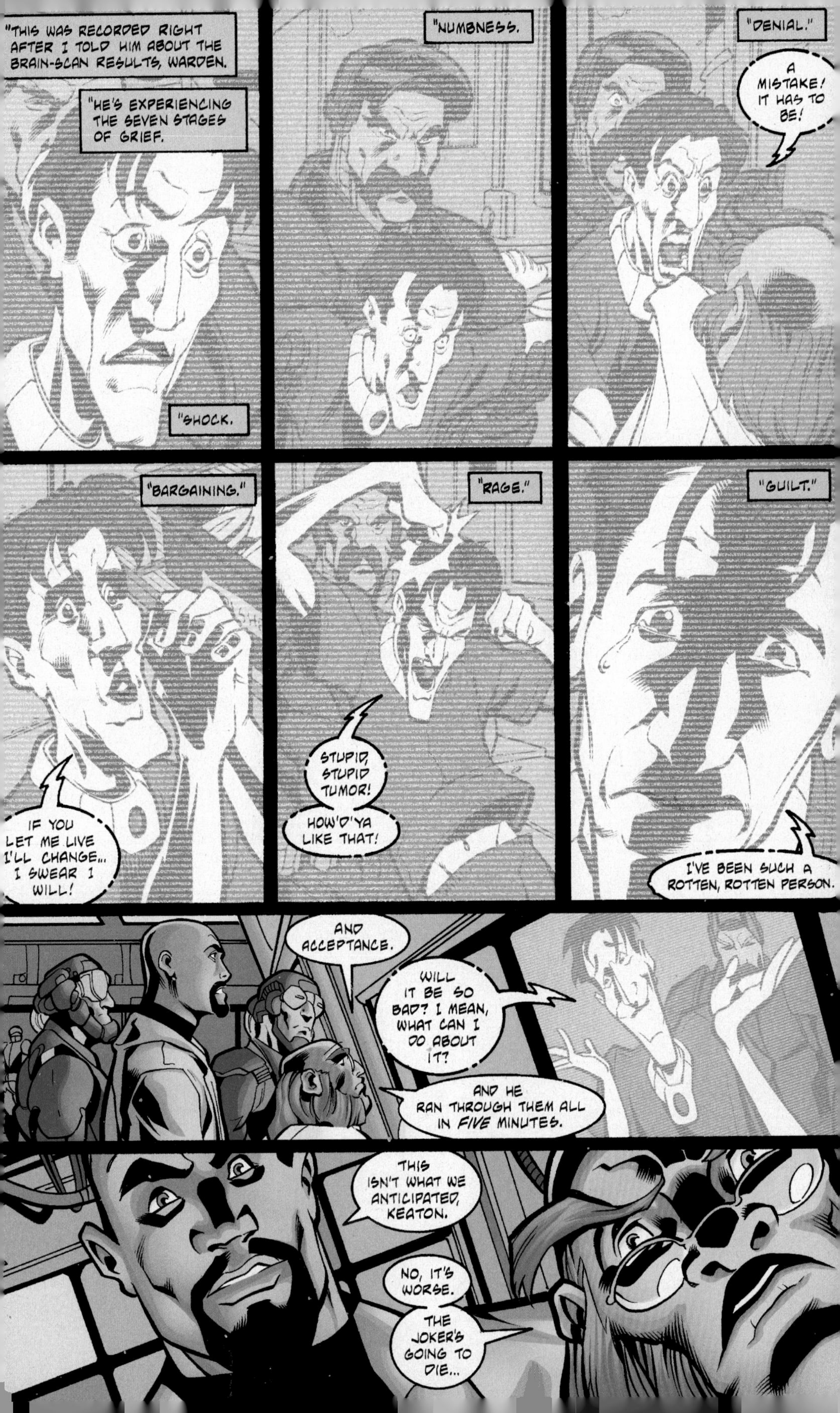

"THIS WAS RECORDED RIGHT AFTER I TOLD HIM ABOUT THE BRAIN-SCAN RESULTS, WARDEN.
"HE'S EXPERIENCING THE SEVEN STAGES OF GRIEF.
"SHOCK.
"NUMBNESS.
"DENIAL."
A MISTAKE! IT HAS TO BE!
"BARGAINING."
IF YOU LET ME LIVE I'LL CHANGE... I SWEAR I WILL!
"RAGE."
STUPID, STUPID TUMOR!
HOW'D'YA LIKE THAT!
"GUILT."
I'VE BEEN SUCH A ROTTEN, ROTTEN PERSON.
AND ACCEPTANCE.
WILL IT BE SO BAD? I MEAN, WHAT CAN I DO ABOUT IT?
AND HE RAN THROUGH THEM ALL IN FIVE MINUTES.
THIS ISN'T WHAT WE ANTICIPATED, KEATON.
NO, IT'S WORSE.
THE JOKER'S GOING TO DIE...

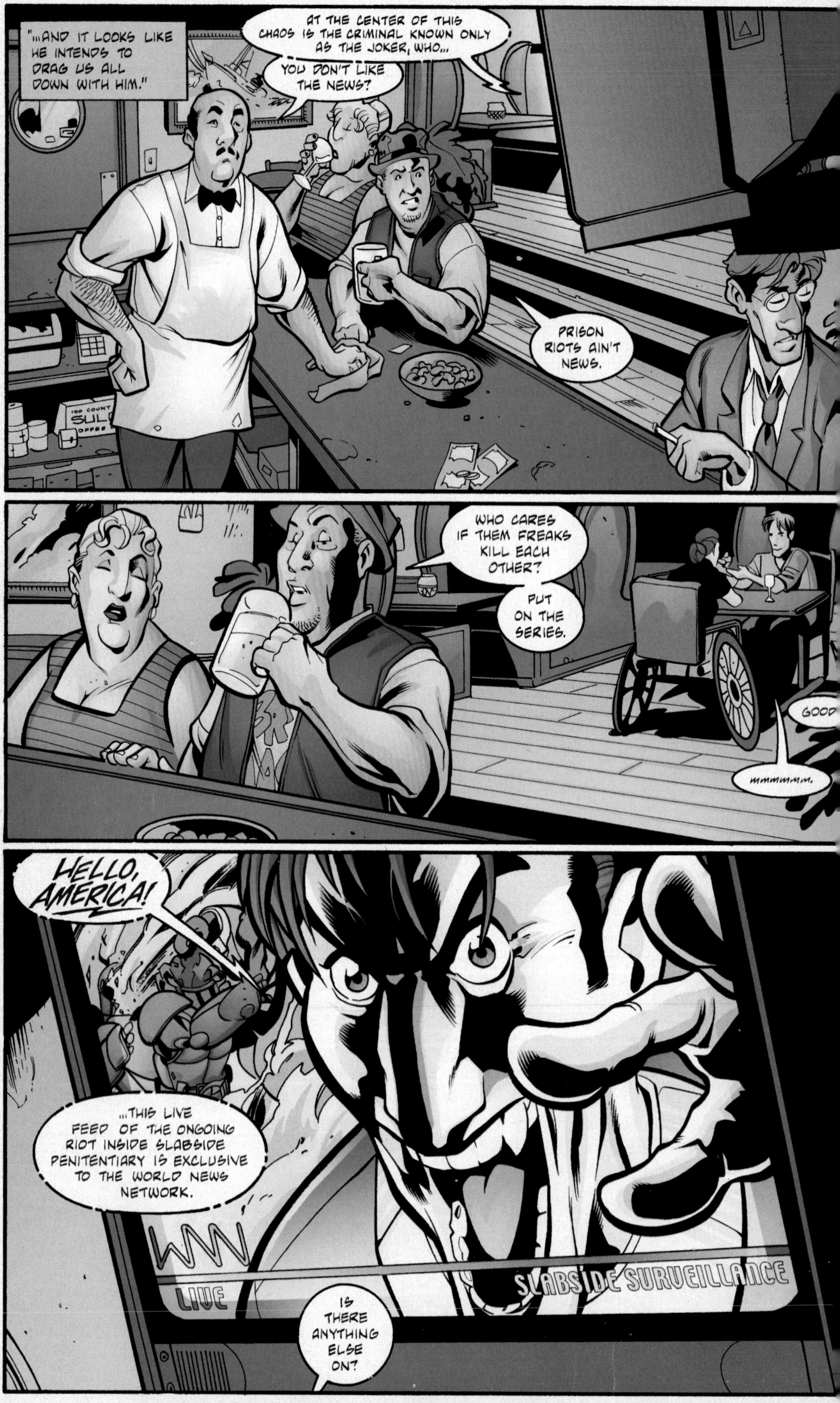
"...AND IT LOOKS LIKE HE INTENDS TO DRAG US ALL DOWN WITH HIM."
AT THE CENTER OF THIS CHAOS IS THE CRIMINAL KNOWN ONLY AS THE JOKER, WHO...
YOU DON'T LIKE THE NEWS?
PRISON RIOTS AIN'T NEWS.
WHO CARES IF THEM FREAKS KILL EACH OTHER?
PUT ON THE SERIES.
GOOD
mmmmmm.
HELLO, AMERICA!
...THIS LIVE FEED OF THE ONGOING RIOT INSIDE SLABSIDE PENITENTIARY IS EXCLUSIVE TO THE WORLD NEWS NETWORK.
WNN
LIVE
SLABSIDE SURVEILLANCE
IS THERE ANYTHING ELSE ON?

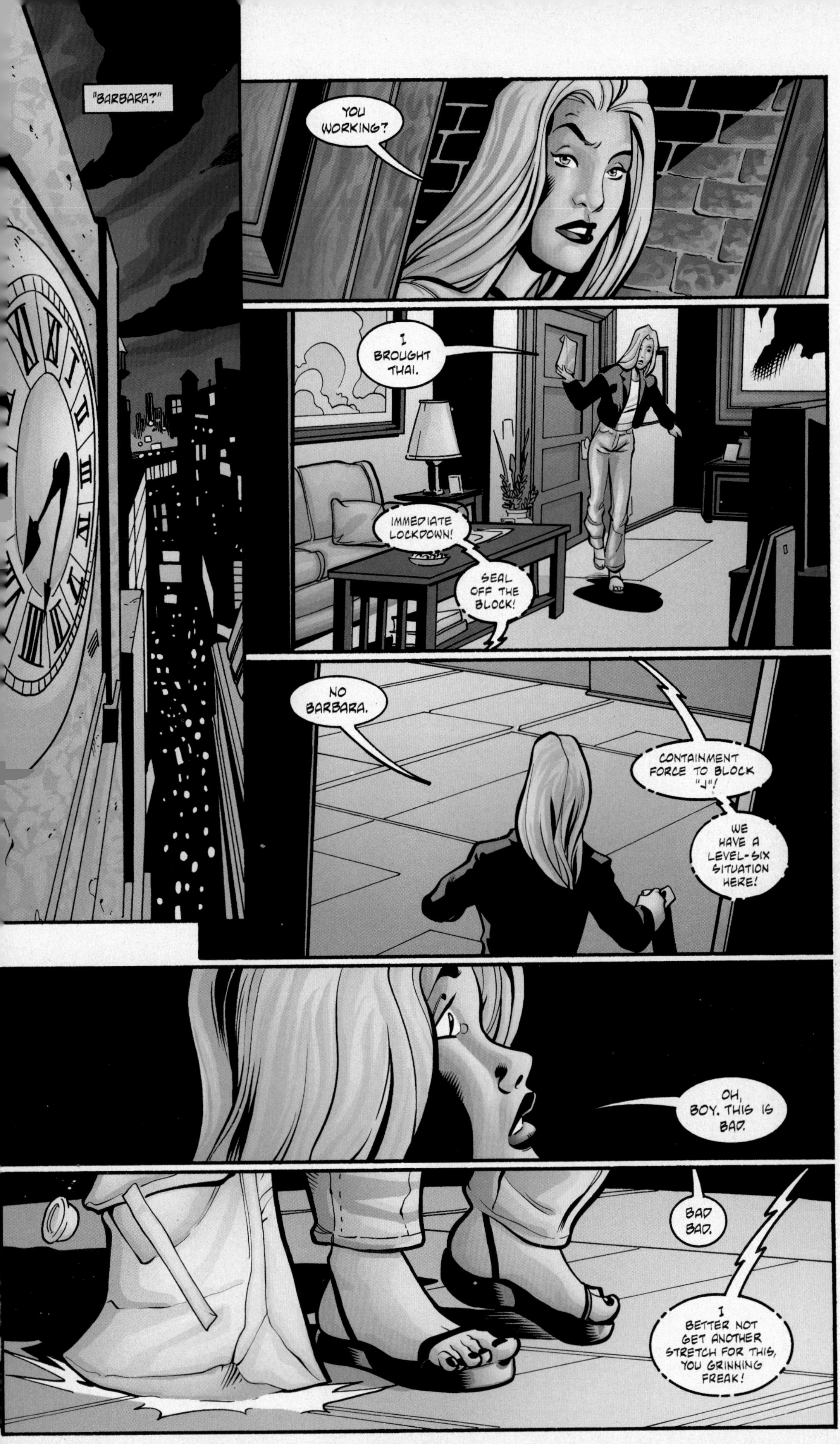
"BARBARA?"
YOU WORKING?
I BROUGHT THAI.
IMMEDIATE LOCKDOWN!
SEAL OFF THE BLOCK!
NO BARBARA.
CONTAINMENT FORCE TO BLOCK "J"!
WE HAVE A LEVEL-SIX SITUATION HERE!
OH, BOY. THIS IS BAD.
BAD BAD.
I BETTER NOT GET ANOTHER STRETCH FOR THIS, YOU GRINNING FREAK!

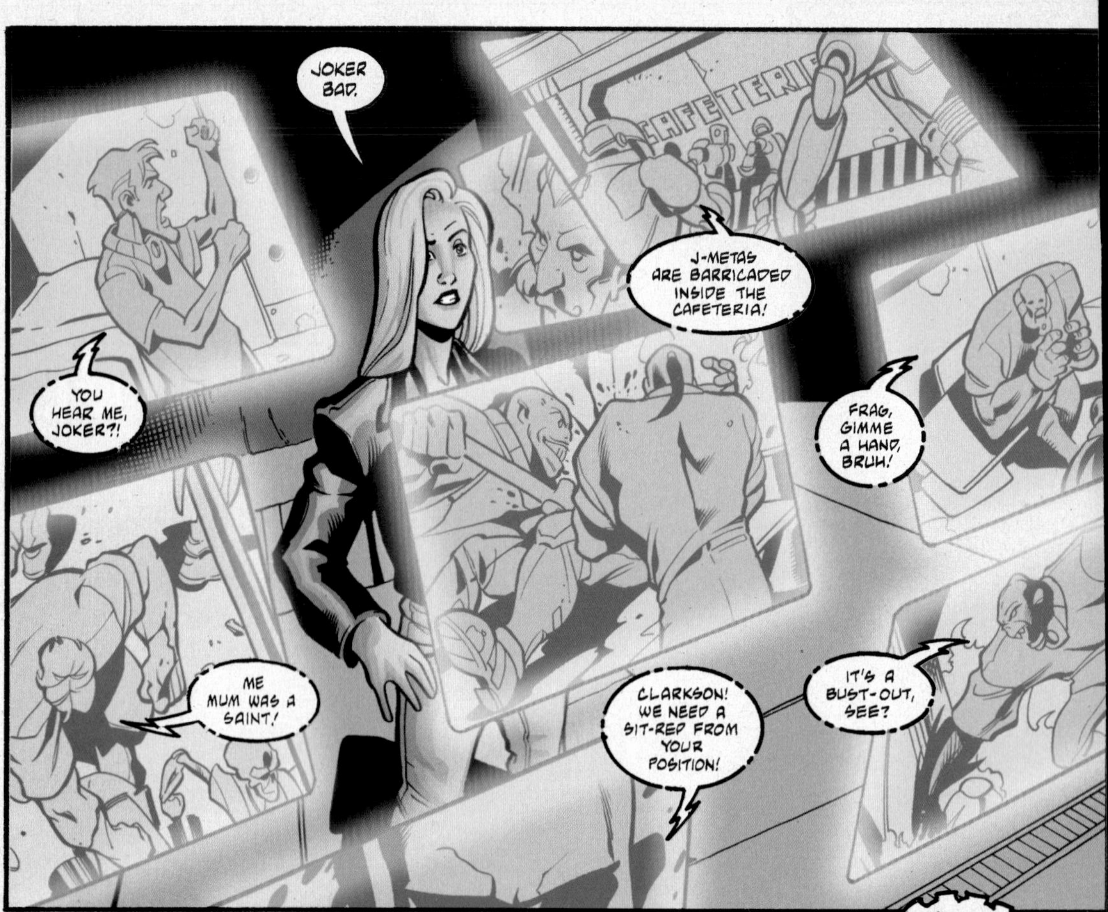
JOKER BAD.
J-METAS ARE BARRICADED INSIDE THE CAFETERIA!
YOU HEAR ME, JOKER?!
FRAG, GIMME A HAND, BRUH!
ME MUM WAS A SAINT!
CLARKSON! WE NEED A SIT-REP FROM YOUR POSITION!
IT'S A BUST-OUT, SEE?

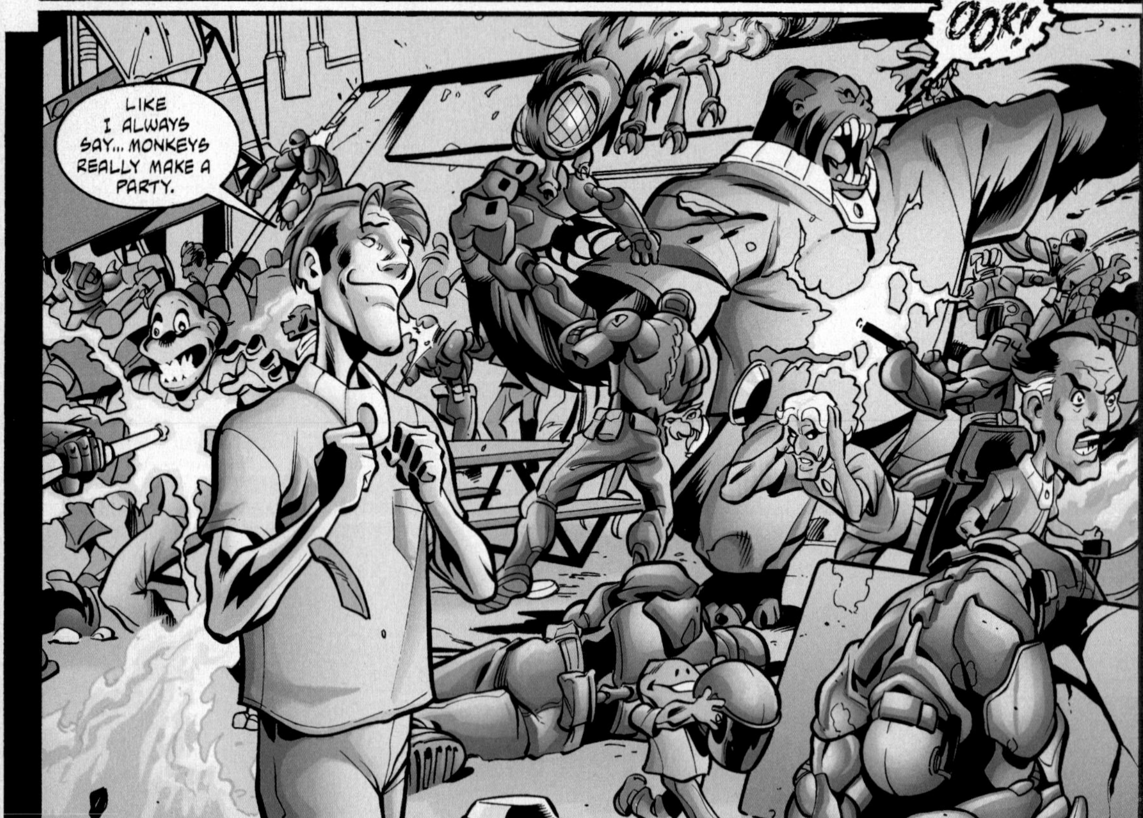
LIKE I ALWAYS SAY... MONKEYS REALLY MAKE A PARTY.
OOK!

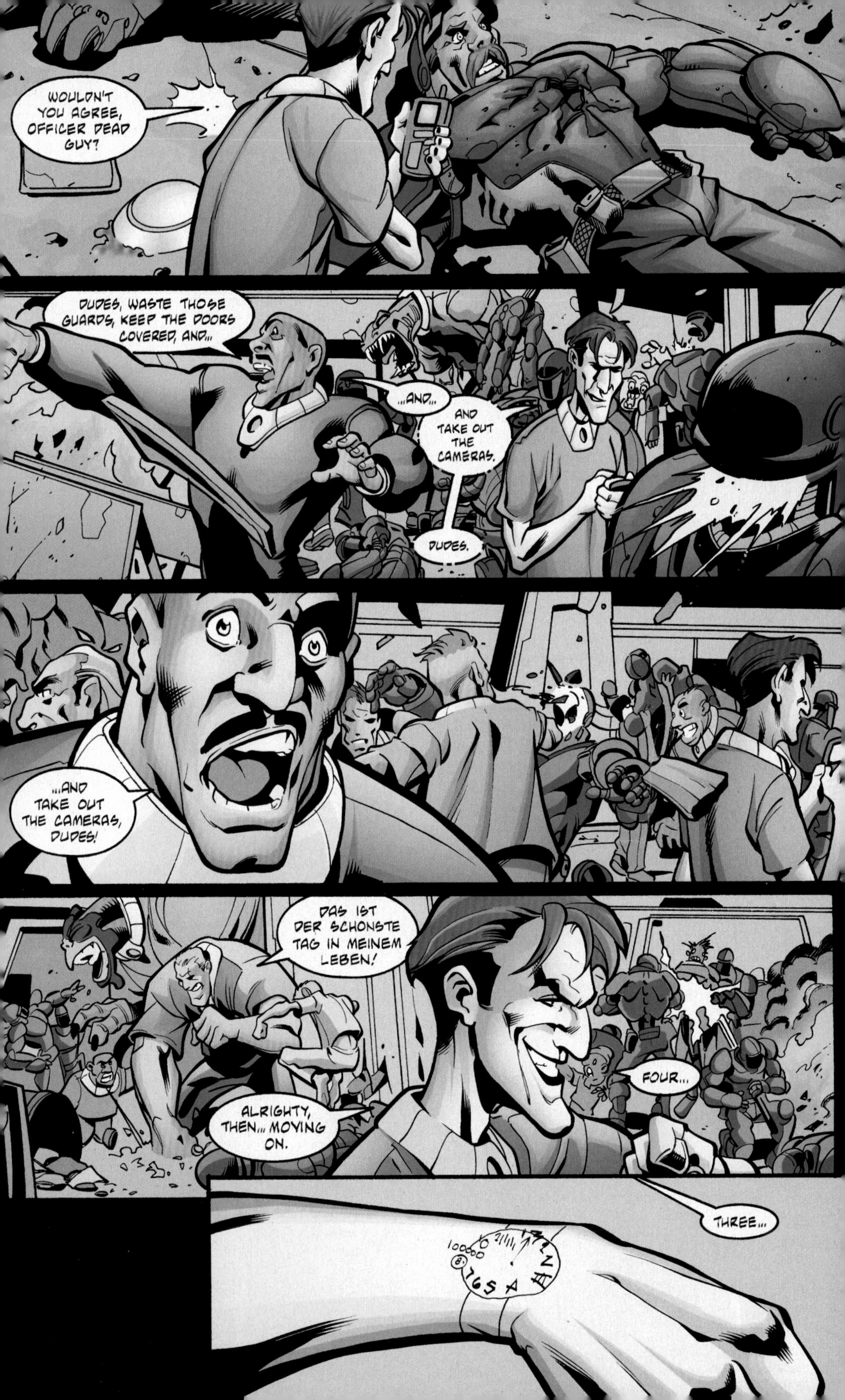
WOULDN'T YOU AGREE, OFFICER DEAD GUY?
DUDES, WASTE THOSE GUARDS, KEEP THE DOORS COVERED, AND...
...AND...
AND TAKE OUT THE CAMERAS.
DUDES.
...AND TAKE OUT THE CAMERAS, DUDES!
DAS IST DER SCHONSTE TAG IN MEINEM LEBEN!
FOUR...
ALRIGHTY, THEN... MOVING ON.
THREE...

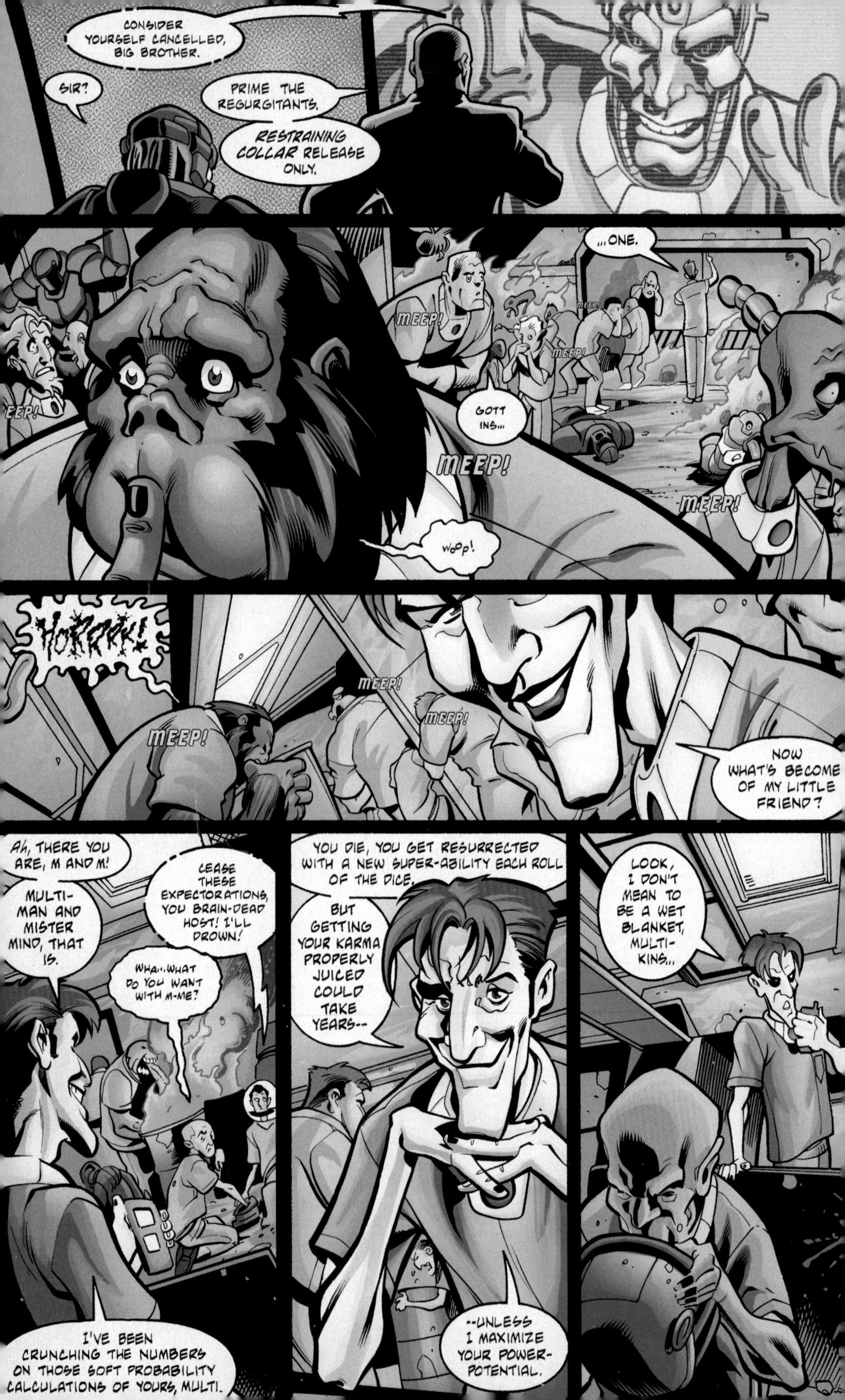
CONSIDER YOURSELF CANCELLED, BIG BROTHER.
SIR?
PRIME THE REGURGITANTS.
RESTRAINING COLLAR RELEASE ONLY.
...ONE.
MEEP!
EEP!
MEEP!
MEEP!
GOTT INS...
MEEP!
MEEP!
WOOP!
HORRRK!
MEEP!
MEEP!
MEEP!
NOW WHAT'S BECOME OF MY LITTLE FRIEND?
AH, THERE YOU ARE, M AND M!
MULTI-MAN AND MISTER MIND, THAT IS.
CEASE THESE EXPECTORATIONS, YOU BRAIN-DEAD HOST! I'LL DROWN!
WHA...WHAT DO YOU WANT WITH M-ME?
I'VE BEEN CRUNCHING THE NUMBERS ON THOSE SOFT PROBABILITY CALCULATIONS OF YOURS, MULTI.
YOU DIE, YOU GET RESURRECTED WITH A NEW SUPER-ABILITY EACH ROLL OF THE DICE.
BUT GETTING YOUR KARMA PROPERLY JUICED COULD TAKE YEARS--
--UNLESS I MAXIMIZE YOUR POWER-POTENTIAL.
LOOK, I DON'T MEAN TO BE A WET BLANKET, MULTI-KINS...

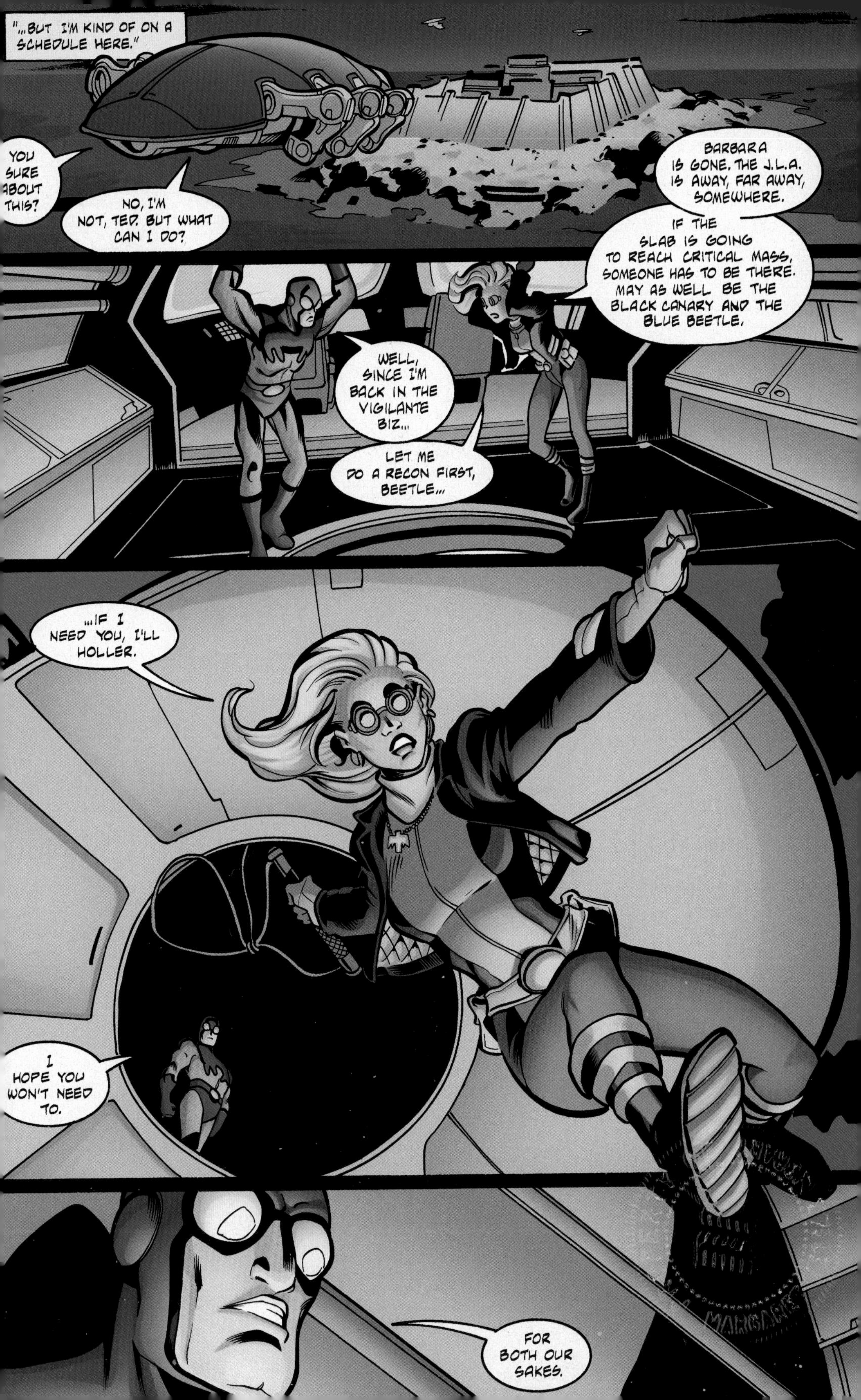
"...BUT I'M KIND OF ON A SCHEDULE HERE."
YOU SURE ABOUT THIS?
NO, I'M NOT, TED. BUT WHAT CAN I DO?
BARBARA IS GONE. THE J.L.A. IS AWAY, FAR AWAY, SOMEWHERE.
IF THE SLAB IS GOING TO REACH CRITICAL MASS, SOMEONE HAS TO BE THERE. MAY AS WELL BE THE BLACK CANARY AND THE BLUE BEETLE.
WELL, SINCE I'M BACK IN THE VIGILANTE BIZ...
LET ME DO A RECON FIRST, BEETLE...
...IF I NEED YOU, I'LL HOLLER.
I HOPE YOU WON'T NEED TO.
FOR BOTH OUR SAKES.

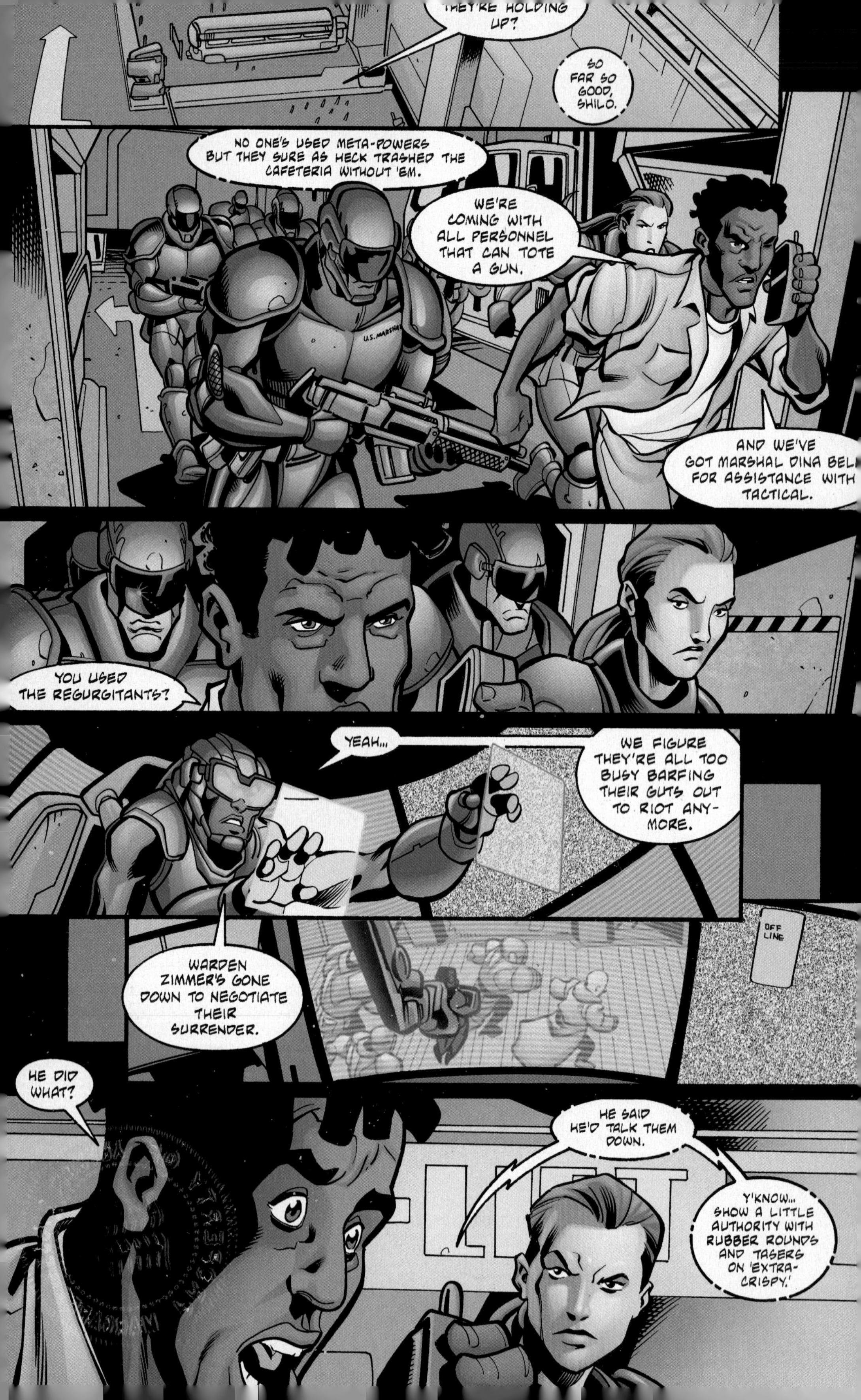
THEY'RE HOLDING UP?
SO FAR SO GOOD, SHILO.
NO ONE'S USED META-POWERS BUT THEY SURE AS HECK TRASHED THE CAFETERIA WITHOUT 'EM.
WE'RE COMING WITH ALL PERSONNEL THAT CAN TOTE A GUN.
U.S. MARSHAL
AND WE'VE GOT MARSHAL DINA BELL FOR ASSISTANCE WITH TACTICAL.
YOU USED THE REGURGITANTS?
YEAH...
WE FIGURE THEY'RE ALL TOO BUSY BARFING THEIR GUTS OUT TO RIOT ANY-MORE.
WARDEN ZIMMER'S GONE DOWN TO NEGOTIATE THEIR SURRENDER.
OFF LINE
HE DID WHAT?
HE SAID HE'D TALK THEM DOWN.
Y'KNOW... SHOW A LITTLE AUTHORITY WITH RUBBER ROUNDS AND TASERS ON 'EXTRA-CRISPY.'

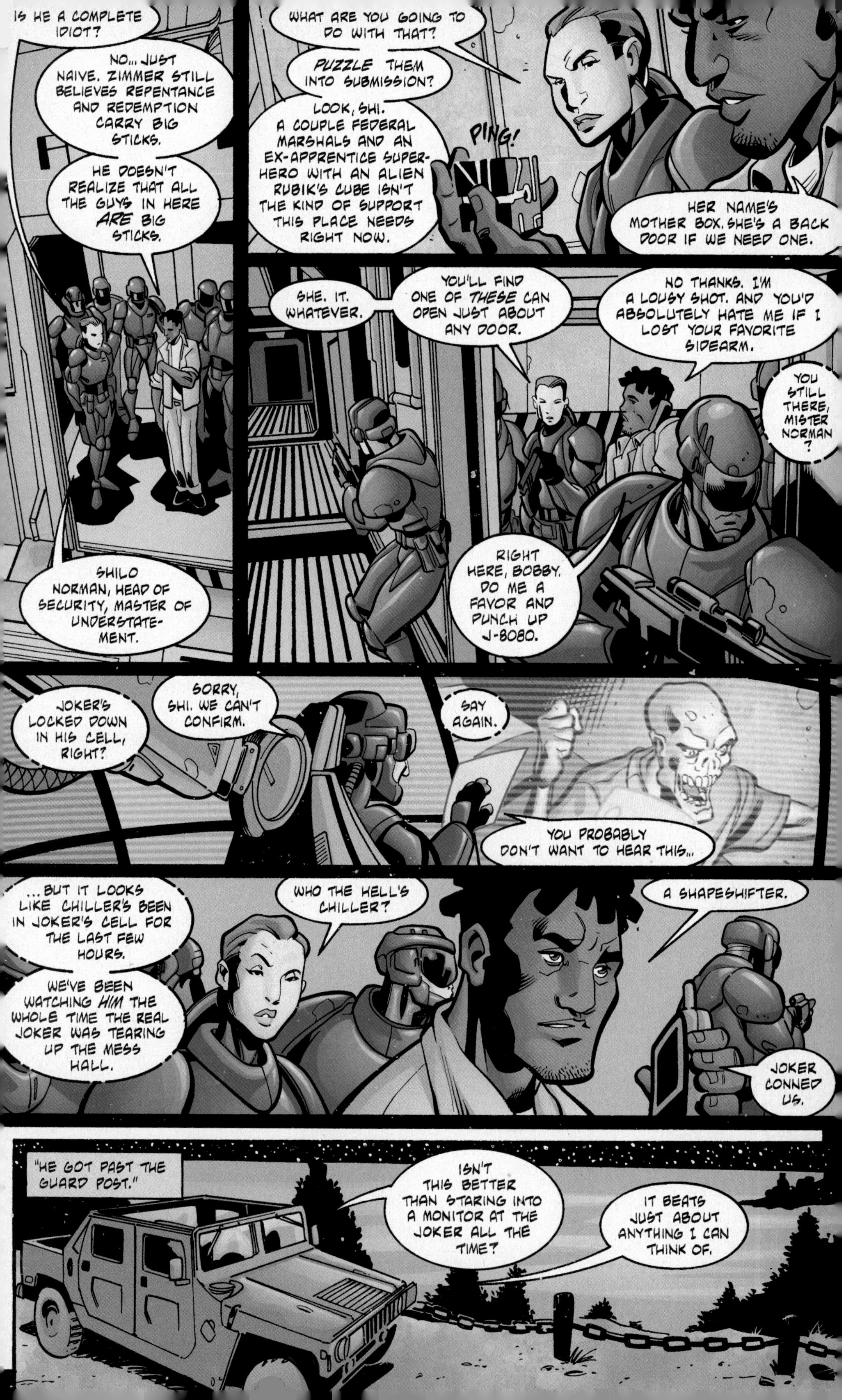
IS HE A COMPLETE IDIOT?
NO... JUST NAIVE. ZIMMER STILL BELIEVES REPENTANCE AND REDEMPTION CARRY BIG STICKS.
HE DOESN'T REALIZE THAT ALL THE GUYS IN HERE *ARE* BIG STICKS.
SHILO NORMAN, HEAD OF SECURITY, MASTER OF UNDERSTATE-MENT.
WHAT ARE YOU GOING TO DO WITH THAT?
*PUZZLE* THEM INTO SUBMISSION?
LOOK, SHI. A COUPLE FEDERAL MARSHALS AND AN EX-APPRENTICE SUPER-HERO WITH AN ALIEN RUBIK'S CUBE ISN'T THE KIND OF SUPPORT THIS PLACE NEEDS RIGHT NOW.
PING!
HER NAME'S MOTHER BOX. SHE'S A BACK DOOR IF WE NEED ONE.
SHE. IT. WHATEVER.
YOU'LL FIND ONE OF *THESE* CAN OPEN JUST ABOUT ANY DOOR.
NO THANKS. I'M A LOUSY SHOT. AND YOU'D ABSOLUTELY HATE ME IF I LOST YOUR FAVORITE SIDEARM.
YOU STILL THERE, MISTER NORMAN?
RIGHT HERE, BOBBY. DO ME A FAVOR AND PUNCH UP J-8080.
JOKER'S LOCKED DOWN IN HIS CELL, RIGHT?
SORRY, SHI. WE CAN'T CONFIRM.
SAY AGAIN.
YOU PROBABLY DON'T WANT TO HEAR THIS...
...BUT IT LOOKS LIKE CHILLER'S BEEN IN JOKER'S CELL FOR THE LAST FEW HOURS.
WE'VE BEEN WATCHING *HIM* THE WHOLE TIME THE REAL JOKER WAS TEARING UP THE MESS HALL.
WHO THE HELL'S CHILLER?
A SHAPESHIFTER.
JOKER CONNED US.
"HE GOT PAST THE GUARD POST."
ISN'T THIS BETTER THAN STARING INTO A MONITOR AT THE JOKER ALL THE TIME?
IT BEATS JUST ABOUT ANYTHING I CAN THINK OF.

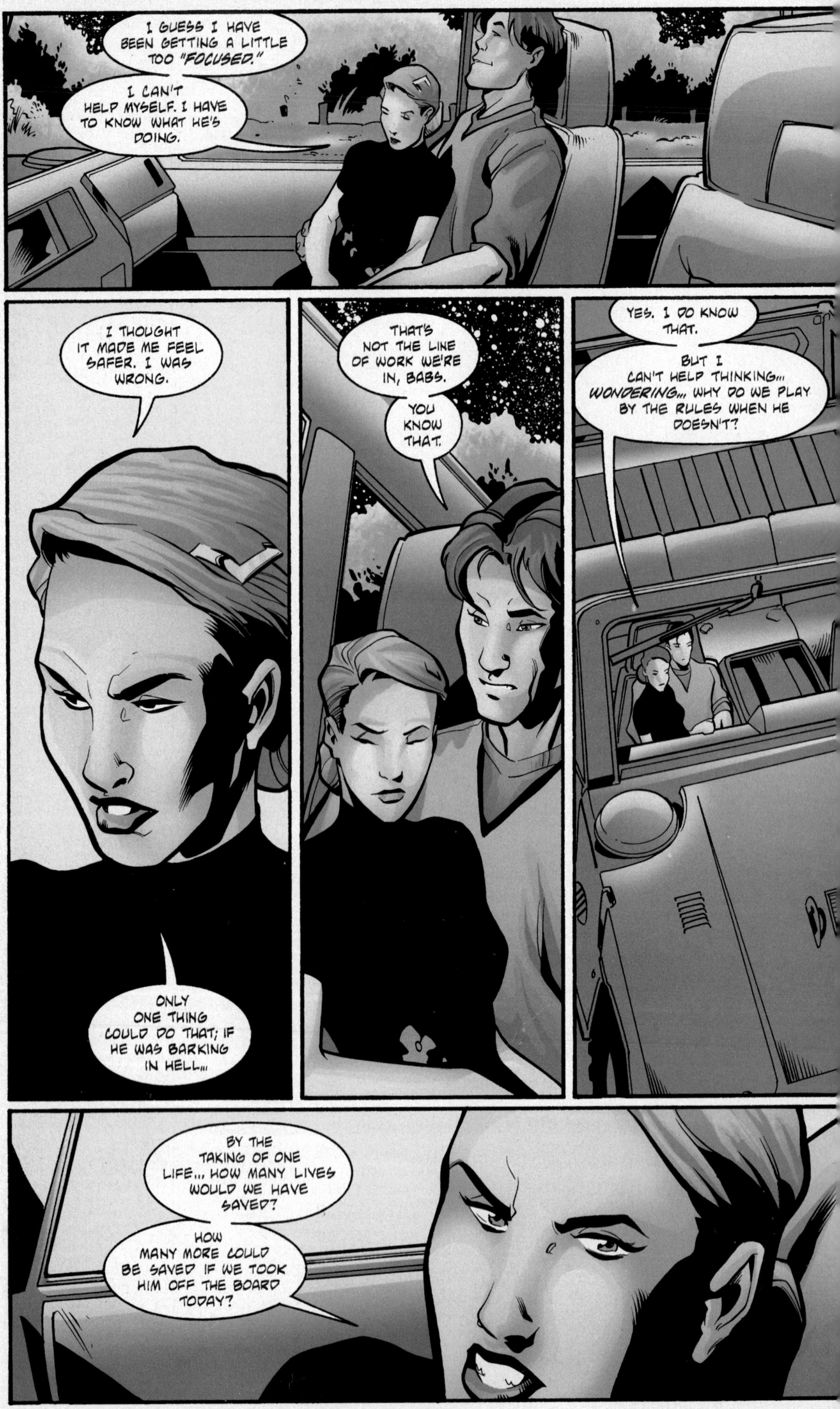
I GUESS I HAVE BEEN GETTING A LITTLE TOO "FOCUSED."
I CAN'T HELP MYSELF. I HAVE TO KNOW WHAT HE'S DOING.
I THOUGHT IT MADE ME FEEL SAFER. I WAS WRONG.
ONLY ONE THING COULD DO THAT; IF HE WAS BARKING IN HELL...
THAT'S NOT THE LINE OF WORK WE'RE IN, BABS.
YOU KNOW THAT.
YES. I DO KNOW THAT.
BUT I CAN'T HELP THINKING... WONDERING... WHY DO WE PLAY BY THE RULES WHEN HE DOESN'T?
BY THE TAKING OF ONE LIFE... HOW MANY LIVES WOULD WE HAVE SAVED?
HOW MANY MORE COULD BE SAVED IF WE TOOK HIM OFF THE BOARD TODAY?

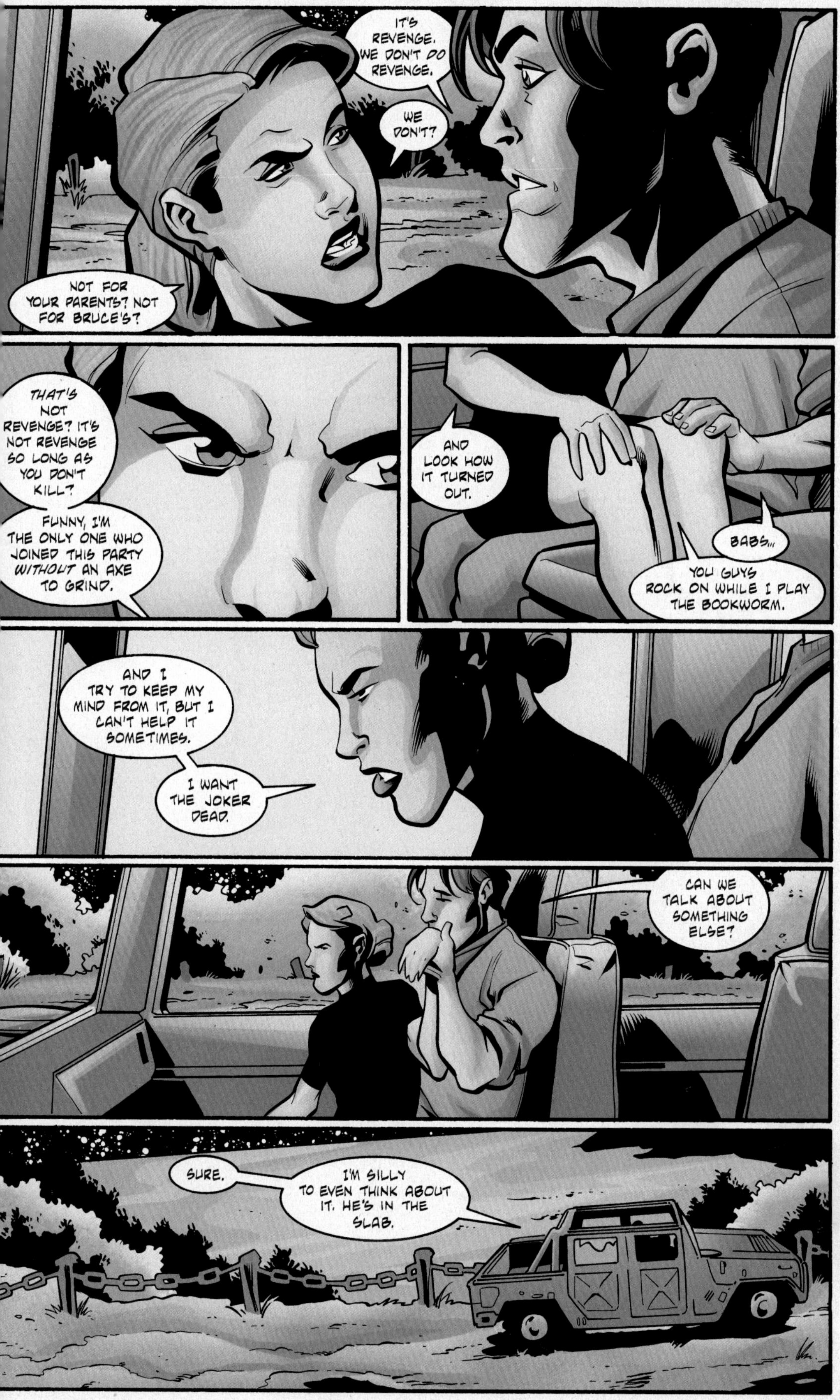
IT'S REVENGE. WE DON'T DO REVENGE.
WE DON'T?
NOT FOR YOUR PARENTS? NOT FOR BRUCE'S?
THAT'S NOT REVENGE? IT'S NOT REVENGE SO LONG AS YOU DON'T KILL?
FUNNY, I'M THE ONLY ONE WHO JOINED THIS PARTY WITHOUT AN AXE TO GRIND.
AND LOOK HOW IT TURNED OUT.
BABS...
YOU GUYS ROCK ON WHILE I PLAY THE BOOKWORM.
AND I TRY TO KEEP MY MIND FROM IT, BUT I CAN'T HELP IT SOMETIMES.
I WANT THE JOKER DEAD.
CAN WE TALK ABOUT SOMETHING ELSE?
SURE.
I'M SILLY TO EVEN THINK ABOUT IT. HE'S IN THE SLAB.

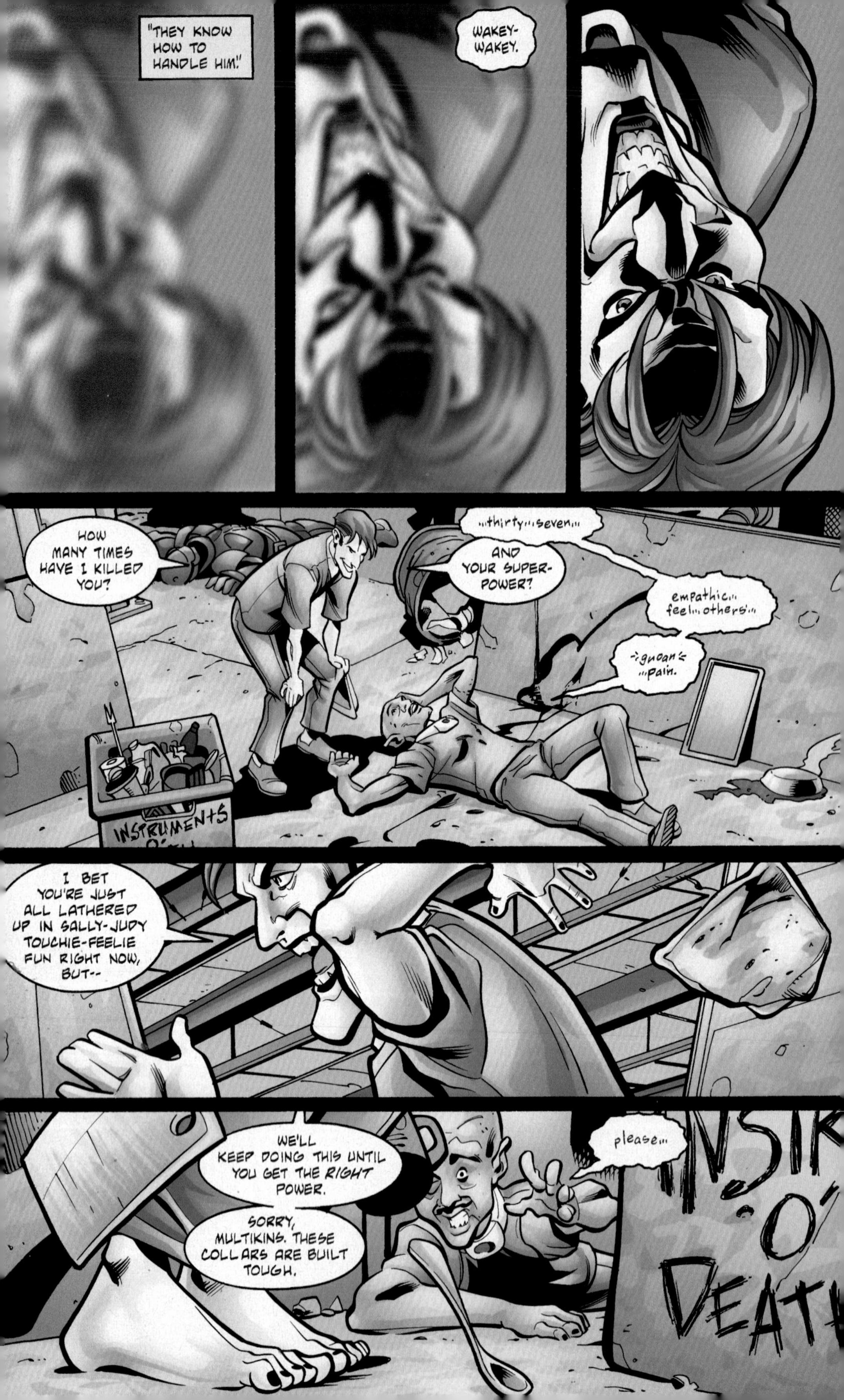
"THEY KNOW HOW TO HANDLE HIM."
WAKEY-WAKEY.
HOW MANY TIMES HAVE I KILLED YOU?
...thirty...seven...
AND YOUR SUPER-POWER?
empathic... feel...others'...
-groan- ...pain.
INSTRUMENTS
I BET YOU'RE JUST ALL LATHERED UP IN SALLY-JUDY TOUCHIE-FEELIE FUN RIGHT NOW, BUT--
WE'LL KEEP DOING THIS UNTIL YOU GET THE *RIGHT* POWER.
SORRY, MULTIKINS. THESE COLLARS ARE BUILT TOUGH.
please...

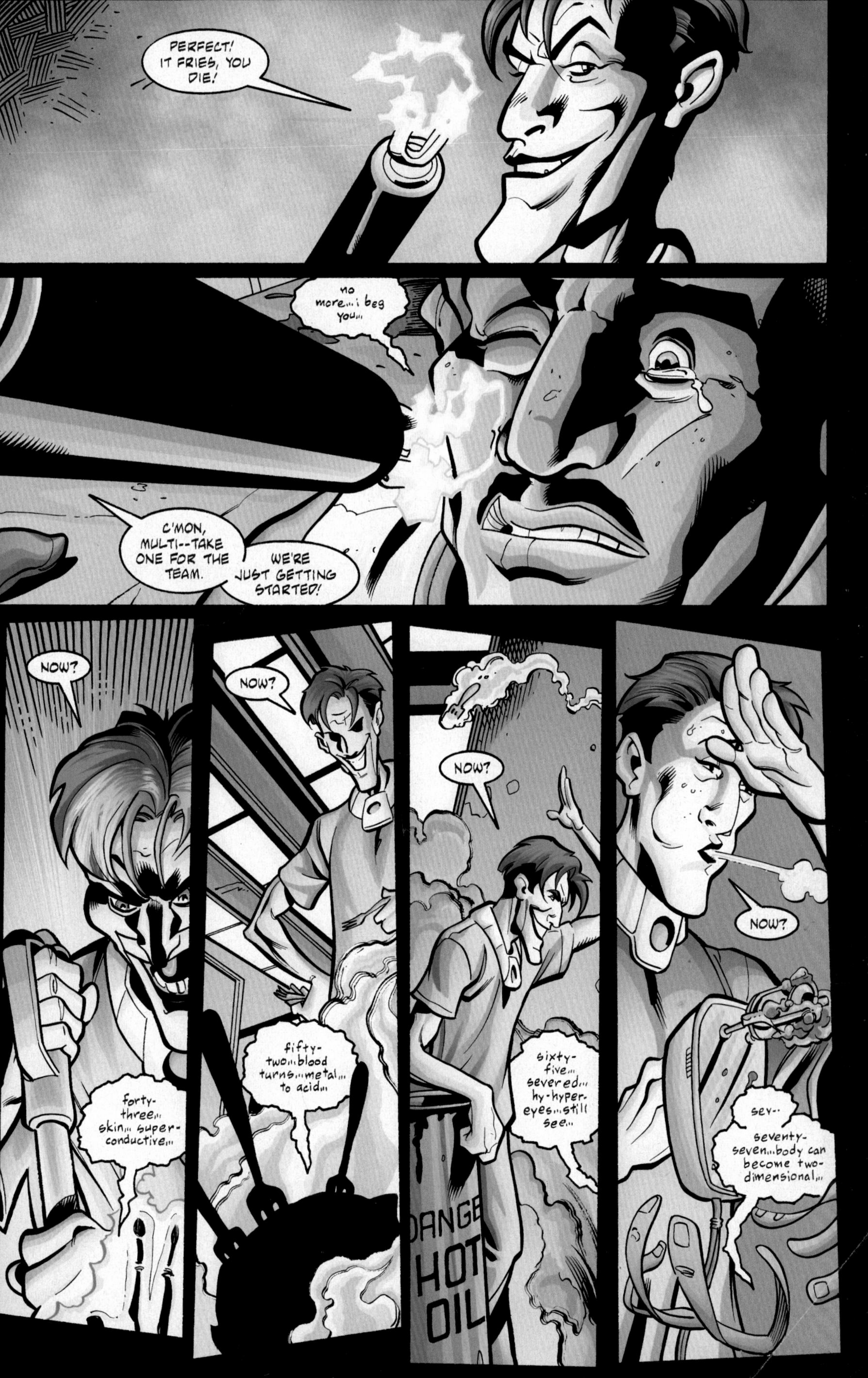
PERFECT! IT FRIES, YOU DIE!
no more... i beg you...
C'MON, MULTI--TAKE ONE FOR THE TEAM.
WE'RE JUST GETTING STARTED!
NOW?
forty-three... skin... super-conductive...
NOW?
fifty-two... blood turns... metal... to acid...
NOW?
sixty-five... severed... hy-hyper-eyes... still see...
DANGER HOT OIL
NOW?
sev--
seventy-seven... body can become two-dimensional...

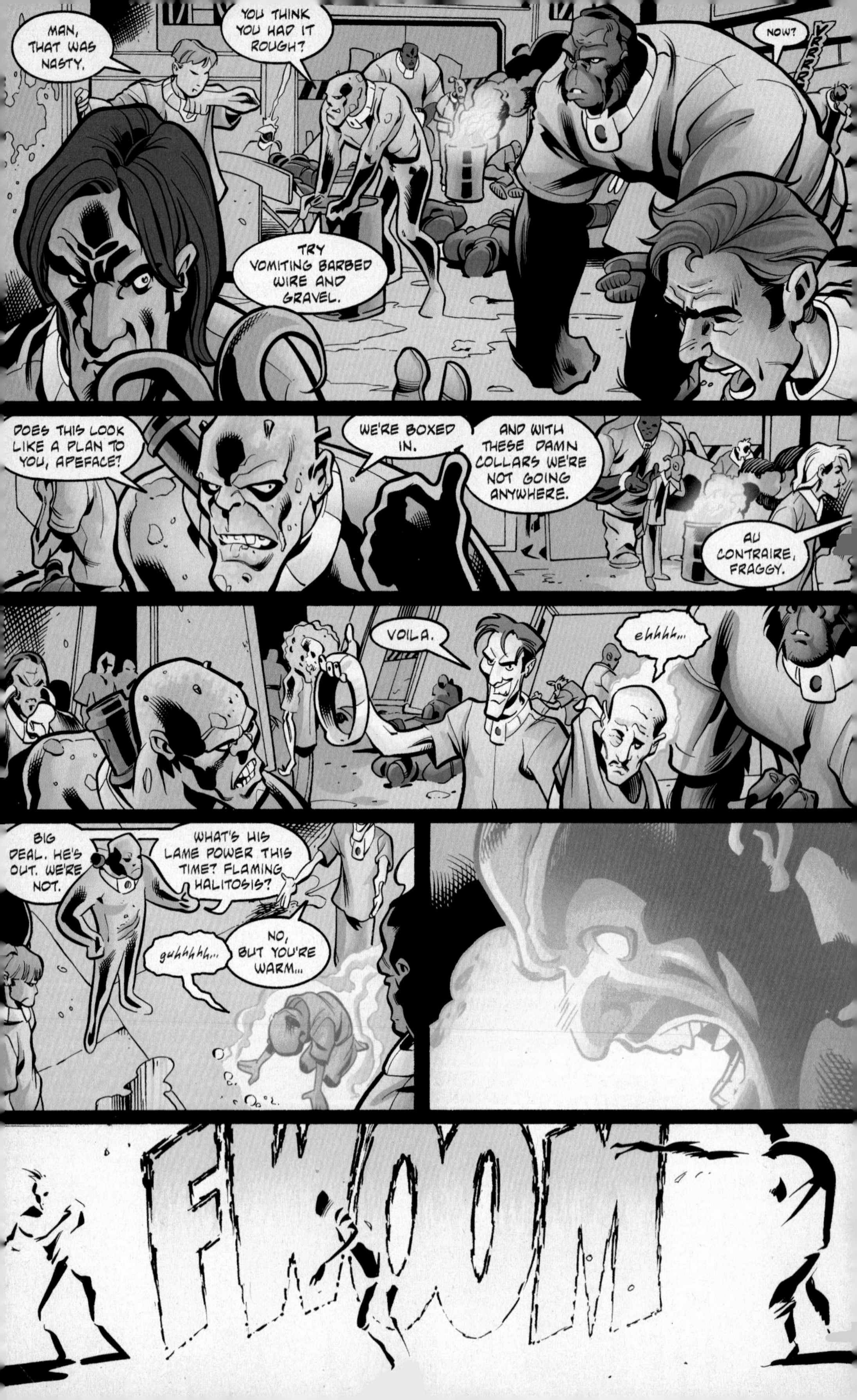
MAN, THAT WAS NASTY.
YOU THINK YOU HAD IT ROUGH?
NOW?
VRRRR
TRY VOMITING BARBED WIRE AND GRAVEL.
DOES THIS LOOK LIKE A PLAN TO YOU, APEFACE?
WE'RE BOXED IN.
AND WITH THESE DAMN COLLARS WE'RE NOT GOING ANYWHERE.
AU CONTRAIRE, FRAGGY.
VOILA.
ehhhh...
BIG DEAL. HE'S OUT. WE'RE NOT.
WHAT'S HIS LAME POWER THIS TIME? FLAMING HALITOSIS?
guhhhhh...
NO, BUT YOU'RE WARM...
FWOOM

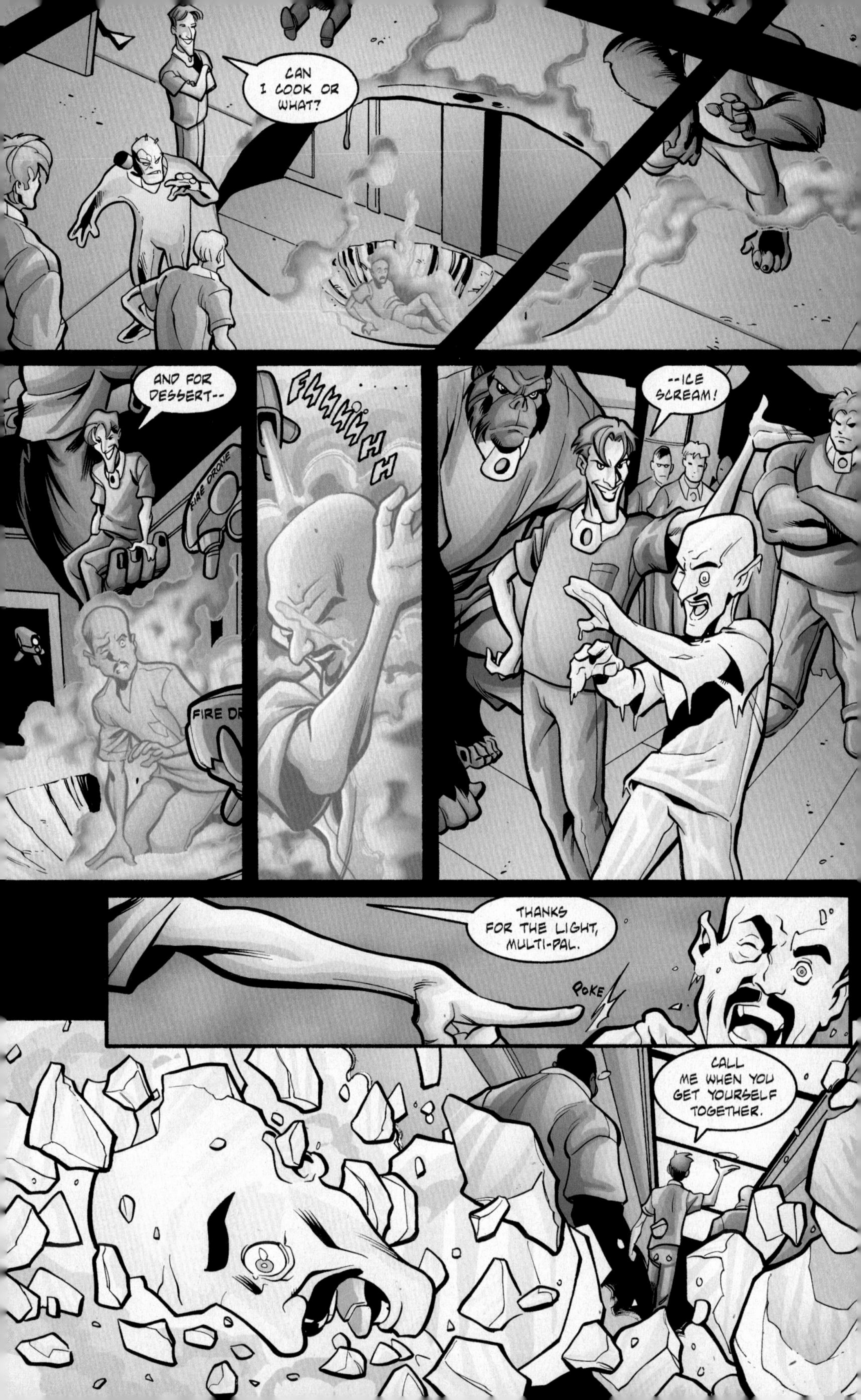
CAN I COOK OR WHAT?
AND FOR DESSERT--
FIRE DRONE
FWWWWHHH
--ICE SCREAM!
THANKS FOR THE LIGHT, MULTI-PAL.
POKE
CALL ME WHEN YOU GET YOURSELF TOGETHER.

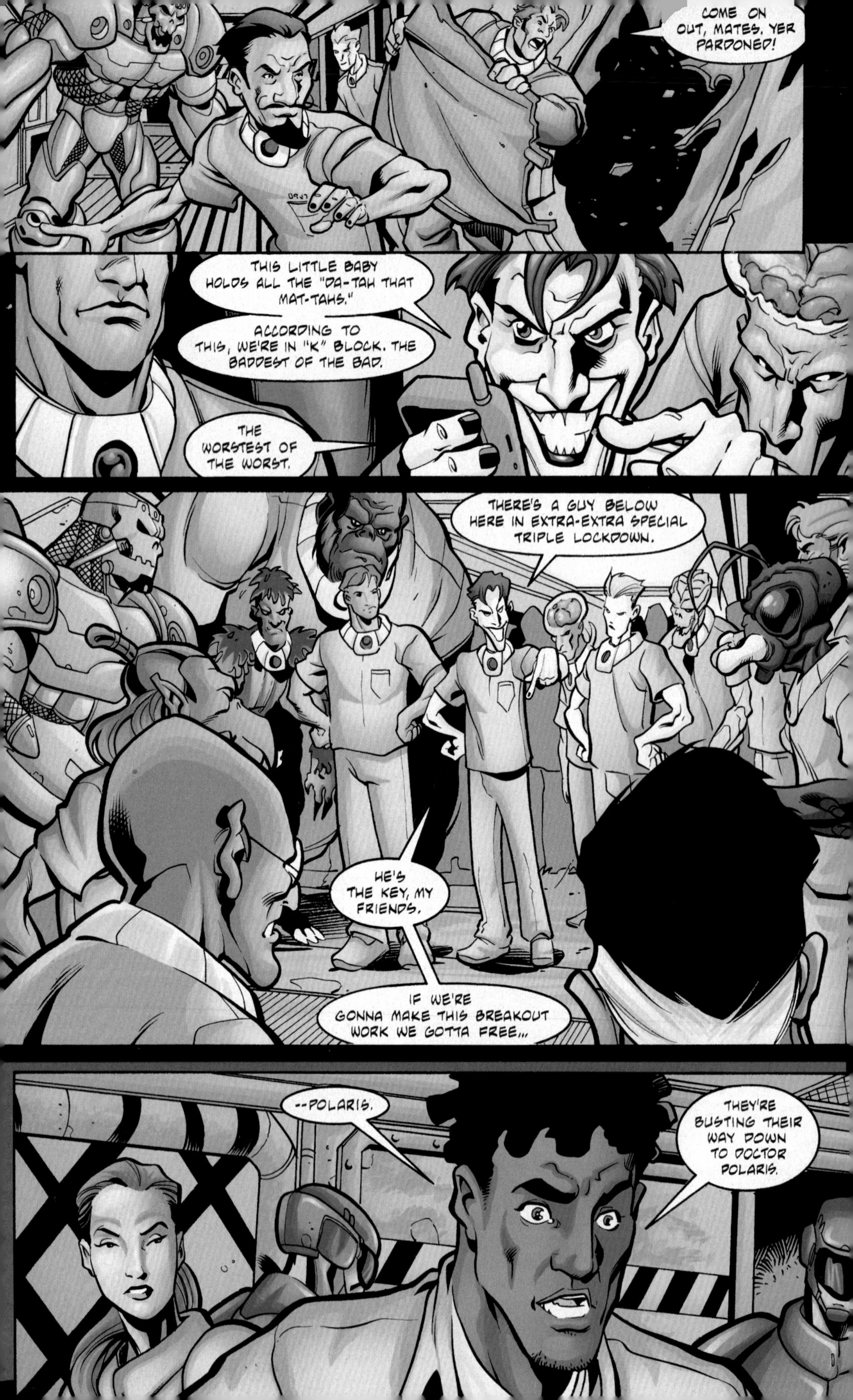
COME ON OUT, MATES. YER PARDONED!
THIS LITTLE BABY HOLDS ALL THE "DA-TAH THAT MAT-TAHS."
ACCORDING TO THIS, WE'RE IN "K" BLOCK. THE BADDEST OF THE BAD.
THE WORSTEST OF THE WORST.
THERE'S A GUY BELOW HERE IN EXTRA-EXTRA SPECIAL TRIPLE LOCKDOWN.
HE'S THE KEY, MY FRIENDS.
IF WE'RE GONNA MAKE THIS BREAKOUT WORK WE GOTTA FREE...
--POLARIS.
THEY'RE BUSTING THEIR WAY DOWN TO DOCTOR POLARIS.

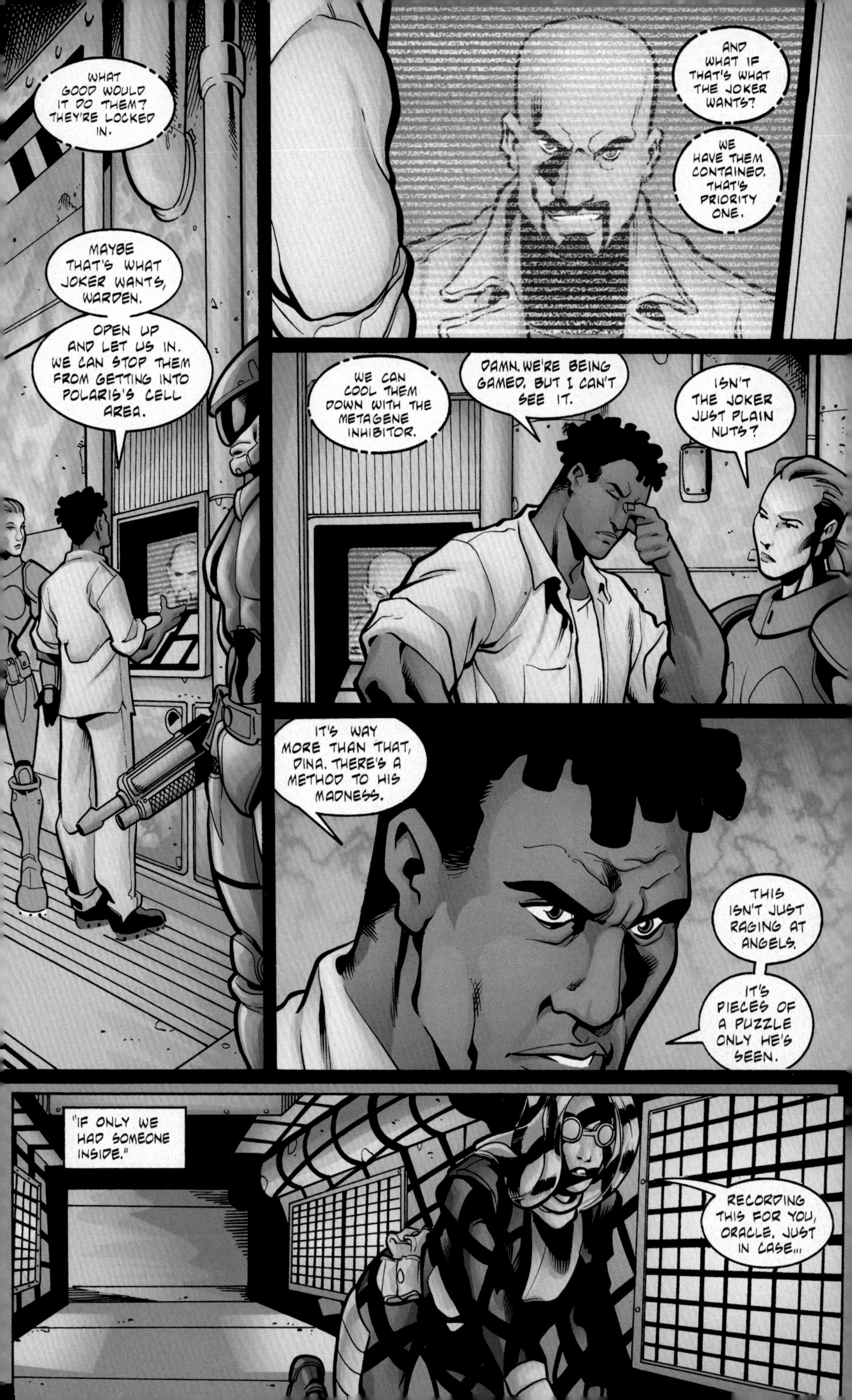
WHAT GOOD WOULD IT DO THEM? THEY'RE LOCKED IN.
AND WHAT IF THAT'S WHAT THE JOKER WANTS?
WE HAVE THEM CONTAINED. THAT'S PRIORITY ONE.
MAYBE THAT'S WHAT JOKER WANTS, WARDEN.
OPEN UP AND LET US IN. WE CAN STOP THEM FROM GETTING INTO POLARIS'S CELL AREA.
WE CAN COOL THEM DOWN WITH THE METAGENE INHIBITOR.
DAMN. WE'RE BEING GAMED, BUT I CAN'T SEE IT.
ISN'T THE JOKER JUST PLAIN NUTS?
IT'S WAY MORE THAN THAT, DINA. THERE'S A METHOD TO HIS MADNESS.
THIS ISN'T JUST RAGING AT ANGELS.
IT'S PIECES OF A PUZZLE ONLY HE'S SEEN.
"IF ONLY WE HAD SOMEONE INSIDE."
RECORDING THIS FOR YOU, ORACLE. JUST IN CASE...

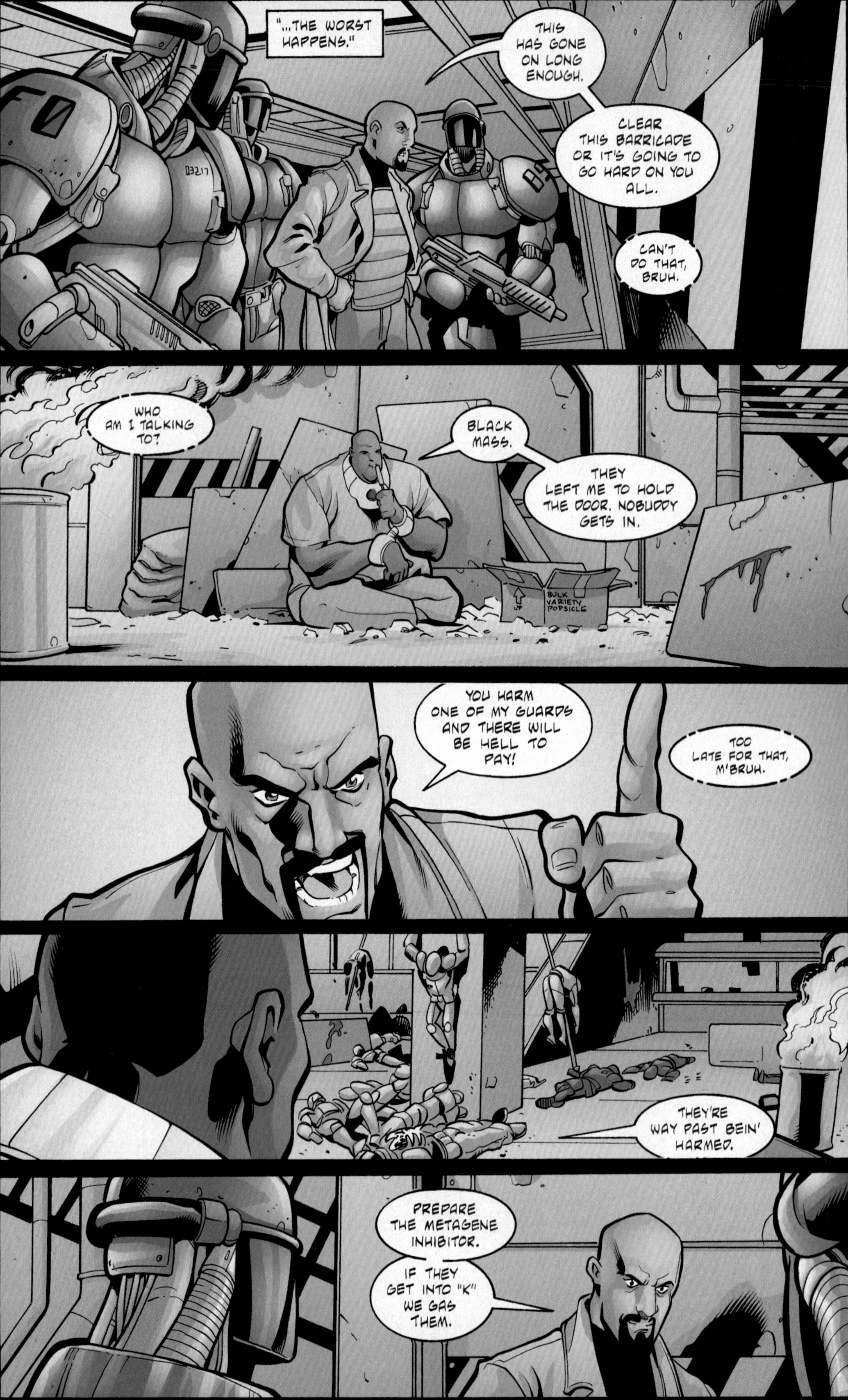
"...THE WORST HAPPENS."
THIS HAS GONE ON LONG ENOUGH.
CLEAR THIS BARRICADE OR IT'S GOING TO GO HARD ON YOU ALL.
CAN'T DO THAT, BRUH.
WHO AM I TALKING TO?
BLACK MASS.
THEY LEFT ME TO HOLD THE DOOR. NOBUDDY GETS IN.
BULK VARIETY POPSICLE
UP
YOU HARM ONE OF MY GUARDS AND THERE WILL BE HELL TO PAY!
TOO LATE FOR THAT, M'BRUH.
THEY'RE WAY PAST BEIN' HARMED.
PREPARE THE METAGENE INHIBITOR.
IF THEY GET INTO "K" WE GAS THEM.

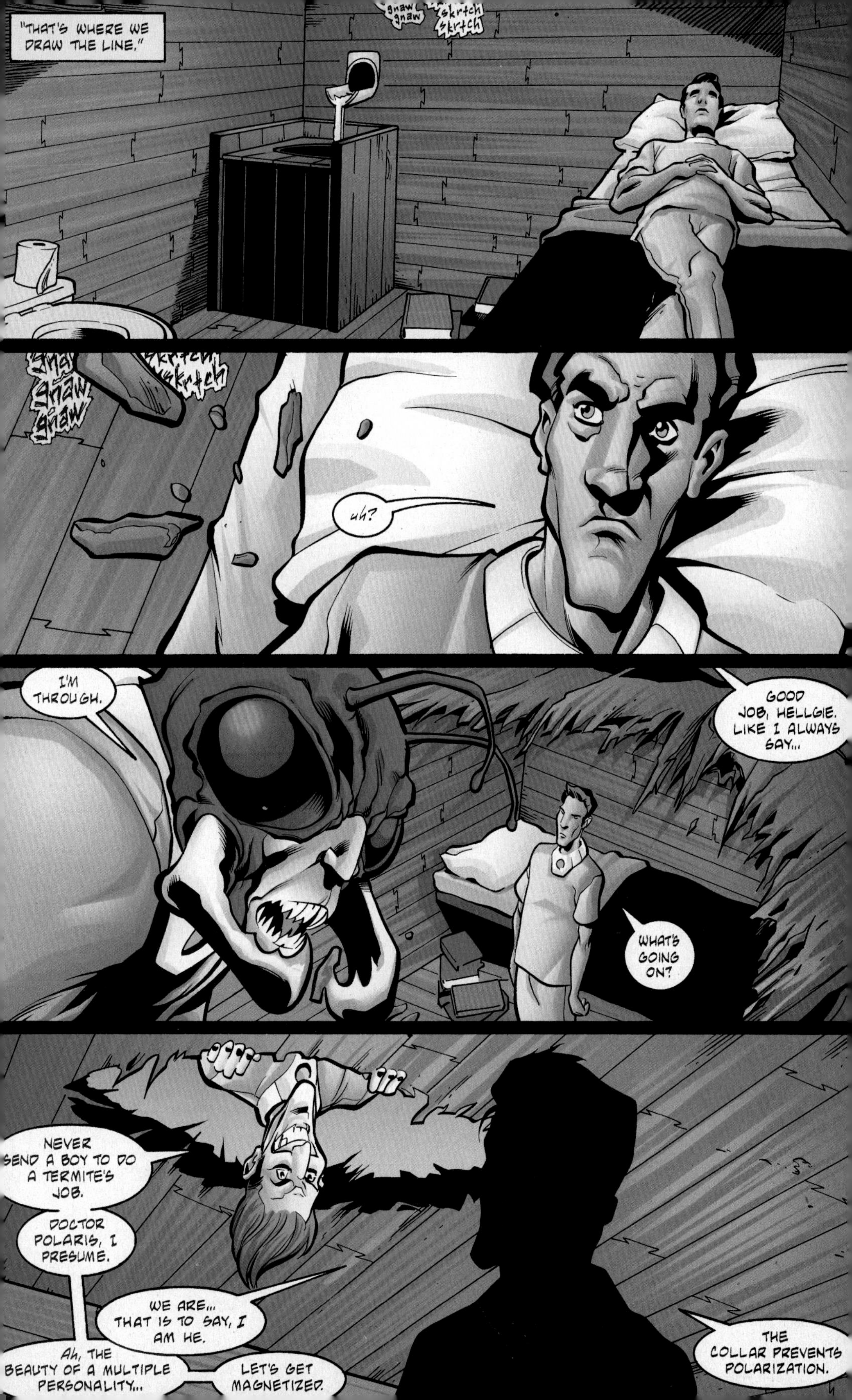
"THAT'S WHERE WE DRAW THE LINE."
gnaw gnaw
skrtch skrtch
gnaw gnaw gnaw
skrtch skrtch
uh?
I'M THROUGH.
GOOD JOB, HELLGIE. LIKE I ALWAYS SAY...
WHAT'S GOING ON?
NEVER SEND A BOY TO DO A TERMITE'S JOB.
DOCTOR POLARIS, I PRESUME.
WE ARE... THAT IS TO SAY, I AM HE.
AH, THE BEAUTY OF A MULTIPLE PERSONALITY...
LET'S GET MAGNETIZED.
THE COLLAR PREVENTS POLARIZATION.

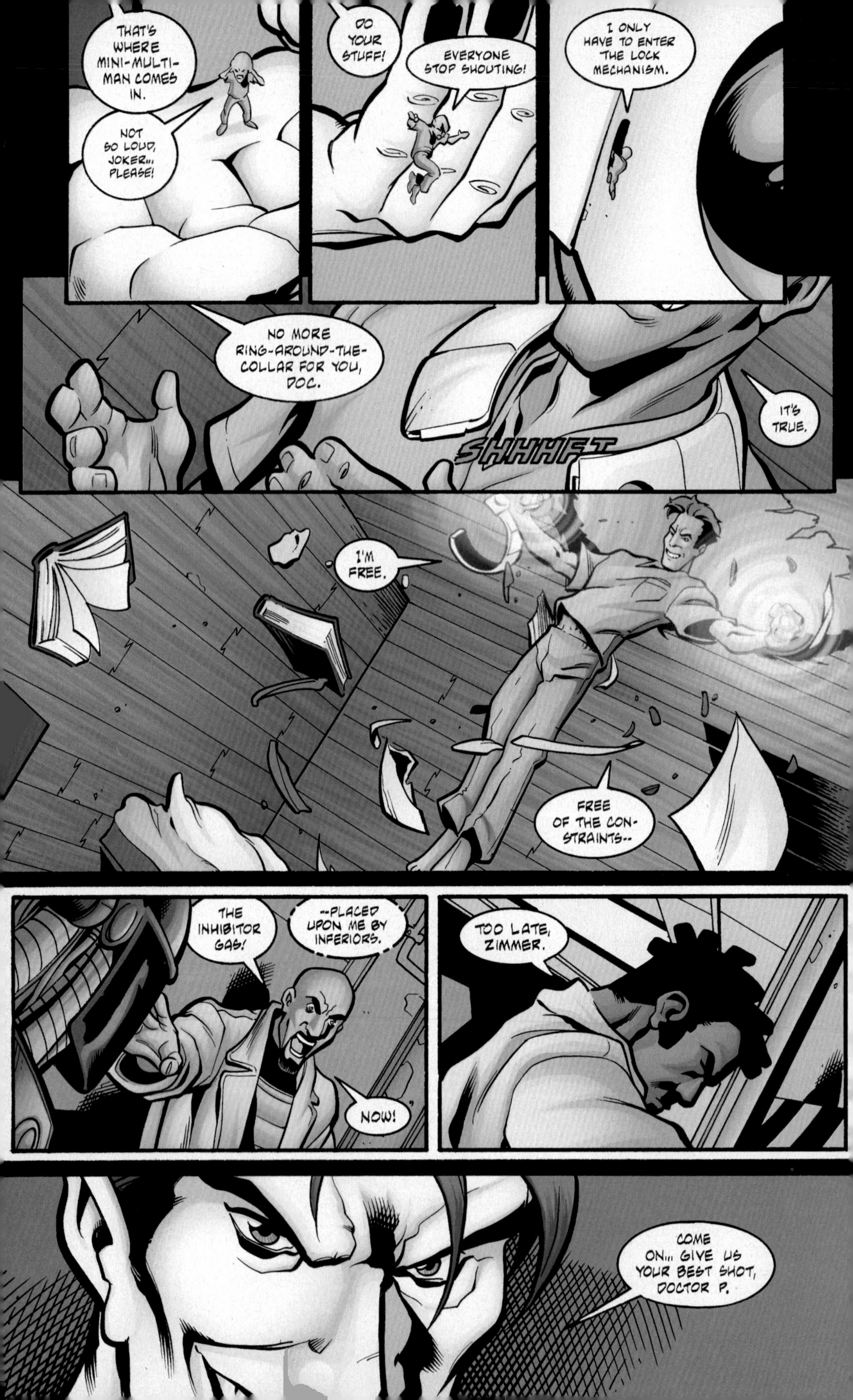
THAT'S WHERE MINI-MULTI-MAN COMES IN.
NOT SO LOUD, JOKER... PLEASE!
DO YOUR STUFF!
EVERYONE STOP SHOUTING!
I ONLY HAVE TO ENTER THE LOCK MECHANISM.
NO MORE RING-AROUND-THE-COLLAR FOR YOU, DOC.
IT'S TRUE.
SHHHFT
I'M FREE.
FREE OF THE CON-STRAINTS--
THE INHIBITOR GAS!
--PLACED UPON ME BY INFERIORS.
NOW!
TOO LATE, ZIMMER.
COME ON... GIVE US YOUR BEST SHOT, DOCTOR P.

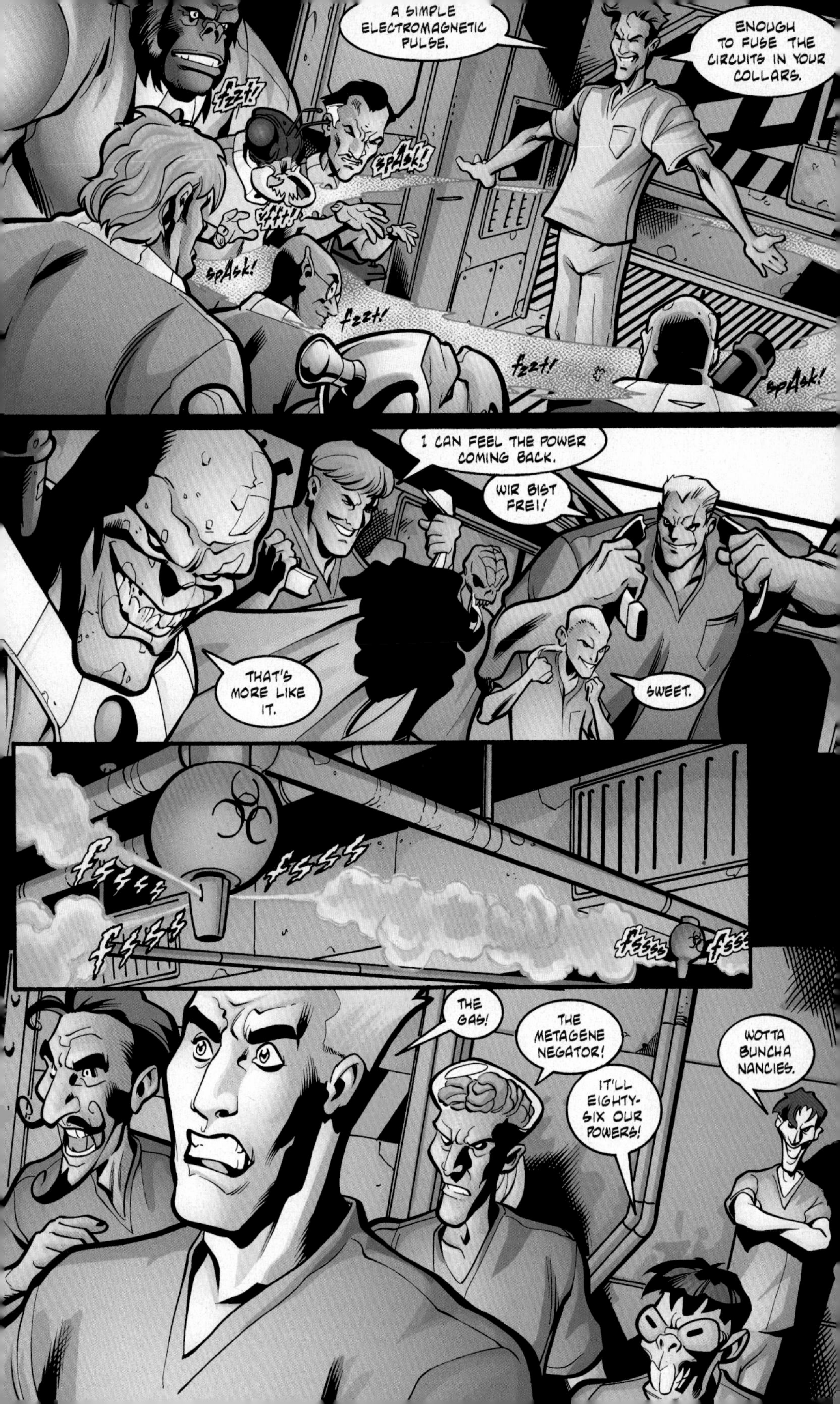
A SIMPLE ELECTROMAGNETIC PULSE.
ENOUGH TO FUSE THE CIRCUITS IN YOUR COLLARS.
fzzt!
spAsk!
spAsk!
fzzt!
fzzt!
spAsk!
I CAN FEEL THE POWER COMING BACK.
WIR BIST FREI!
THAT'S MORE LIKE IT.
SWEET.
fssss
fssss
fssss
THE GAS!
THE METAGENE NEGATOR!
IT'LL EIGHTY-SIX OUR POWERS!
WOTTA BUNCHA NANCIES.

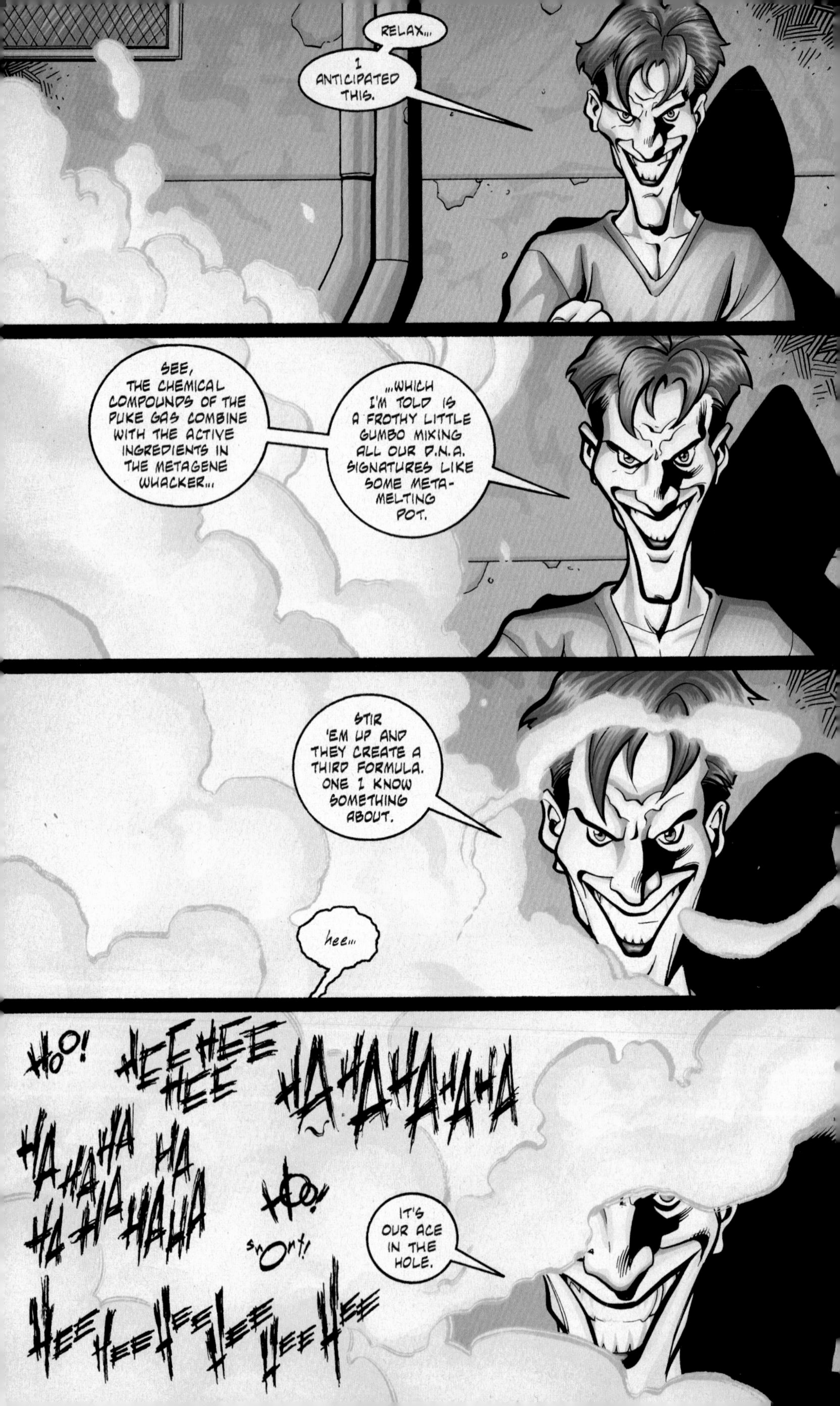

RELAX...
I ANTICIPATED THIS.
SEE, THE CHEMICAL COMPOUNDS OF THE PUKE GAS COMBINE WITH THE ACTIVE INGREDIENTS IN THE METAGENE WHACKER...
...WHICH I'M TOLD IS A FROTHY LITTLE GUMBO MIXING ALL OUR D.N.A. SIGNATURES LIKE SOME META-MELTING POT.
STIR 'EM UP AND THEY CREATE A THIRD FORMULA. ONE I KNOW SOMETHING ABOUT.
hee...
HOO! HEEHEE HEE HAHAHAHAHA
HAHAHA HA HAHAHA HAHA
HOO!
snort!
IT'S OUR ACE IN THE HOLE.
HEE HEE HEE HEE HEE HEE

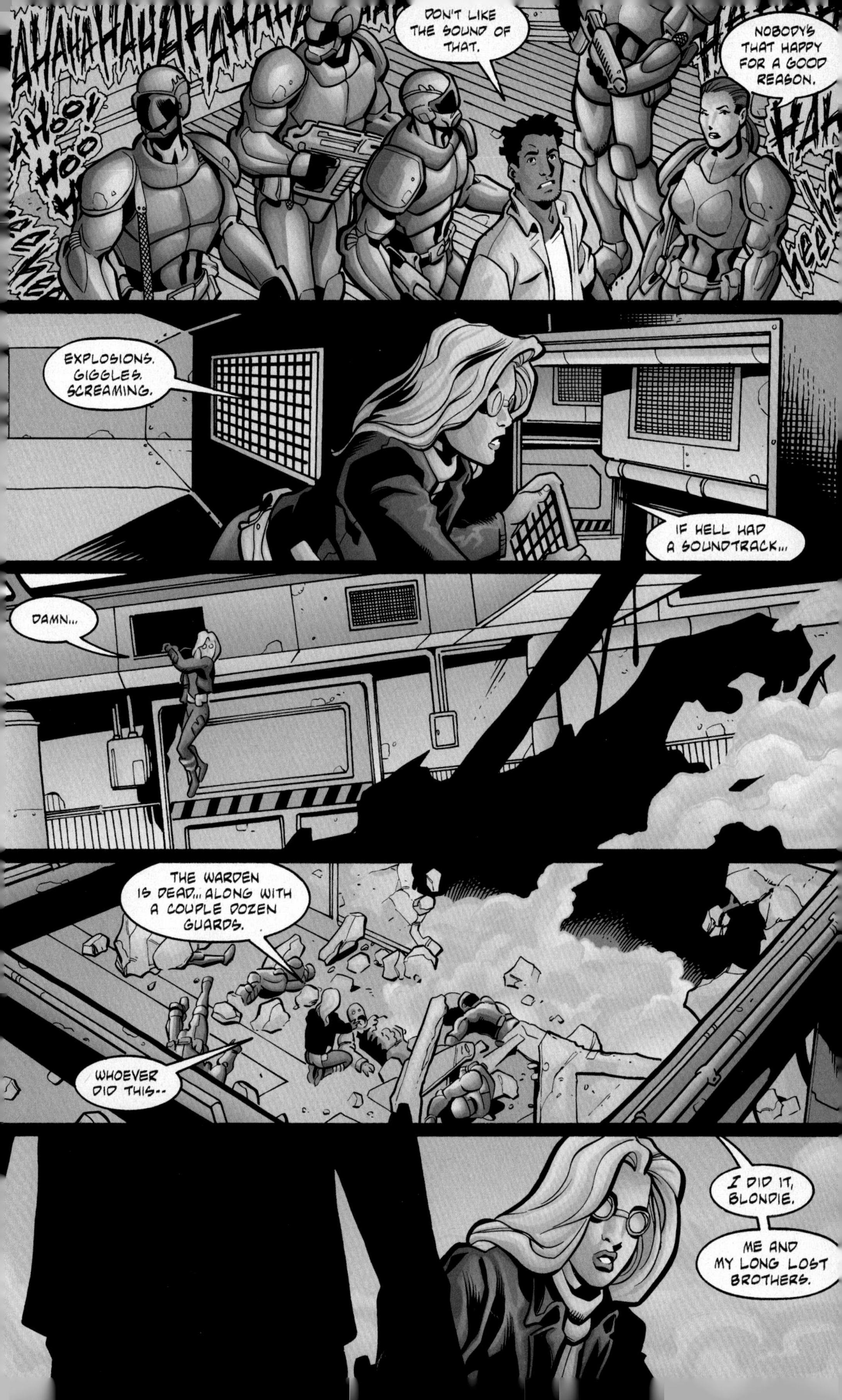
AHAHAHAHAHAHAHAHA
AHOO! HOO
DON'T LIKE THE SOUND OF THAT.
NOBODY'S THAT HAPPY FOR A GOOD REASON.
HAH
EXPLOSIONS. GIGGLES. SCREAMING.
IF HELL HAD A SOUNDTRACK...
DAMN...
THE WARDEN IS DEAD... ALONG WITH A COUPLE DOZEN GUARDS.
WHOEVER DID THIS--
I DID IT, BLONDIE.
ME AND MY LONG LOST BROTHERS.

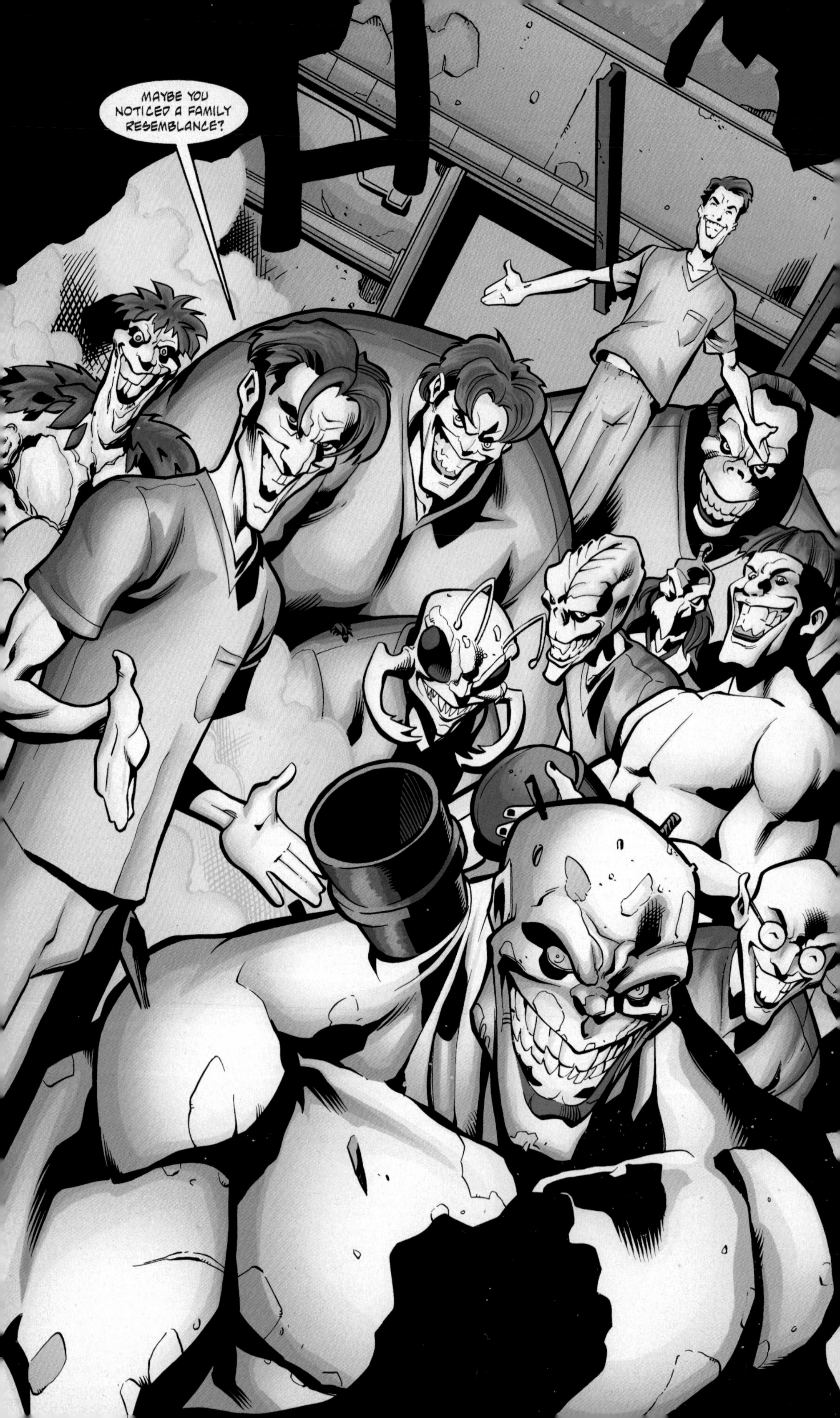
MAYBE YOU NOTICED A FAMILY RESEMBLANCE?

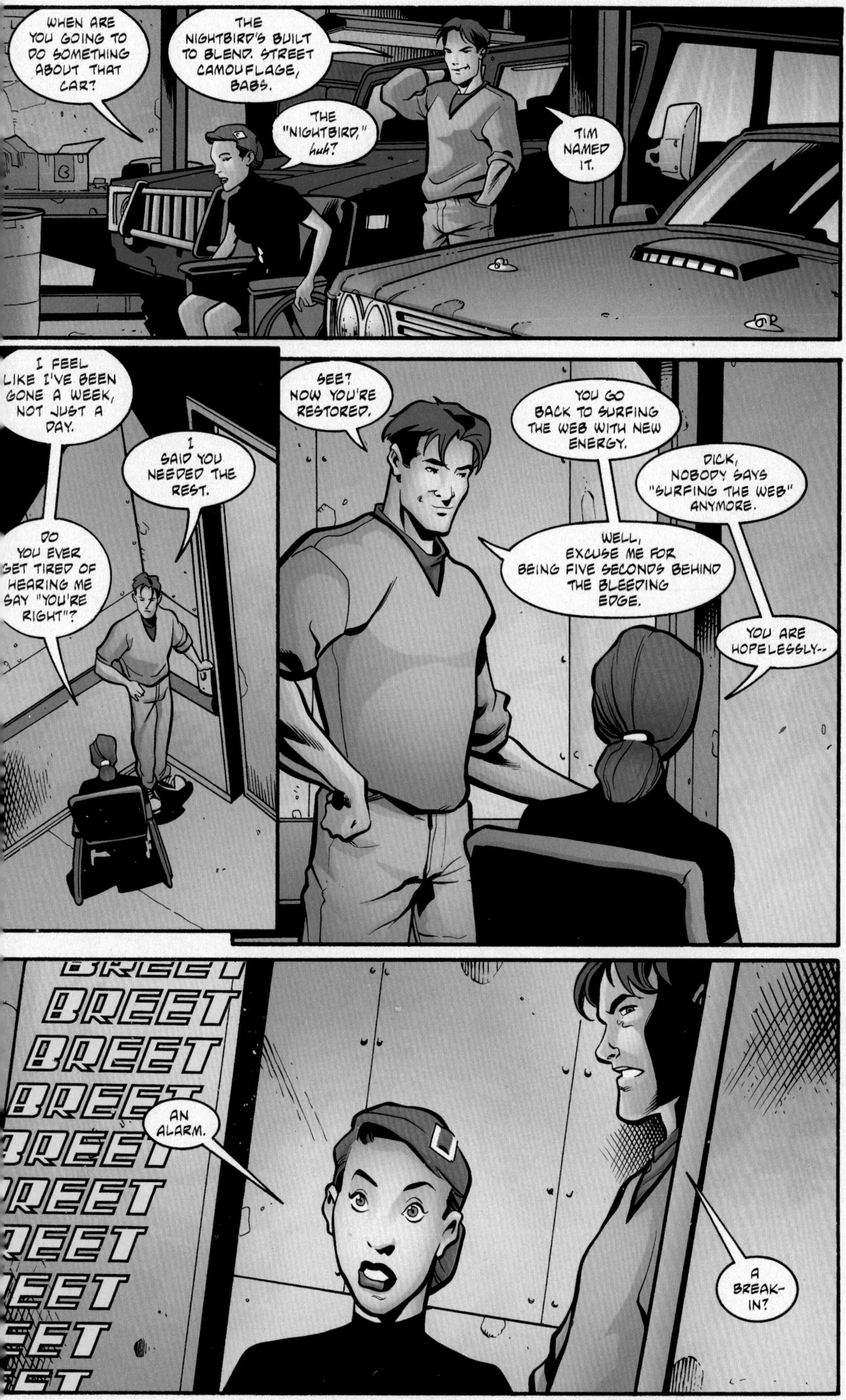
WHEN ARE YOU GOING TO DO SOMETHING ABOUT THAT CAR?
THE NIGHTBIRD'S BUILT TO BLEND. STREET CAMOUFLAGE, BABS.
THE "NIGHTBIRD," huh?
TIM NAMED IT.
I FEEL LIKE I'VE BEEN GONE A WEEK, NOT JUST A DAY.
I SAID YOU NEEDED THE REST.
DO YOU EVER GET TIRED OF HEARING ME SAY "YOU'RE RIGHT"?
SEE? NOW YOU'RE RESTORED.
YOU GO BACK TO SURFING THE WEB WITH NEW ENERGY.
DICK, NOBODY SAYS "SURFING THE WEB" ANYMORE.
WELL, EXCUSE ME FOR BEING FIVE SECONDS BEHIND THE BLEEDING EDGE.
YOU ARE HOPELESSLY--
BREET BREET BREET BREET BREET BREET BREET BREET
AN ALARM.
A BREAK-IN?

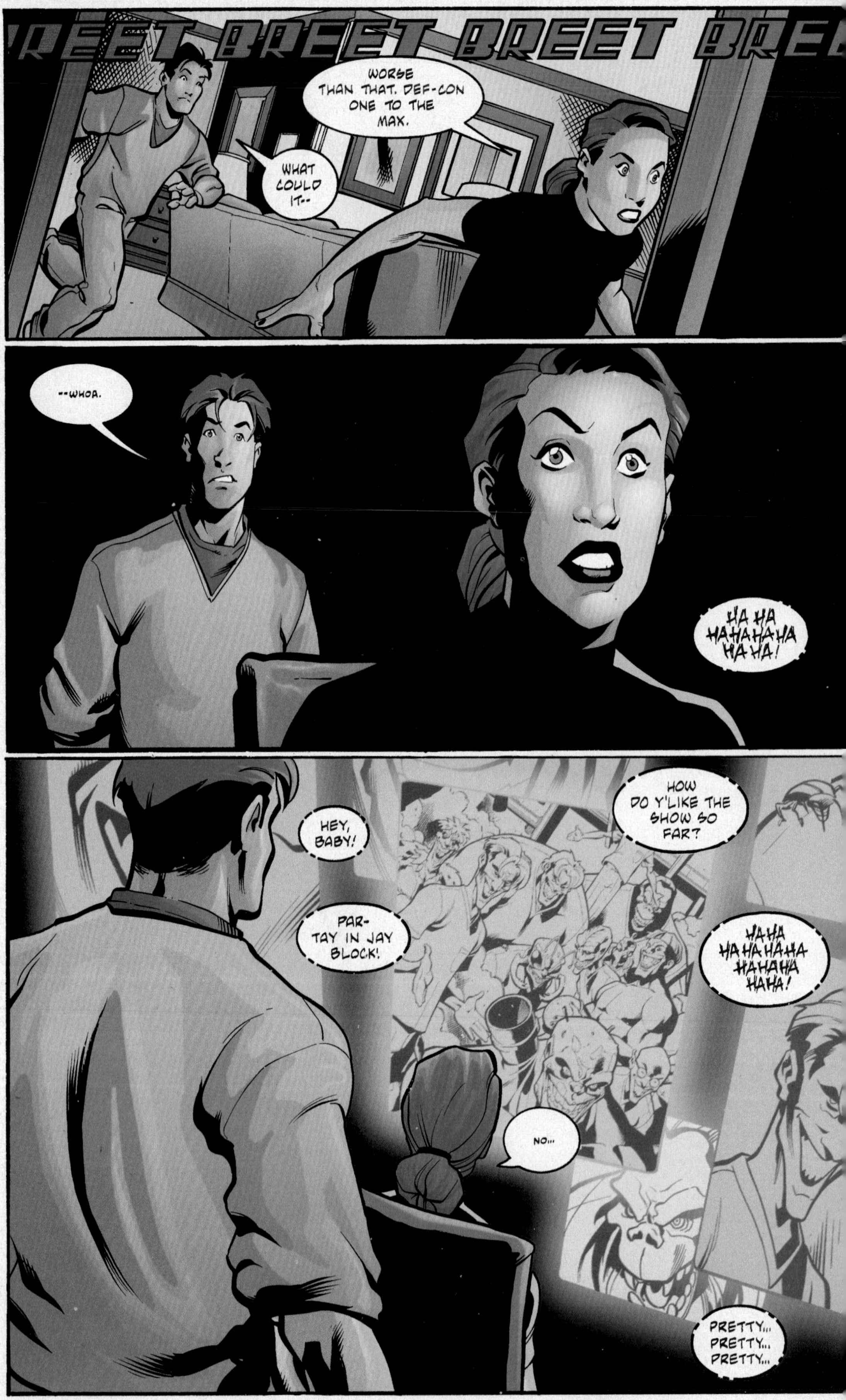
BREET BREET BREET BRE
WORSE THAN THAT. DEF-CON ONE TO THE MAX.
WHAT COULD IT--
--WHOA.
HA HA HAHAHAHA HA HA!
HEY, BABY!
PAR-TAY IN JAY BLOCK!
HOW DO Y'LIKE THE SHOW SO FAR?
HAHA HAHAHAHA HAHAHA HAHA!
NO...
PRETTY... PRETTY... PRETTY...

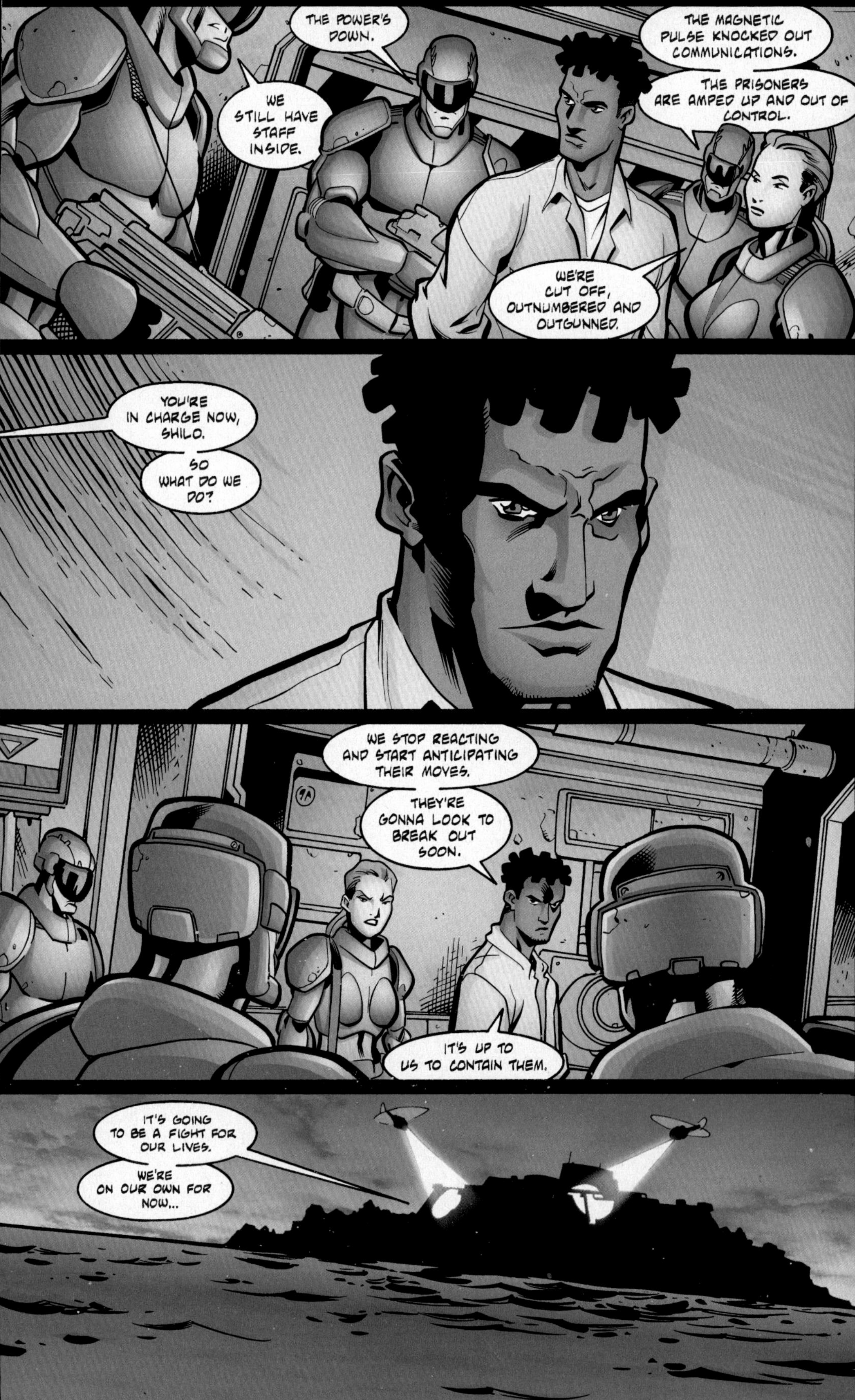
THE POWER'S DOWN.
WE STILL HAVE STAFF INSIDE.
THE MAGNETIC PULSE KNOCKED OUT COMMUNICATIONS.
THE PRISONERS ARE AMPED UP AND OUT OF CONTROL.
WE'RE CUT OFF, OUTNUMBERED AND OUTGUNNED.
YOU'RE IN CHARGE NOW, SHILO.
SO WHAT DO WE DO?
WE STOP REACTING AND START ANTICIPATING THEIR MOVES.
THEY'RE GONNA LOOK TO BREAK OUT SOON.
IT'S UP TO US TO CONTAIN THEM.
IT'S GOING TO BE A FIGHT FOR OUR LIVES.
WE'RE ON OUR OWN FOR NOW...

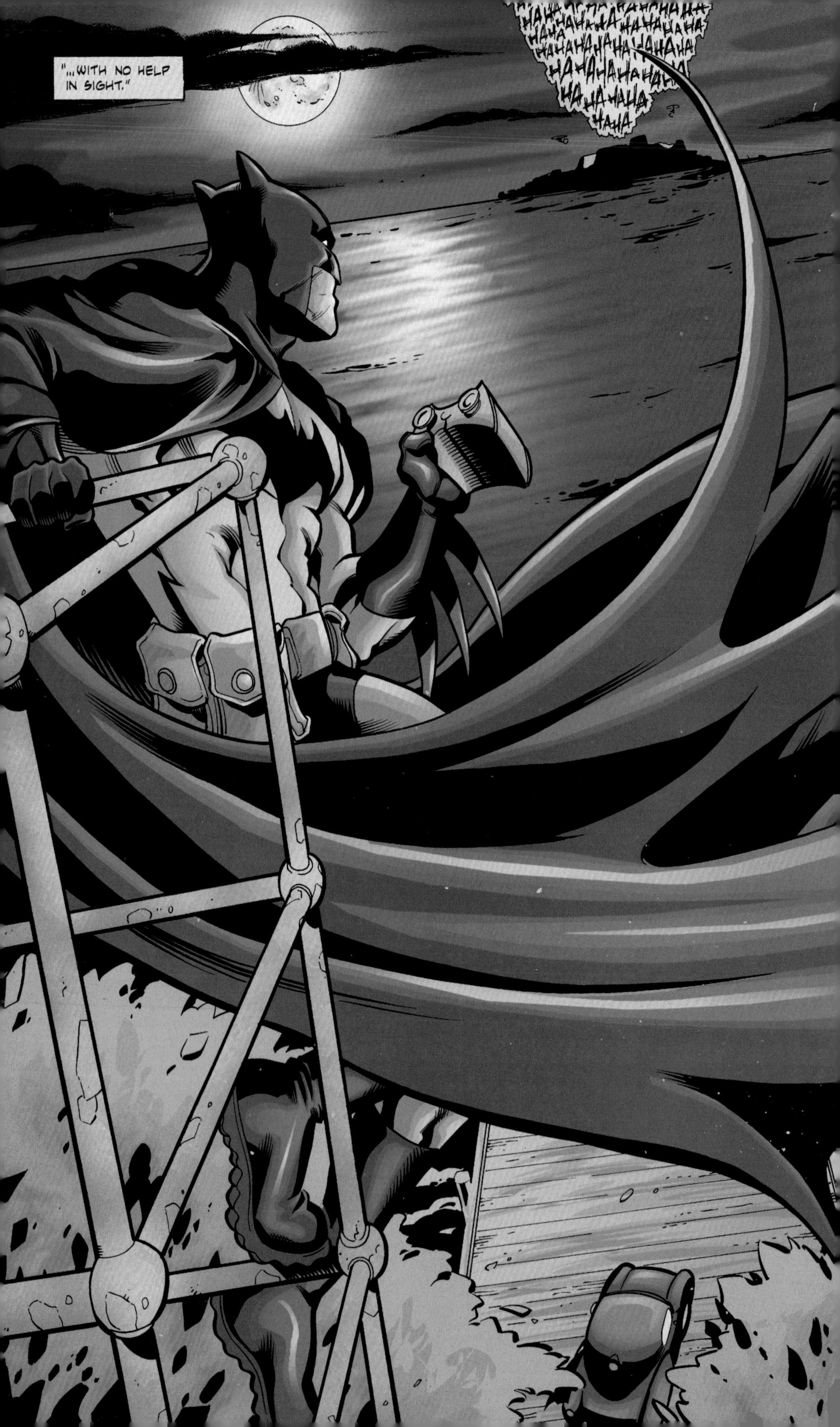
"...WITH NO HELP IN SIGHT."
HA HA HA HA HA HA HA HA HA HA HA HA HA HA HA HA HA HA HA HA HA HA HA HA HA HA HA HA HA

# Joker: Last Laugh

## part two: siege mentality

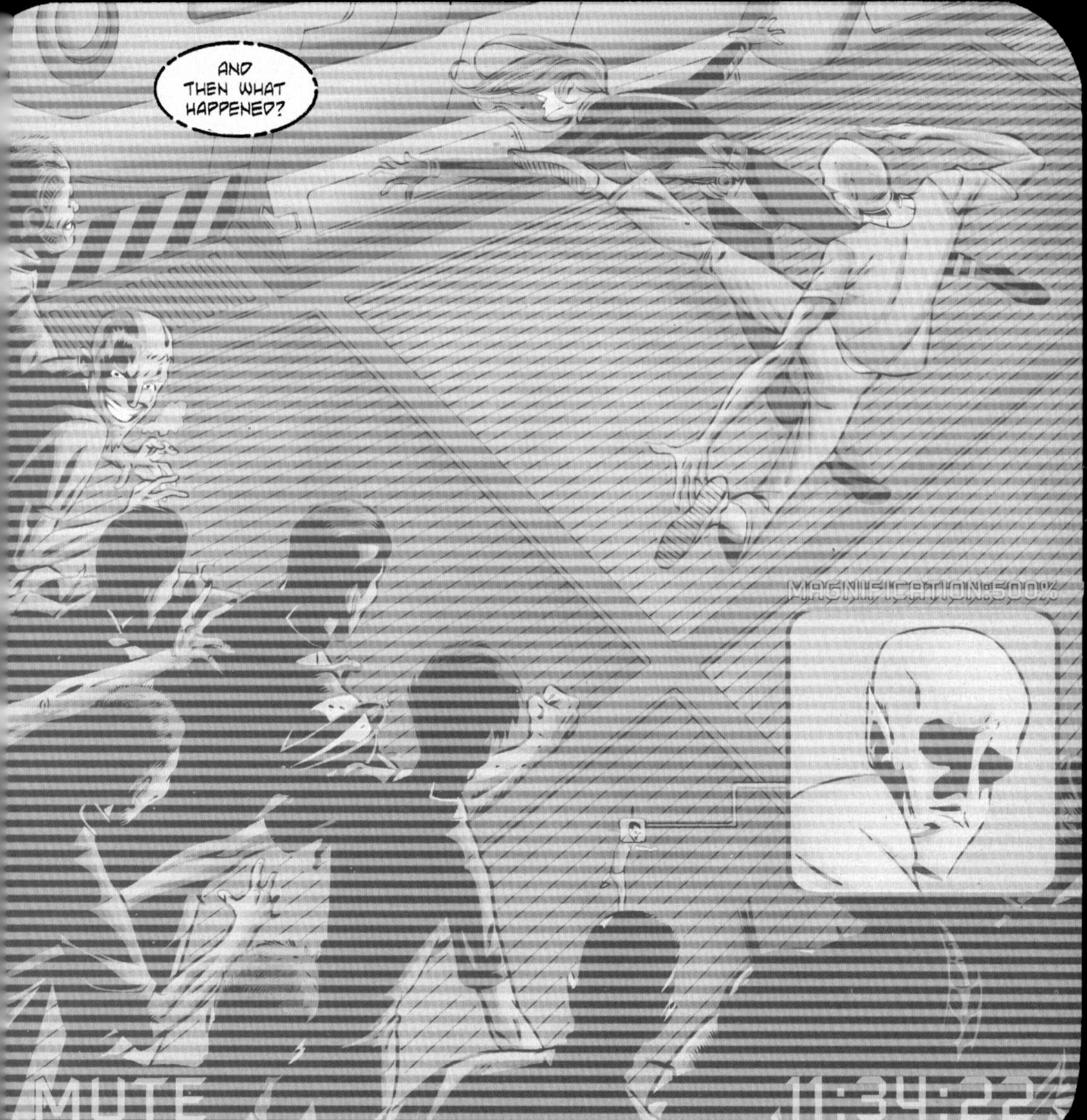

AND THEN WHAT HAPPENED?
MAGNIFICATION:500%
MUTE
11:34:22


written by Chuck Dixon & Scott Beatty pencils by Marcos Martin
inks by Mark Farmer & Alvaro Lopez
colors by Tom McCraw separations by Digital Chameleon
letters by Willie Schubert
assistant editor Nachie Castro editor Matt Idelson

Batman created by Bob Kane

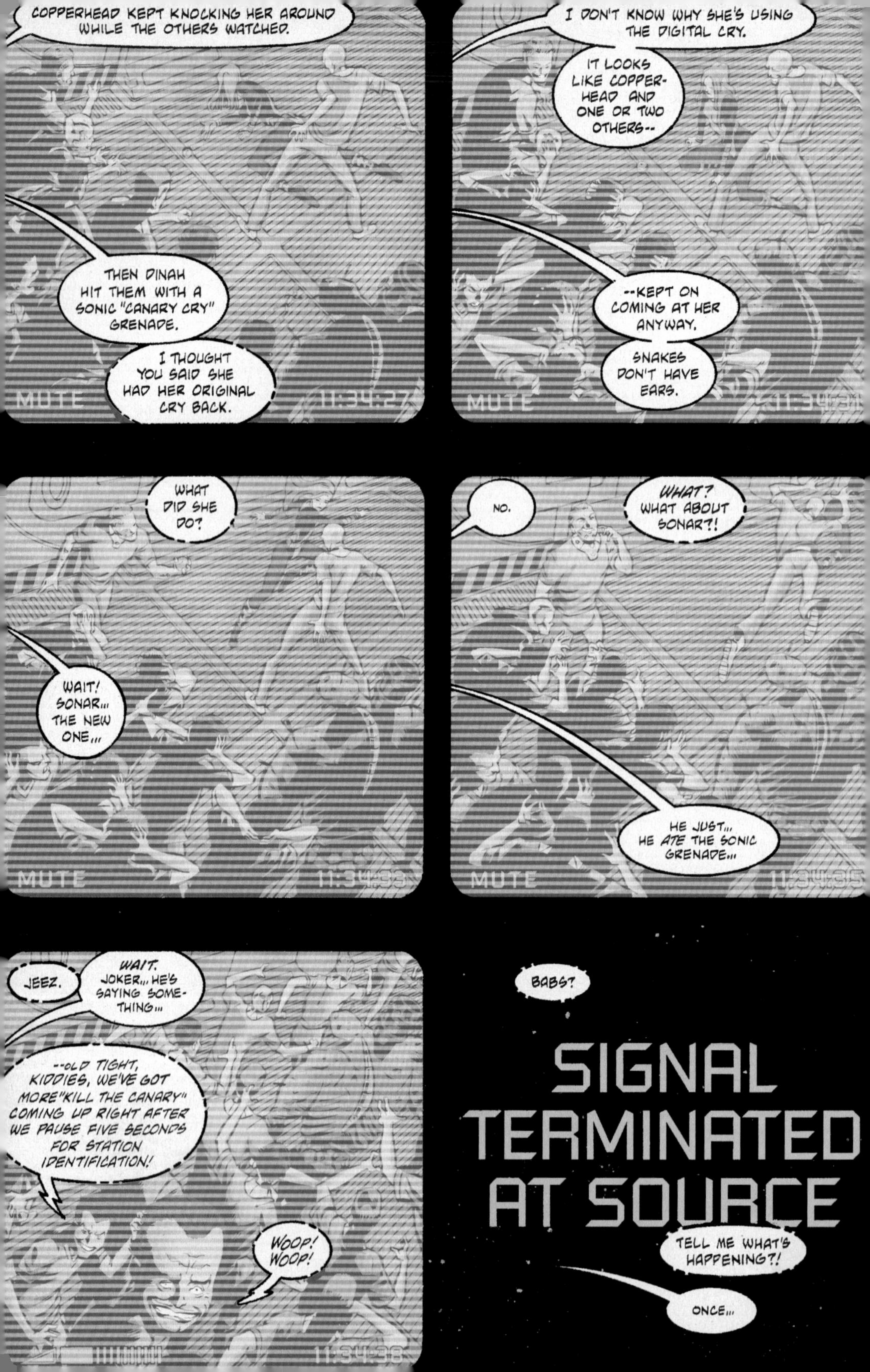
COPPERHEAD KEPT KNOCKING HER AROUND WHILE THE OTHERS WATCHED.
THEN DINAH HIT THEM WITH A SONIC "CANARY CRY" GRENADE.
I THOUGHT YOU SAID SHE HAD HER ORIGINAL CRY BACK.
MUTE
11:34:27
I DON'T KNOW WHY SHE'S USING THE DIGITAL CRY.
IT LOOKS LIKE COPPER-HEAD AND ONE OR TWO OTHERS--
--KEPT ON COMING AT HER ANYWAY.
SNAKES DON'T HAVE EARS.
MUTE
WHAT DID SHE DO?
WAIT! SONAR... THE NEW ONE...
MUTE
NO.
WHAT? WHAT ABOUT SONAR?!
HE JUST... HE ATE THE SONIC GRENADE...
MUTE
JEEZ.
WAIT. JOKER... HE'S SAYING SOME-THING...
--OLD TIGHT, KIDDIES, WE'VE GOT MORE "KILL THE CANARY" COMING UP RIGHT AFTER WE PAUSE FIVE SECONDS FOR STATION IDENTIFICATION!
WOOP! WOOP!
BABS?
SIGNAL TERMINATED AT SOURCE
TELL ME WHAT'S HAPPENING?!
ONCE...

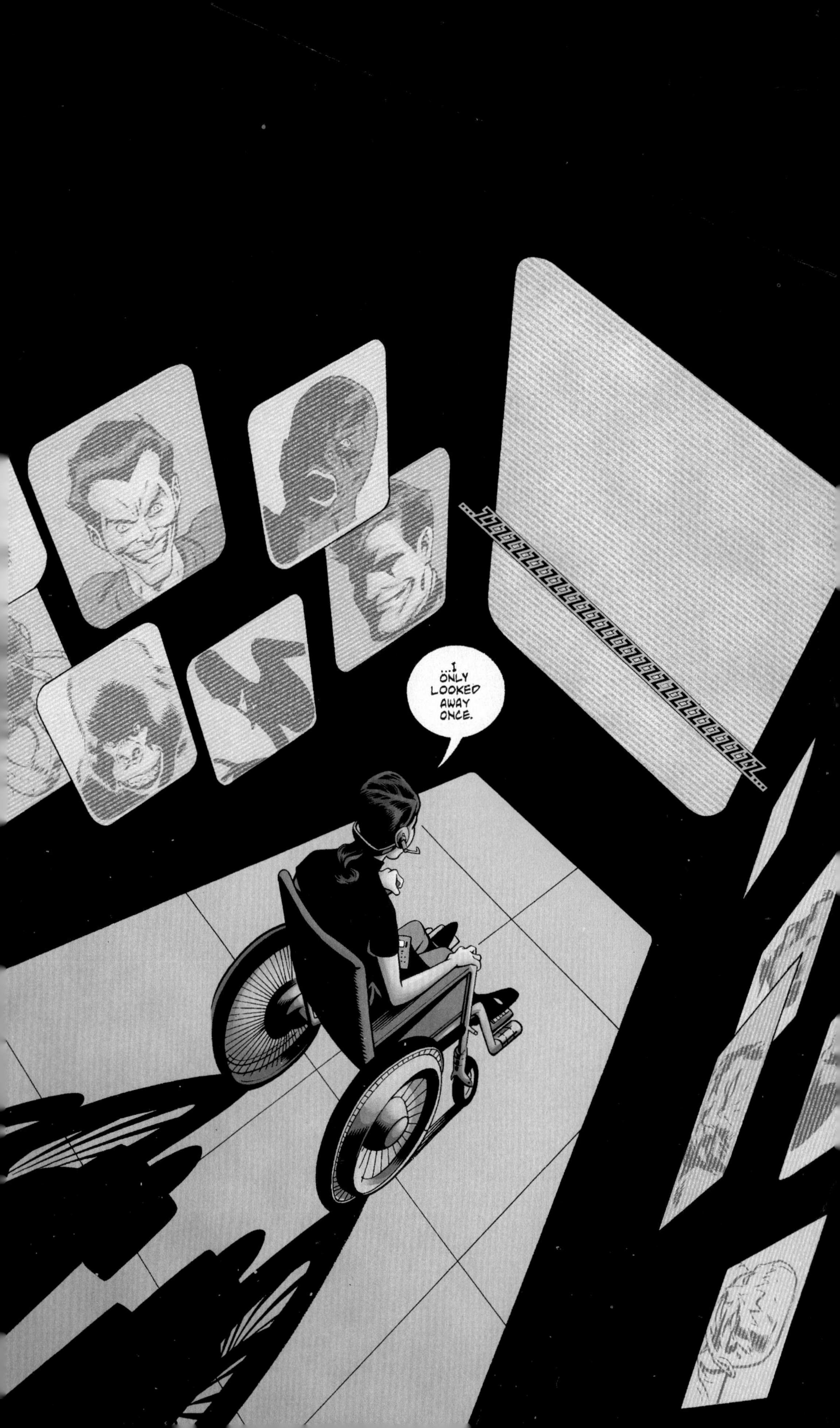

...I ONLY LOOKED AWAY ONCE.

DINAH'S OKAY, BABS.

JUST FOCUS ON THAT RIGHT NOW--

SCREEEEEER!

--AND TRY TO GET THE LOCAL COPS OFF MY TAIL.

I BROKE ABOUT SIXTEEN SPEED LIMITS GETTING HERE.

I KNEW THIS WOULD HAPPEN.

NONE OF THIS IS YOUR FAULT, BABS.

I SHOULDN'T HAVE LET YOU DRAG ME AWAY.

I TRIED TO TELL YOU....

VEET-VEET-DOOT-VEET

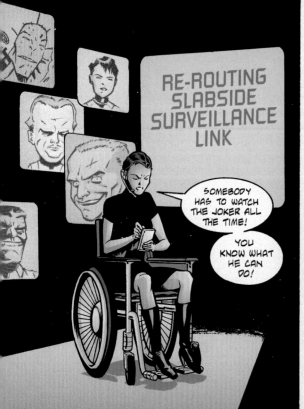

RE-ROUTING SLABSIDE SURVEILLANCE LINK

SOMEBODY HAS TO WATCH THE JOKER ALL THE TIME!

YOU KNOW WHAT HE CAN DO!

LOOK, BATMAN'S ALREADY ON-SCENE...AND I'LL BET THE JUSTICE LEAGUE'S GOT THE PLACE WRAPPED UP IN A FORCE FIELD OR SOMETHING BY NOW.

DICK, THE J.L.A.'S OFF-WORLD. IT'S JUST THE HOME TEAM.

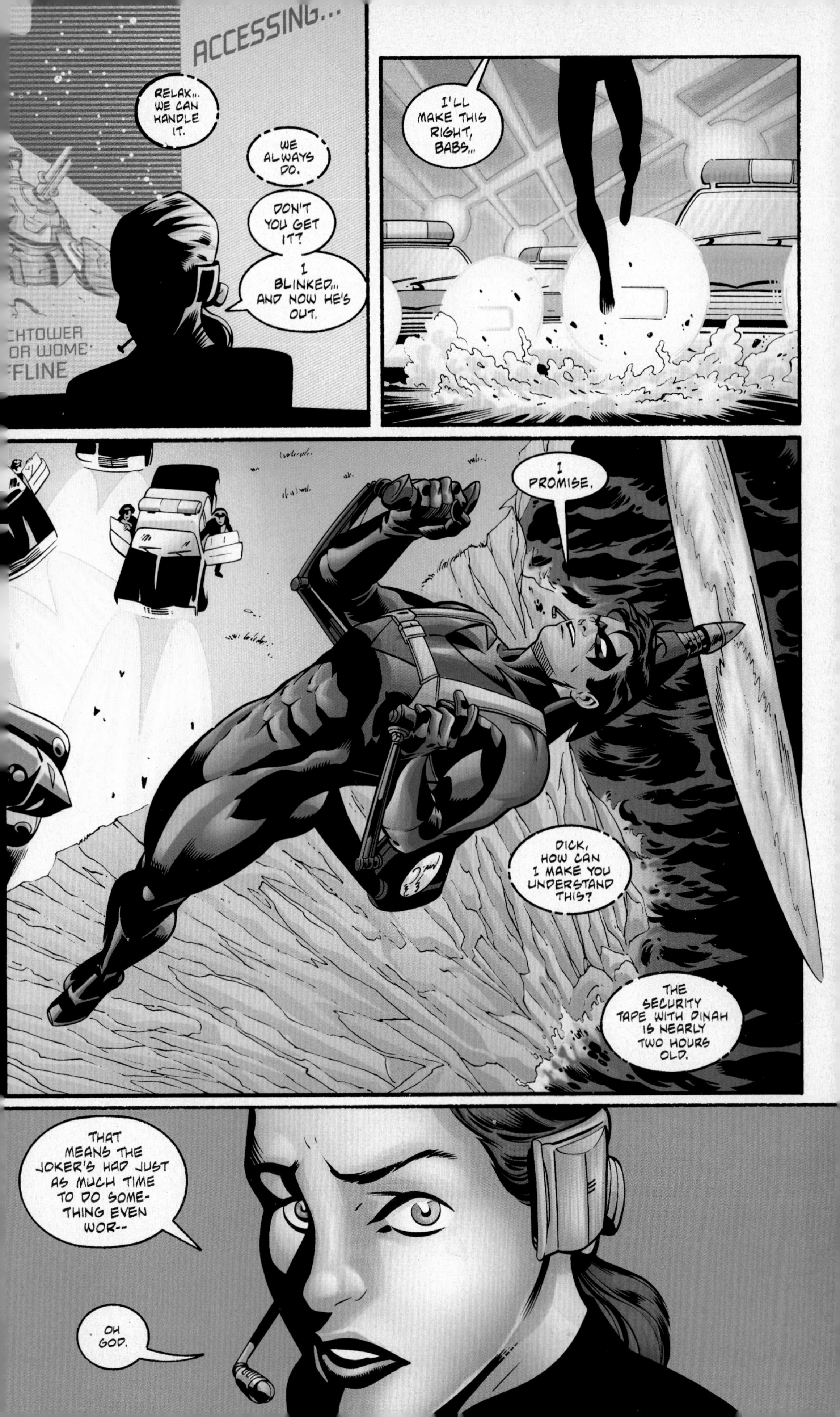
ACCESSING...
RELAX... WE CAN HANDLE IT.
WE ALWAYS DO.
DON'T YOU GET IT?
I BLINKED... AND NOW HE'S OUT.
CHTOWER
OR WOME
FFLINE
I'LL MAKE THIS RIGHT, BABS...
I PROMISE.
DICK, HOW CAN I MAKE YOU UNDERSTAND THIS?
THE SECURITY TAPE WITH DINAH IS NEARLY TWO HOURS OLD.
THAT MEANS THE JOKER'S HAD JUST AS MUCH TIME TO DO SOME-THING EVEN WOR--
OH GOD.

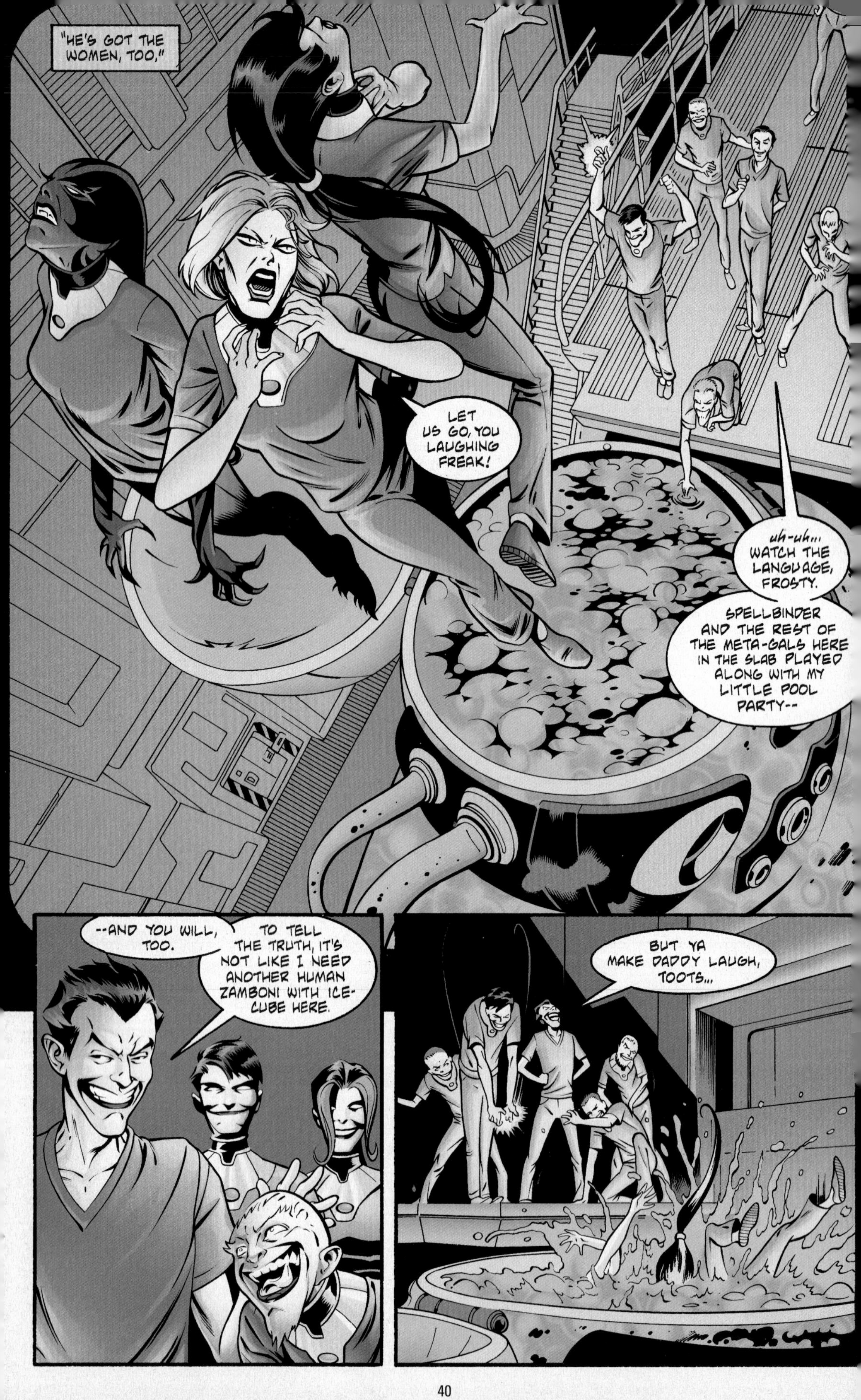
"HE'S GOT THE WOMEN, TOO,"
LET US GO, YOU LAUGHING FREAK!
uh-uh... WATCH THE LANGUAGE, FROSTY.
SPELLBINDER AND THE REST OF THE META-GALS HERE IN THE SLAB PLAYED ALONG WITH MY LITTLE POOL PARTY--
--AND YOU WILL, TOO.
TO TELL THE TRUTH, IT'S NOT LIKE I NEED ANOTHER HUMAN ZAMBONI WITH ICE-CUBE HERE.
BUT YA MAKE DADDY LAUGH, TOOTS...

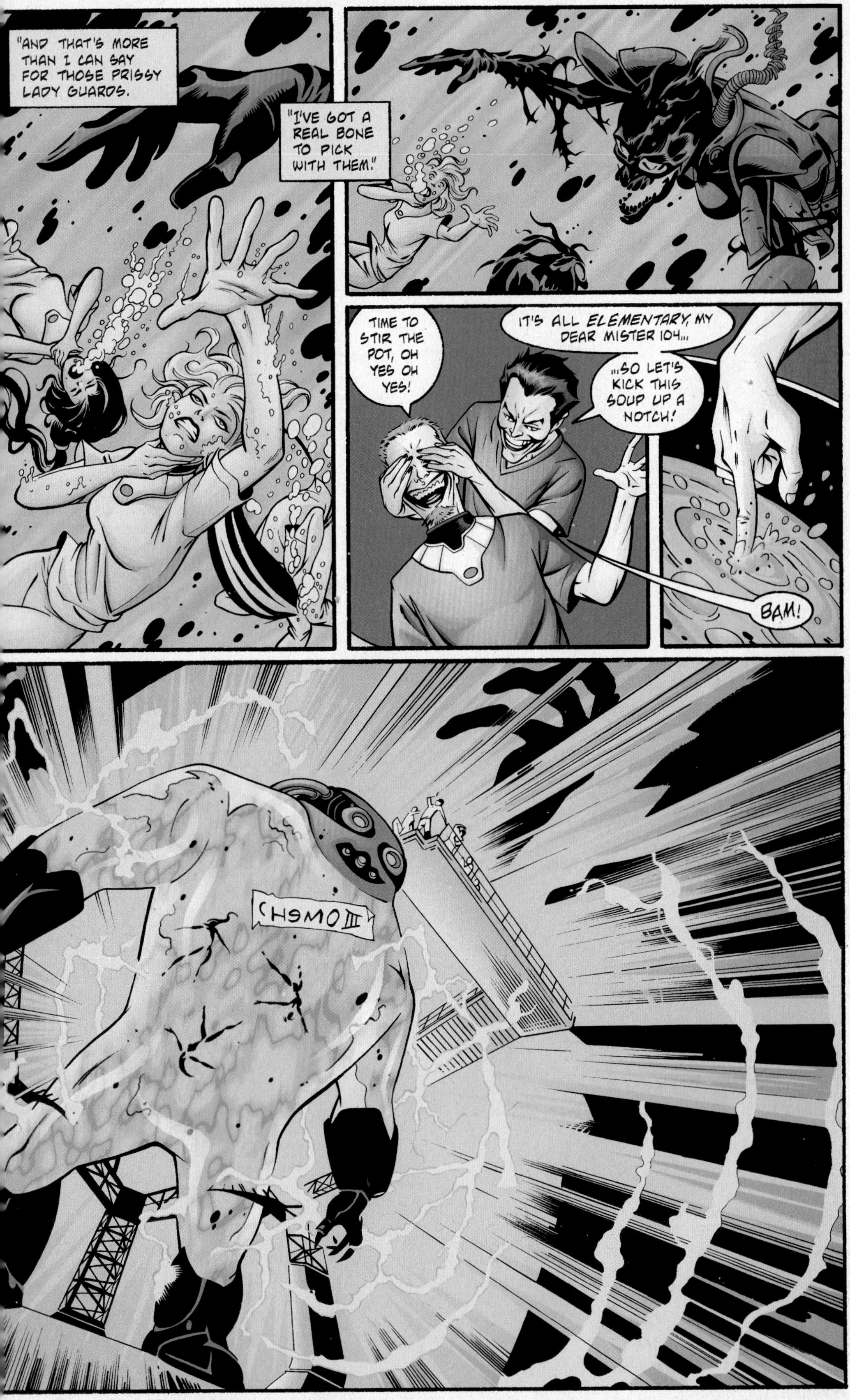

"AND THAT'S MORE THAN I CAN SAY FOR THOSE PRISSY LADY GUARDS.
"I'VE GOT A REAL BONE TO PICK WITH THEM."
TIME TO STIR THE POT, OH YES OH YES!
IT'S ALL ELEMENTARY, MY DEAR MISTER 104...
...SO LET'S KICK THIS SOUP UP A NOTCH!
BAM!
CHEMO III

SURVEILLANCE HUB, WHERE THE HELL ARE YOU?

THIS IS SHILO NORMAN. YOU KNOW, *HEAD* OF SECURITY?

SUB-LEVEL M

HELLO?

FZSST... TZZL...

SHI, RUN THIS BY ME AGAIN.

WHY ARE WE GOING DOWN WHEN THE FIGHT'S ALL UPSTAIRS?

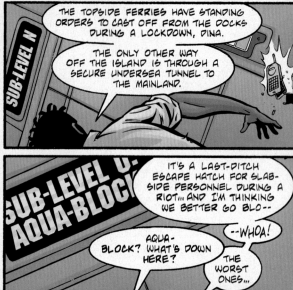

SUB-LEVEL N

THE TOPSIDE FERRIES HAVE STANDING ORDERS TO CAST OFF FROM THE DOCKS DURING A LOCKDOWN, DINA.

THE ONLY OTHER WAY OFF THE ISLAND IS THROUGH A SECURE UNDERSEA TUNNEL TO THE MAINLAND.

SUB-LEVEL O: AQUA-BLOCK

IT'S A LAST-DITCH ESCAPE HATCH FOR SLAB-SIDE PERSONNEL DURING A RIOT... AND I'M THINKING WE BETTER GO BLO--

--WHOA!

AQUA-BLOCK? WHAT'S DOWN HERE?

THE WORST ONES...

HI. HOWYADOING?

THE MAN-EATERS!

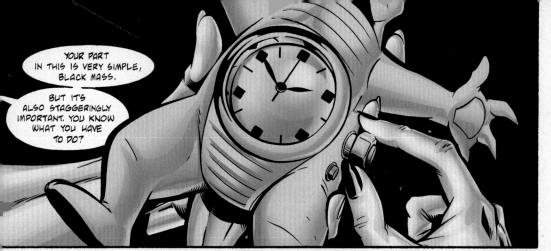

YOUR PART IN THIS IS VERY SIMPLE, BLACK MASS.

BUT IT'S ALSO STAGGERINGLY IMPORTANT. YOU KNOW WHAT YOU HAVE TO DO?

THE ALARM CLOCK RINGS, M'BRUH.

I SLAM MY BANDS TOGETHER.

CHAIN REACTION AND THEN--

ZOOP! hee hee hee hee!

THAT'S RIGHT, RANCOR. A BIG SUCKING SOUND.

EVERYTHING GOES INTO A GRAVITY WELL.

giggle. snort.

GUARDS. MARSHALS. ME.

giggle.

IT ALL GOES IN AND NOTHIN' COMES OUT.

tictictic

WELL, SEE YOU ON THE OTHER SIDE, BLACK MASS.

"OTHER SIDE."

GOOD ONE! Hee!

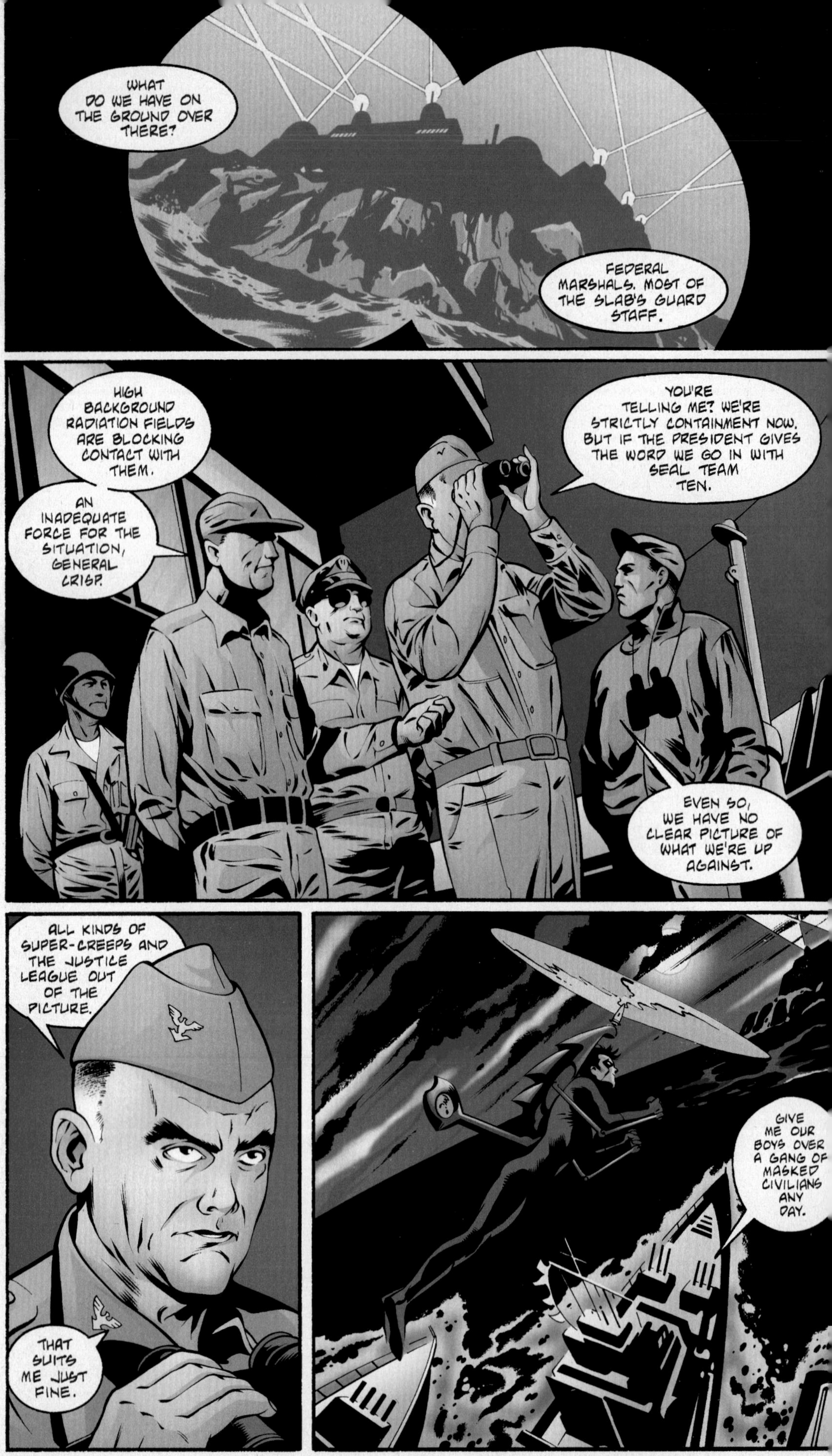
WHAT DO WE HAVE ON THE GROUND OVER THERE?
FEDERAL MARSHALS. MOST OF THE SLAB'S GUARD STAFF.
HIGH BACKGROUND RADIATION FIELDS ARE BLOCKING CONTACT WITH THEM.
AN INADEQUATE FORCE FOR THE SITUATION, GENERAL CRISP.
YOU'RE TELLING ME? WE'RE STRICTLY CONTAINMENT NOW. BUT IF THE PRESIDENT GIVES THE WORD WE GO IN WITH SEAL TEAM TEN.
EVEN SO, WE HAVE NO CLEAR PICTURE OF WHAT WE'RE UP AGAINST.
ALL KINDS OF SUPER-CREEPS AND THE JUSTICE LEAGUE OUT OF THE PICTURE.
THAT SUITS ME JUST FINE.
GIVE ME OUR BOYS OVER A GANG OF MASKED CIVILIANS ANY DAY.

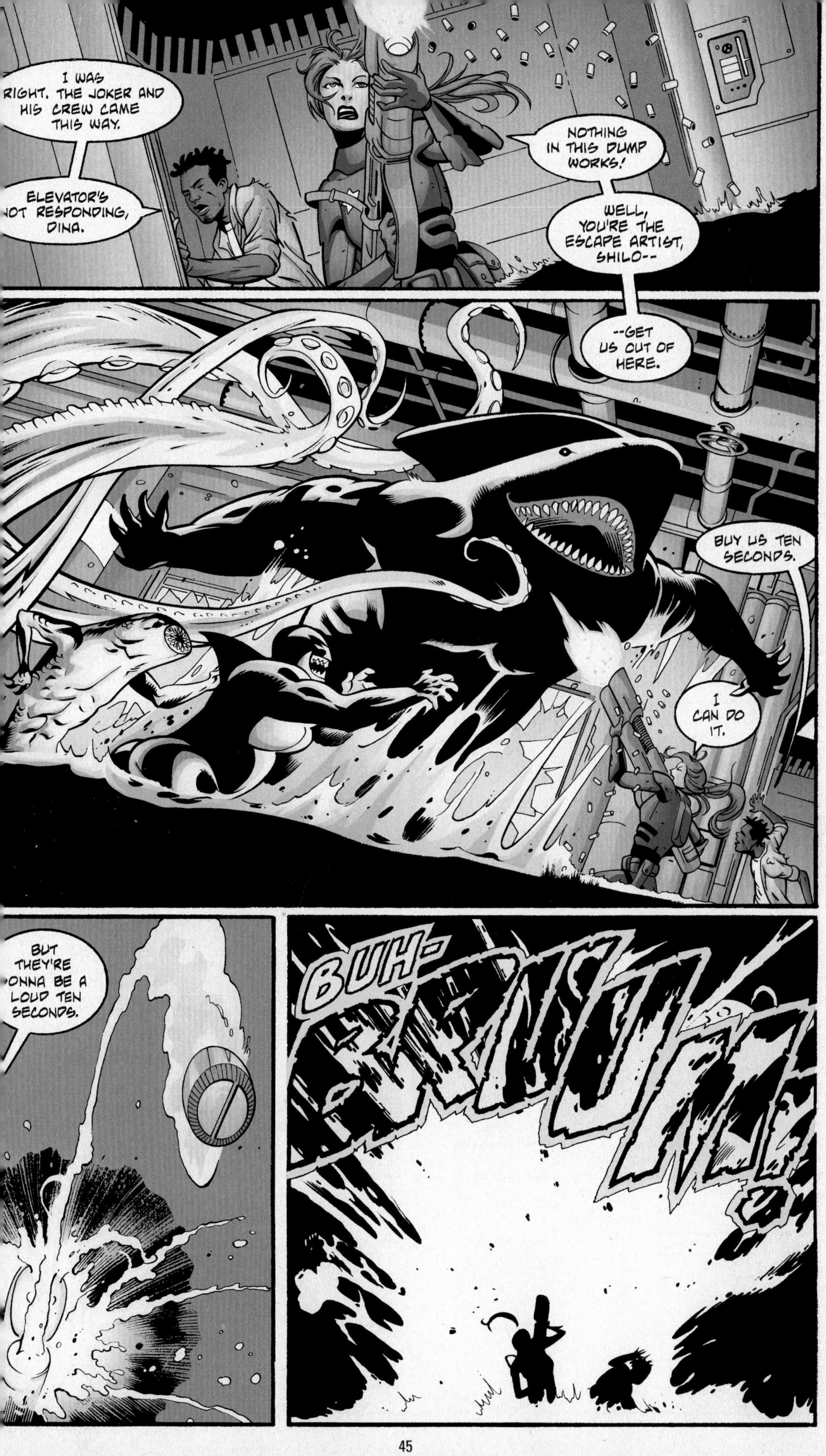
I WAS RIGHT. THE JOKER AND HIS CREW CAME THIS WAY.
ELEVATOR'S NOT RESPONDING, DINA.
NOTHING IN THIS DUMP WORKS!
WELL, YOU'RE THE ESCAPE ARTIST, SHILO--
--GET US OUT OF HERE.
BUY US TEN SECONDS.
I CAN DO IT.
BUT THEY'RE GONNA BE A LOUD TEN SECONDS.
BUH-

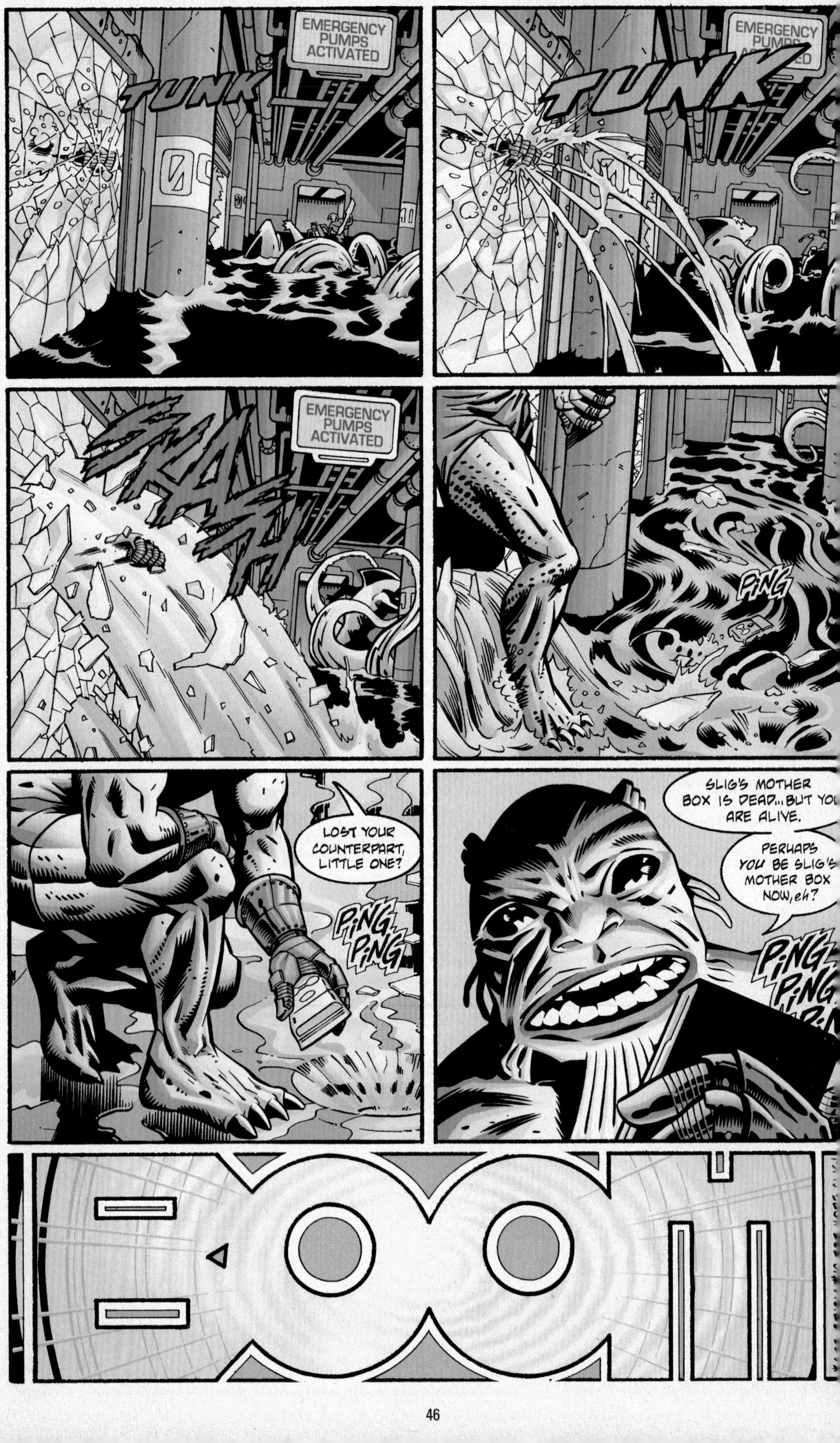

EMERGENCY PUMPS ACTIVATED
TUNK
EMERGENCY PUMPS
TUNK
EMERGENCY PUMPS ACTIVATED
PING
LOST YOUR COUNTERPART, LITTLE ONE?
PING PING
SLIG'S MOTHER BOX IS DEAD...BUT YOU ARE ALIVE.
PERHAPS YOU BE SLIG'S MOTHER BOX NOW, eh?
PING PING

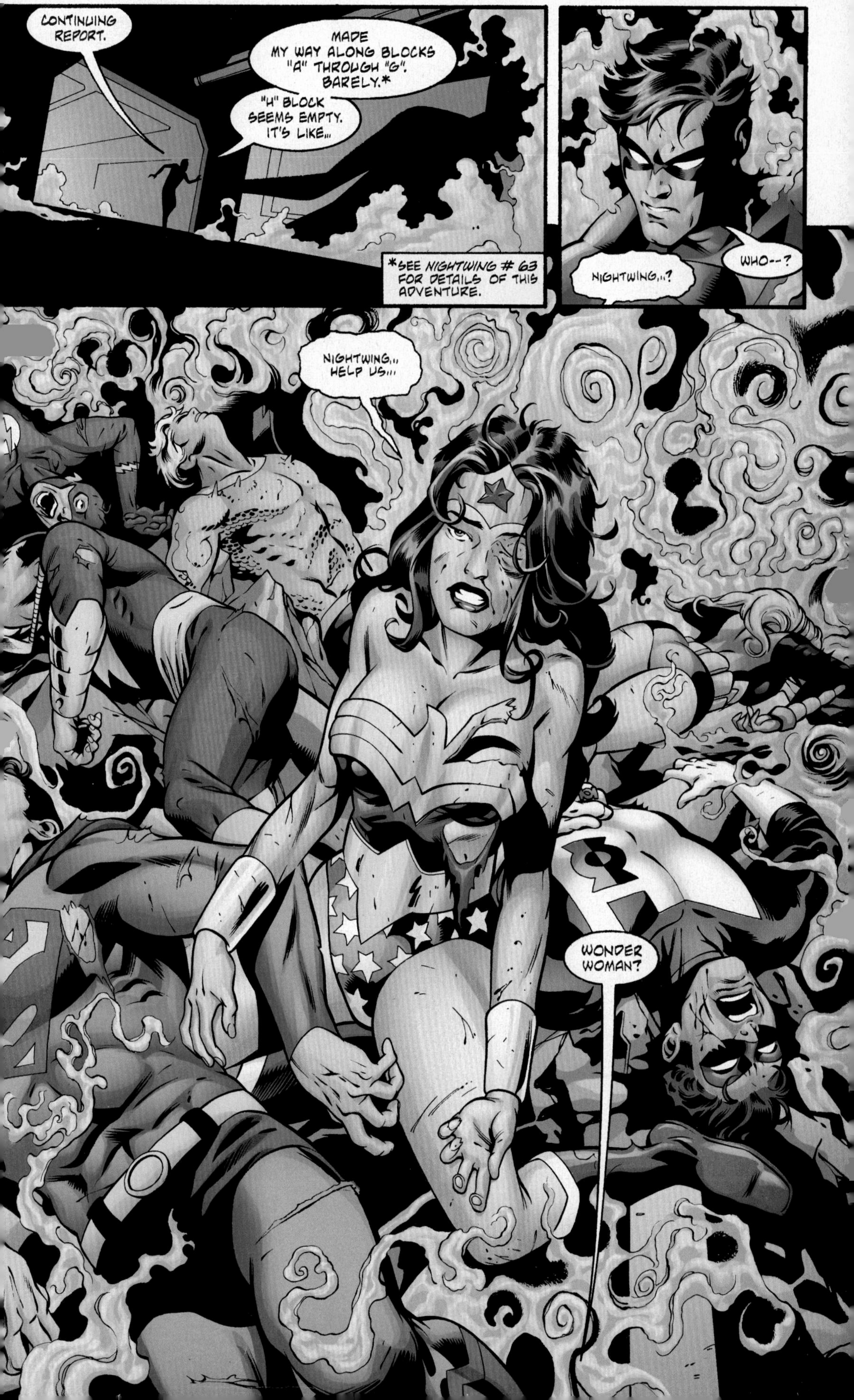
CONTINUING REPORT.
MADE MY WAY ALONG BLOCKS "A" THROUGH "G". BARELY.*
"H" BLOCK SEEMS EMPTY. IT'S LIKE...
*SEE NIGHTWING # 63 FOR DETAILS OF THIS ADVENTURE.
NIGHTWING...?
WHO--?
NIGHTWING... HELP US...
WONDER WOMAN?

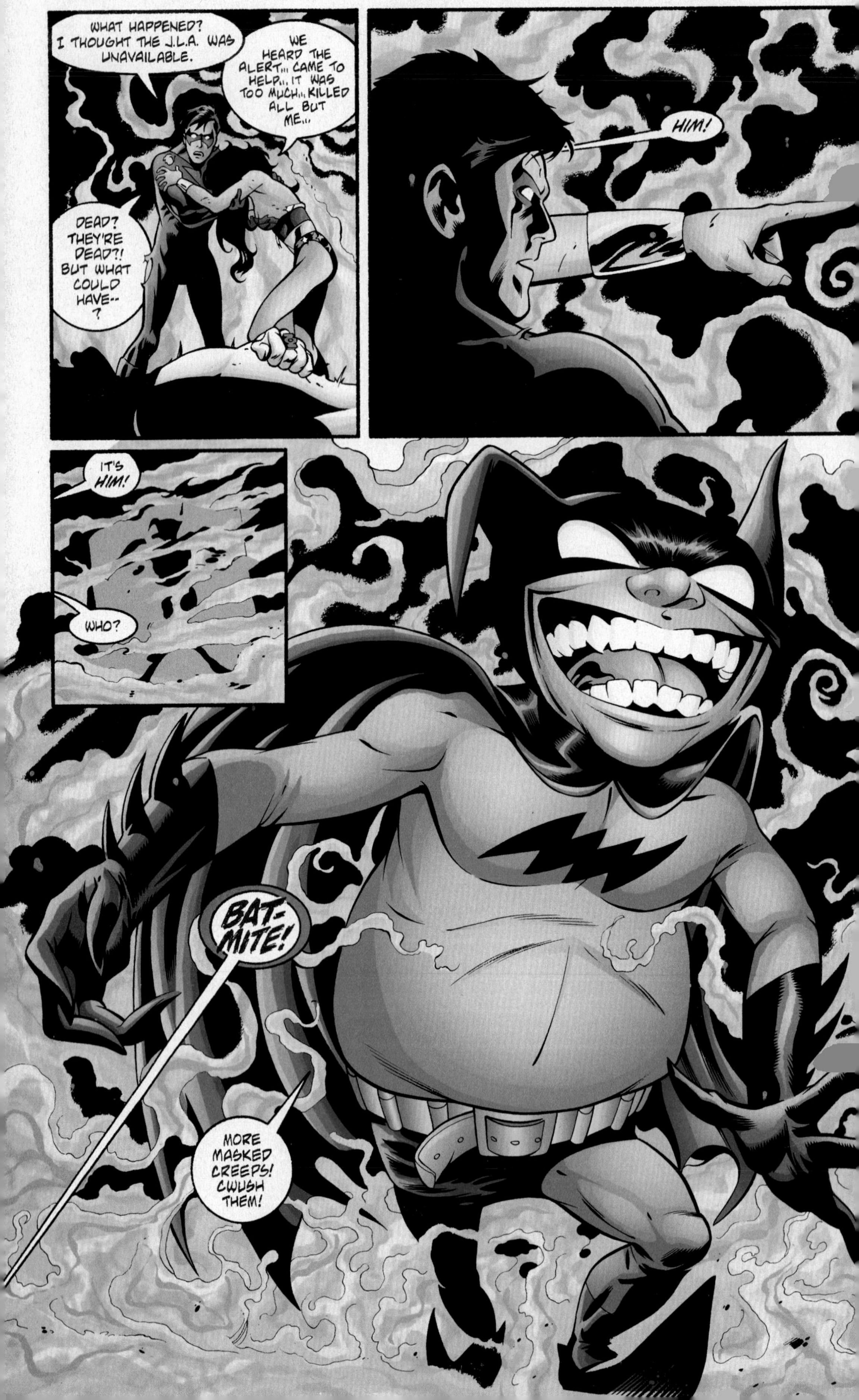
WHAT HAPPENED? I THOUGHT THE J.L.A. WAS UNAVAILABLE.
WE HEARD THE ALERT... CAME TO HELP... IT WAS TOO MUCH... KILLED ALL BUT ME...
DEAD? THEY'RE DEAD?! BUT WHAT COULD HAVE-- ?
HIM!
IT'S HIM!
WHO?
BAT-MITE!
MORE MASKED CREEPS! CWUSH THEM!

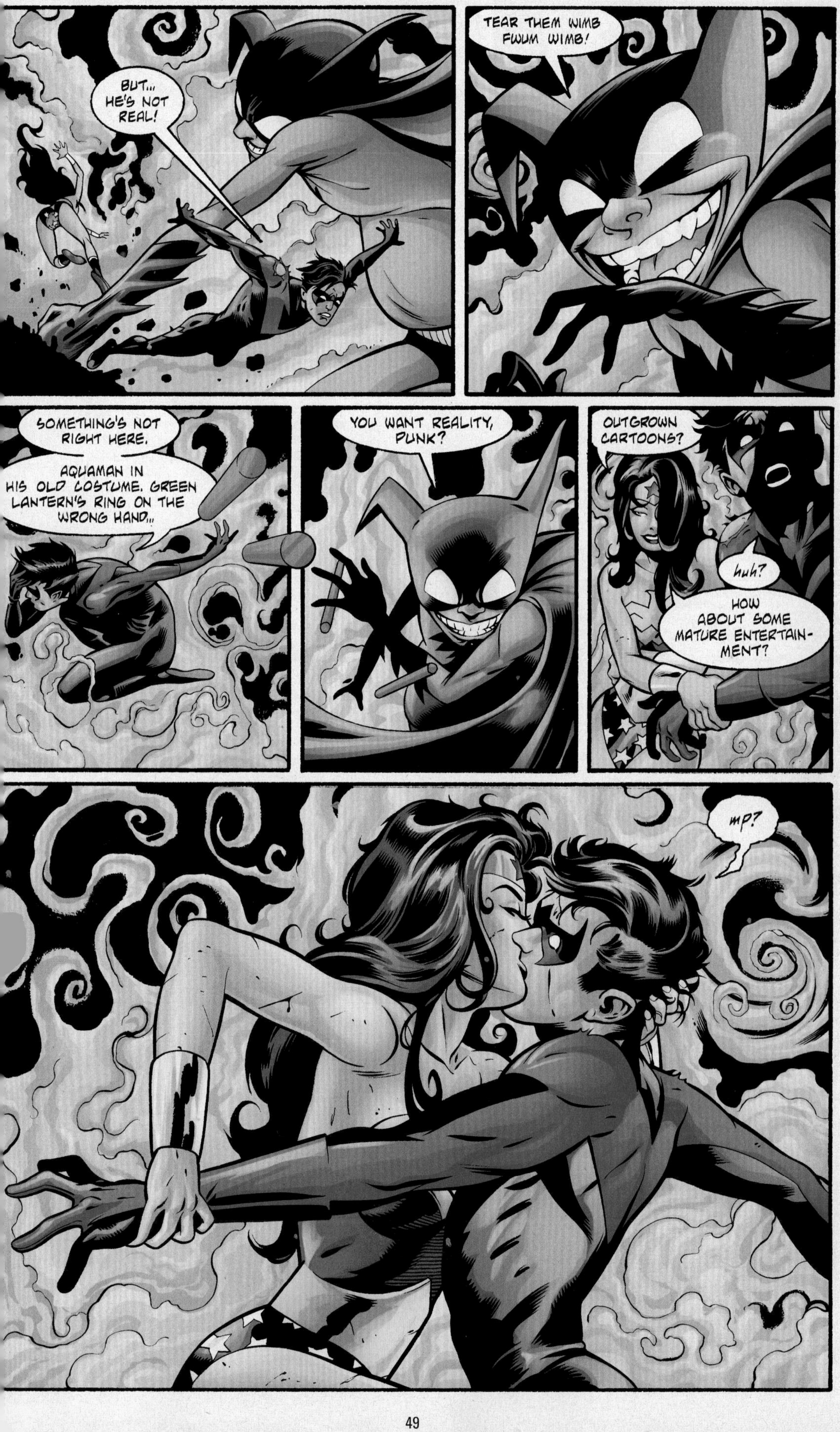
BUT... HE'S NOT REAL!
TEAR THEM WIMB FWUM WIMB!
SOMETHING'S NOT RIGHT HERE.
AQUAMAN IN HIS OLD COSTUME. GREEN LANTERN'S RING ON THE WRONG HAND...
YOU WANT REALITY, PUNK?
OUTGROWN CARTOONS?
huh?
HOW ABOUT SOME MATURE ENTERTAIN-MENT?
mp?

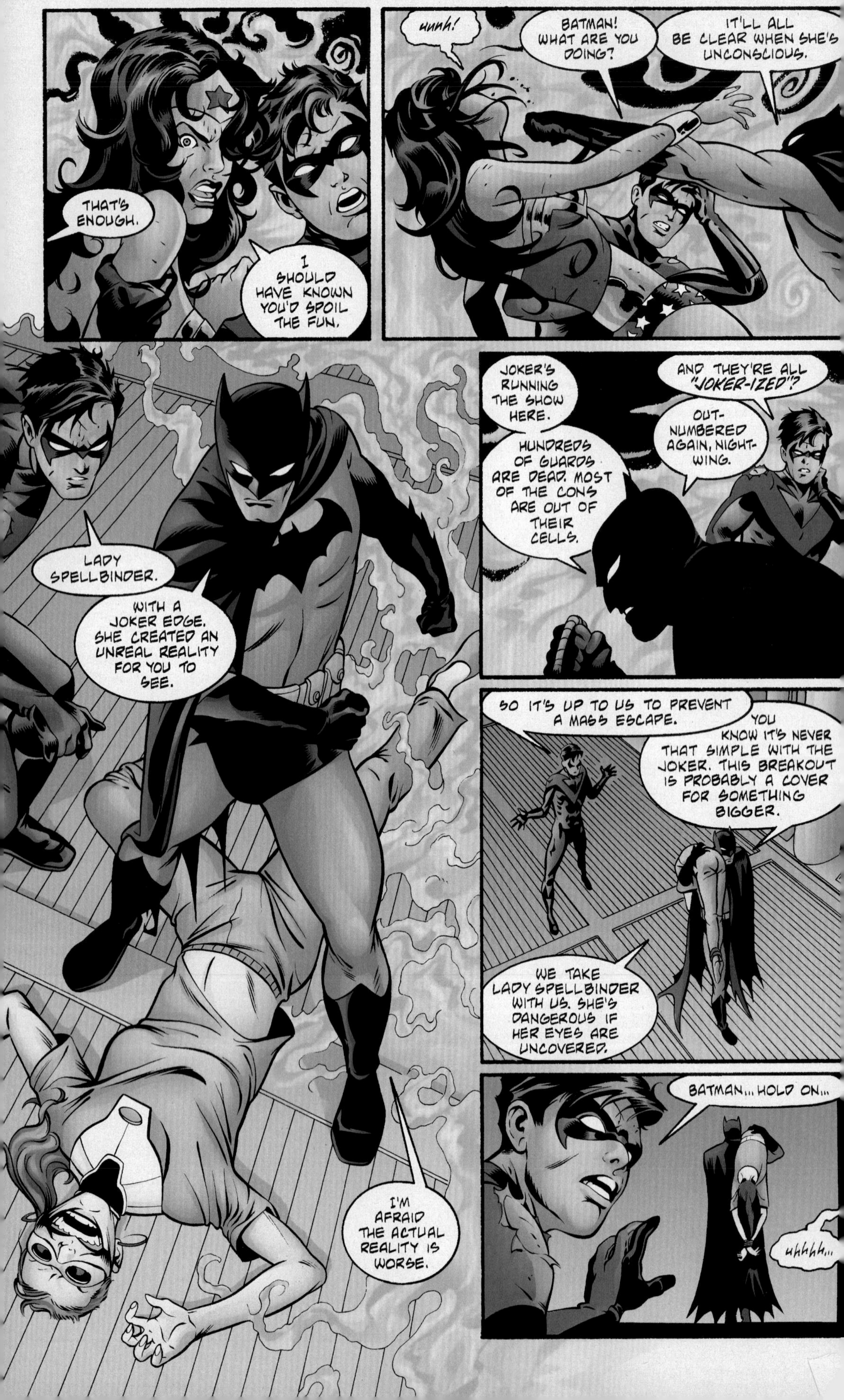
THAT'S ENOUGH.
I SHOULD HAVE KNOWN YOU'D SPOIL THE FUN.
unnh!
BATMAN! WHAT ARE YOU DOING?
IT'LL ALL BE CLEAR WHEN SHE'S UNCONSCIOUS.
LADY SPELLBINDER.
WITH A JOKER EDGE. SHE CREATED AN UNREAL REALITY FOR YOU TO SEE.
I'M AFRAID THE ACTUAL REALITY IS WORSE.
JOKER'S RUNNING THE SHOW HERE.
HUNDREDS OF GUARDS ARE DEAD. MOST OF THE CONS ARE OUT OF THEIR CELLS.
AND THEY'RE ALL "JOKER-IZED"?
OUT-NUMBERED AGAIN, NIGHT-WING.
SO IT'S UP TO US TO PREVENT A MASS ESCAPE.
YOU KNOW IT'S NEVER THAT SIMPLE WITH THE JOKER. THIS BREAKOUT IS PROBABLY A COVER FOR SOMETHING BIGGER.
WE TAKE LADY SPELLBINDER WITH US. SHE'S DANGEROUS IF HER EYES ARE UNCOVERED.
BATMAN... HOLD ON...
uhhhh...

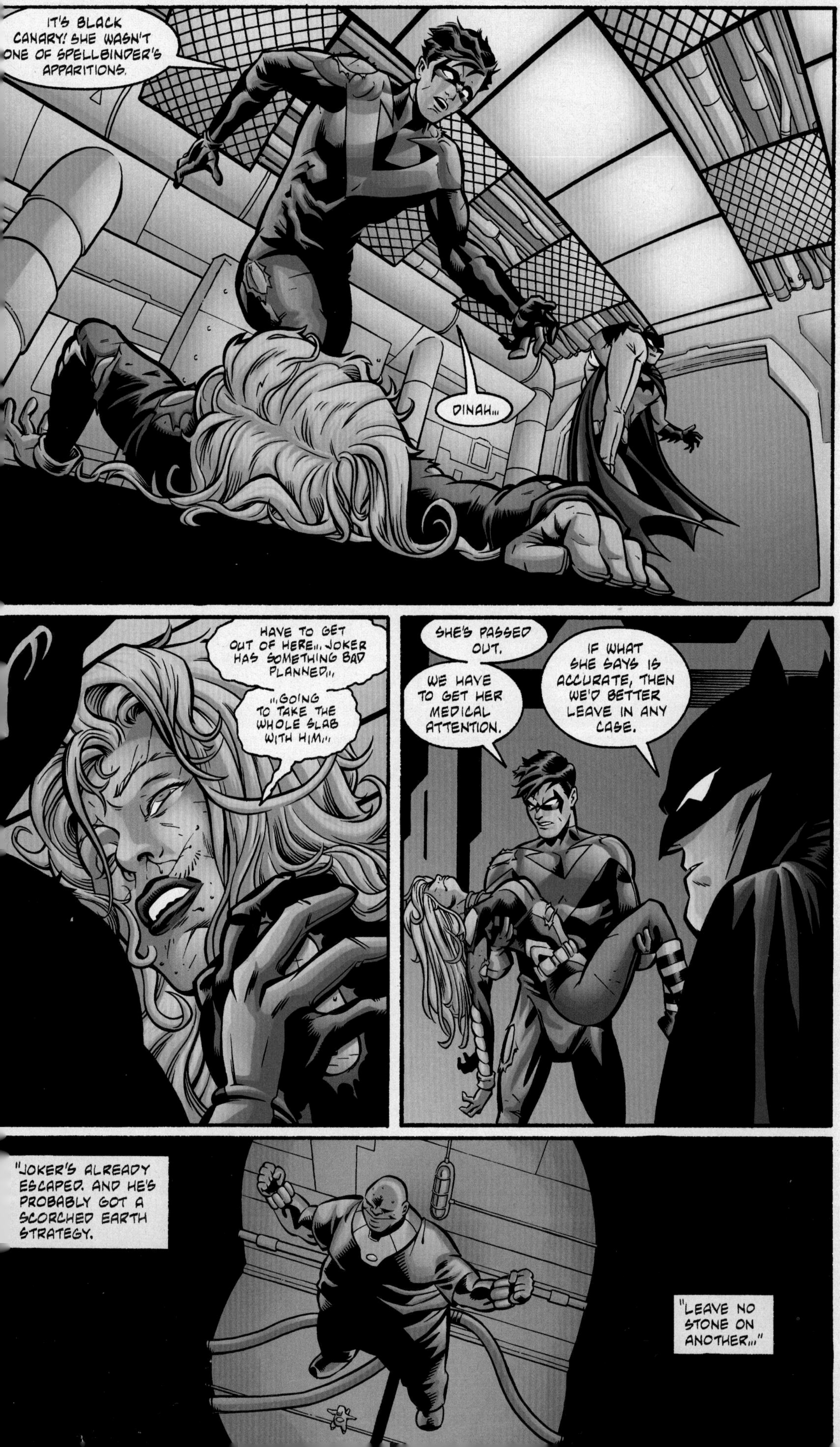
IT'S BLACK CANARY! SHE WASN'T ONE OF SPELLBINDER'S APPARITIONS.
DINAH...
HAVE TO GET OUT OF HERE... JOKER HAS SOMETHING BAD PLANNED...
...GOING TO TAKE THE WHOLE SLAB WITH HIM...
SHE'S PASSED OUT.
WE HAVE TO GET HER MEDICAL ATTENTION.
IF WHAT SHE SAYS IS ACCURATE, THEN WE'D BETTER LEAVE IN ANY CASE.
"JOKER'S ALREADY ESCAPED. AND HE'S PROBABLY GOT A SCORCHED EARTH STRATEGY.
"LEAVE NO STONE ON ANOTHER..."

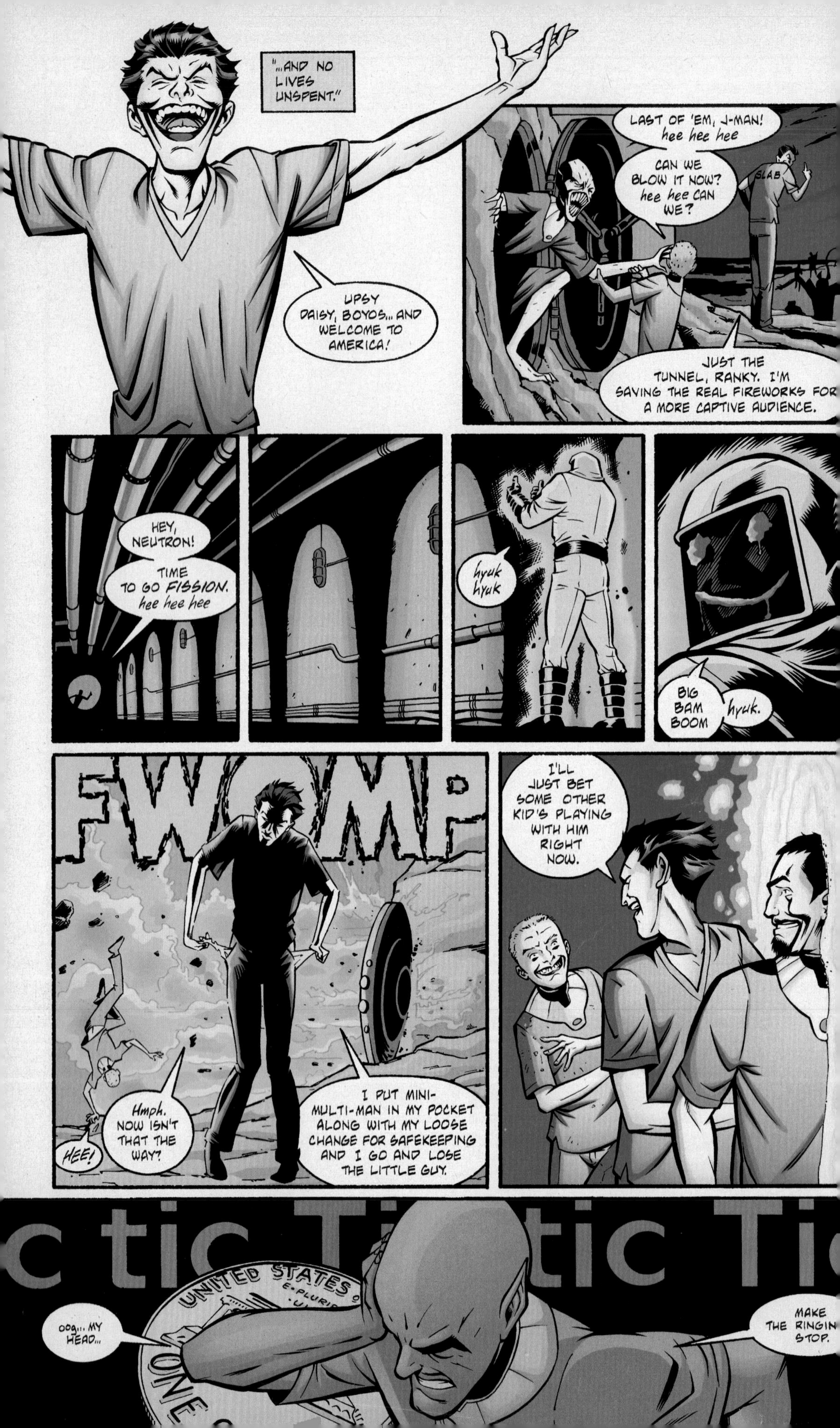
"...AND NO LIVES UNSPENT."
UPSY DAISY, BOYOS... AND WELCOME TO AMERICA!
LAST OF 'EM, J-MAN! hee hee hee
CAN WE BLOW IT NOW? hee hee CAN WE?
SLAB
JUST THE TUNNEL, RANKY. I'M SAVING THE REAL FIREWORKS FOR A MORE CAPTIVE AUDIENCE.
HEY, NEUTRON!
TIME TO GO FISSION. hee hee hee
hyuk hyuk
BIG BAM BOOM
hyuk.
FWOMP
HEE!
Hmph. NOW ISN'T THAT THE WAY?
I PUT MINI-MULTI-MAN IN MY POCKET ALONG WITH MY LOOSE CHANGE FOR SAFEKEEPING AND I GO AND LOSE THE LITTLE GUY.
I'LL JUST BET SOME OTHER KID'S PLAYING WITH HIM RIGHT NOW.
c tic Tic tic Tic
UNITED STATES
ONE
oog... MY HEAD...
MAKE THE RINGIN STOP.

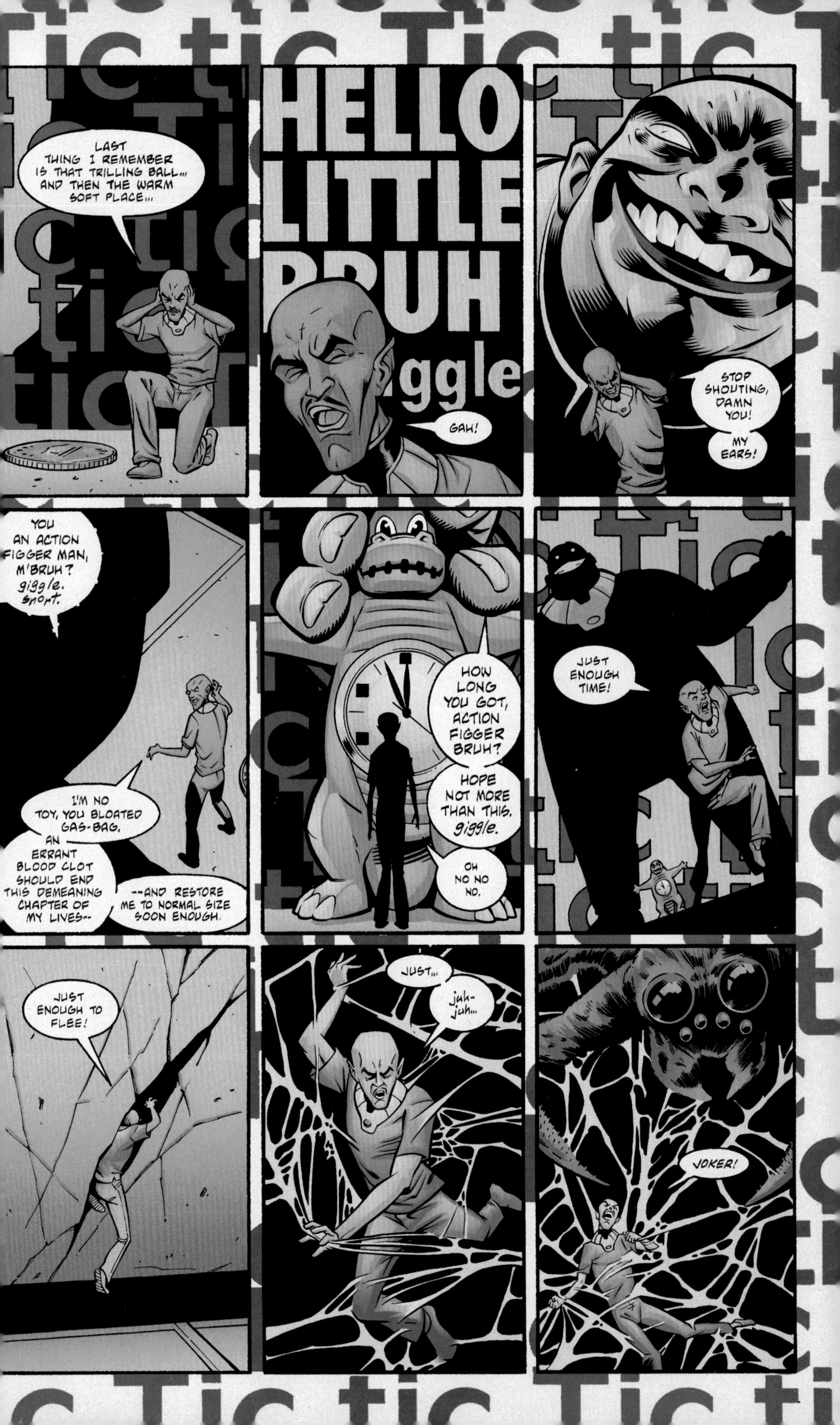
LAST THING I REMEMBER IS THAT TRILLING BALL... AND THEN THE WARM SOFT PLACE...
HELLO LITTLE BRUH
giggle
GAH!
STOP SHOUTING, DAMN YOU!
MY EARS!
YOU AN ACTION FIGGER MAN, M'BRUH? giggle. snort.
I'M NO TOY, YOU BLOATED GAS-BAG.
AN ERRANT BLOOD CLOT SHOULD END THIS DEMEANING CHAPTER OF MY LIVES--
--AND RESTORE ME TO NORMAL SIZE SOON ENOUGH.
HOW LONG YOU GOT, ACTION FIGGER BRUH?
HOPE NOT MORE THAN THIS. giggle.
OH NO NO NO.
JUST ENOUGH TIME!
JUST ENOUGH TO FLEE!
JUST...
juh-juh...
JOKER!

WE COULD REALLY USE THAT "BACK DOOR" OF YOURS RIGHT ABOUT NOW, SHI.

I LOST MOTHER BOX...nggh... BACK WHEN THAT WAVE HIT US.

GHOON GHOON

MOTHER WHO!?

DOESN'T MATTER. WE'RE SAFE FOR NOW AT LEAST.

DON'T BET ON IT. I THINK I SAW--

KRANK

--KING SHARK GETTING BACK UP.

AND YOU JUST BACKED US INTO A CORNER.

Uh-uh... WE CAN GO UP.

TRUNK

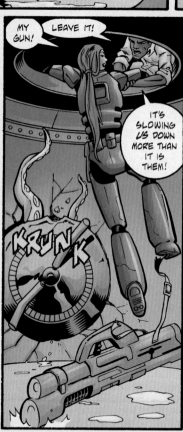

MY GUN!

LEAVE IT!

IT'S SLOWING US DOWN MORE THAN IT IS THEM!

KRUNK

THERE AREN'T ANY LADDERS.

OUT-VENTING TUBES. THEY PURGE EXCESS WATER IN CASE THE CELL BLOCK FLOODS.

SO PURGE US OUT OF HERE, SHI.

I'M WORKING ON IT... I'M WORKING ON IT...

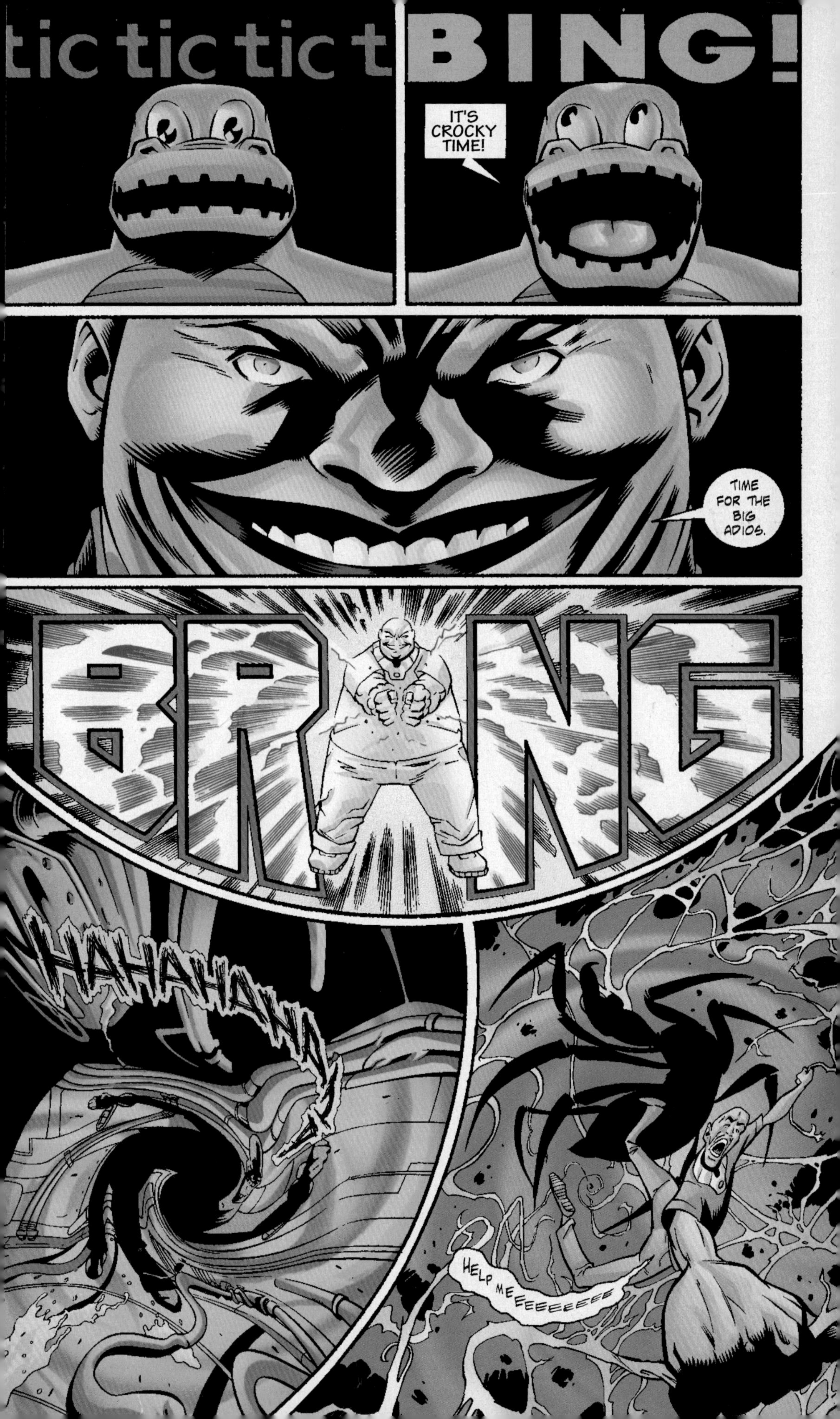

tic tic tic tic t
BING!
IT'S CROCKY TIME!
TIME FOR THE BIG ADIOS.
BRING
HAHAHAHA
HELP MEEEEEEEEEE

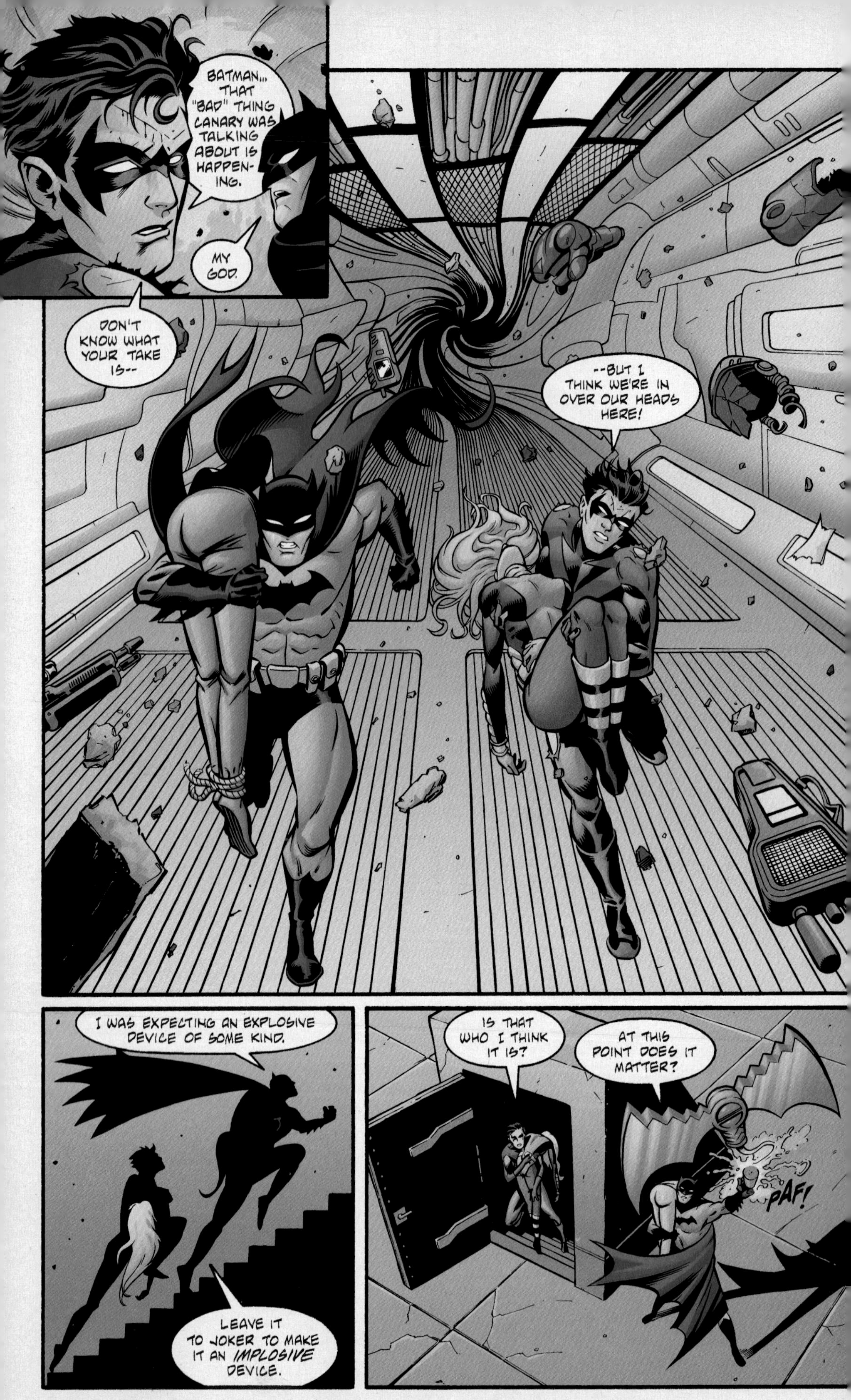
BATMAN... THAT "BAD" THING CANARY WAS TALKING ABOUT IS HAPPEN-ING.
MY GOD.
DON'T KNOW WHAT YOUR TAKE IS--
--BUT I THINK WE'RE IN OVER OUR HEADS HERE!
I WAS EXPECTING AN EXPLOSIVE DEVICE OF SOME KIND.
LEAVE IT TO JOKER TO MAKE IT AN *IMPLOSIVE* DEVICE.
IS THAT WHO I THINK IT IS?
AT THIS POINT DOES IT MATTER?
PAF!

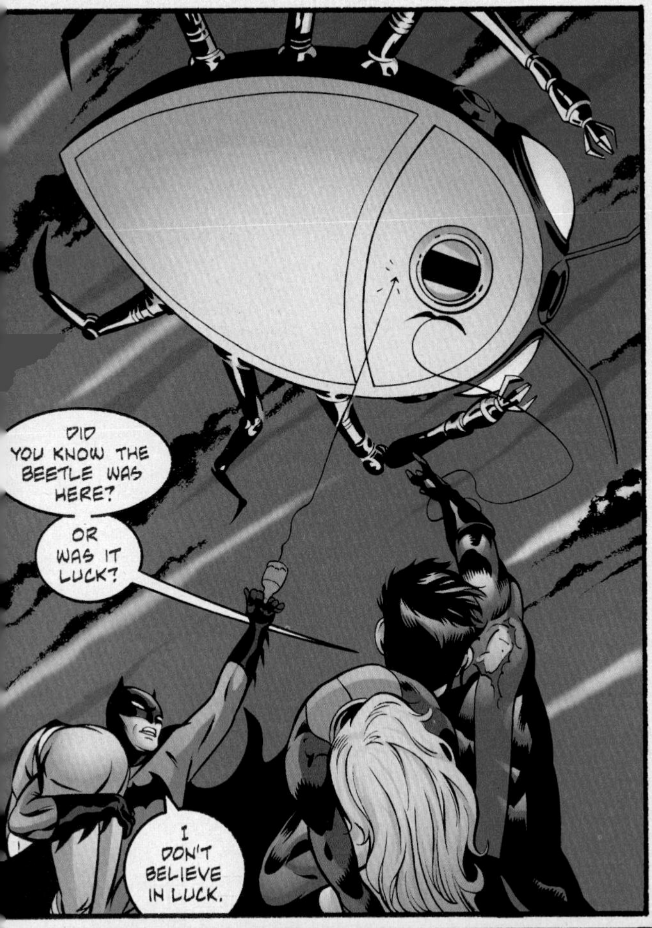
DID YOU KNOW THE BEETLE WAS HERE?
OR WAS IT LUCK?
I DON'T BELIEVE IN LUCK.

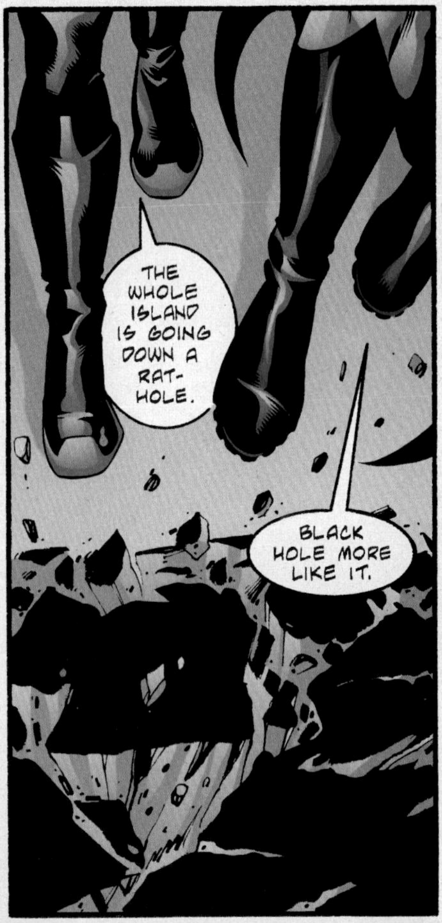
THE WHOLE ISLAND IS GOING DOWN A RAT-HOLE.
BLACK HOLE MORE LIKE IT.

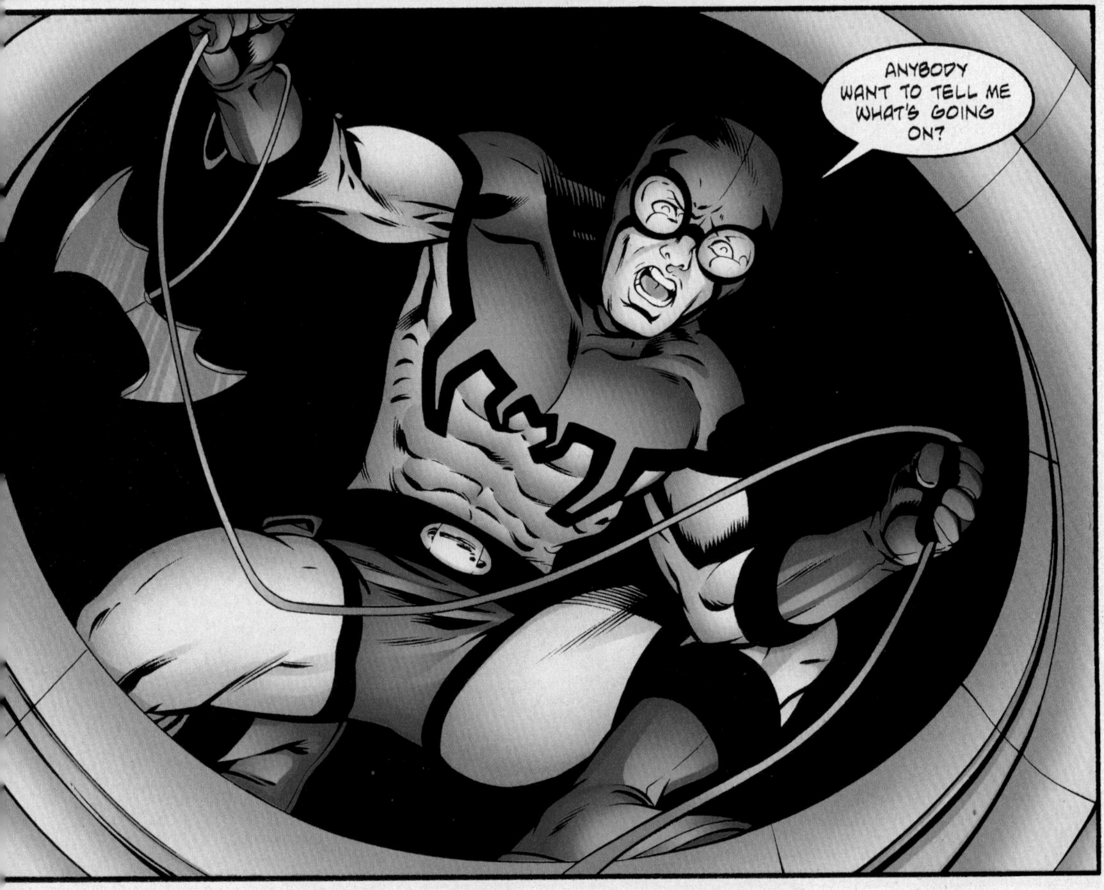
ANYBODY WANT TO TELL ME WHAT'S GOING ON?

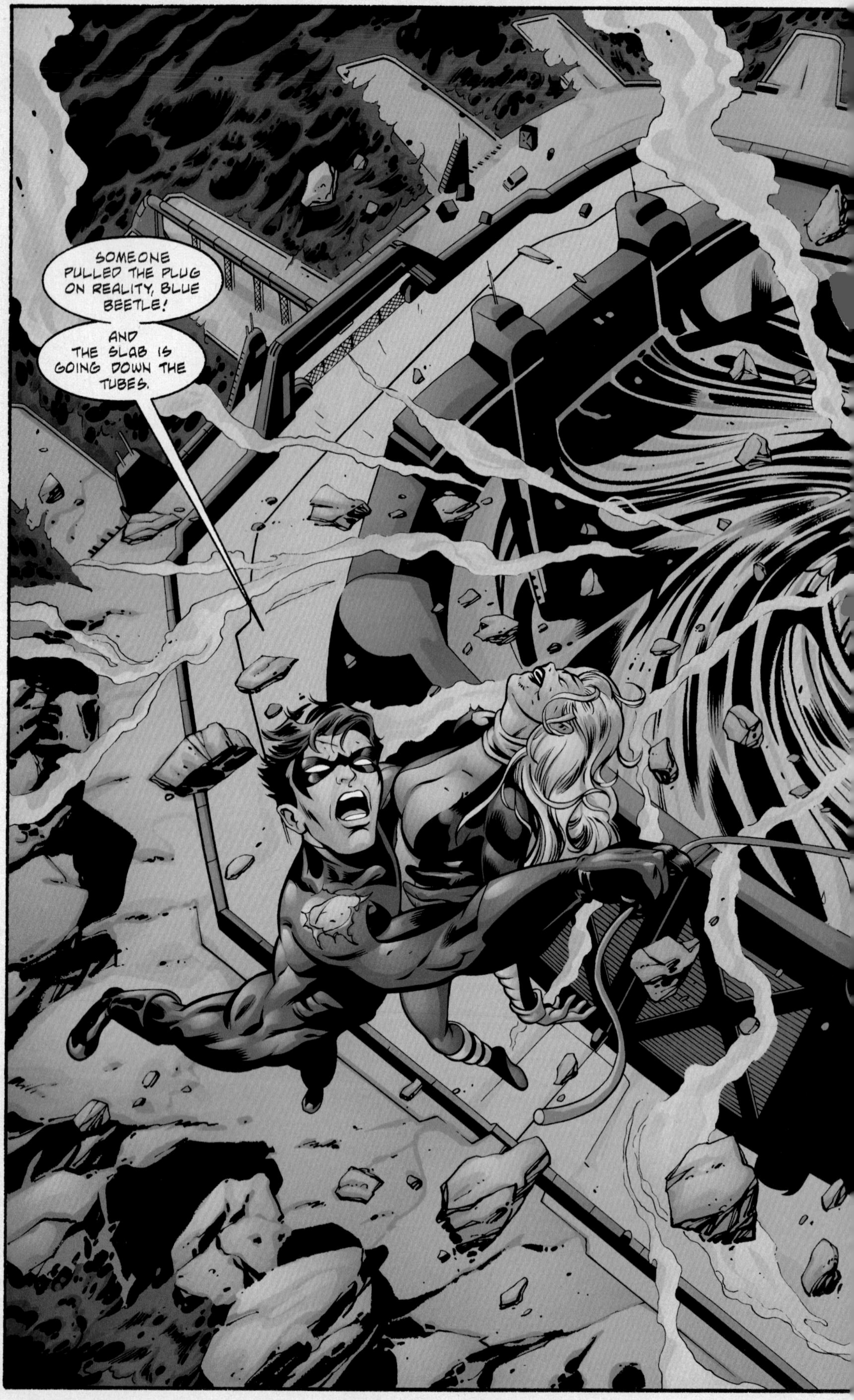
SOMEONE PULLED THE PLUG ON REALITY, BLUE BEETLE!
AND THE SLAB IS GOING DOWN THE TUBES.

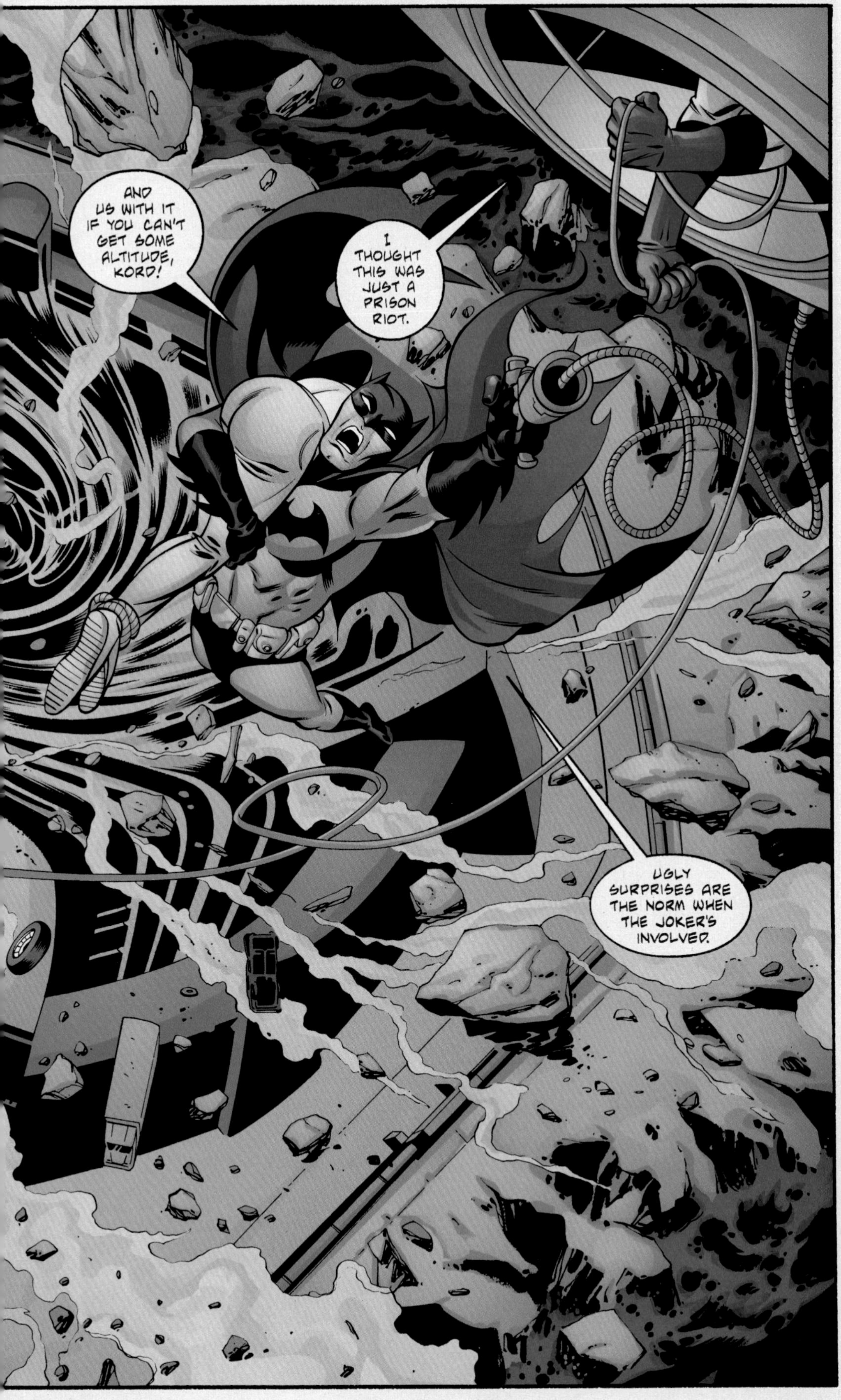
AND US WITH IT IF YOU CAN'T GET SOME ALTITUDE, KORD!
I THOUGHT THIS WAS JUST A PRISON RIOT.
UGLY SURPRISES ARE THE NORM WHEN THE JOKER'S INVOLVED.

I TOLD THE CANARY I'D HOVER IN CASE SHE NEEDED A QUICK GETAWAY.

LUCKY FOR ALL OF US.

AND THE OTHER LADY?

SPELL-BINDER ALL JOKERED-UP.

INTRODUCTIONS LATER. PULL US OUT OF THIS GRAVITY WELL *NOW*, BEETLE!

GOOD IDEA!

BUT I GOTTA WARN YOU--

--THE BUG'S NOT BUILT FOR SPEED... OR POWER!

unng.

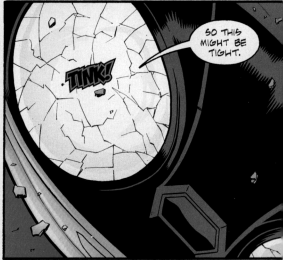

SO THIS MIGHT BE TIGHT.

TINK!

IS THIS EFFECT GOING TO STOP, BATMAN?

IF IT DOESN'T, THEN NONE OF US WILL BE HERE TO WORRY ABOUT IT.

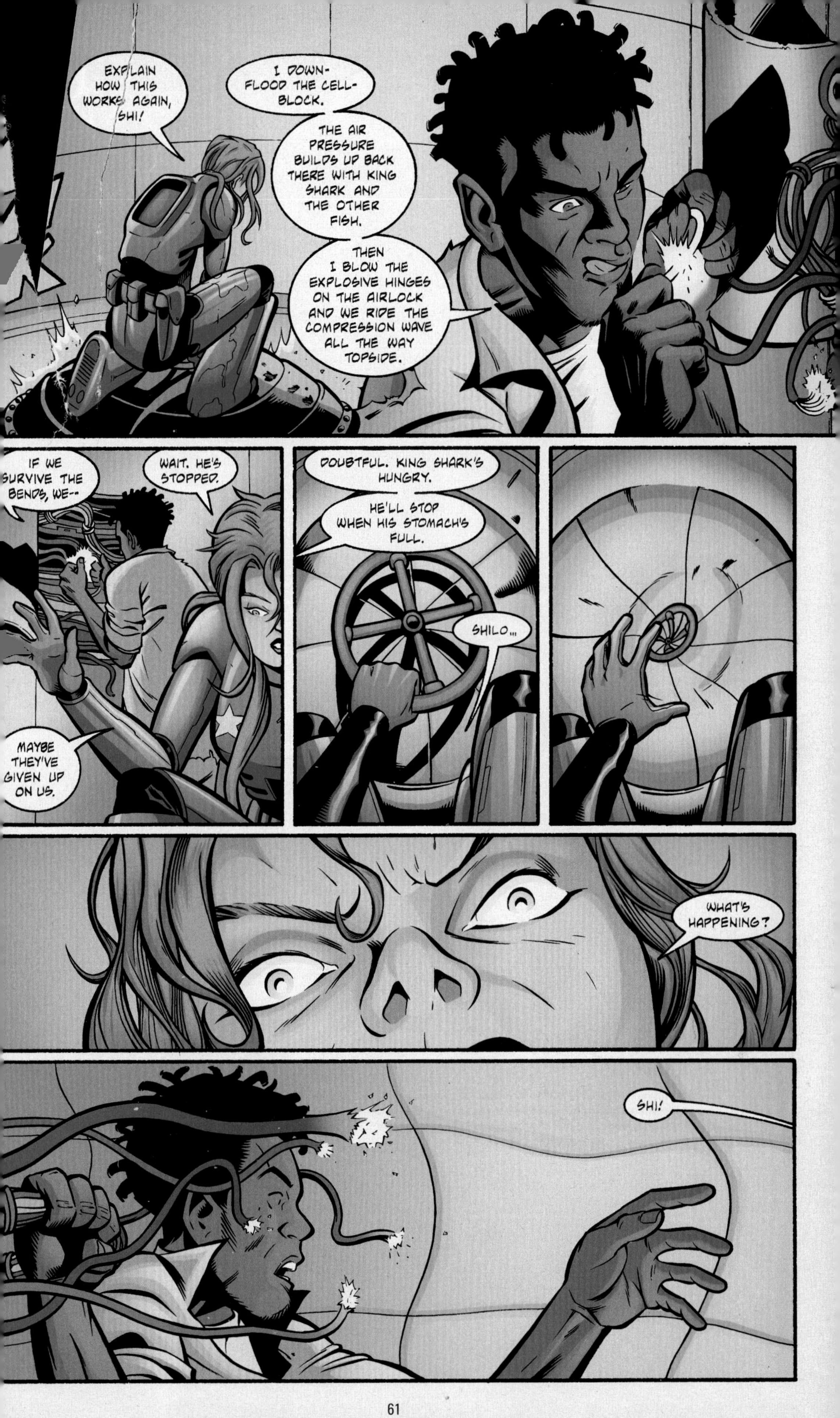
EXPLAIN HOW THIS WORKS AGAIN, SHI!
I DOWN-FLOOD THE CELL-BLOCK.
THE AIR PRESSURE BUILDS UP BACK THERE WITH KING SHARK AND THE OTHER FISH.
THEN I BLOW THE EXPLOSIVE HINGES ON THE AIRLOCK AND WE RIDE THE COMPRESSION WAVE ALL THE WAY TOPSIDE.
IF WE SURVIVE THE BENDS, WE--
WAIT. HE'S STOPPED.
MAYBE THEY'VE GIVEN UP ON US.
DOUBTFUL. KING SHARK'S HUNGRY.
HE'LL STOP WHEN HIS STOMACH'S FULL.
SHILO...
WHAT'S HAPPENING?
SHI!

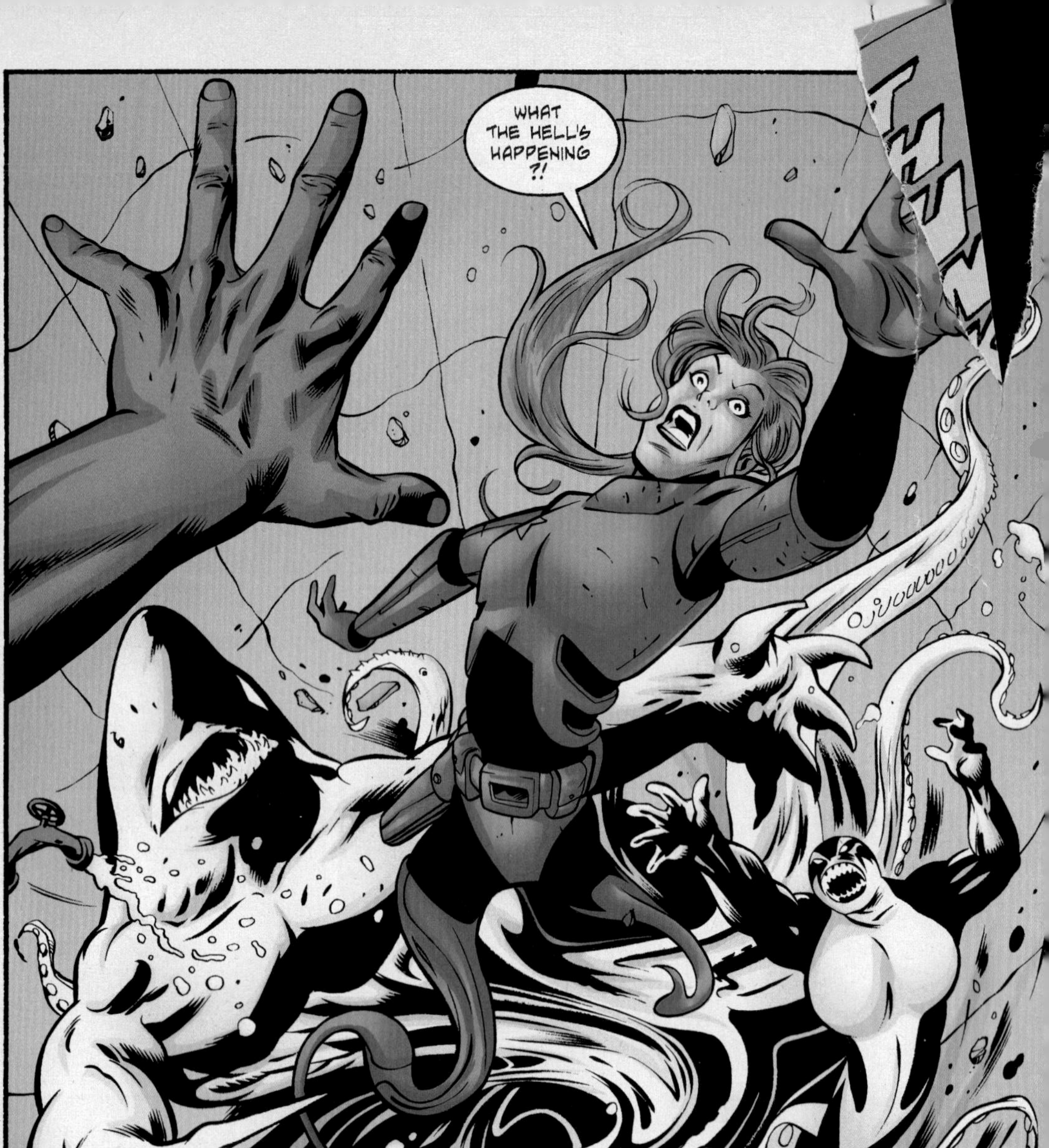
WHAT THE HELL'S HAPPENING ?!
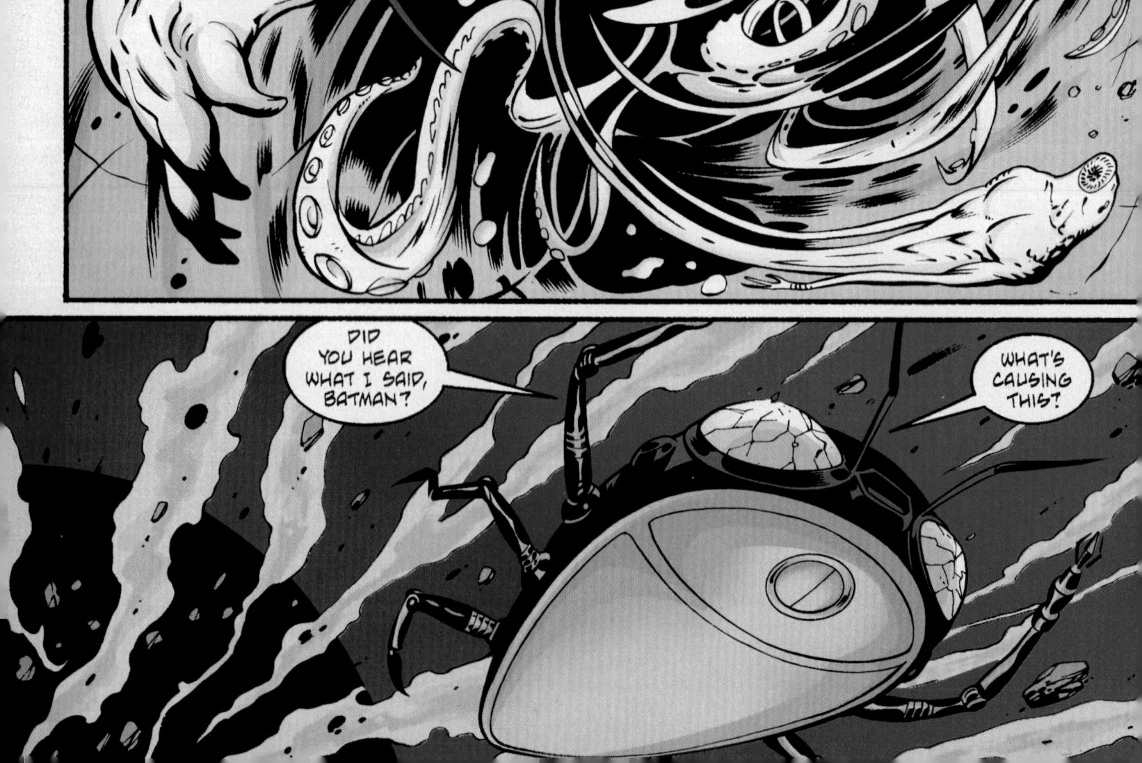
DID YOU HEAR WHAT I SAID, BATMAN?
WHAT'S CAUSING THIS?

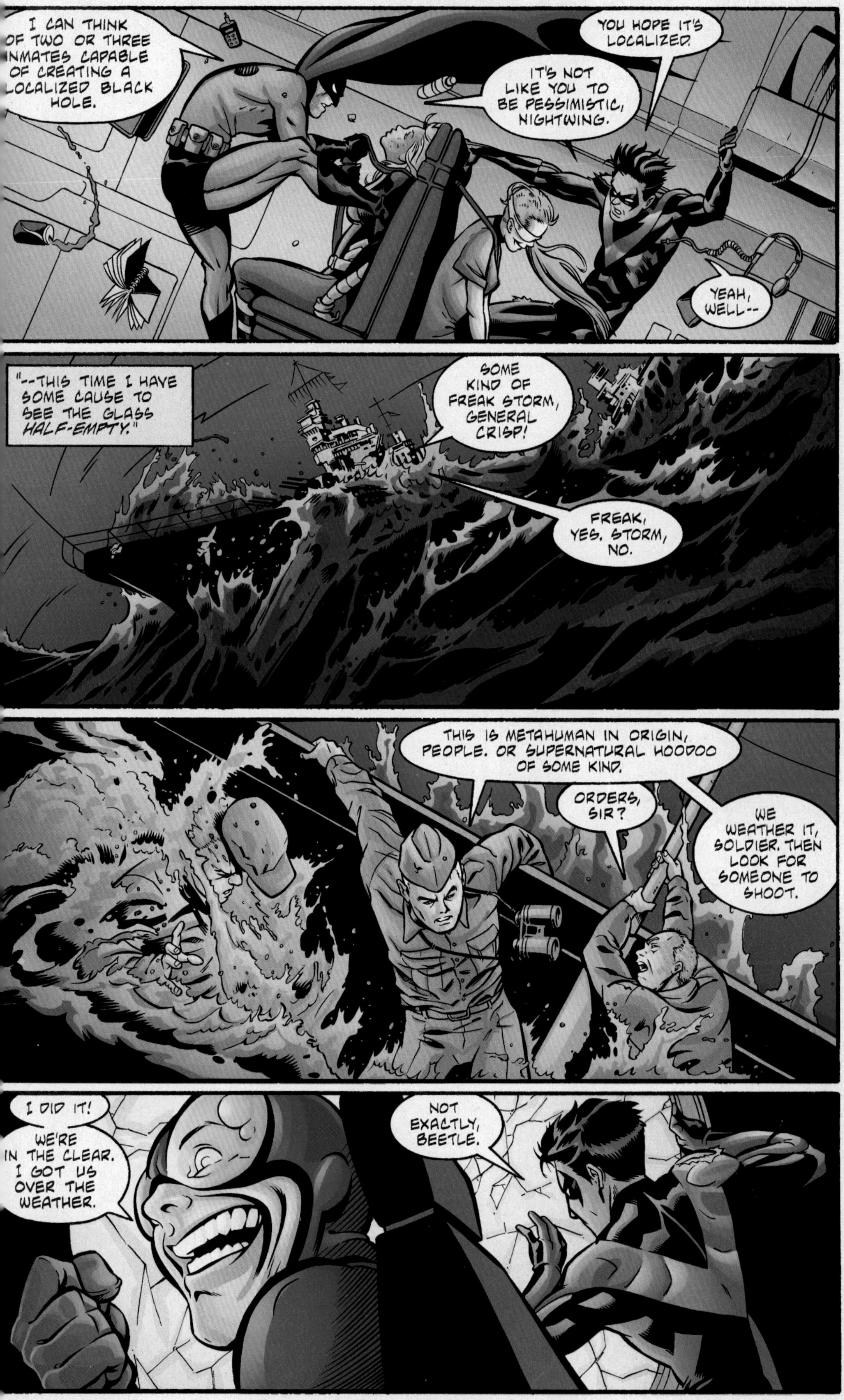
I CAN THINK OF TWO OR THREE INMATES CAPABLE OF CREATING A LOCALIZED BLACK HOLE.
YOU HOPE IT'S LOCALIZED.
IT'S NOT LIKE YOU TO BE PESSIMISTIC, NIGHTWING.
YEAH, WELL--
"--THIS TIME I HAVE SOME CAUSE TO SEE THE GLASS *HALF-EMPTY.*"
SOME KIND OF FREAK STORM, GENERAL CRISP!
FREAK, YES. STORM, NO.
THIS IS METAHUMAN IN ORIGIN, PEOPLE. OR SUPERNATURAL HOODOO OF SOME KIND.
ORDERS, SIR?
WE WEATHER IT, SOLDIER. THEN LOOK FOR SOMEONE TO SHOOT.
I DID IT!
WE'RE IN THE CLEAR. I GOT US OVER THE WEATHER.
NOT EXACTLY, BEETLE.

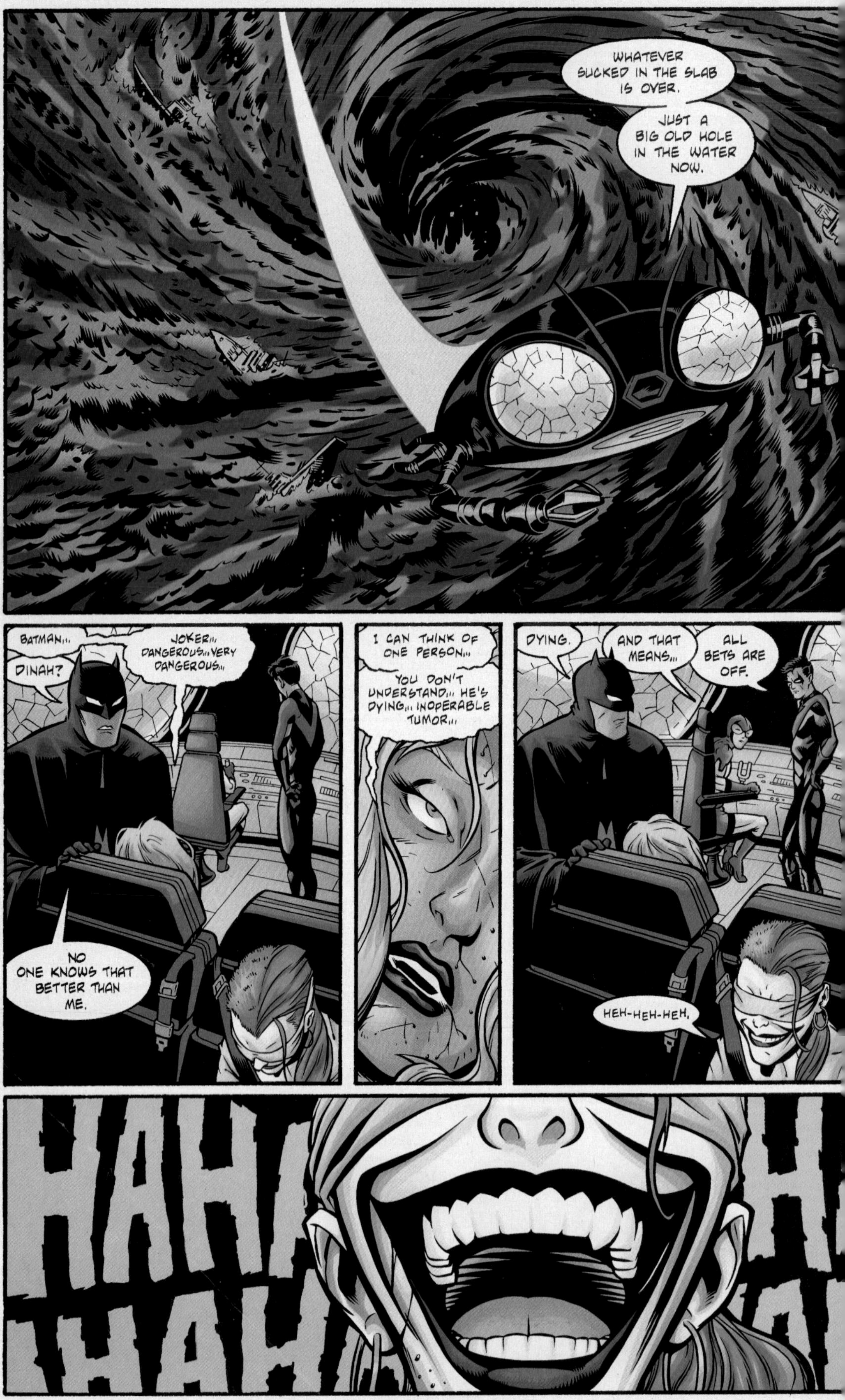
WHATEVER SUCKED IN THE SLAB IS OVER.
JUST A BIG OLD HOLE IN THE WATER NOW.
BATMAN...
DINAH?
JOKER... DANGEROUS... VERY DANGEROUS...
NO ONE KNOWS THAT BETTER THAN ME.
I CAN THINK OF ONE PERSON...
YOU DON'T UNDERSTAND... HE'S DYING... INOPERABLE TUMOR...
DYING.
AND THAT MEANS...
ALL BETS ARE OFF.
HEH-HEH-HEH.

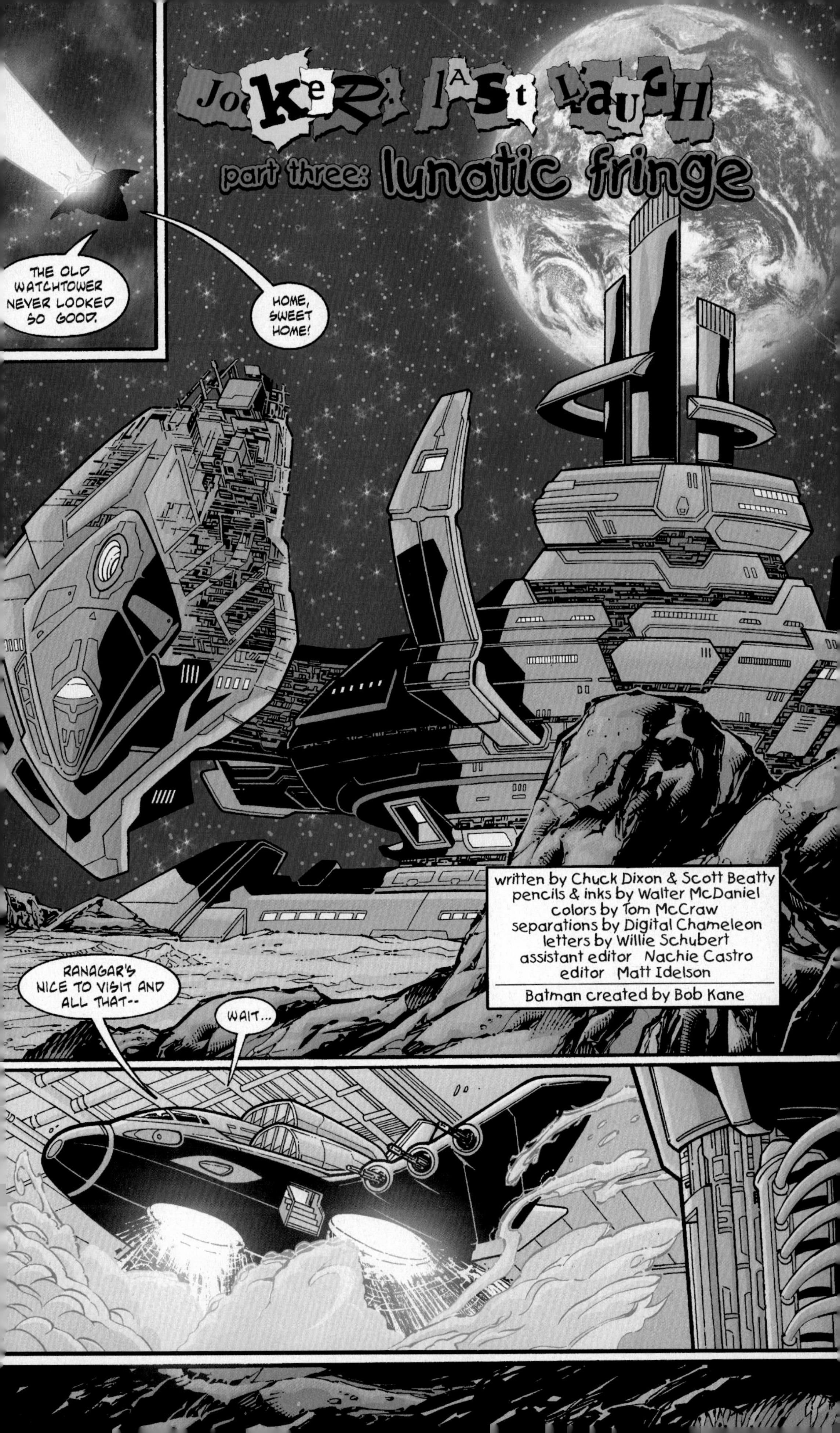

JOKER: LAST LAUGH
part three: lunatic fringe
THE OLD WATCHTOWER NEVER LOOKED SO GOOD.
HOME, SWEET HOME!
written by Chuck Dixon & Scott Beatty
pencils & inks by Walter McDaniel
colors by Tom McCraw
separations by Digital Chameleon
letters by Willie Schubert
assistant editor Nachie Castro
editor Matt Idelson
Batman created by Bob Kane
RANAGAR'S NICE TO VISIT AND ALL THAT--
WAIT...

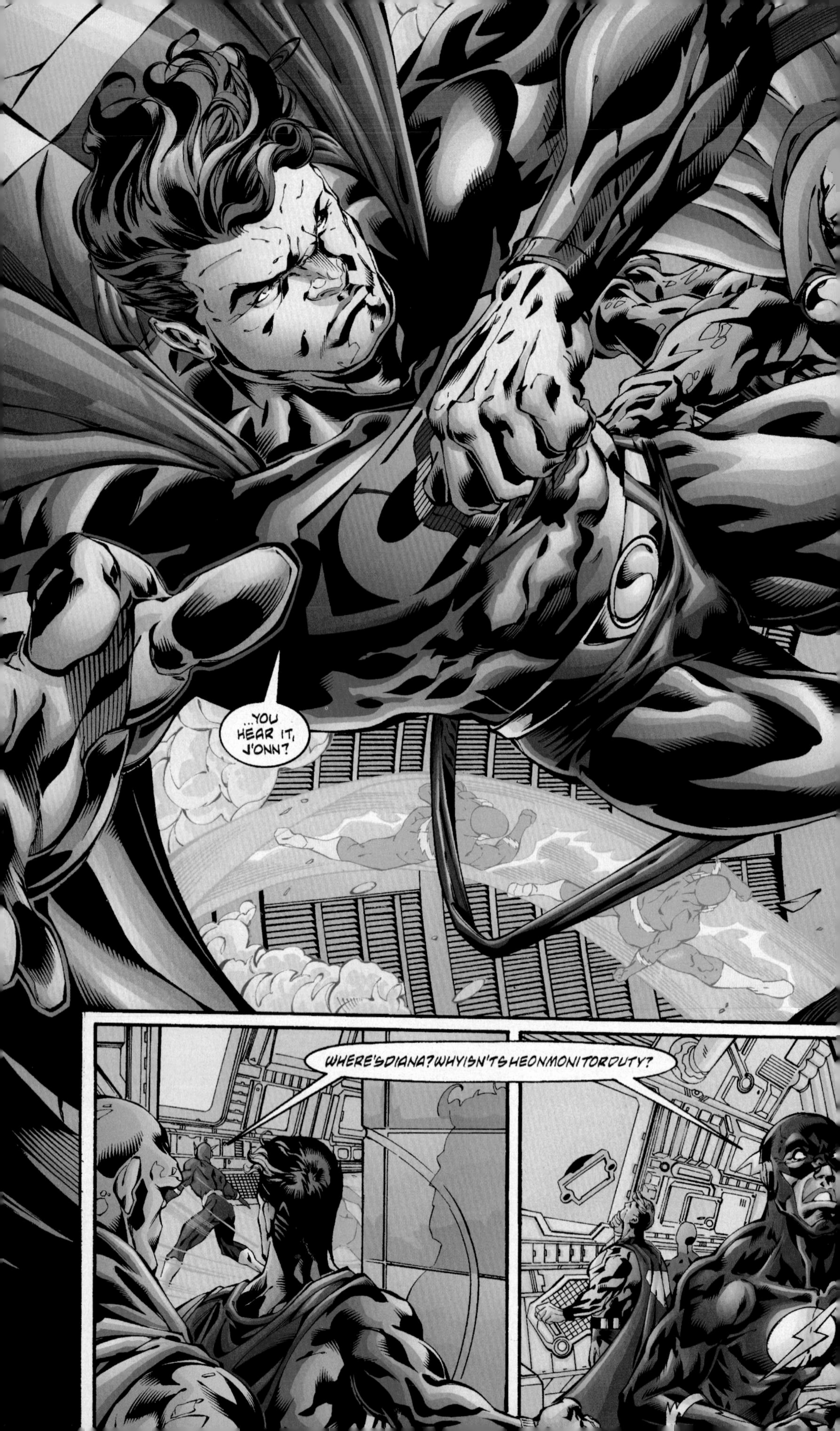
...YOU HEAR IT, J'ONN?
WHERE'S DIANA? WHY ISN'T SHE ON MONITOR DUTY?

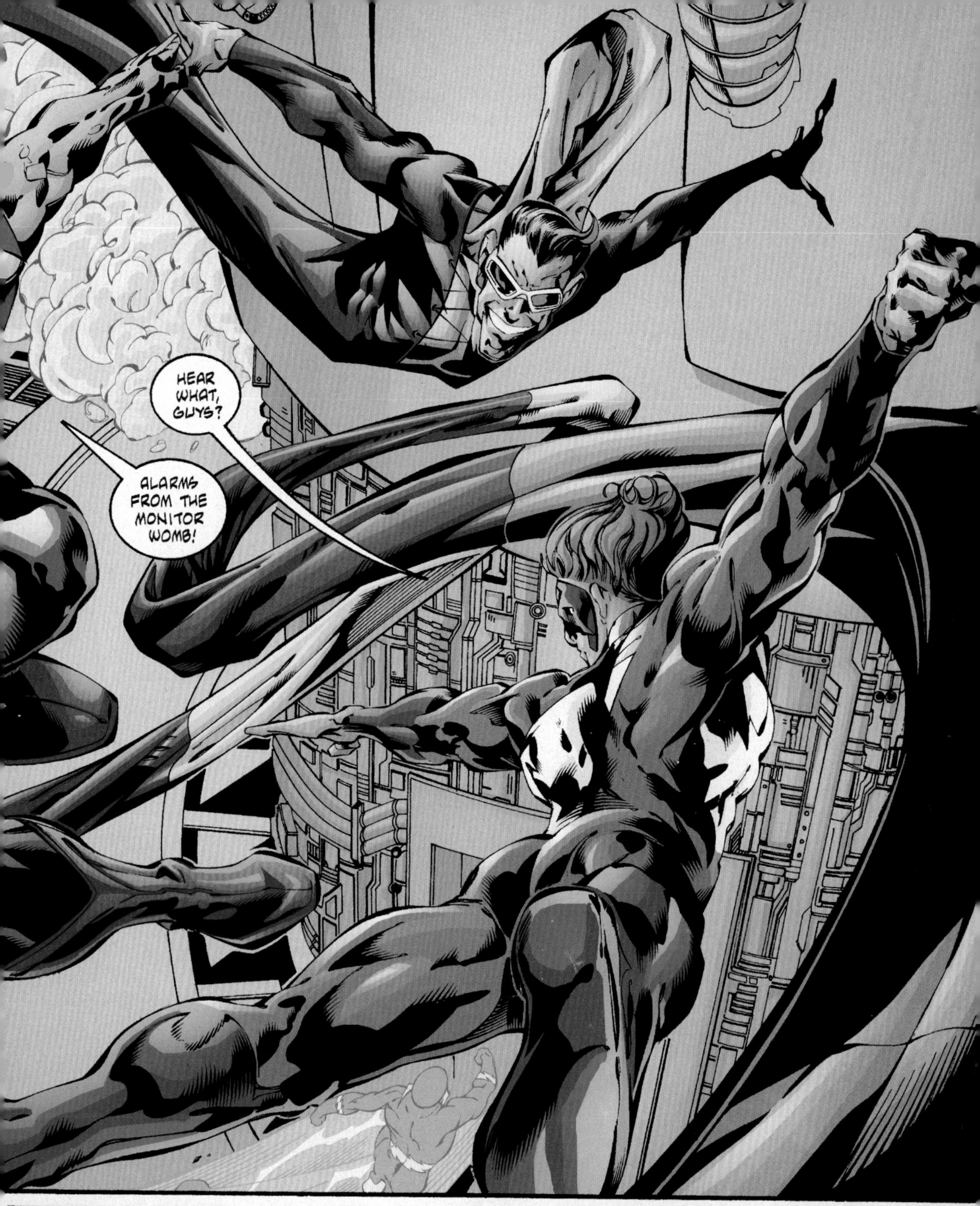
HEAR WHAT, GUYS?
ALARMS FROM THE MONITOR WOMB!

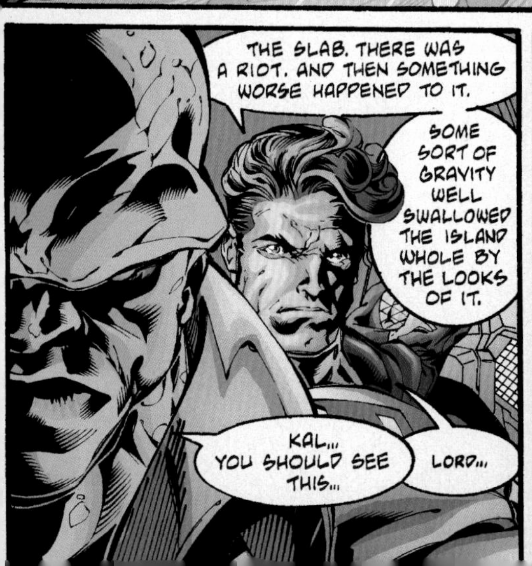
THE SLAB. THERE WAS A RIOT. AND THEN SOMETHING WORSE HAPPENED TO IT.
SOME SORT OF GRAVITY WELL SWALLOWED THE ISLAND WHOLE BY THE LOOKS OF IT.
KAL... YOU SHOULD SEE THIS...
LORD...

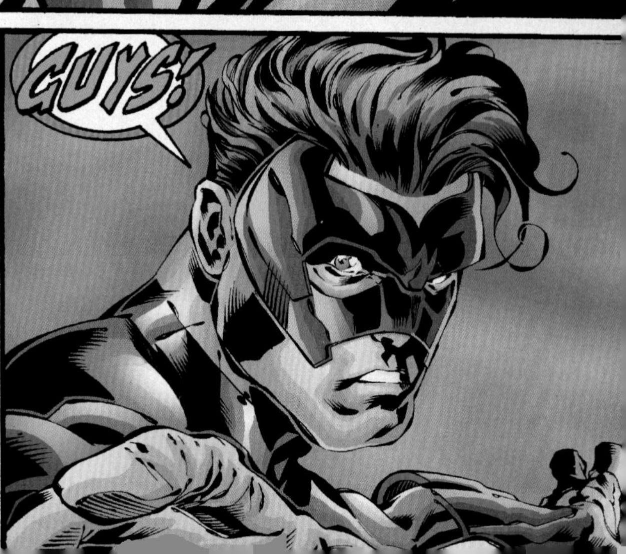
GUYS!

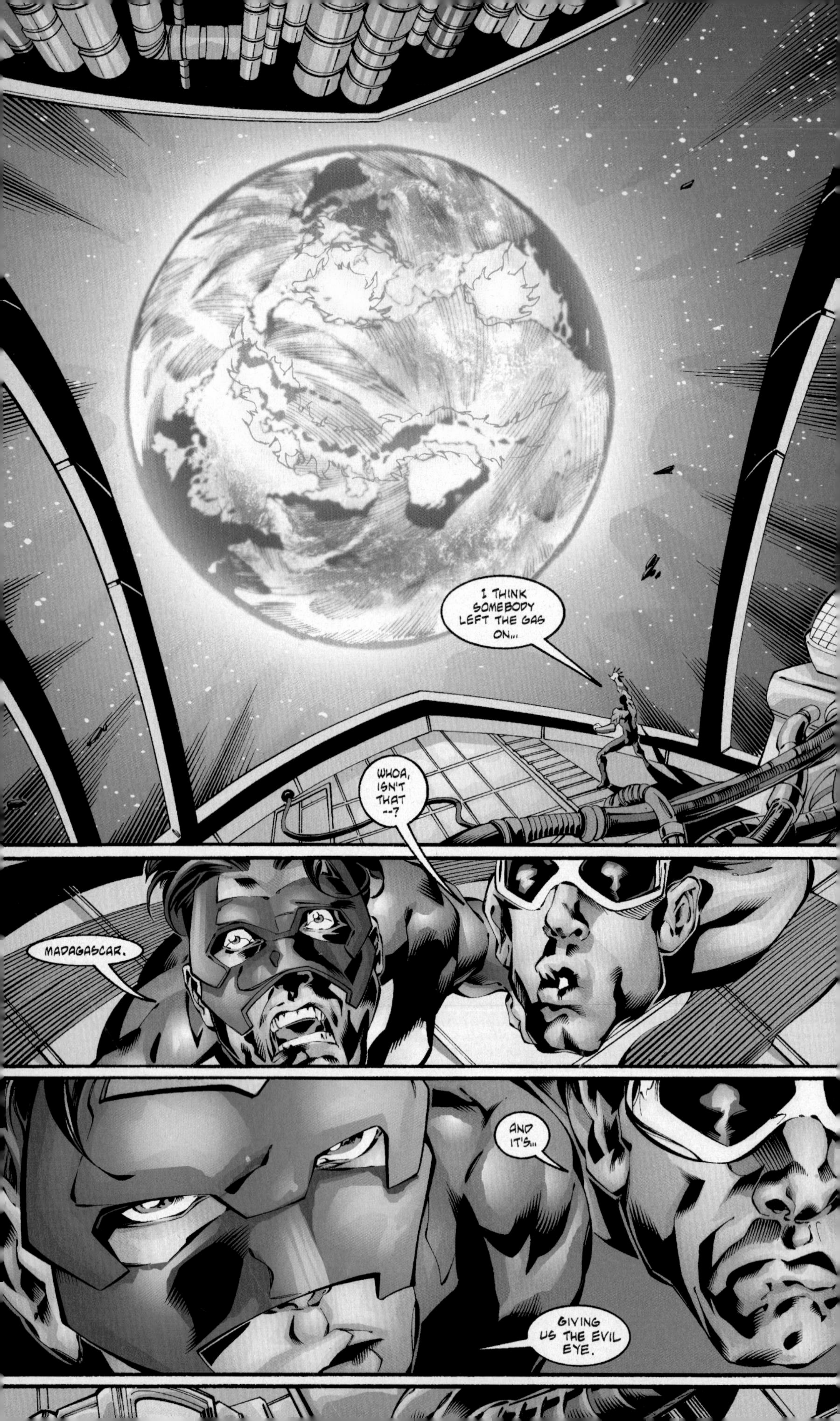
I THINK SOMEBODY LEFT THE GAS ON...
WHOA, ISN'T THAT --?
MADAGASCAR.
AND IT'S...
GIVING US THE EVIL EYE.

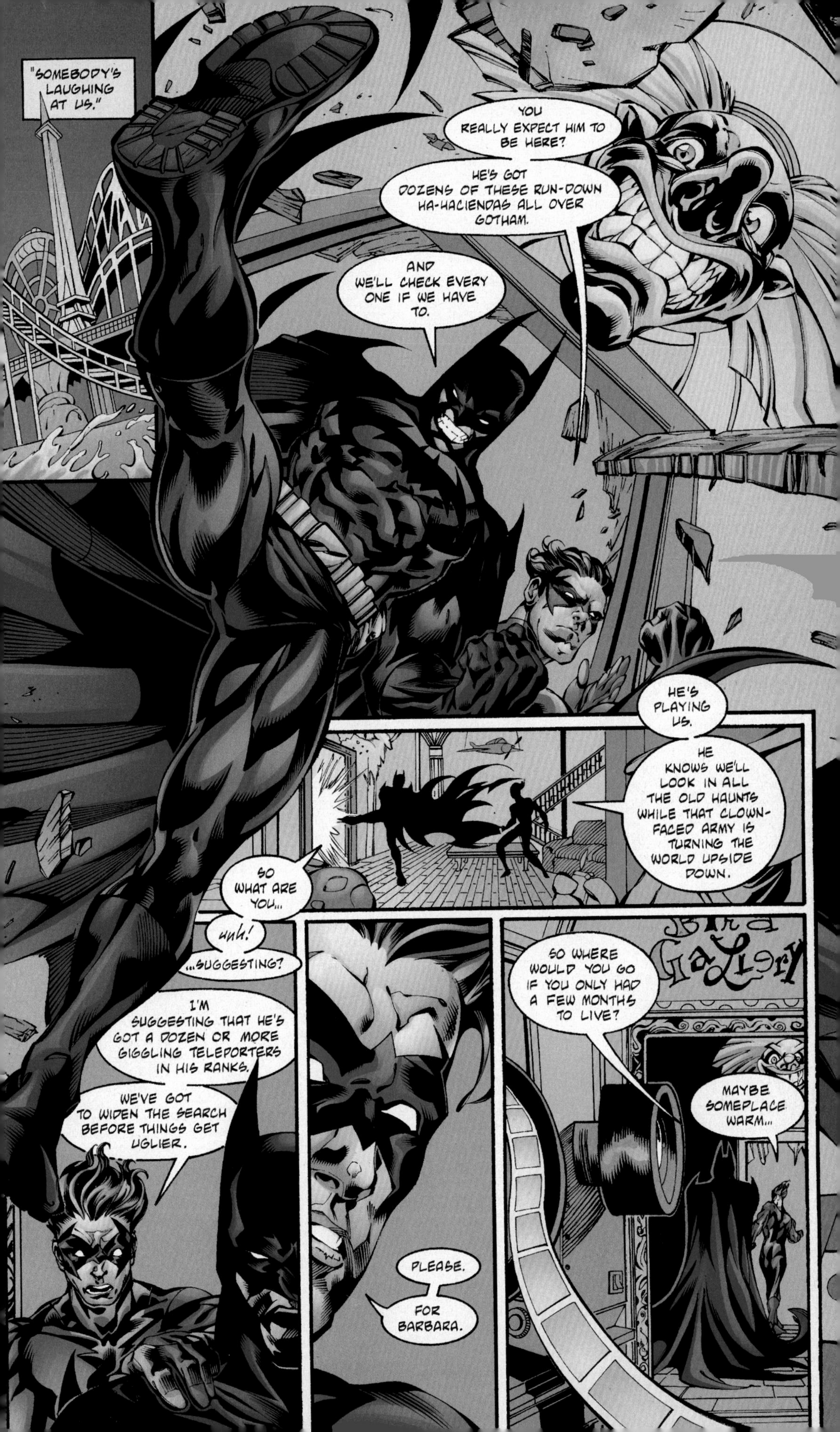
"SOMEBODY'S LAUGHING AT US."
YOU REALLY EXPECT HIM TO BE HERE?
HE'S GOT DOZENS OF THESE RUN-DOWN HA-HACIENDAS ALL OVER GOTHAM.
AND WE'LL CHECK EVERY ONE IF WE HAVE TO.
HE'S PLAYING US.
HE KNOWS WE'LL LOOK IN ALL THE OLD HAUNTS WHILE THAT CLOWN-FACED ARMY IS TURNING THE WORLD UPSIDE DOWN.
SO WHAT ARE YOU...
unh!
...SUGGESTING?
I'M SUGGESTING THAT HE'S GOT A DOZEN OR MORE GIGGLING TELEPORTERS IN HIS RANKS.
WE'VE GOT TO WIDEN THE SEARCH BEFORE THINGS GET UGLIER.
PLEASE.
FOR BARBARA.
SO WHERE WOULD YOU GO IF YOU ONLY HAD A FEW MONTHS TO LIVE?
MAYBE SOMEPLACE WARM...

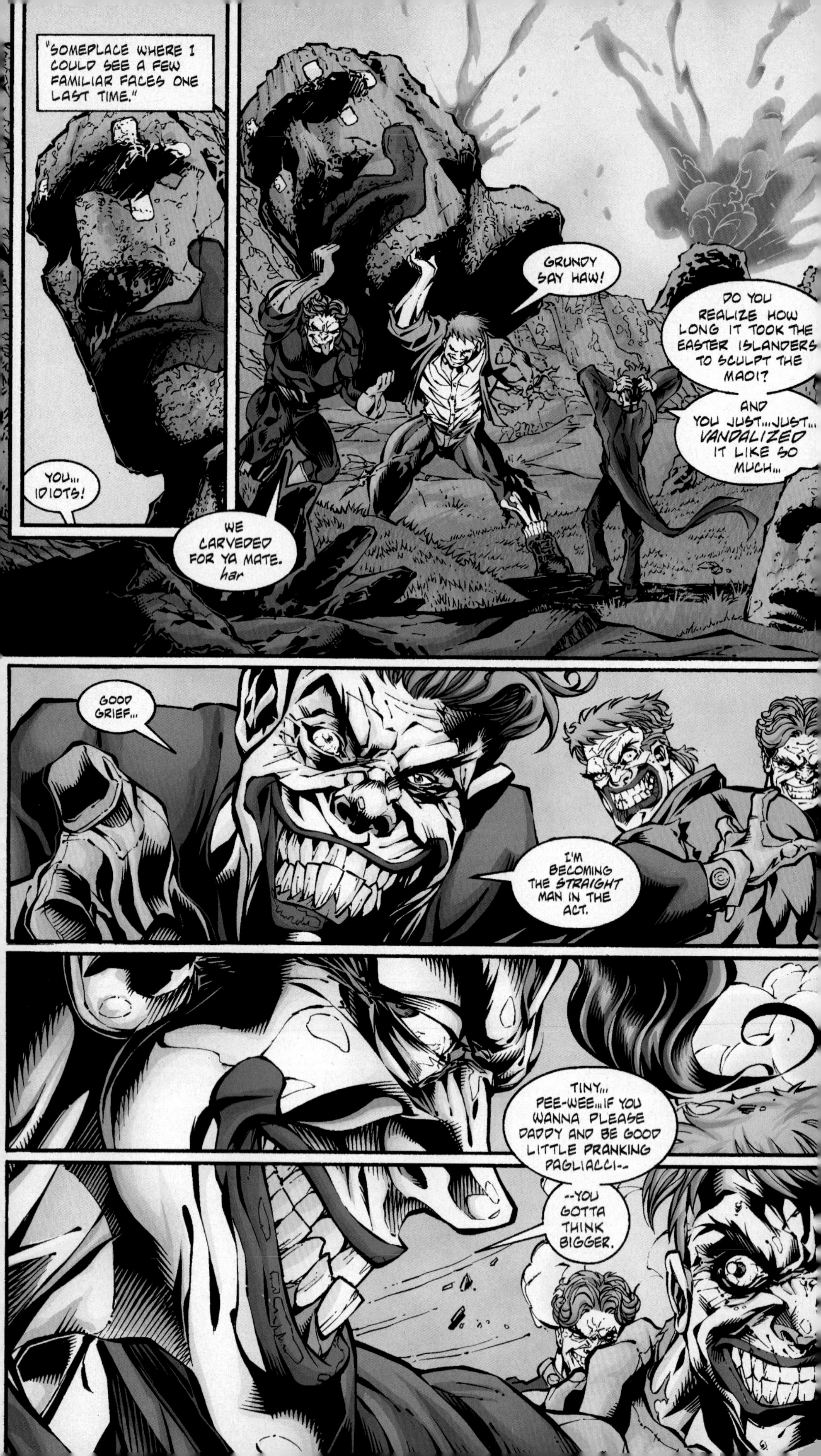
"SOMEPLACE WHERE I COULD SEE A FEW FAMILIAR FACES ONE LAST TIME."
YOU... IDIOTS!
WE CARVEDED FOR YA MATE. har
GRUNDY SAY HAW!
DO YOU REALIZE HOW LONG IT TOOK THE EASTER ISLANDERS TO SCULPT THE MAOI?
AND YOU JUST...JUST...JUST... VANDALIZED IT LIKE SO MUCH...
GOOD GRIEF...
I'M BECOMING THE STRAIGHT MAN IN THE ACT.
TINY... PEE-WEE...IF YOU WANNA PLEASE DADDY AND BE GOOD LITTLE PRANKING PAGLIACCI--
--YOU GOTTA THINK BIGGER.

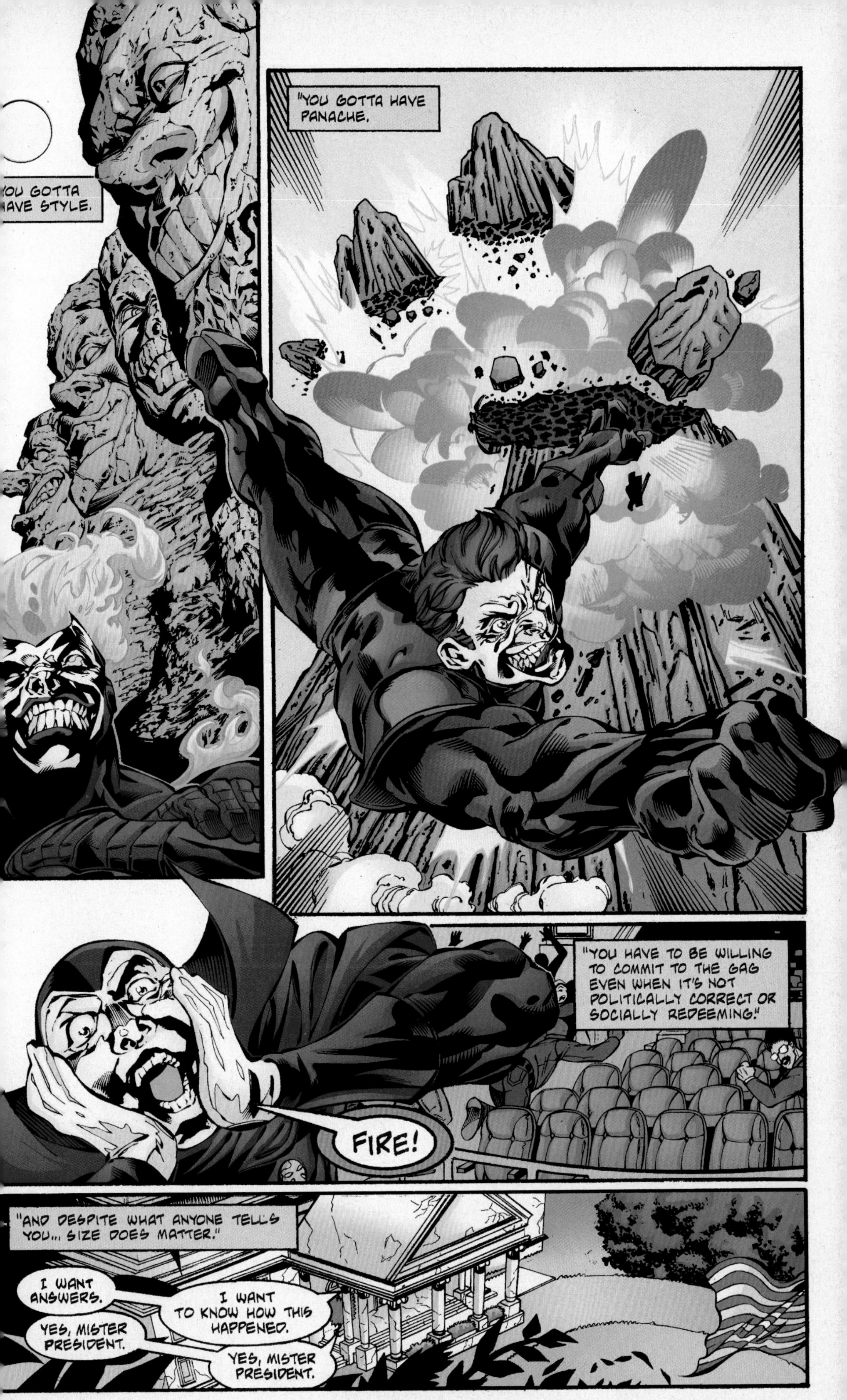
YOU GOTTA
HAVE STYLE.
"YOU GOTTA HAVE
PANACHE.
"YOU HAVE TO BE WILLING TO COMMIT TO THE GAG EVEN WHEN IT'S NOT POLITICALLY CORRECT OR SOCIALLY REDEEMING."
FIRE!
"AND DESPITE WHAT ANYONE TELLS YOU... SIZE DOES MATTER."
I WANT ANSWERS.
I WANT TO KNOW HOW THIS HAPPENED.
YES, MISTER PRESIDENT.
YES, MISTER PRESIDENT.

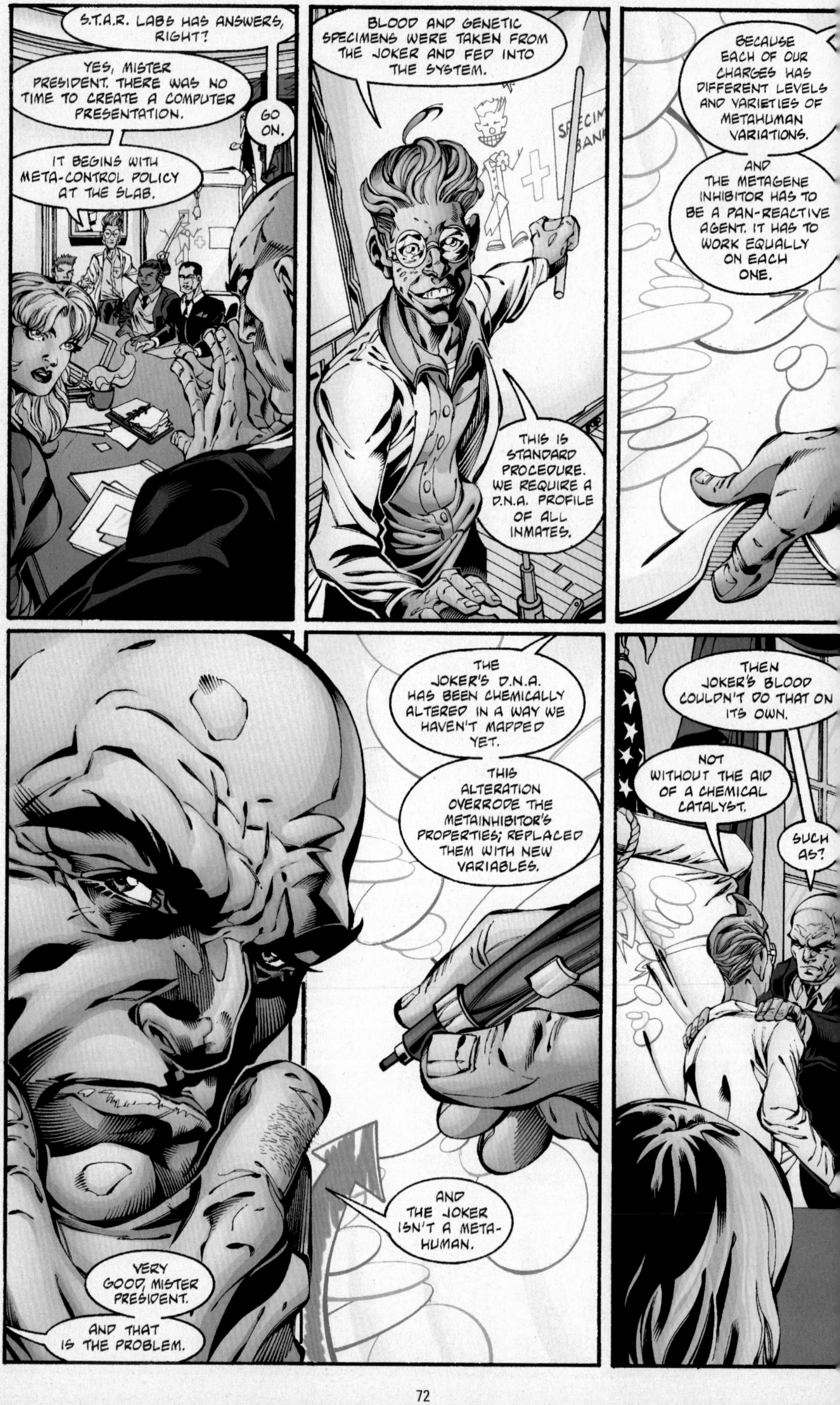
S.T.A.R. LABS HAS ANSWERS, RIGHT?
YES, MISTER PRESIDENT. THERE WAS NO TIME TO CREATE A COMPUTER PRESENTATION.
GO ON.
IT BEGINS WITH META-CONTROL POLICY AT THE SLAB.
BLOOD AND GENETIC SPECIMENS WERE TAKEN FROM THE JOKER AND FED INTO THE SYSTEM.
THIS IS STANDARD PROCEDURE. WE REQUIRE A D.N.A. PROFILE OF ALL INMATES.
BECAUSE EACH OF OUR CHARGES HAS DIFFERENT LEVELS AND VARIETIES OF METAHUMAN VARIATIONS.
AND THE METAGENE INHIBITOR HAS TO BE A PAN-REACTIVE AGENT. IT HAS TO WORK EQUALLY ON EACH ONE.
THE JOKER'S D.N.A. HAS BEEN CHEMICALLY ALTERED IN A WAY WE HAVEN'T MAPPED YET.
THIS ALTERATION OVERRODE THE METAINHIBITOR'S PROPERTIES; REPLACED THEM WITH NEW VARIABLES.
AND THE JOKER ISN'T A META-HUMAN.
VERY GOOD, MISTER PRESIDENT.
AND THAT IS THE PROBLEM.
THEN JOKER'S BLOOD COULDN'T DO THAT ON ITS OWN.
NOT WITHOUT THE AID OF A CHEMICAL CATALYST.
SUCH AS?

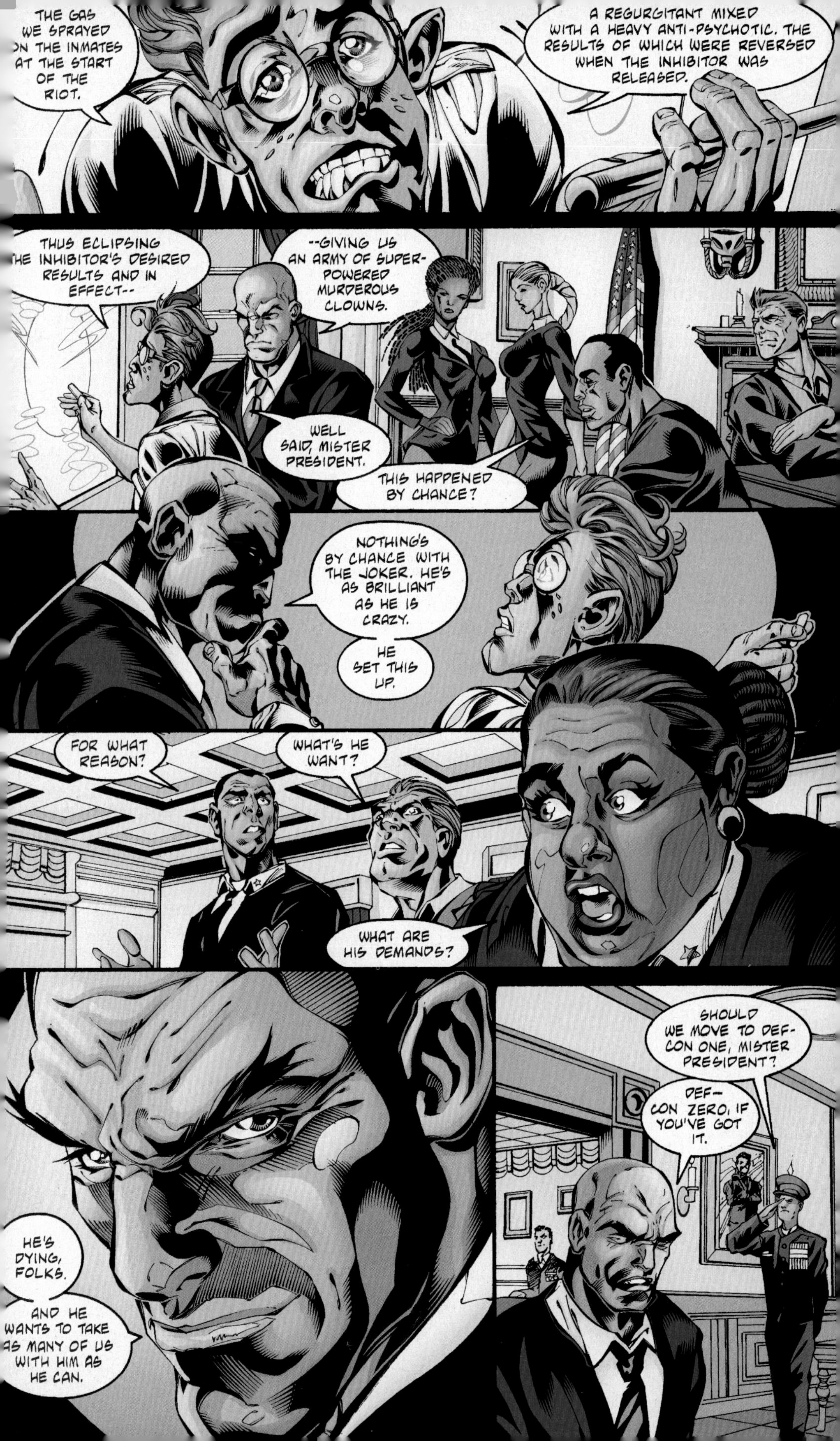
THE GAS WE SPRAYED ON THE INMATES AT THE START OF THE RIOT.
A REGURGITANT MIXED WITH A HEAVY ANTI-PSYCHOTIC. THE RESULTS OF WHICH WERE REVERSED WHEN THE INHIBITOR WAS RELEASED.
THUS ECLIPSING THE INHIBITOR'S DESIRED RESULTS AND IN EFFECT--
--GIVING US AN ARMY OF SUPER-POWERED MURDEROUS CLOWNS.
WELL SAID, MISTER PRESIDENT.
THIS HAPPENED BY CHANCE?
NOTHING'S BY CHANCE WITH THE JOKER. HE'S AS BRILLIANT AS HE IS CRAZY.
HE SET THIS UP.
FOR WHAT REASON?
WHAT'S HE WANT?
WHAT ARE HIS DEMANDS?
HE'S DYING, FOLKS.
AND HE WANTS TO TAKE AS MANY OF US WITH HIM AS HE CAN.
SHOULD WE MOVE TO DEF-CON ONE, MISTER PRESIDENT?
DEF-CON ZERO, IF YOU'VE GOT IT.

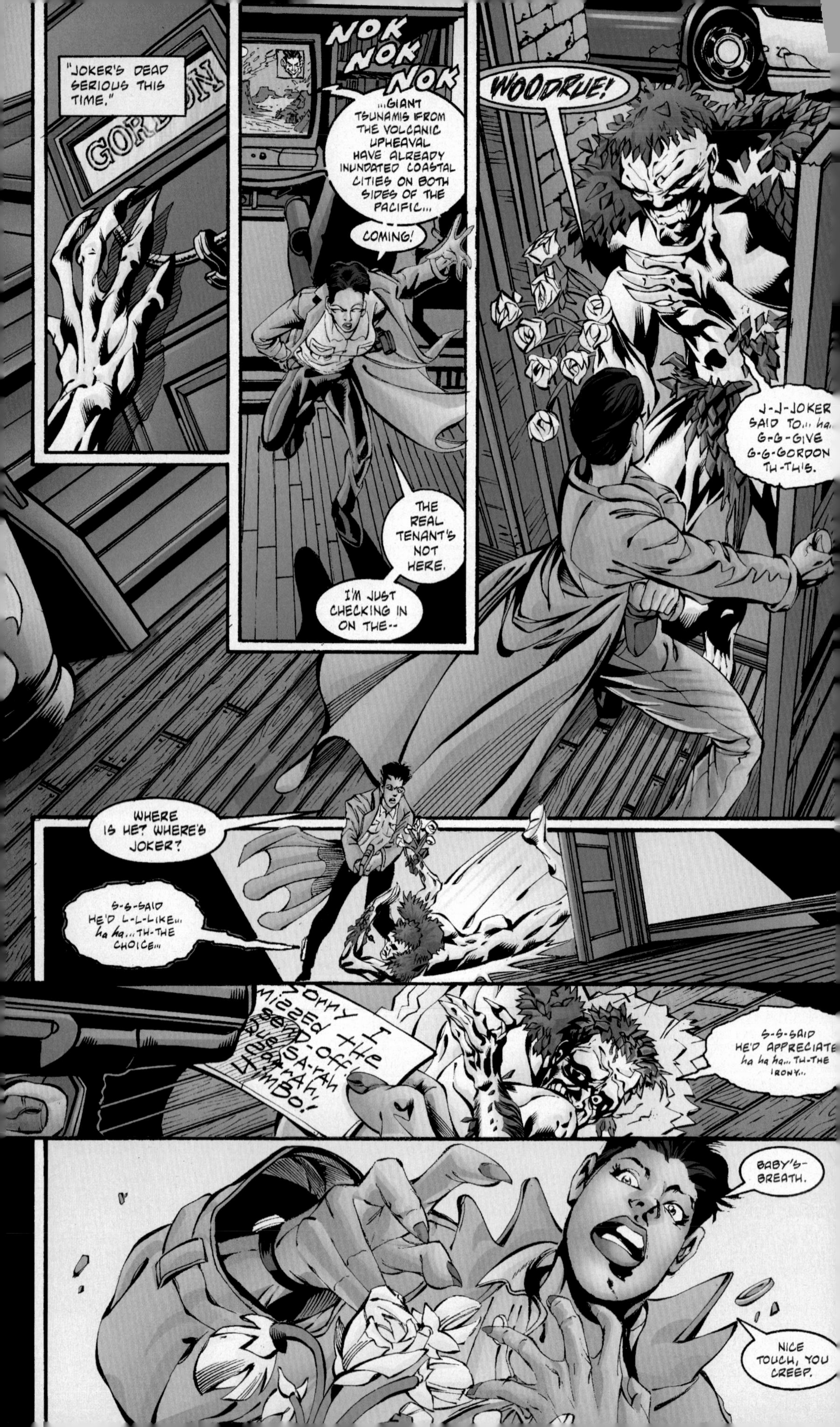
"JOKER'S DEAD SERIOUS THIS TIME."
GORDON
NOK NOK NOK
...GIANT TSUNAMIS FROM THE VOLCANIC UPHEAVAL HAVE ALREADY INUNDATED COASTAL CITIES ON BOTH SIDES OF THE PACIFIC...
COMING!
THE REAL TENANT'S NOT HERE.
I'M JUST CHECKING IN ON THE--
WOODRUE!
J-J-JOKER SAID TO... ha. G-G-GIVE G-G-GORDON TH-TH'S.
WHERE IS HE? WHERE'S JOKER?
S-S-SAID HE'D L-L-LIKE... ha ha... TH-THE CHOICE...
S-S-SAID HE'D APPRECIATE ha ha ha... TH-THE IRONY...
BABY'S-BREATH.
NICE TOUCH, YOU CREEP.

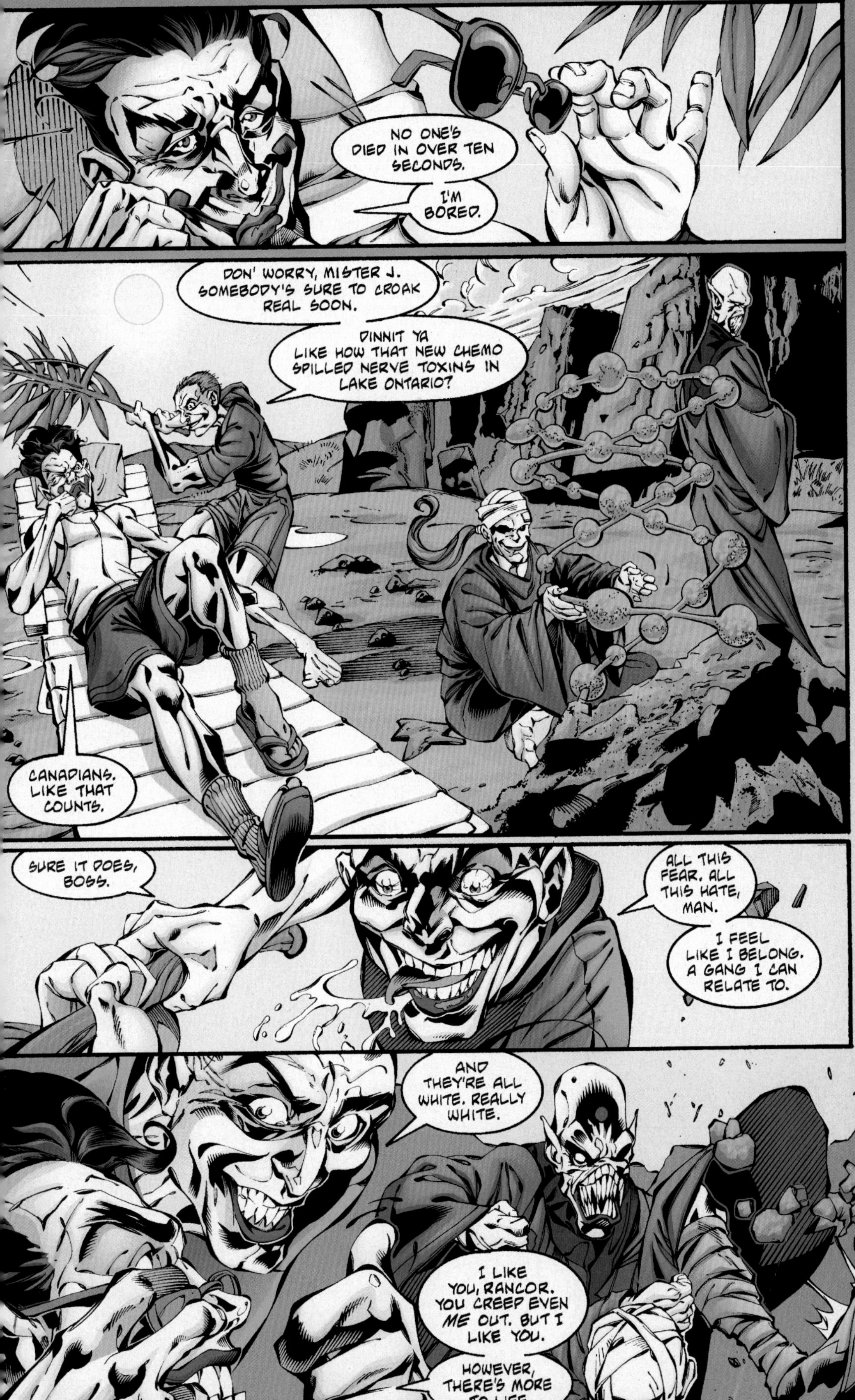
NO ONE'S DIED IN OVER TEN SECONDS.
I'M BORED.
DON' WORRY, MISTER J. SOMEBODY'S SURE TO CROAK REAL SOON.
DINNIT YA LIKE HOW THAT NEW CHEMO SPILLED NERVE TOXINS IN LAKE ONTARIO?
CANADIANS. LIKE THAT COUNTS.
SURE IT DOES, BOSS.
ALL THIS FEAR. ALL THIS HATE, MAN.
I FEEL LIKE I BELONG. A GANG I CAN RELATE TO.
AND THEY'RE ALL WHITE. REALLY WHITE.
I LIKE YOU, RANCOR. YOU CREEP EVEN ME OUT. BUT I LIKE YOU.
HOWEVER, THERE'S MORE TO LIFE.

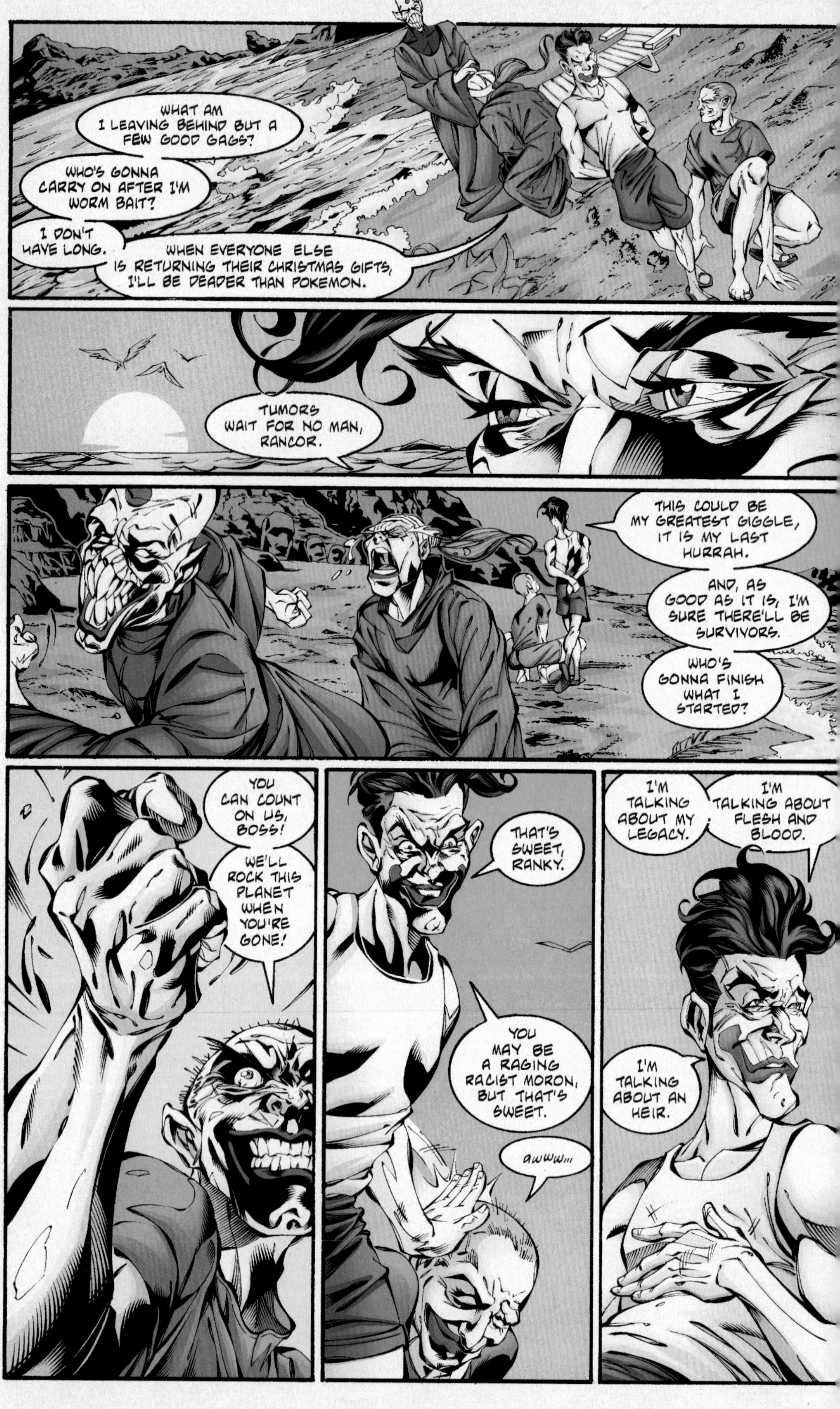
WHAT AM I LEAVING BEHIND BUT A FEW GOOD GAGS?
WHO'S GONNA CARRY ON AFTER I'M WORM BAIT?
I DON'T HAVE LONG.
WHEN EVERYONE ELSE IS RETURNING THEIR CHRISTMAS GIFTS, I'LL BE DEADER THAN POKEMON.
TUMORS WAIT FOR NO MAN, RANCOR.
THIS COULD BE MY GREATEST GIGGLE, IT IS MY LAST HURRAH.
AND, AS GOOD AS IT IS, I'M SURE THERE'LL BE SURVIVORS.
WHO'S GONNA FINISH WHAT I STARTED?
YOU CAN COUNT ON US, BOSS!
WE'LL ROCK THIS PLANET WHEN YOU'RE GONE!
THAT'S SWEET, RANKY.
YOU MAY BE A RAGING RACIST MORON, BUT THAT'S SWEET.
awww...
I'M TALKING ABOUT MY LEGACY.
I'M TALKING ABOUT FLESH AND BLOOD.
I'M TALKING ABOUT AN HEIR.

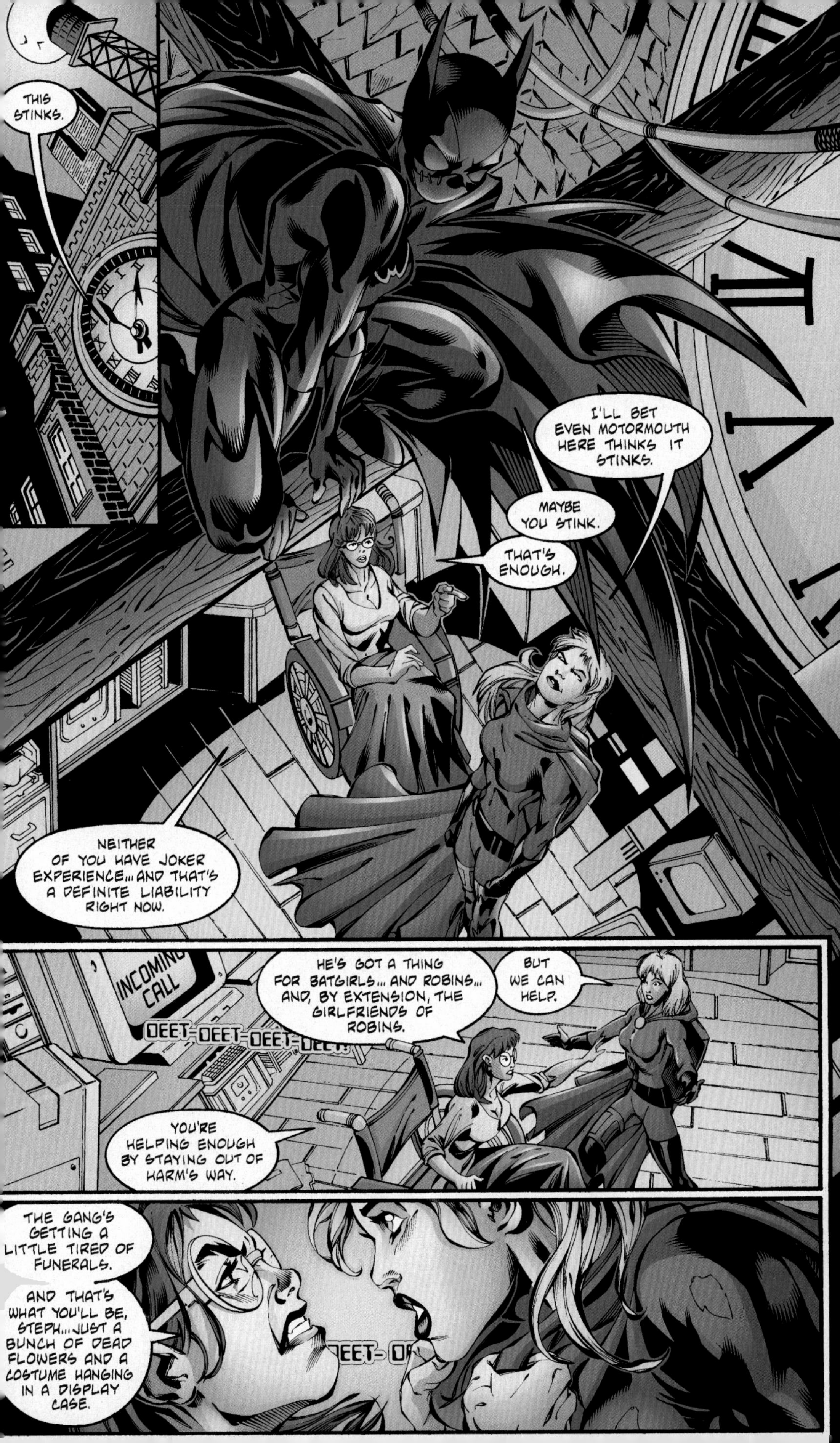

THIS STINKS.
I'LL BET EVEN MOTORMOUTH HERE THINKS IT STINKS.
MAYBE YOU STINK.
THAT'S ENOUGH.
NEITHER OF YOU HAVE JOKER EXPERIENCE... AND THAT'S A DEFINITE LIABILITY RIGHT NOW.
INCOMING CALL
DEET-DEET-DEET-DEET!
HE'S GOT A THING FOR BATGIRLS... AND ROBINS... AND, BY EXTENSION, THE GIRLFRIENDS OF ROBINS.
BUT WE CAN HELP.
YOU'RE HELPING ENOUGH BY STAYING OUT OF HARM'S WAY.
THE GANG'S GETTING A LITTLE TIRED OF FUNERALS.
AND THAT'S WHAT YOU'LL BE, STEPH... JUST A BUNCH OF DEAD FLOWERS AND A COSTUME HANGING IN A DISPLAY CASE.
DEET-

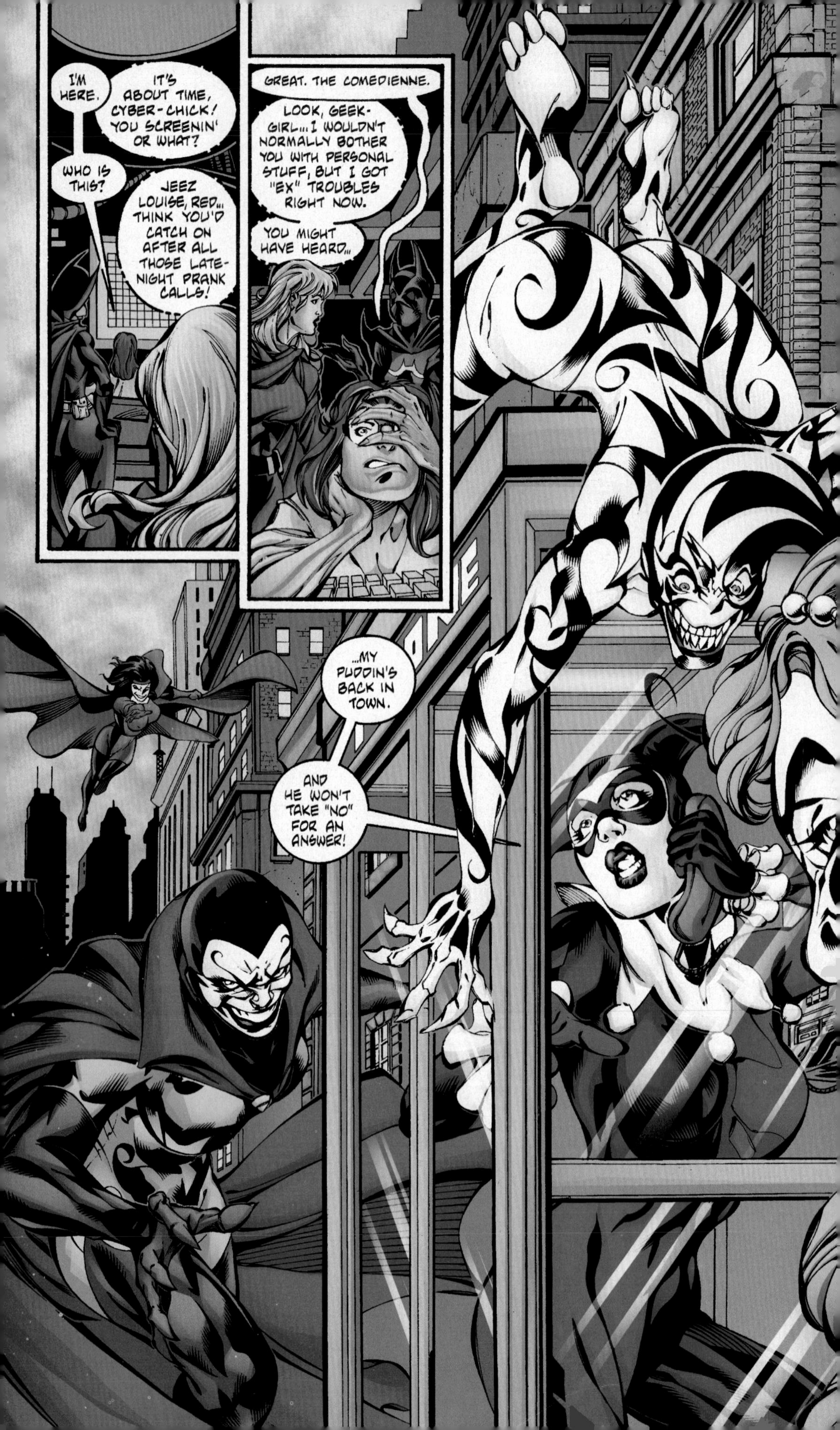
I'M HERE.
IT'S ABOUT TIME, CYBER-CHICK! YOU SCREENIN' OR WHAT?
WHO IS THIS?
JEEZ LOUISE, RED... THINK YOU'D CATCH ON AFTER ALL THOSE LATE-NIGHT PRANK CALLS!
GREAT. THE COMEDIENNE.
LOOK, GEEK-GIRL... I WOULDN'T NORMALLY BOTHER YOU WITH PERSONAL STUFF, BUT I GOT "EX" TROUBLES RIGHT NOW.
YOU MIGHT HAVE HEARD...
...MY PUDDIN'S BACK IN TOWN.
AND HE WON'T TAKE "NO" FOR AN ANSWER!

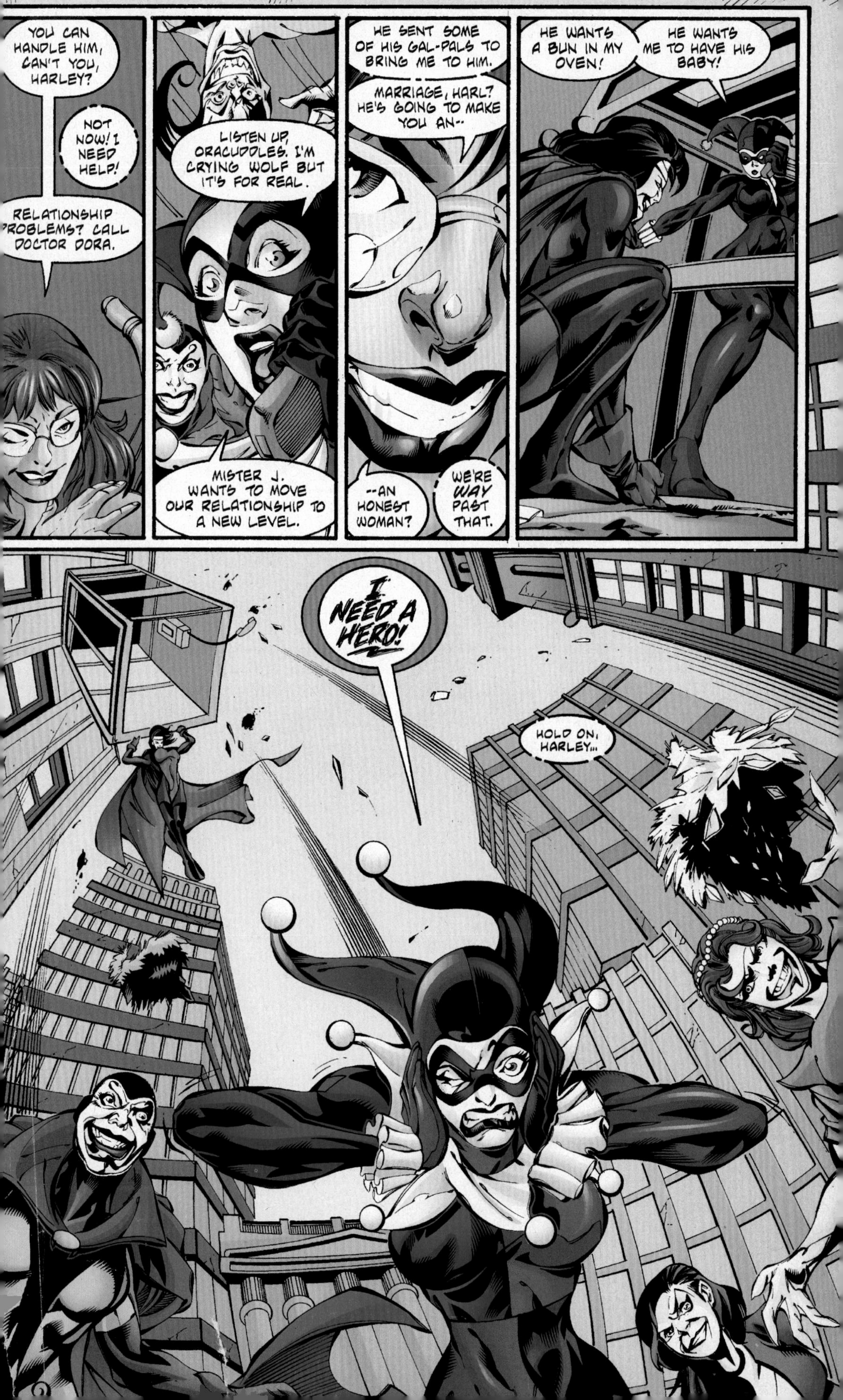
YOU CAN HANDLE HIM, CAN'T YOU, HARLEY?
NOT NOW! I NEED HELP!
RELATIONSHIP PROBLEMS? CALL DOCTOR DORA.
LISTEN UP, ORACUDDLES. I'M CRYING WOLF BUT IT'S FOR REAL.
MISTER J. WANTS TO MOVE OUR RELATIONSHIP TO A NEW LEVEL.
HE SENT SOME OF HIS GAL-PALS TO BRING ME TO HIM.
MARRIAGE, HARL? HE'S GOING TO MAKE YOU AN--
--AN HONEST WOMAN?
WE'RE WAY PAST THAT.
HE WANTS A BUN IN MY OVEN!
HE WANTS ME TO HAVE HIS BABY!
I NEED A HERO!
HOLD ON, HARLEY...

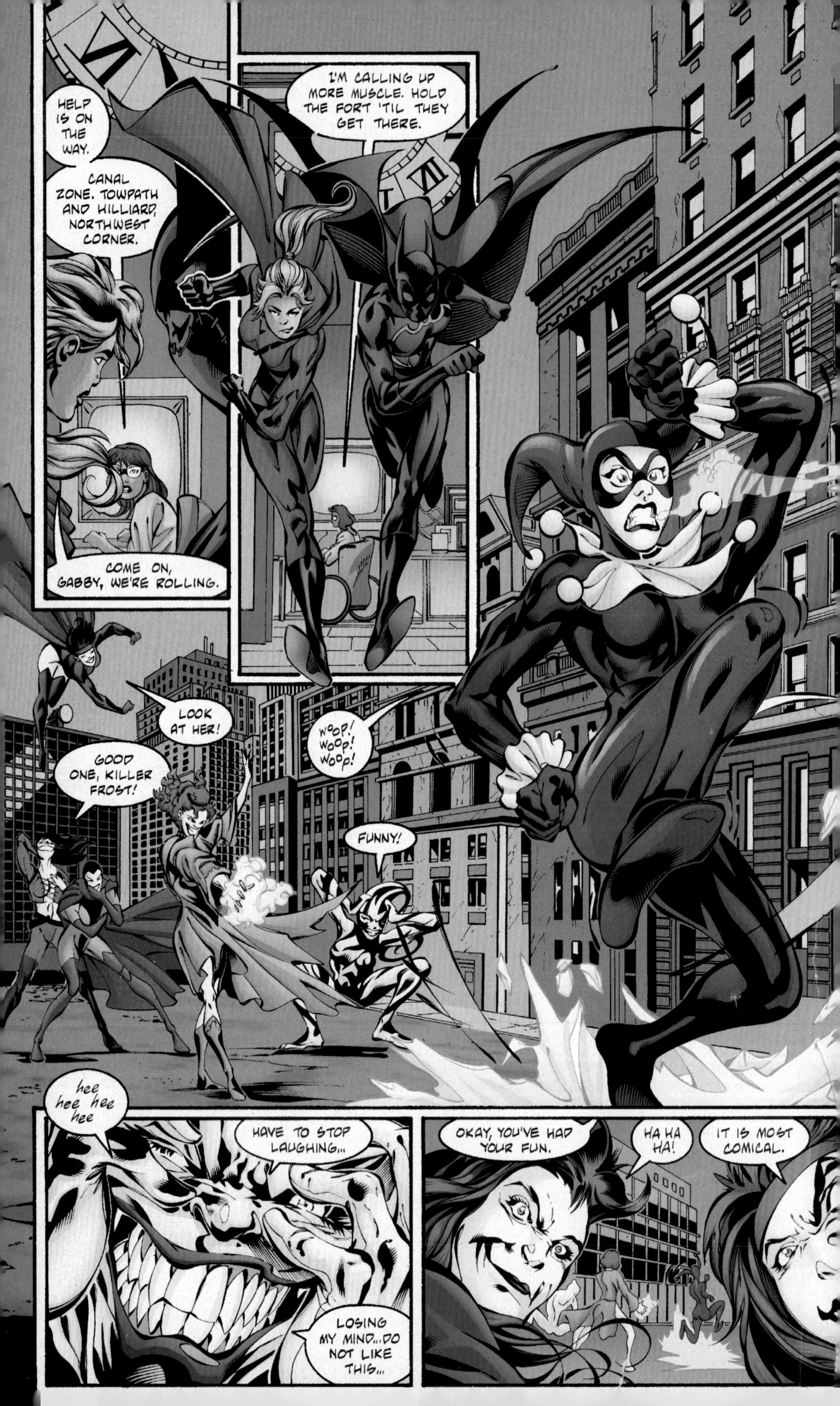

HELP IS ON THE WAY.
CANAL ZONE. TOWPATH AND HILLIARD, NORTHWEST CORNER.
I'M CALLING UP MORE MUSCLE. HOLD THE FORT 'TIL THEY GET THERE.
COME ON, GABBY, WE'RE ROLLING.
LOOK AT HER!
GOOD ONE, KILLER FROST!
WOOP! WOOP! WOOP!
FUNNY!
hee hee hee hee
HAVE TO STOP LAUGHING...
LOSING MY MIND...DO NOT LIKE THIS...
OKAY, YOU'VE HAD YOUR FUN.
HA HA HA!
IT IS MOST COMICAL.

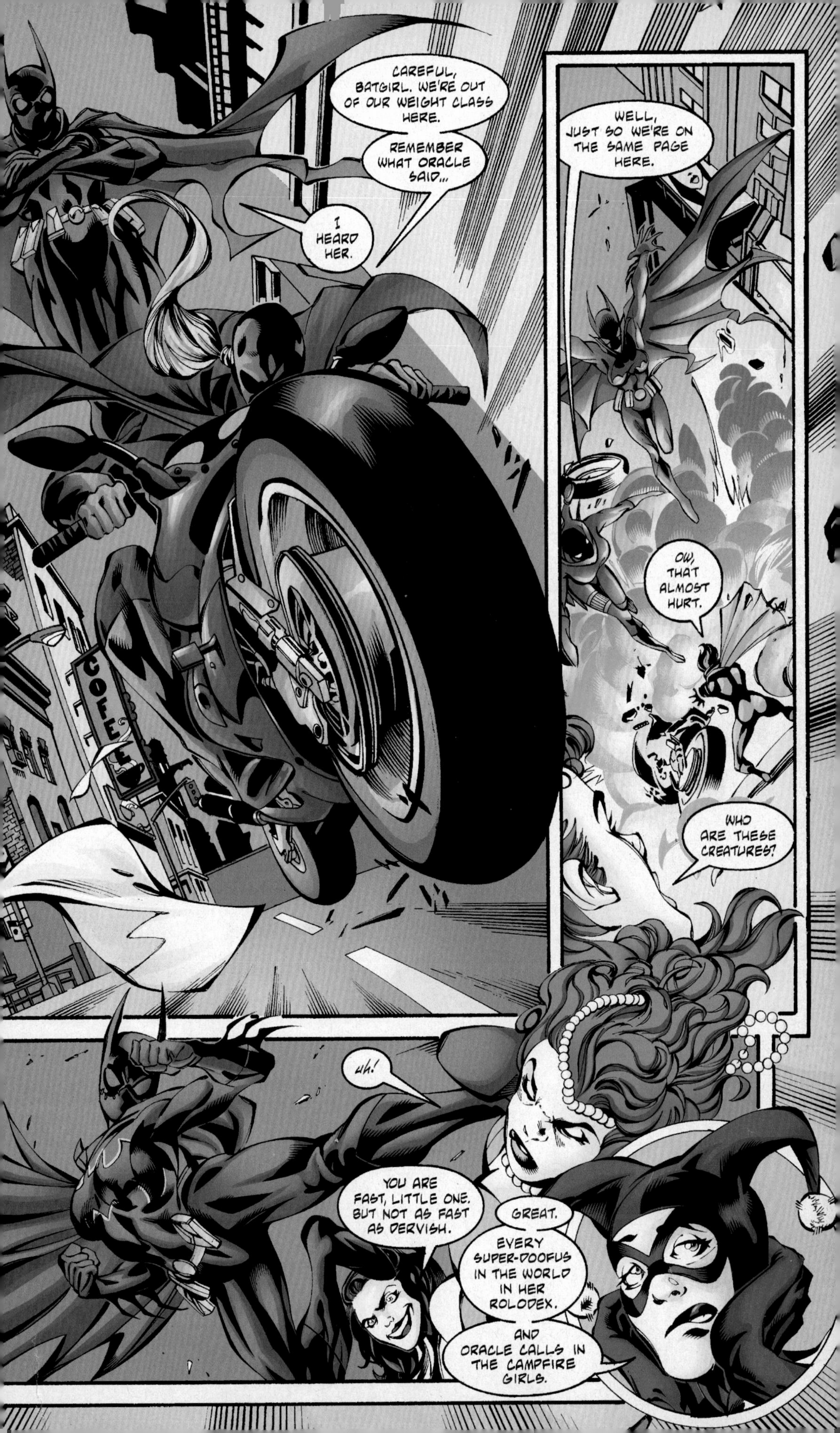
CAREFUL, BATGIRL. WE'RE OUT OF OUR WEIGHT CLASS HERE.
REMEMBER WHAT ORACLE SAID...
I HEARD HER.
WELL, JUST SO WE'RE ON THE SAME PAGE HERE.
OW, THAT ALMOST HURT.
WHO ARE THESE CREATURES?
COFFEE
UH!
YOU ARE FAST, LITTLE ONE. BUT NOT AS FAST AS DERVISH.
GREAT.
EVERY SUPER-DOOFUS IN THE WORLD IN HER ROLODEX.
AND ORACLE CALLS IN THE CAMPFIRE GIRLS.

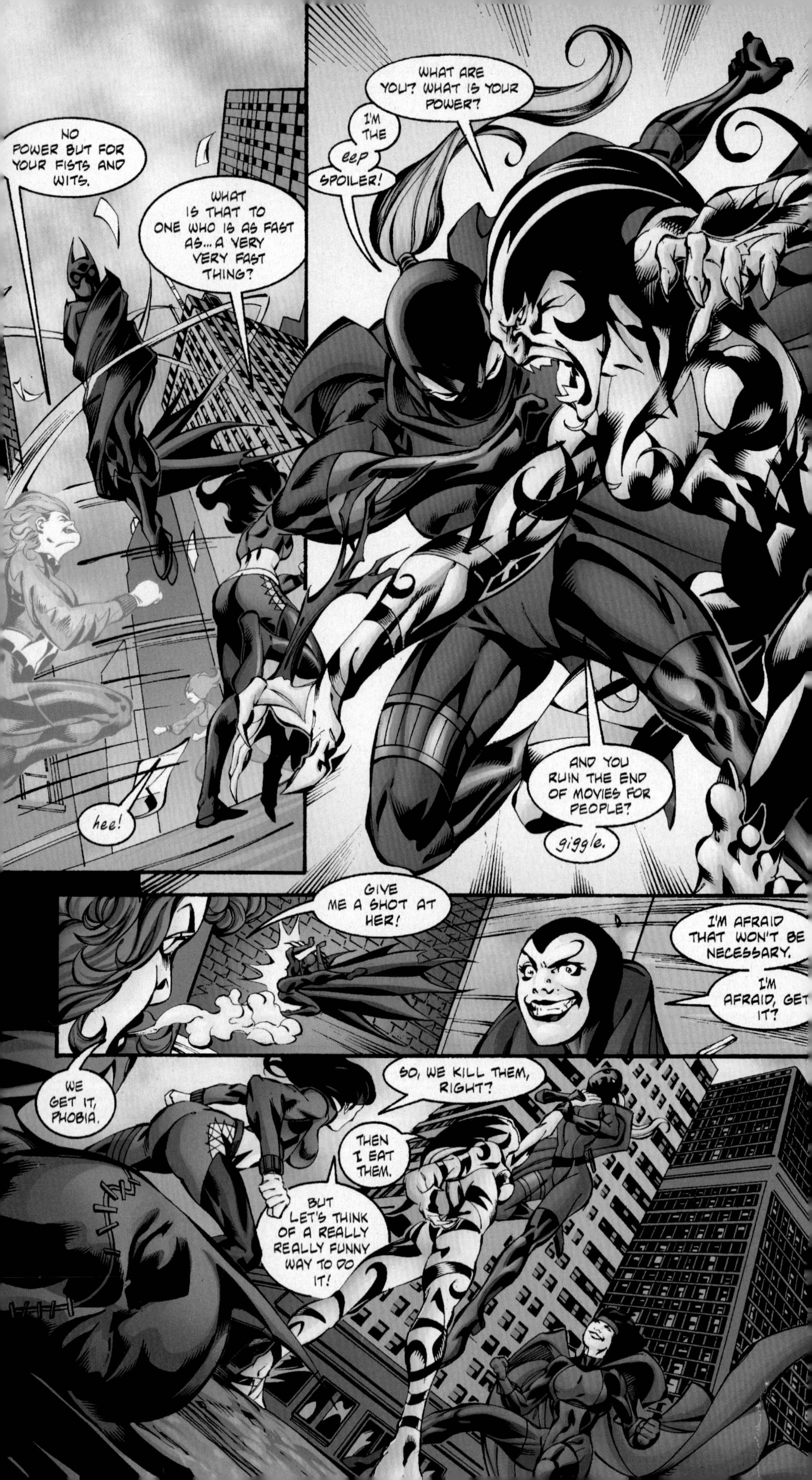
NO POWER BUT FOR YOUR FISTS AND WITS.
WHAT IS THAT TO ONE WHO IS AS FAST AS... A VERY VERY FAST THING?
WHAT ARE YOU? WHAT IS YOUR POWER?
I'M THE eep SPOILER!
hee!
AND YOU RUIN THE END OF MOVIES FOR PEOPLE?
giggle.
GIVE ME A SHOT AT HER!
I'M AFRAID THAT WON'T BE NECESSARY.
I'M AFRAID, GET IT?
WE GET IT, PHOBIA.
SO, WE KILL THEM, RIGHT?
THEN I EAT THEM.
BUT LET'S THINK OF A REALLY REALLY FUNNY WAY TO DO IT!

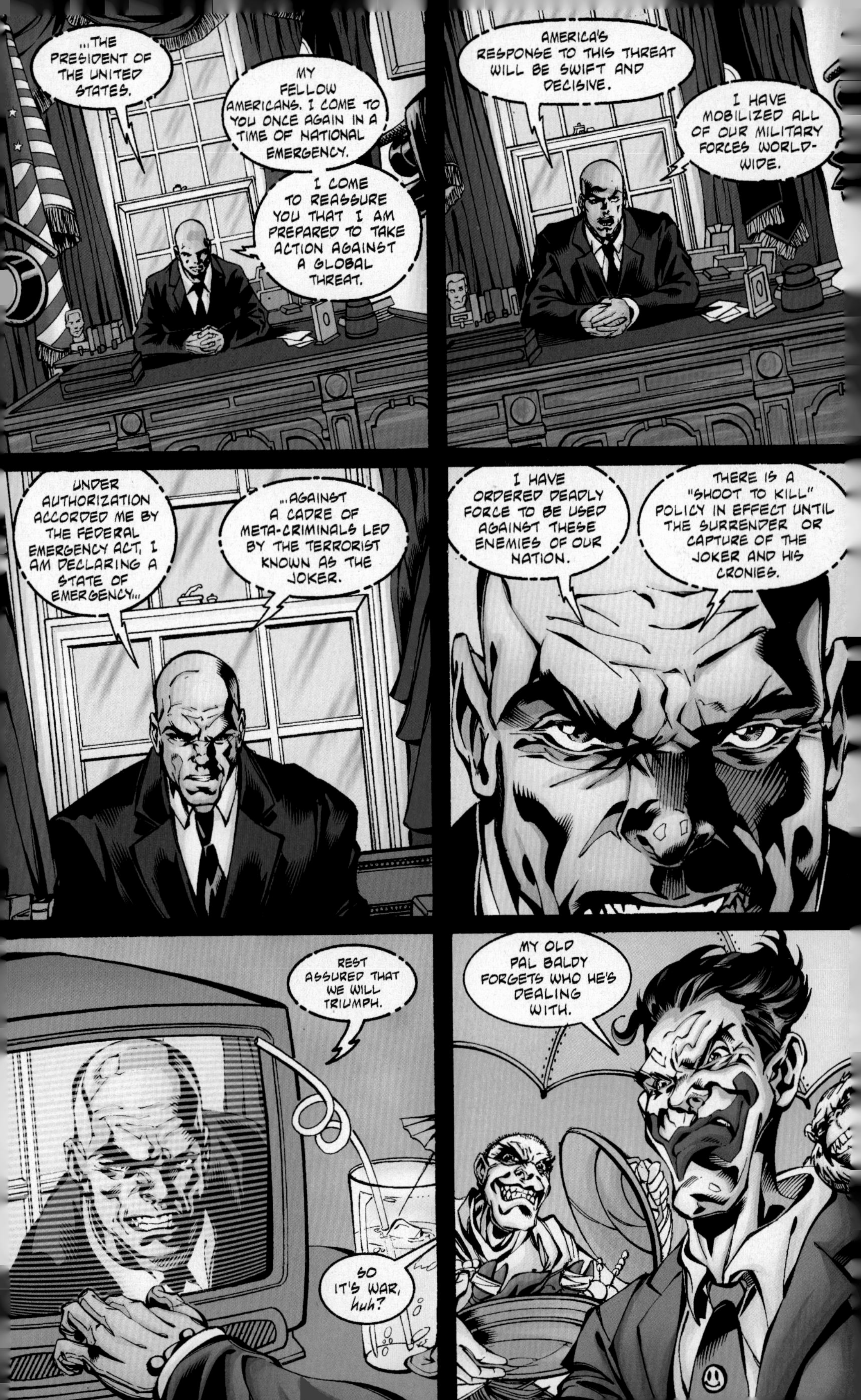
...THE PRESIDENT OF THE UNITED STATES.
MY FELLOW AMERICANS. I COME TO YOU ONCE AGAIN IN A TIME OF NATIONAL EMERGENCY.
I COME TO REASSURE YOU THAT I AM PREPARED TO TAKE ACTION AGAINST A GLOBAL THREAT.
AMERICA'S RESPONSE TO THIS THREAT WILL BE SWIFT AND DECISIVE.
I HAVE MOBILIZED ALL OF OUR MILITARY FORCES WORLD-WIDE.
UNDER AUTHORIZATION ACCORDED ME BY THE FEDERAL EMERGENCY ACT, I AM DECLARING A STATE OF EMERGENCY...
...AGAINST A CADRE OF META-CRIMINALS LED BY THE TERRORIST KNOWN AS THE JOKER.
I HAVE ORDERED DEADLY FORCE TO BE USED AGAINST THESE ENEMIES OF OUR NATION.
THERE IS A "SHOOT TO KILL" POLICY IN EFFECT UNTIL THE SURRENDER OR CAPTURE OF THE JOKER AND HIS CRONIES.
REST ASSURED THAT WE WILL TRIUMPH.
SO IT'S WAR, huh?
MY OLD PAL BALDY FORGETS WHO HE'S DEALING WITH.

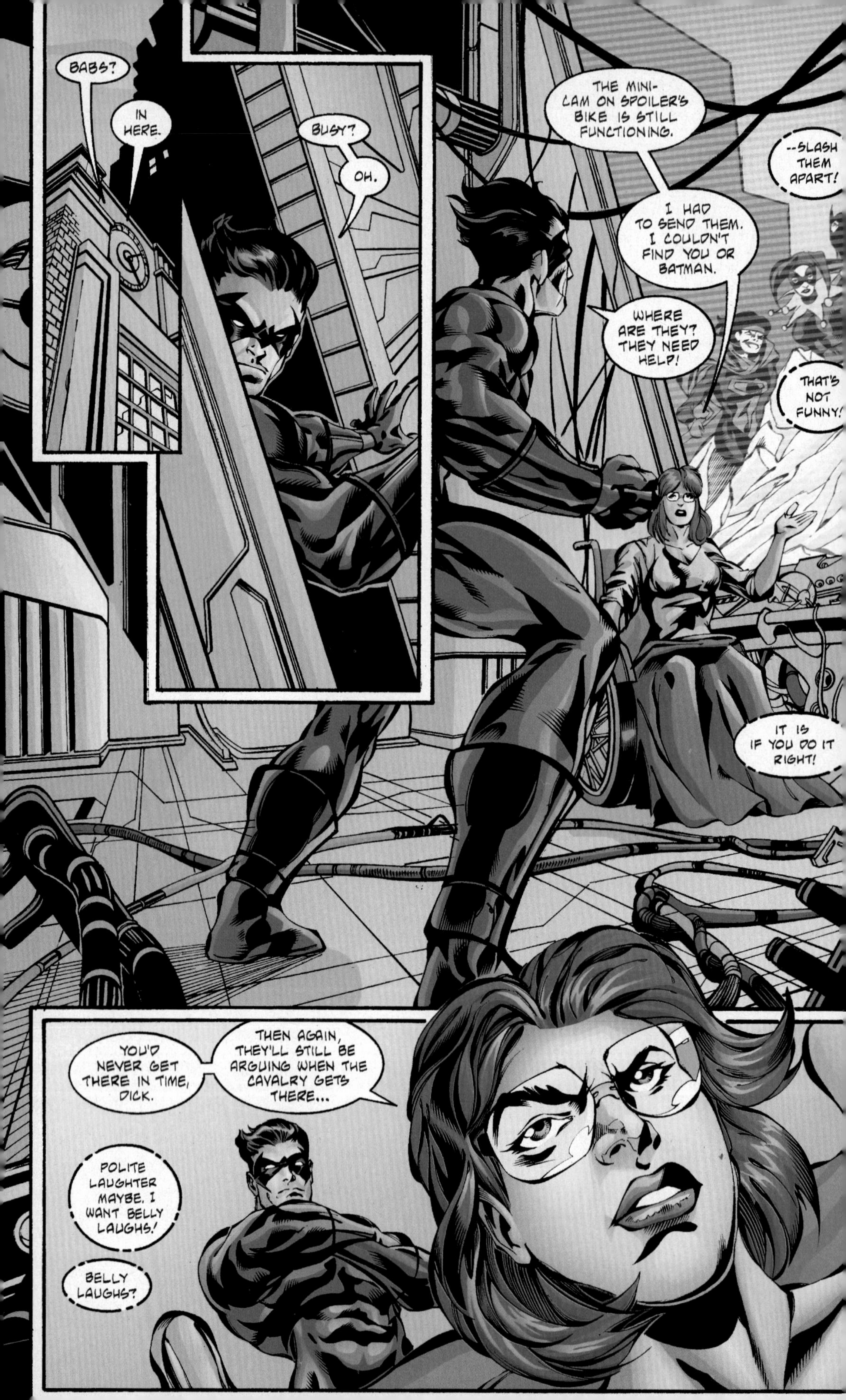

BABS?
IN HERE.
BUSY?
OH.
THE MINI-CAM ON SPOILER'S BIKE IS STILL FUNCTIONING.
--SLASH THEM APART!
I HAD TO SEND THEM. I COULDN'T FIND YOU OR BATMAN.
WHERE ARE THEY? THEY NEED HELP!
THAT'S NOT FUNNY!
IT IS IF YOU DO IT RIGHT!
YOU'D NEVER GET THERE IN TIME, DICK.
THEN AGAIN, THEY'LL STILL BE ARGUING WHEN THE CAVALRY GETS THERE...
POLITE LAUGHTER MAYBE. I WANT BELLY LAUGHS!
BELLY LAUGHS?

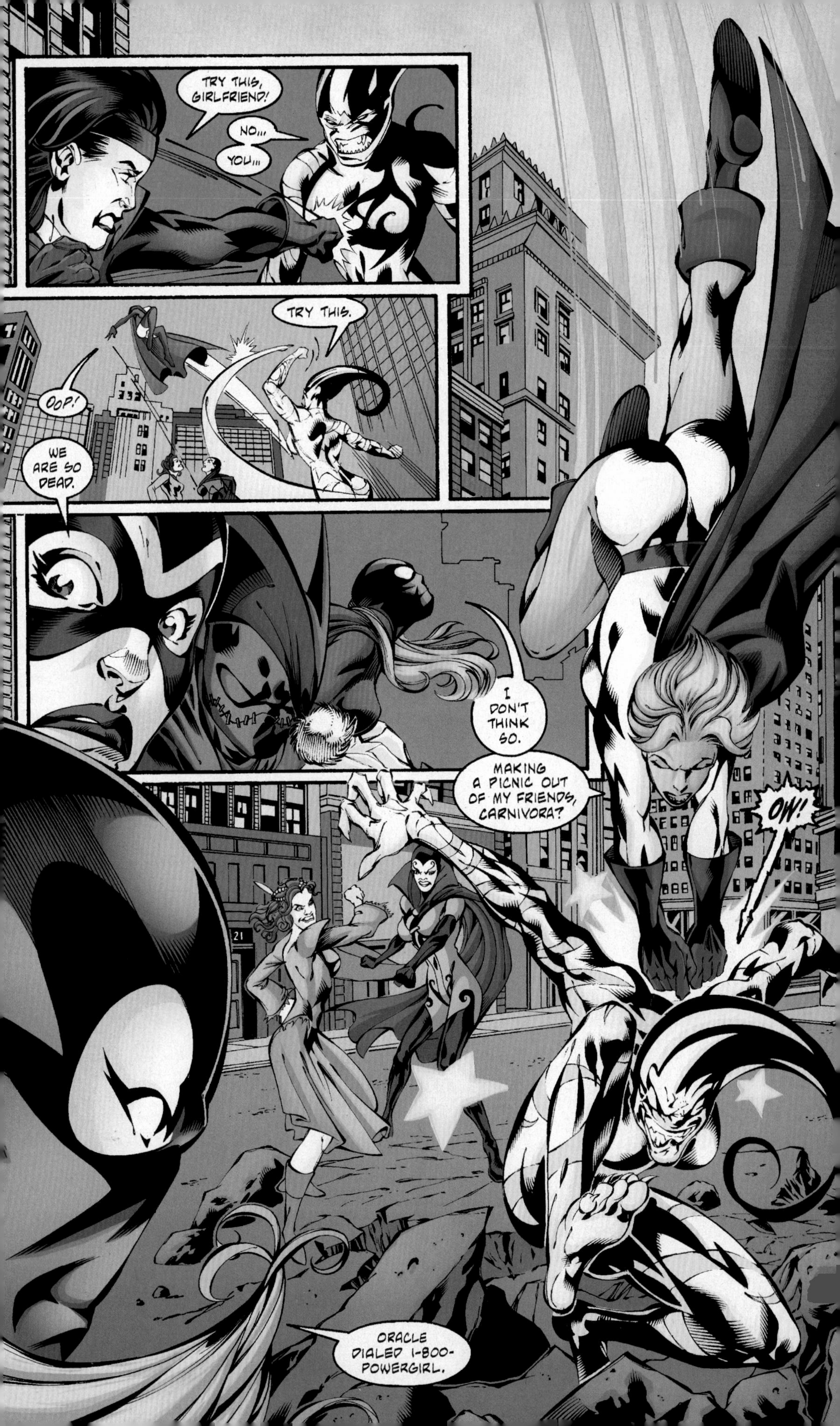
TRY THIS, GIRLFRIEND!
NO...
YOU...
TRY THIS.
OOP!
WE ARE SO DEAD.
I DON'T THINK SO.
MAKING A PICNIC OUT OF MY FRIENDS, CARNIVORA?
OW!
21
ORACLE DIALED 1-800-POWERGIRL.

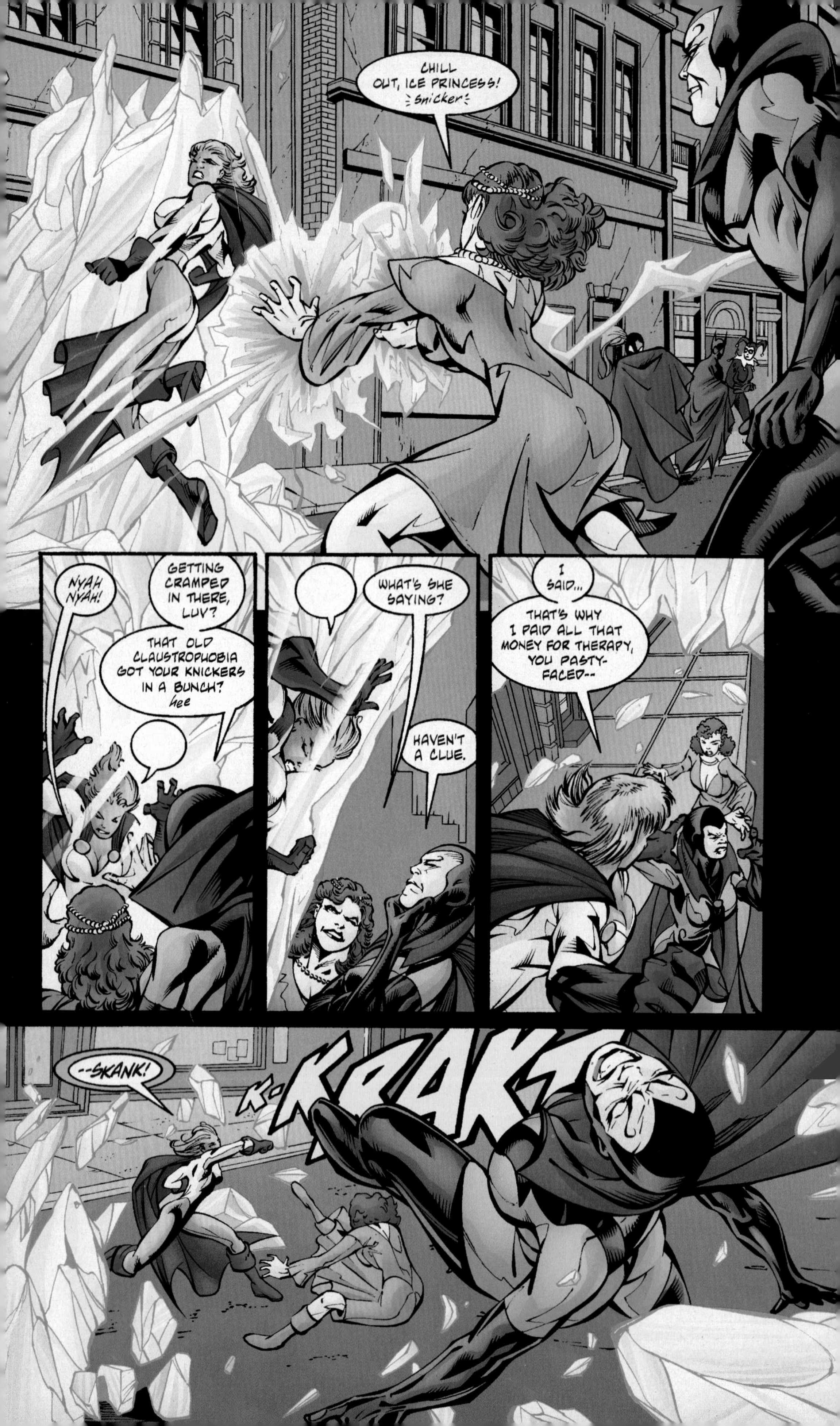
CHILL OUT, ICE PRINCESS! ≷snicker≶
NYAH NYAH!
GETTING CRAMPED IN THERE, LUV?
THAT OLD CLAUSTROPHOBIA GOT YOUR KNICKERS IN A BUNCH? hee
WHAT'S SHE SAYING?
HAVEN'T A CLUE.
I SAID...
THAT'S WHY I PAID ALL THAT MONEY FOR THERAPY, YOU PASTY-FACED--
--SKANK!
K-KRAK

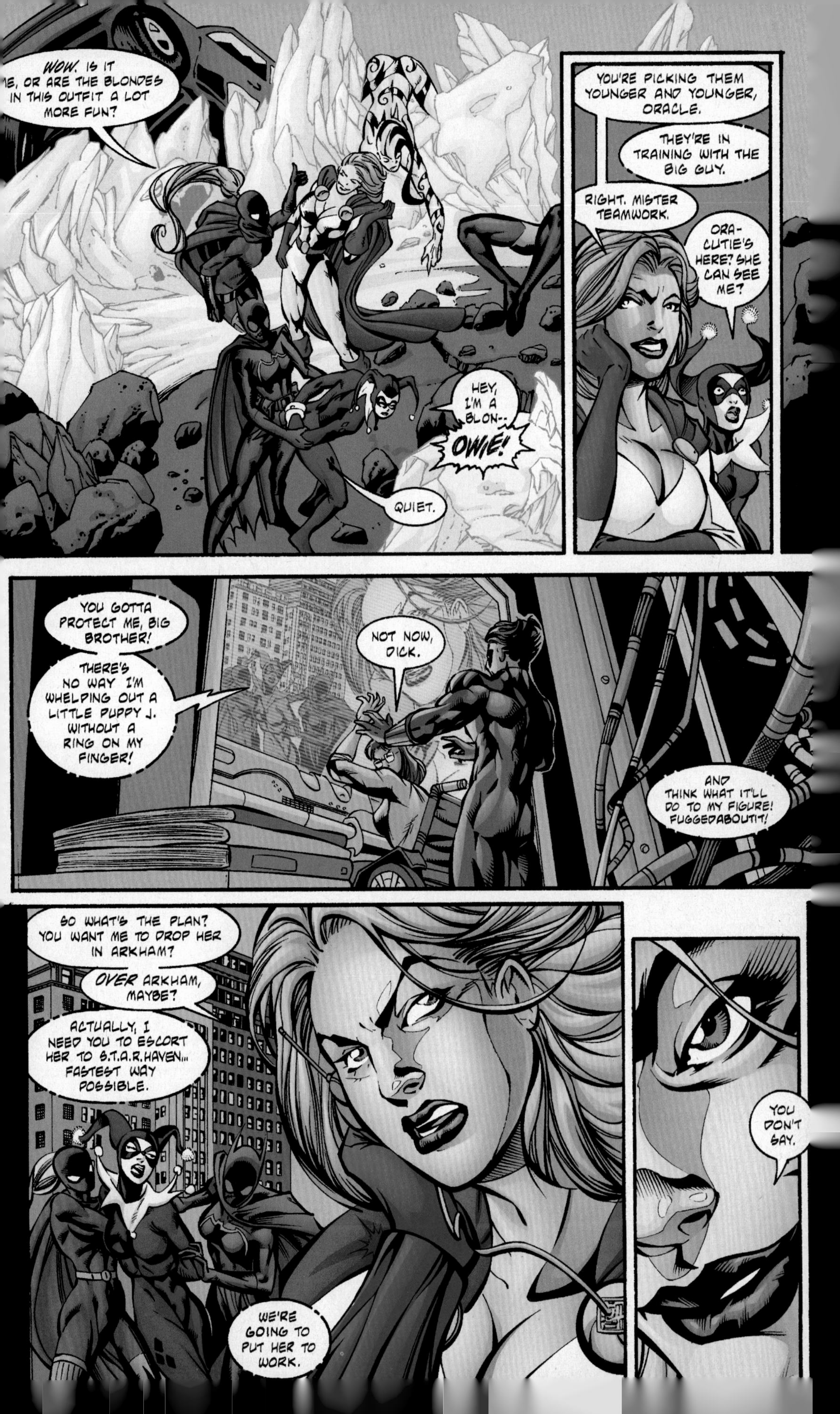
WOW. IS IT ME, OR ARE THE BLONDES IN THIS OUTFIT A LOT MORE FUN?
HEY, I'M A BLON--
OWIE!
QUIET.
YOU'RE PICKING THEM YOUNGER AND YOUNGER, ORACLE.
THEY'RE IN TRAINING WITH THE BIG GUY.
RIGHT. MISTER TEAMWORK.
ORA-CUTIE'S HERE? SHE CAN SEE ME?
YOU GOTTA PROTECT ME, BIG BROTHER!
THERE'S NO WAY I'M WHELPING OUT A LITTLE PUPPY J. WITHOUT A RING ON MY FINGER!
NOT NOW, DICK.
AND THINK WHAT IT'LL DO TO MY FIGURE! FUGGEDABOUTIT!
SO WHAT'S THE PLAN? YOU WANT ME TO DROP HER IN ARKHAM?
OVER ARKHAM, MAYBE?
ACTUALLY, I NEED YOU TO ESCORT HER TO S.T.A.R.HAVEN... FASTEST WAY POSSIBLE.
WE'RE GOING TO PUT HER TO WORK.
YOU DON'T SAY.

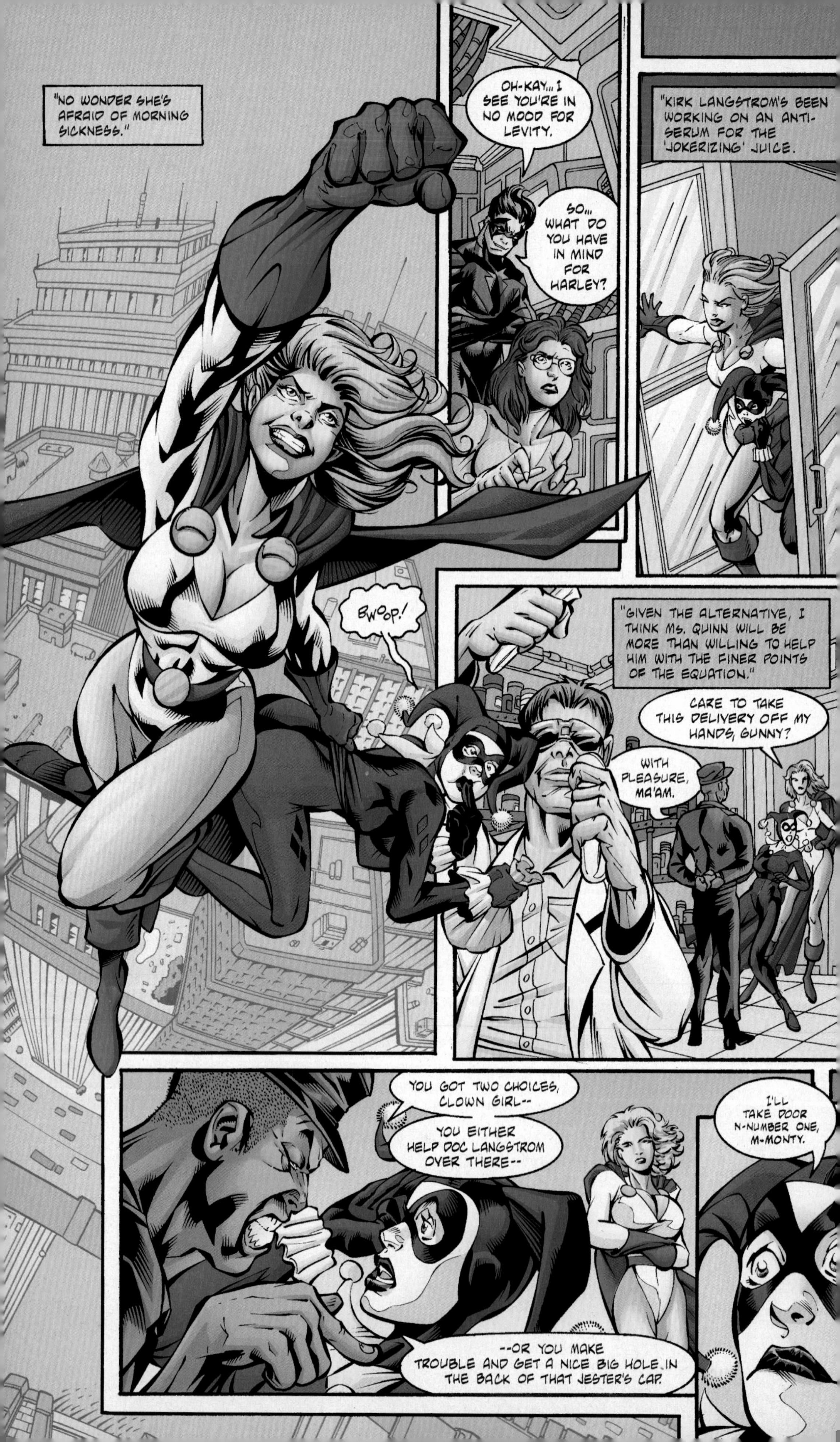
"NO WONDER SHE'S AFRAID OF MORNING SICKNESS."
OH-KAY... I SEE YOU'RE IN NO MOOD FOR LEVITY.
SO... WHAT DO YOU HAVE IN MIND FOR HARLEY?
"KIRK LANGSTROM'S BEEN WORKING ON AN ANTI-SERUM FOR THE 'JOKERIZING' JUICE.
BWOOP!
"GIVEN THE ALTERNATIVE, I THINK MS. QUINN WILL BE MORE THAN WILLING TO HELP HIM WITH THE FINER POINTS OF THE EQUATION."
CARE TO TAKE THIS DELIVERY OFF MY HANDS, GUNNY?
WITH PLEASURE, MA'AM.
YOU GOT TWO CHOICES, CLOWN GIRL--
YOU EITHER HELP DOC LANGSTROM OVER THERE--
--OR YOU MAKE TROUBLE AND GET A NICE BIG HOLE IN THE BACK OF THAT JESTER'S CAP.
I'LL TAKE DOOR N-NUMBER ONE, M-MONTY.

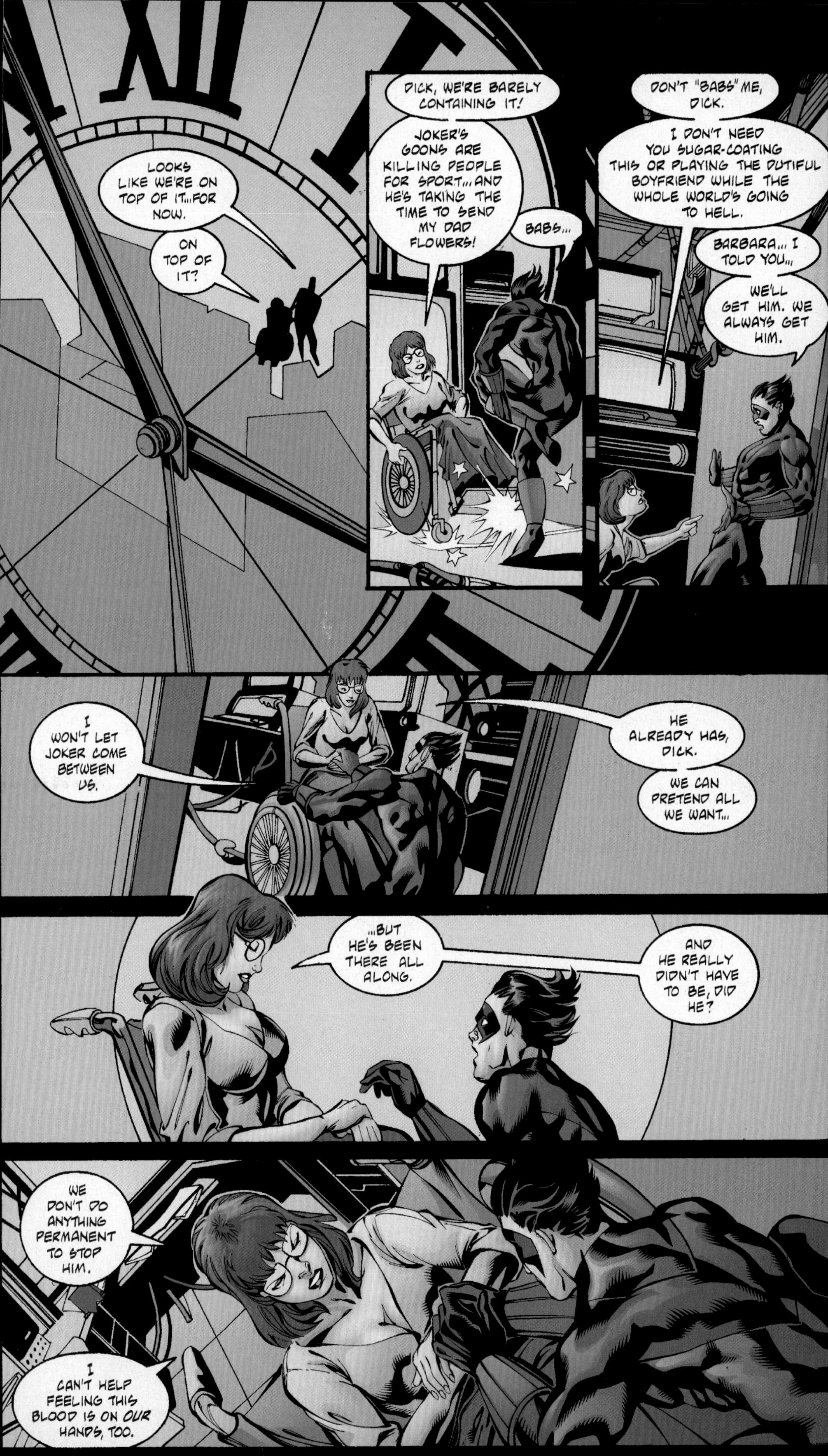
LOOKS LIKE WE'RE ON TOP OF IT...FOR NOW.
ON TOP OF IT?
DICK, WE'RE BARELY CONTAINING IT!
JOKER'S GOONS ARE KILLING PEOPLE FOR SPORT... AND HE'S TAKING THE TIME TO SEND MY DAD FLOWERS!
BABS...
DON'T "BABS" ME, DICK.
I DON'T NEED YOU SUGAR-COATING THIS OR PLAYING THE DUTIFUL BOYFRIEND WHILE THE WHOLE WORLD'S GOING TO HELL.
BARBARA... I TOLD YOU...
WE'LL GET HIM. WE ALWAYS GET HIM.
I WON'T LET JOKER COME BETWEEN US.
HE ALREADY HAS, DICK.
WE CAN PRETEND ALL WE WANT...
...BUT HE'S BEEN THERE ALL ALONG.
AND HE REALLY DIDN'T HAVE TO BE, DID HE?
WE DON'T DO ANYTHING PERMANENT TO STOP HIM.
I CAN'T HELP FEELING THIS BLOOD IS ON OUR HANDS, TOO.

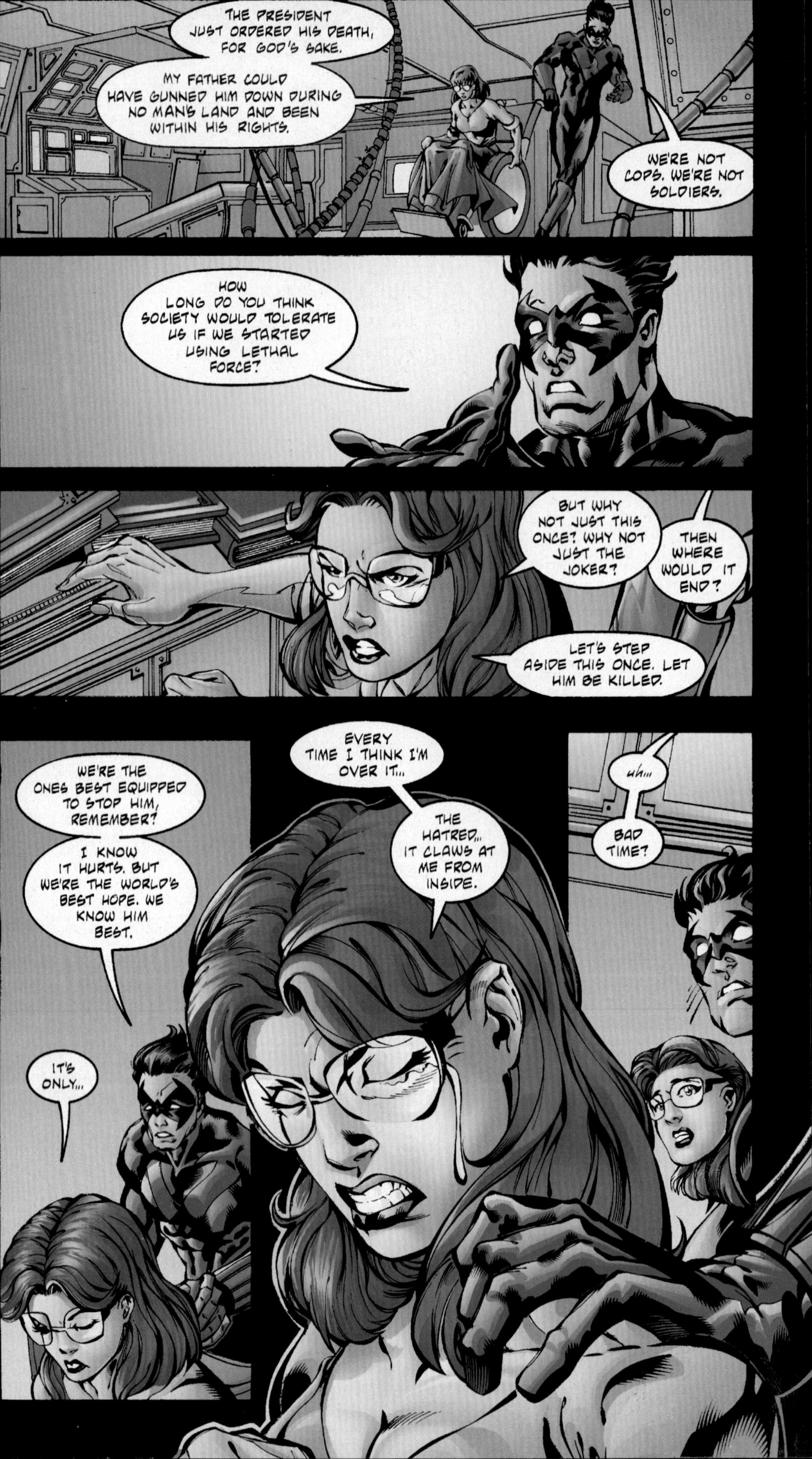
THE PRESIDENT JUST ORDERED HIS DEATH, FOR GOD'S SAKE.
MY FATHER COULD HAVE GUNNED HIM DOWN DURING NO MAN'S LAND AND BEEN WITHIN HIS RIGHTS.
WE'RE NOT COPS. WE'RE NOT SOLDIERS.
HOW LONG DO YOU THINK SOCIETY WOULD TOLERATE US IF WE STARTED USING LETHAL FORCE?
BUT WHY NOT JUST THIS ONCE? WHY NOT JUST THE JOKER?
THEN WHERE WOULD IT END?
LET'S STEP ASIDE THIS ONCE. LET HIM BE KILLED.
WE'RE THE ONES BEST EQUIPPED TO STOP HIM, REMEMBER?
I KNOW IT HURTS. BUT WE'RE THE WORLD'S BEST HOPE. WE KNOW HIM BEST.
IT'S ONLY...
EVERY TIME I THINK I'M OVER IT...
THE HATRED... IT CLAWS AT ME FROM INSIDE.
uh...
BAD TIME?

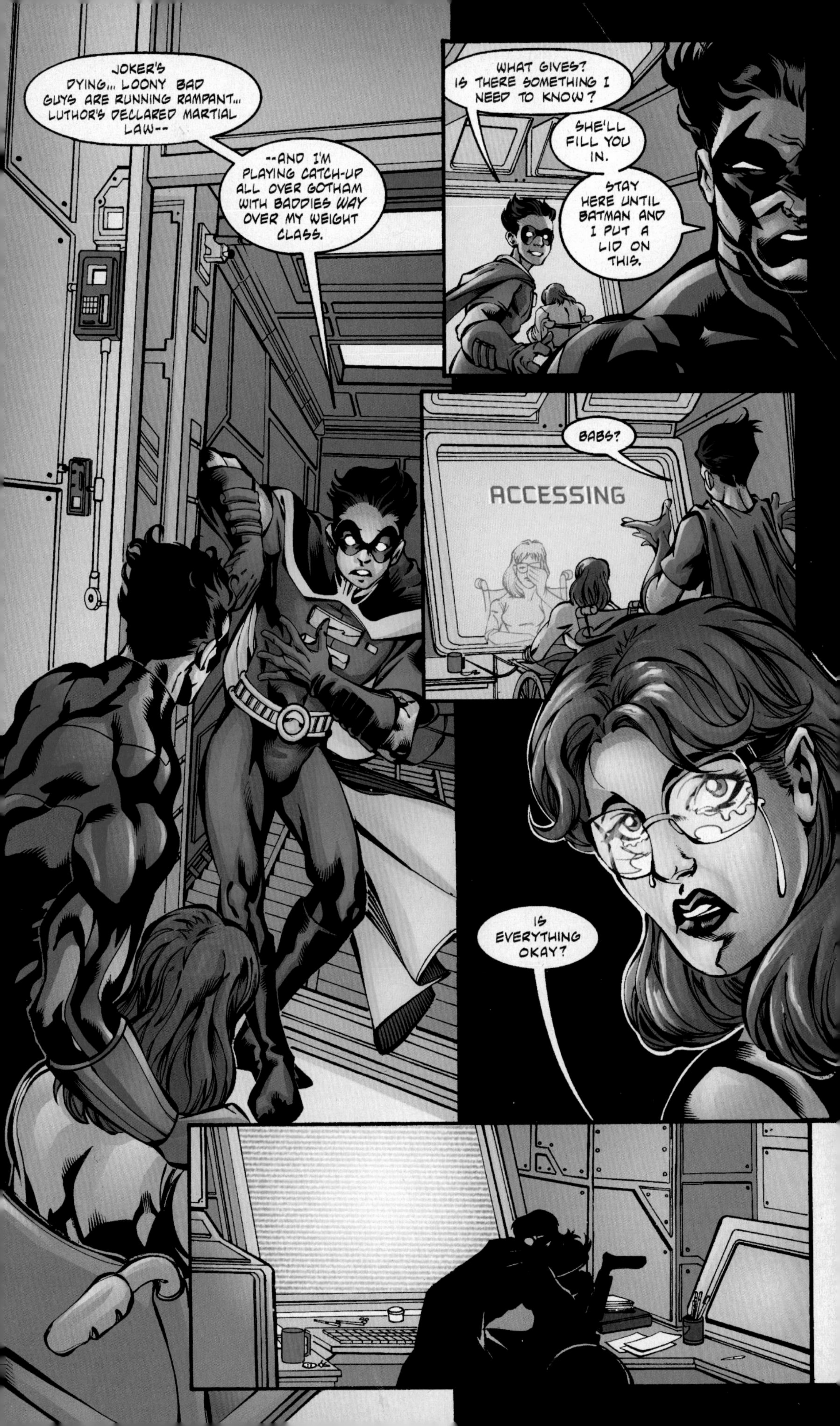
JOKER'S DYING... LOONY BAD GUYS ARE RUNNING RAMPANT... LUTHOR'S DECLARED MARTIAL LAW--
--AND I'M PLAYING CATCH-UP ALL OVER GOTHAM WITH BADDIES WAY OVER MY WEIGHT CLASS.
WHAT GIVES? IS THERE SOMETHING I NEED TO KNOW?
SHE'LL FILL YOU IN.
STAY HERE UNTIL BATMAN AND I PUT A LID ON THIS.
BABS?
ACCESSING
IS EVERYTHING OKAY?

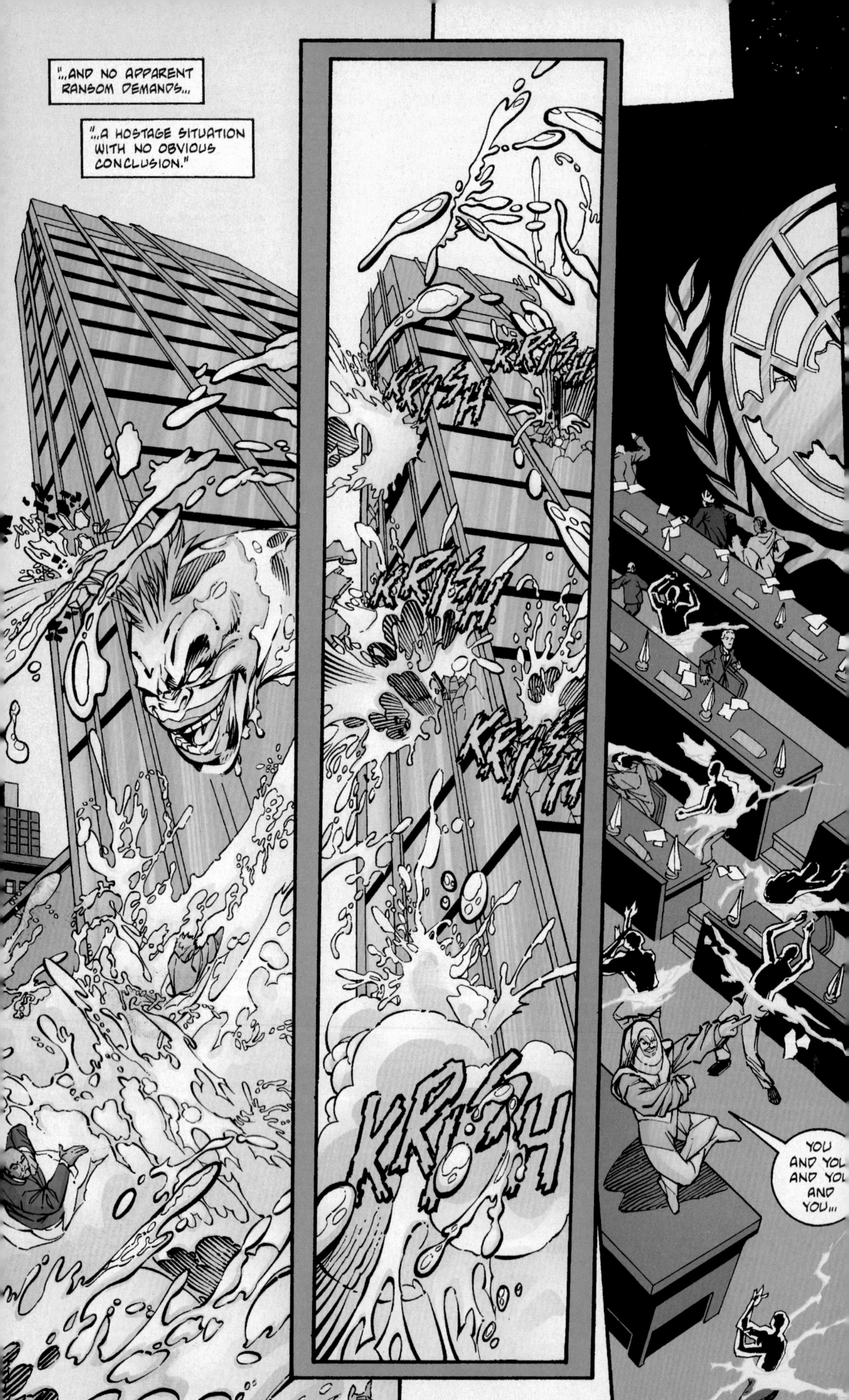
"...AND NO APPARENT RANSOM DEMANDS...
"...A HOSTAGE SITUATION WITH NO OBVIOUS CONCLUSION."
KRASH
KRASH
KRASH
KRASH
KRASH
YOU AND YOU AND YOU AND YOU...

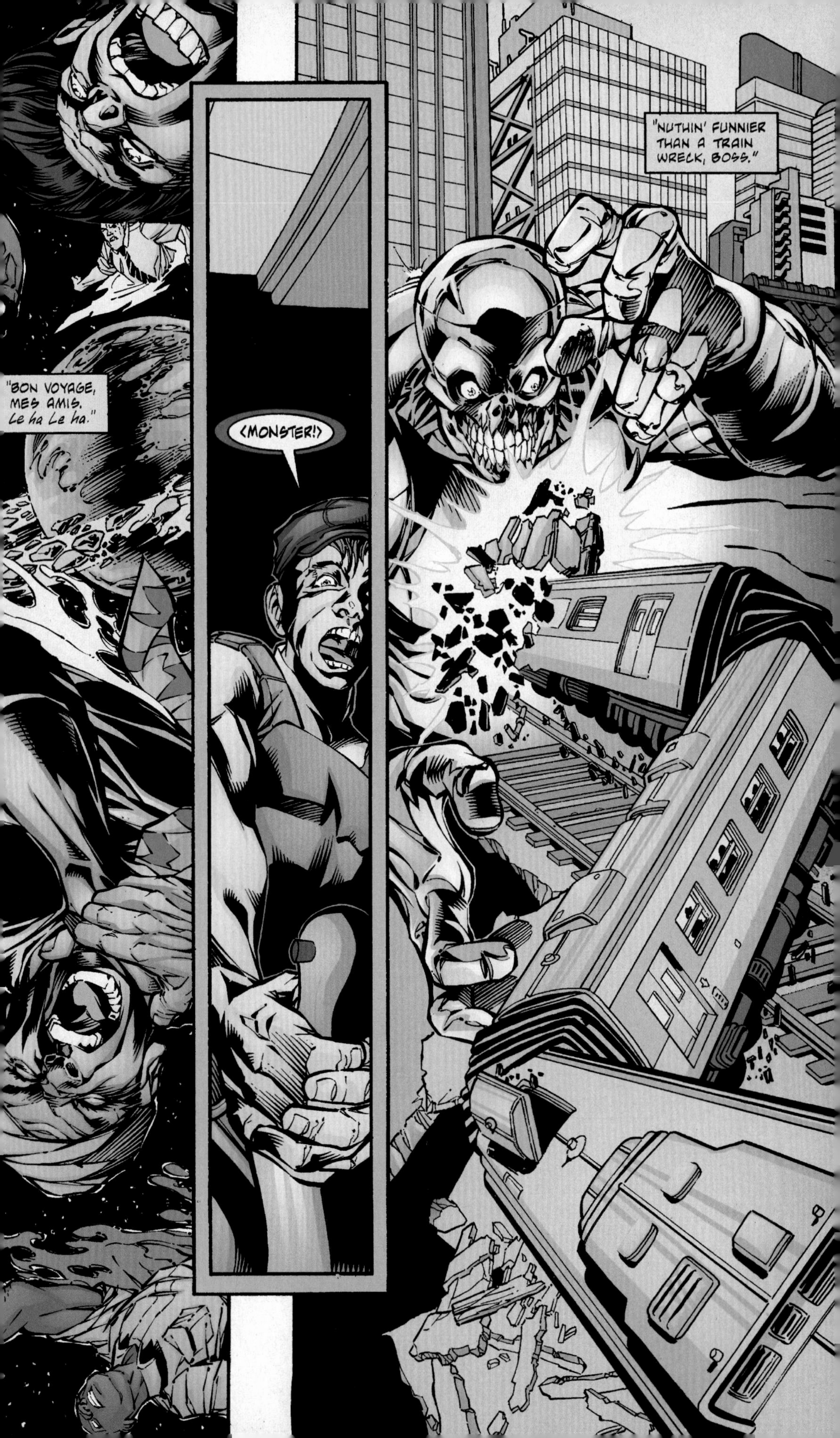
"BON VOYAGE, MES AMIS. Le ha Le ha."
<MONSTER!>
"NUTHIN' FUNNIER THAN A TRAIN WRECK, BOSS."

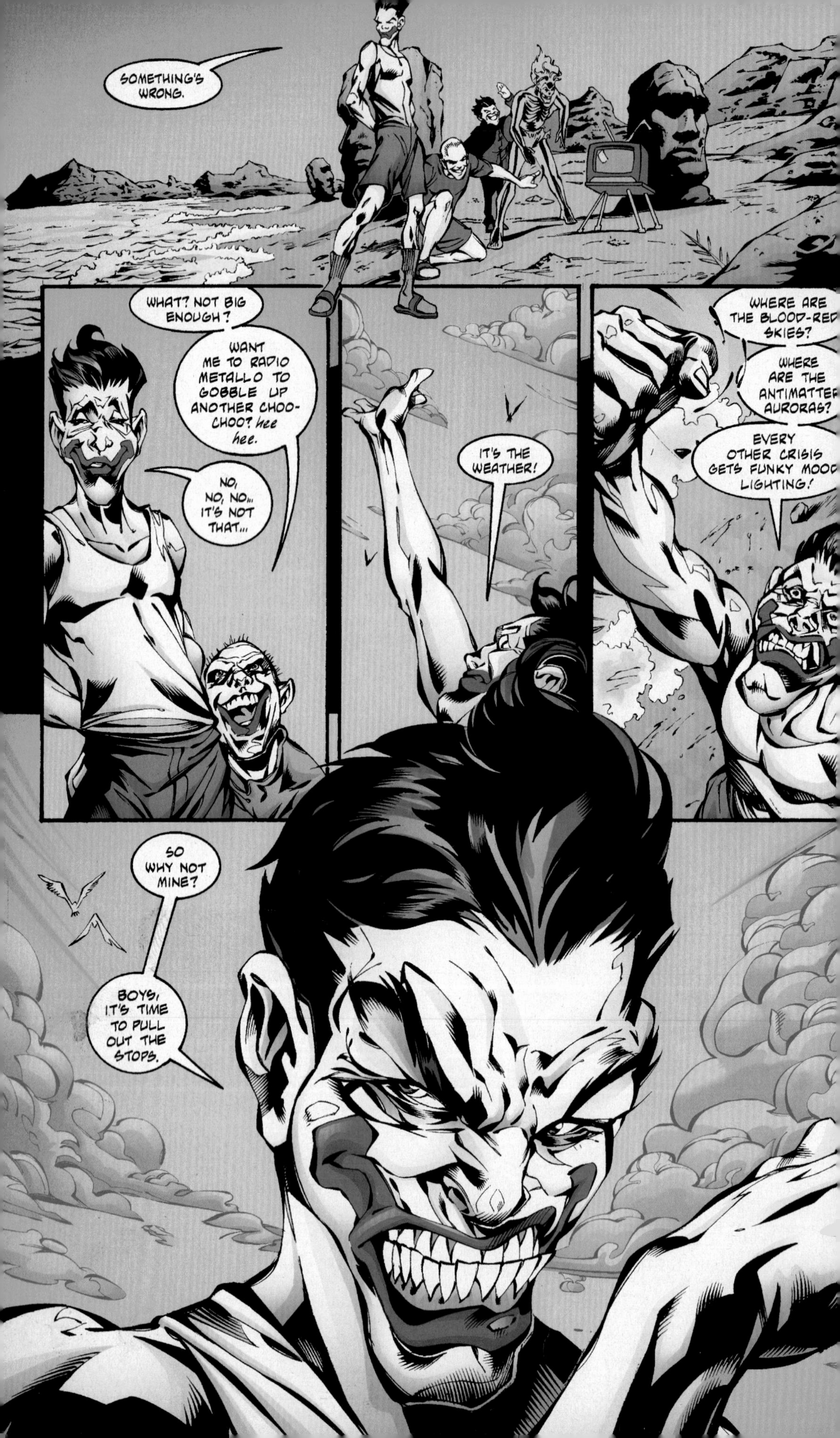
SOMETHING'S WRONG.
WHAT? NOT BIG ENOUGH?
WANT ME TO RADIO METALLO TO GOBBLE UP ANOTHER CHOO-CHOO? hee hee.
NO, NO, NO... IT'S NOT THAT...
IT'S THE WEATHER!
WHERE ARE THE BLOOD-RED SKIES?
WHERE ARE THE ANTIMATTER AURORAS?
EVERY OTHER CRISIS GETS FUNKY MOOD LIGHTING!
SO WHY NOT MINE?
BOYS, IT'S TIME TO PULL OUT THE STOPS.

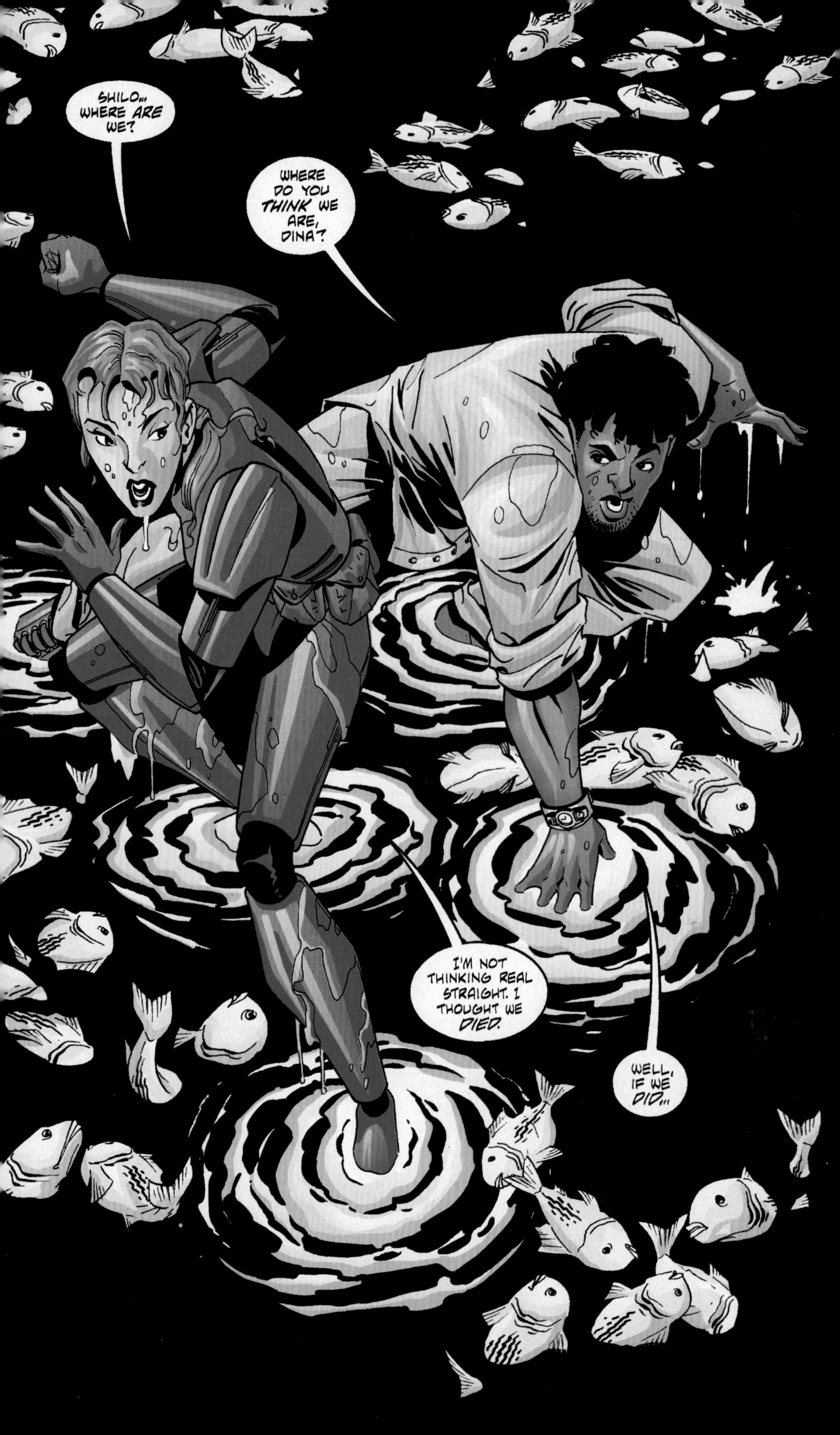
SHILO... WHERE ARE WE?
WHERE DO YOU THINK WE ARE, DINA?
I'M NOT THINKING REAL STRAIGHT. I THOUGHT WE DIED.
WELL, IF WE DID...

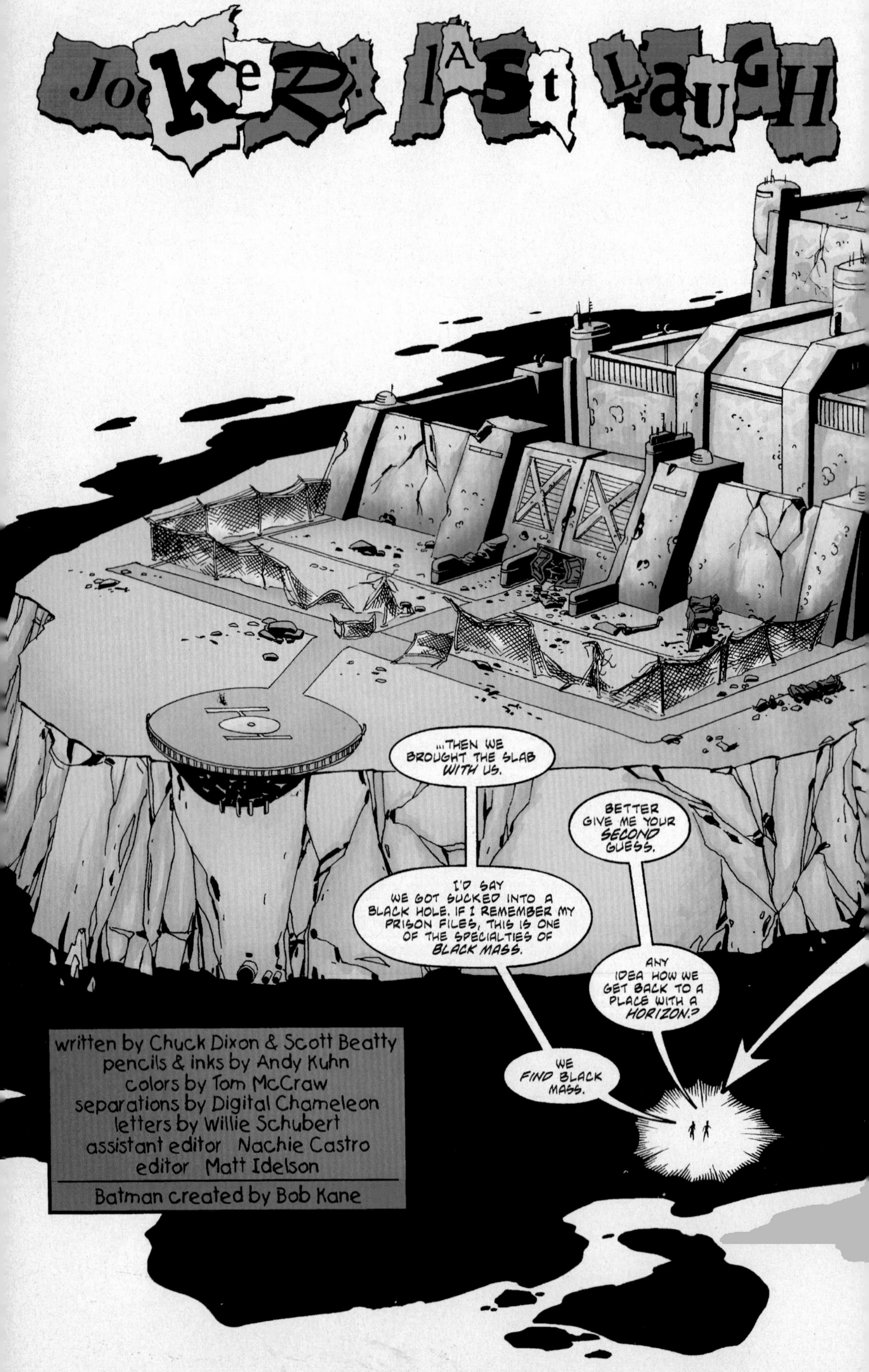
JOKER: LAST LAUGH
...THEN WE BROUGHT THE SLAB WITH US.
BETTER GIVE ME YOUR SECOND GUESS.
I'D SAY WE GOT SUCKED INTO A BLACK HOLE. IF I REMEMBER MY PRISON FILES, THIS IS ONE OF THE SPECIALTIES OF BLACK MASS.
ANY IDEA HOW WE GET BACK TO A PLACE WITH A HORIZON?
WE FIND BLACK MASS.
written by Chuck Dixon & Scott Beatty
pencils & inks by Andy Kuhn
colors by Tom McCraw
separations by Digital Chameleon
letters by Willie Schubert
assistant editor Nachie Castro
editor Matt Idelson
Batman created by Bob Kane

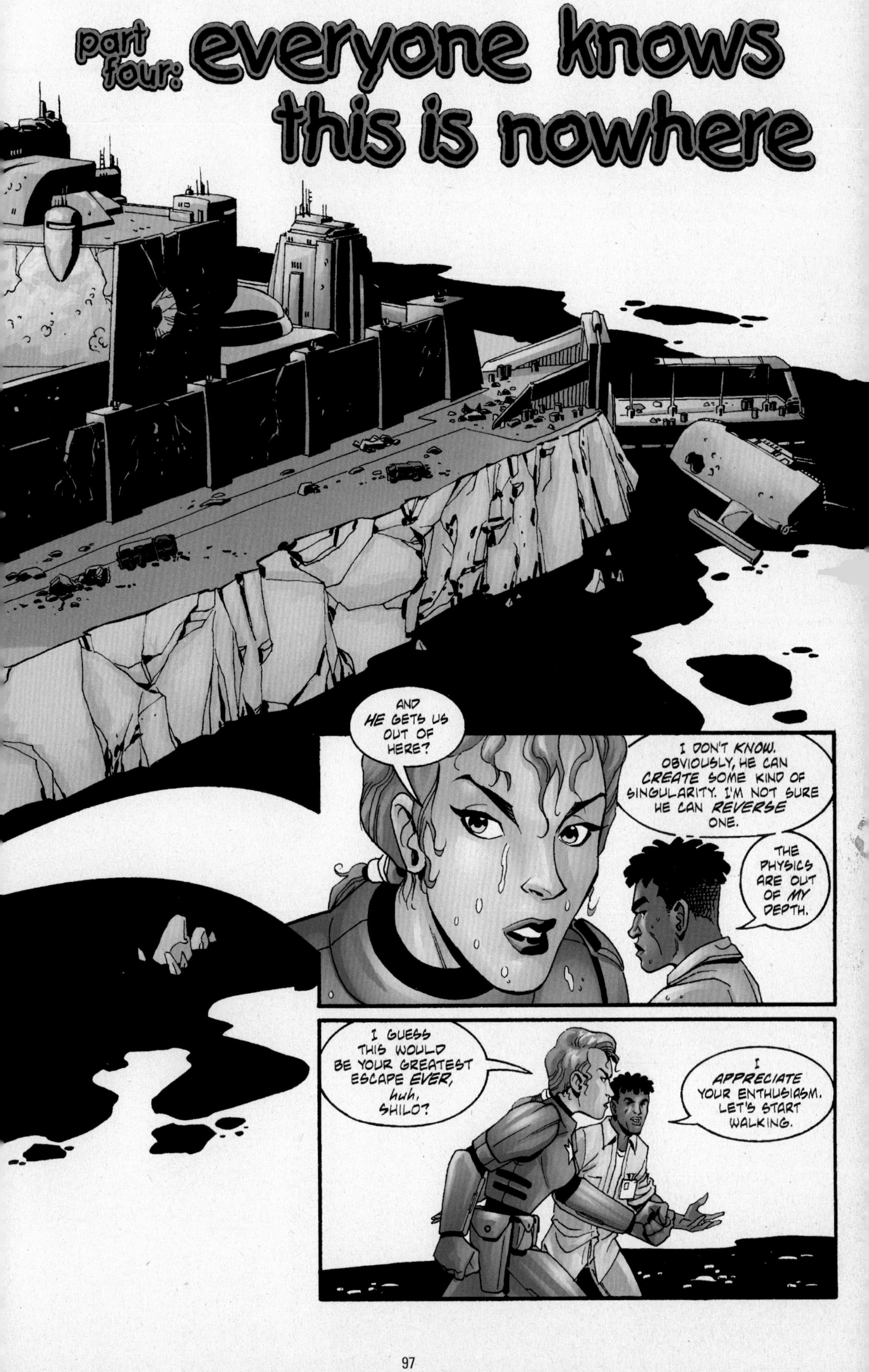
part four: everyone knows this is nowhere
AND HE GETS US OUT OF HERE?
I DON'T KNOW. OBVIOUSLY, HE CAN CREATE SOME KIND OF SINGULARITY. I'M NOT SURE HE CAN REVERSE ONE.
THE PHYSICS ARE OUT OF MY DEPTH.
I GUESS THIS WOULD BE YOUR GREATEST ESCAPE EVER, huh, SHILO?
I APPRECIATE YOUR ENTHUSIASM. LET'S START WALKING.

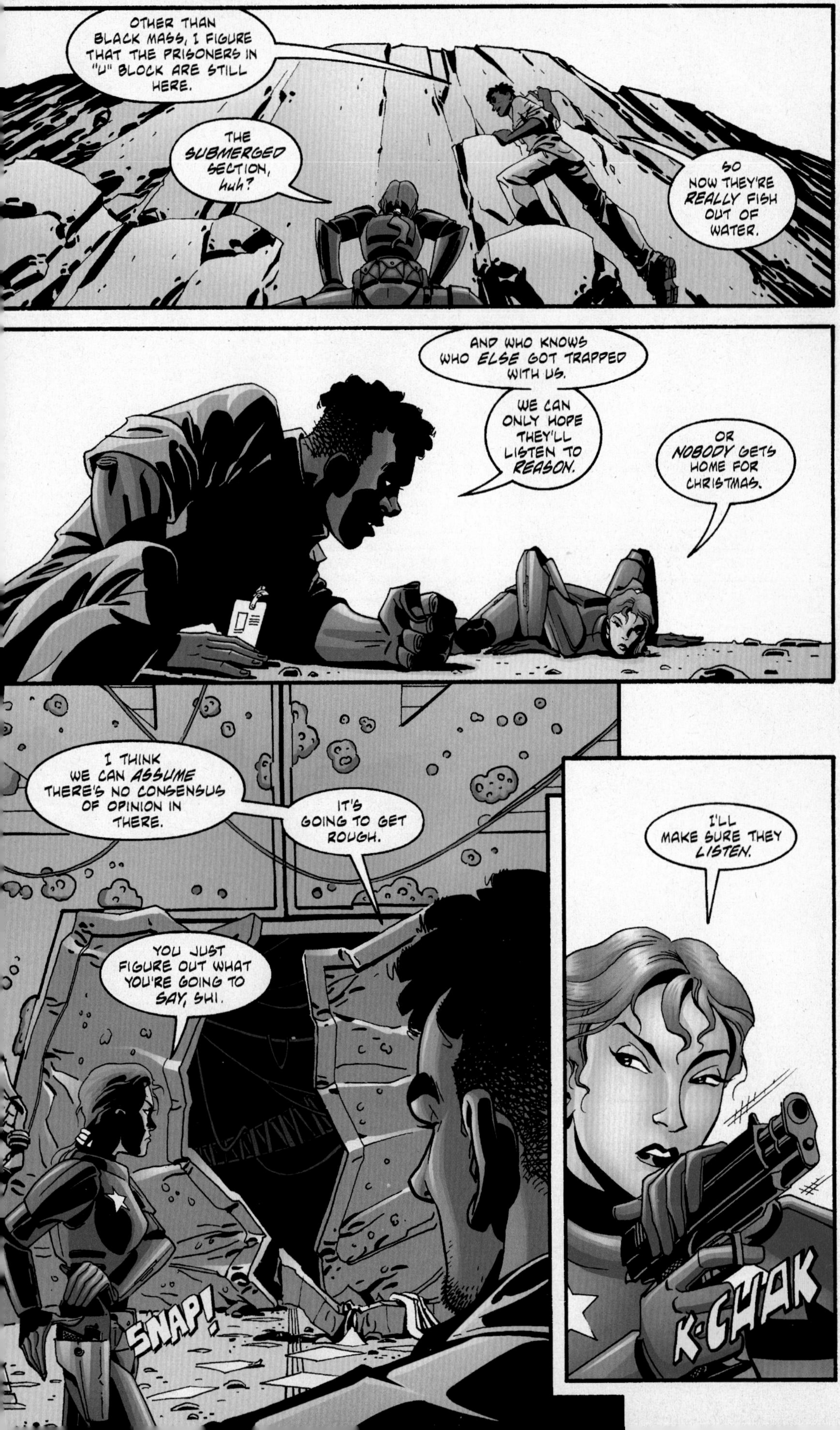
OTHER THAN BLACK MASS, I FIGURE THAT THE PRISONERS IN "U" BLOCK ARE STILL HERE.
THE SUBMERGED SECTION, huh?
SO NOW THEY'RE REALLY FISH OUT OF WATER.
AND WHO KNOWS WHO ELSE GOT TRAPPED WITH US.
WE CAN ONLY HOPE THEY'LL LISTEN TO REASON.
OR NOBODY GETS HOME FOR CHRISTMAS.
I THINK WE CAN ASSUME THERE'S NO CONSENSUS OF OPINION IN THERE.
IT'S GOING TO GET ROUGH.
YOU JUST FIGURE OUT WHAT YOU'RE GOING TO SAY, SHI.
SNAP!
I'LL MAKE SURE THEY LISTEN.
K-CHAK

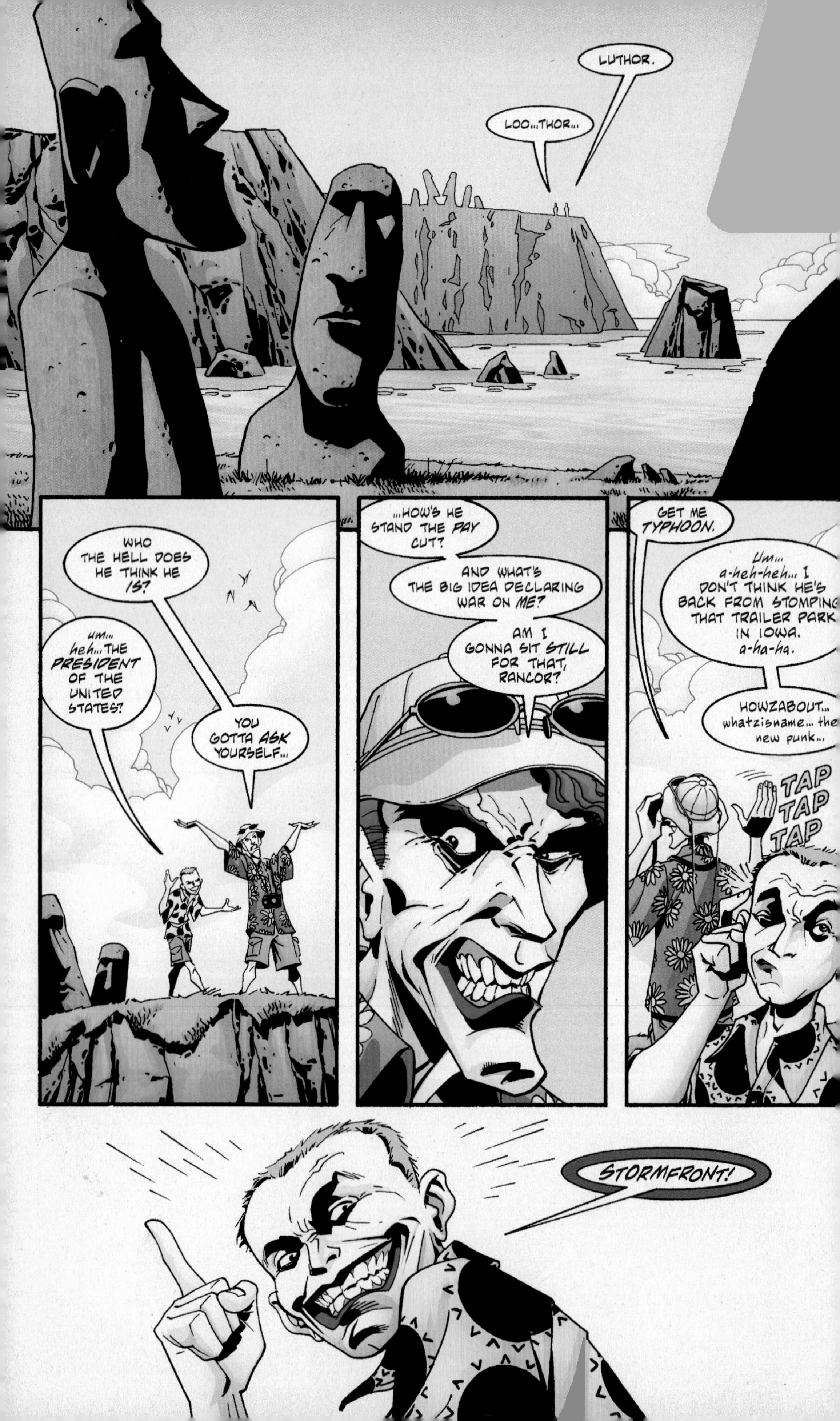
LOO...THOR...
LUTHOR.
WHO THE HELL DOES HE THINK HE IS?
um... heh... THE PRESIDENT OF THE UNITED STATES?
YOU GOTTA ASK YOURSELF...
...HOW'S HE STAND THE PAY CUT?
AND WHAT'S THE BIG IDEA DECLARING WAR ON ME?
AM I GONNA SIT STILL FOR THAT, RANCOR?
GET ME TYPHOON.
Um... a-heh-heh... I DON'T THINK HE'S BACK FROM STOMPING THAT TRAILER PARK IN IOWA. a-ha-ha.
HOWZABOUT... whatzisname... the new punk...
TAP TAP TAP
STORMFRONT!

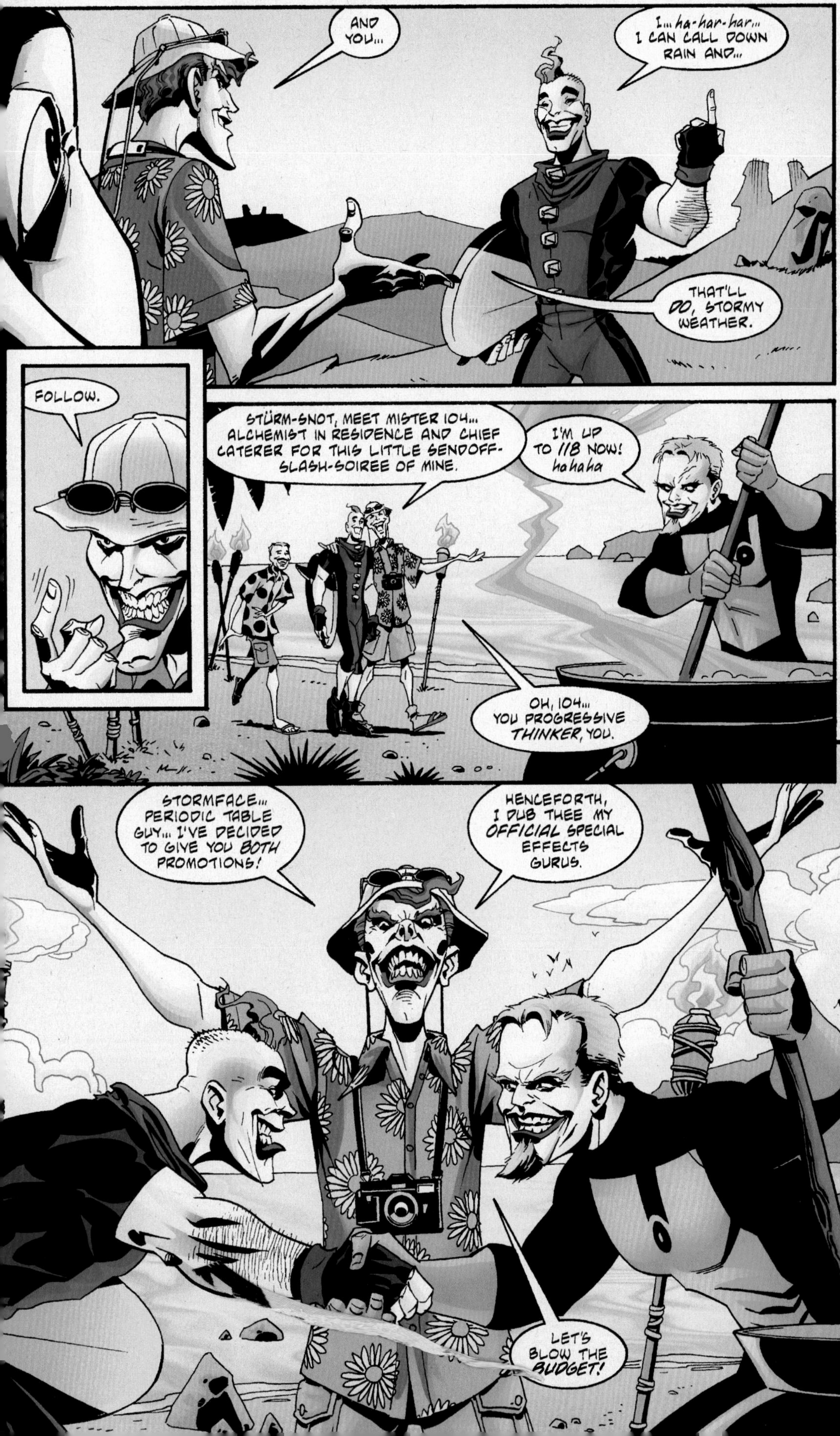
AND YOU...
I... ha-har-har... I CAN CALL DOWN RAIN AND...
THAT'LL DO, STORMY WEATHER.
FOLLOW.
STÜRM-SNOT, MEET MISTER 104... ALCHEMIST IN RESIDENCE AND CHIEF CATERER FOR THIS LITTLE SENDOFF-SLASH-SOIREE OF MINE.
I'M UP TO 118 NOW! hahaha
OH, 104... YOU PROGRESSIVE THINKER, YOU.
STORMFACE... PERIODIC TABLE GUY... I'VE DECIDED TO GIVE YOU BOTH PROMOTIONS!
HENCEFORTH, I DUB THEE MY OFFICIAL SPECIAL EFFECTS GURUS.
LET'S BLOW THE BUDGET!

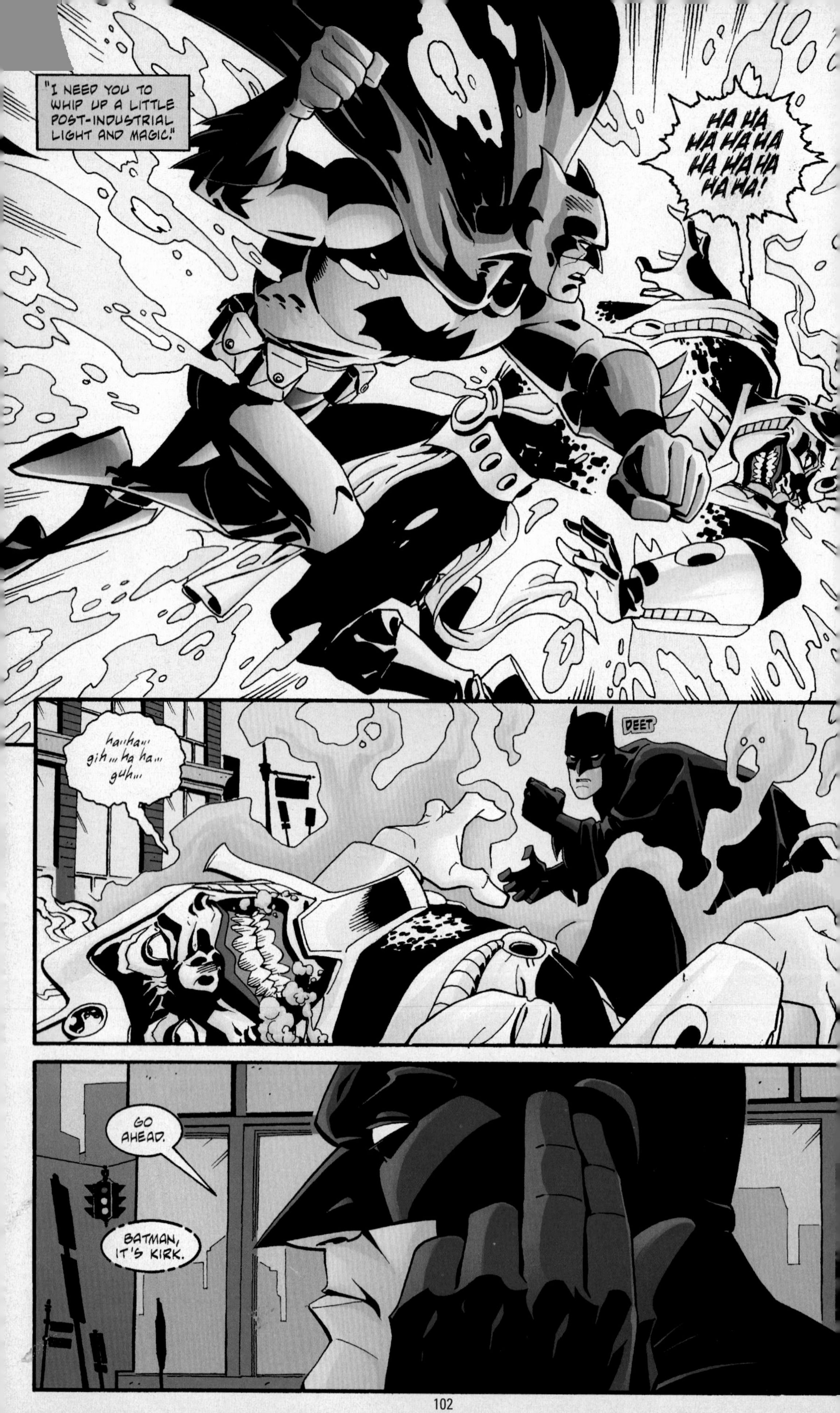
"I NEED YOU TO WHIP UP A LITTLE POST-INDUSTRIAL LIGHT AND MAGIC."
HA HA HA HA HA HA HA HA HA HA!
ha..ha... gih... ha ha... guh...
DEET
GO AHEAD.
BATMAN, IT'S KIRK.

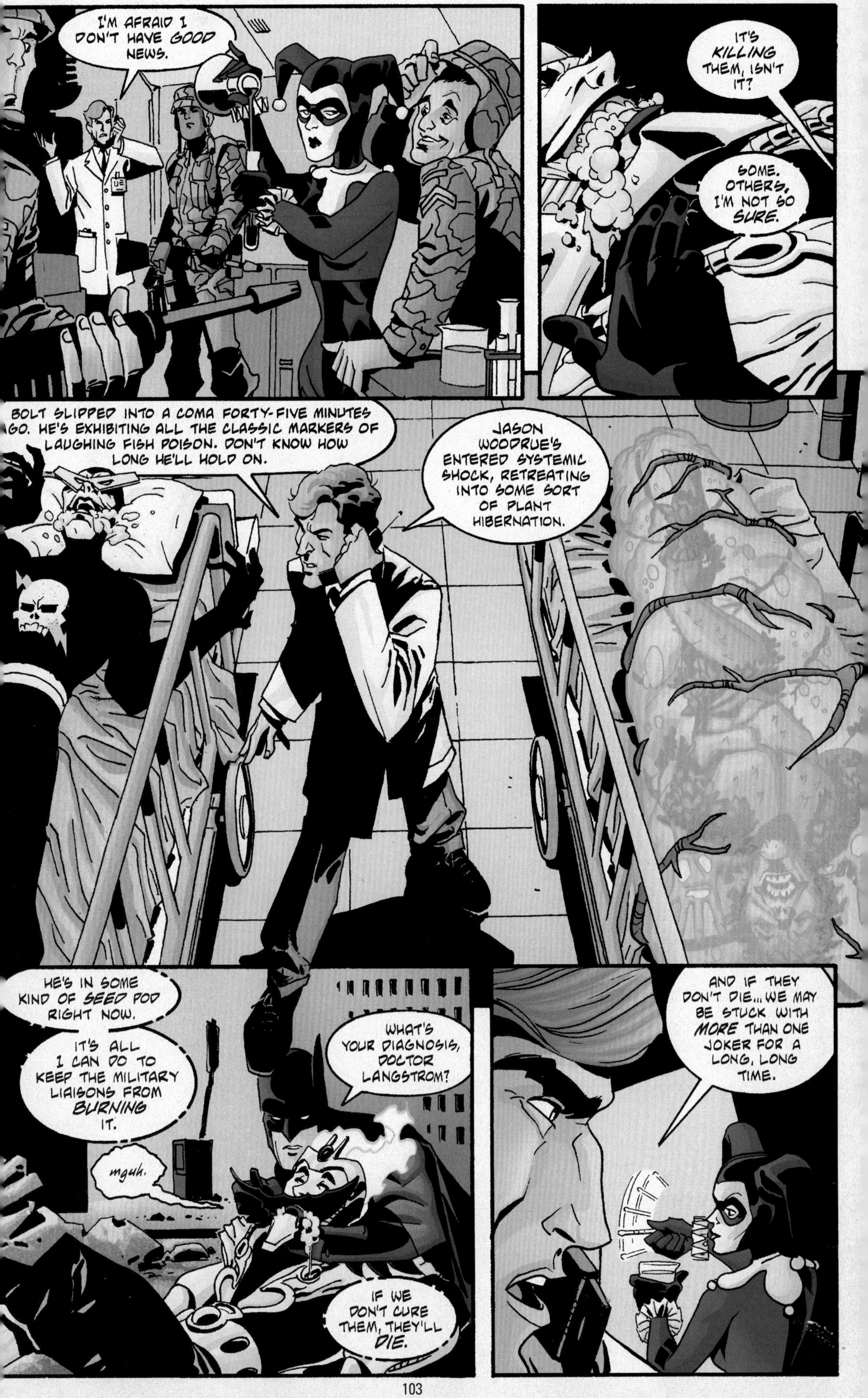
I'M AFRAID I DON'T HAVE GOOD NEWS.
IT'S KILLING THEM, ISN'T IT?
SOME. OTHERS, I'M NOT SO SURE.
BOLT SLIPPED INTO A COMA FORTY-FIVE MINUTES AGO. HE'S EXHIBITING ALL THE CLASSIC MARKERS OF LAUGHING FISH POISON. DON'T KNOW HOW LONG HE'LL HOLD ON.
JASON WOODRUE'S ENTERED SYSTEMIC SHOCK, RETREATING INTO SOME SORT OF PLANT HIBERNATION.
HE'S IN SOME KIND OF SEED POD RIGHT NOW.
IT'S ALL I CAN DO TO KEEP THE MILITARY LIAISONS FROM BURNING IT.
mguh.
WHAT'S YOUR DIAGNOSIS, DOCTOR LANGSTROM?
IF WE DON'T CURE THEM, THEY'LL DIE.
AND IF THEY DON'T DIE... WE MAY BE STUCK WITH MORE THAN ONE JOKER FOR A LONG, LONG TIME.

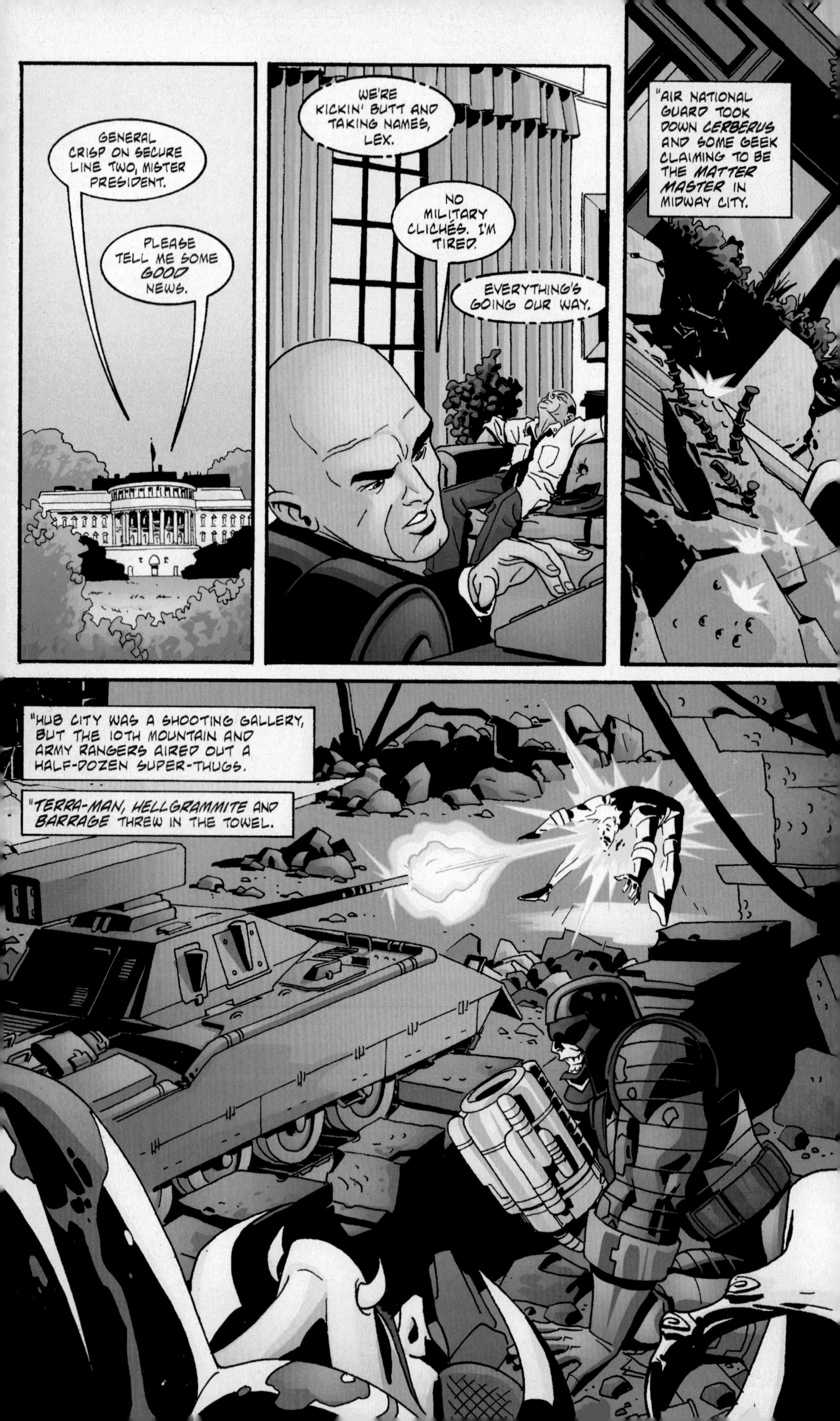
GENERAL CRISP ON SECURE LINE TWO, MISTER PRESIDENT.
PLEASE TELL ME SOME *GOOD* NEWS.
WE'RE KICKIN' BUTT AND TAKING NAMES, LEX.
NO MILITARY CLICHÉS. I'M TIRED.
EVERYTHING'S GOING OUR WAY.
"AIR NATIONAL GUARD TOOK DOWN *CERBERUS* AND SOME GEEK CLAIMING TO BE THE *MATTER MASTER* IN MIDWAY CITY.
"HUB CITY WAS A SHOOTING GALLERY, BUT THE 10TH MOUNTAIN AND ARMY RANGERS AIRED OUT A HALF-DOZEN SUPER-THUGS.
"*TERRA-MAN, HELLGRAMMITE* AND *BARRAGE* THREW IN THE TOWEL.

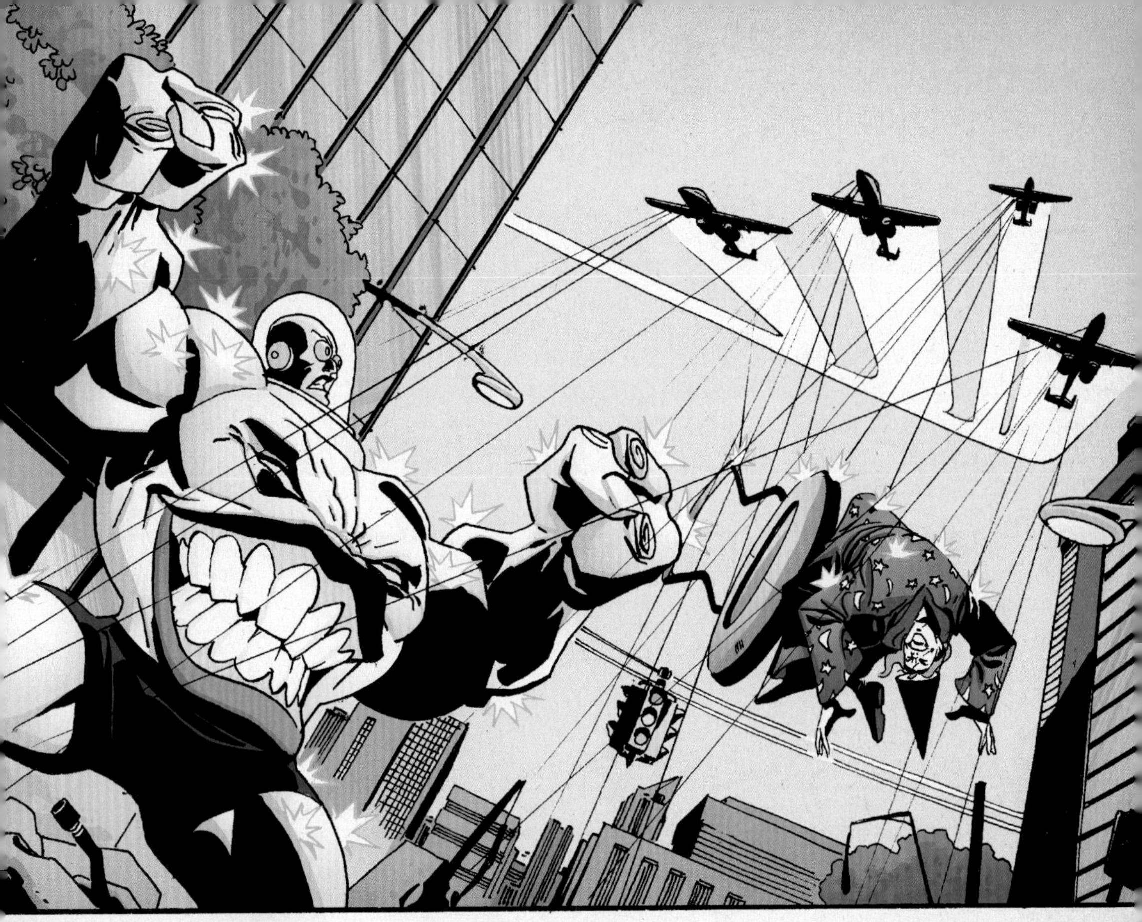

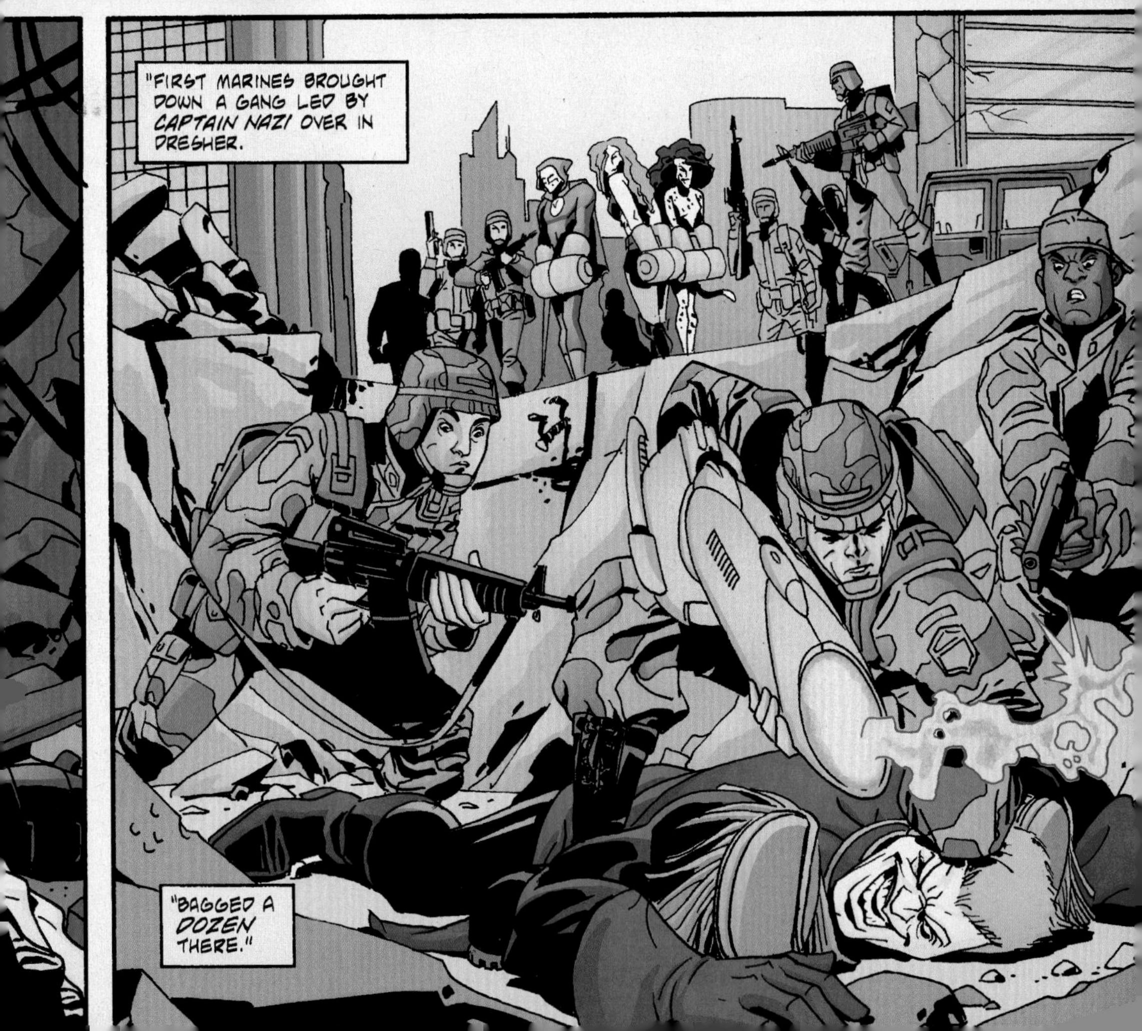
"FIRST MARINES BROUGHT DOWN A GANG LED BY *CAPTAIN NAZI* OVER IN DRESHER.
"BAGGED A *DOZEN* THERE."

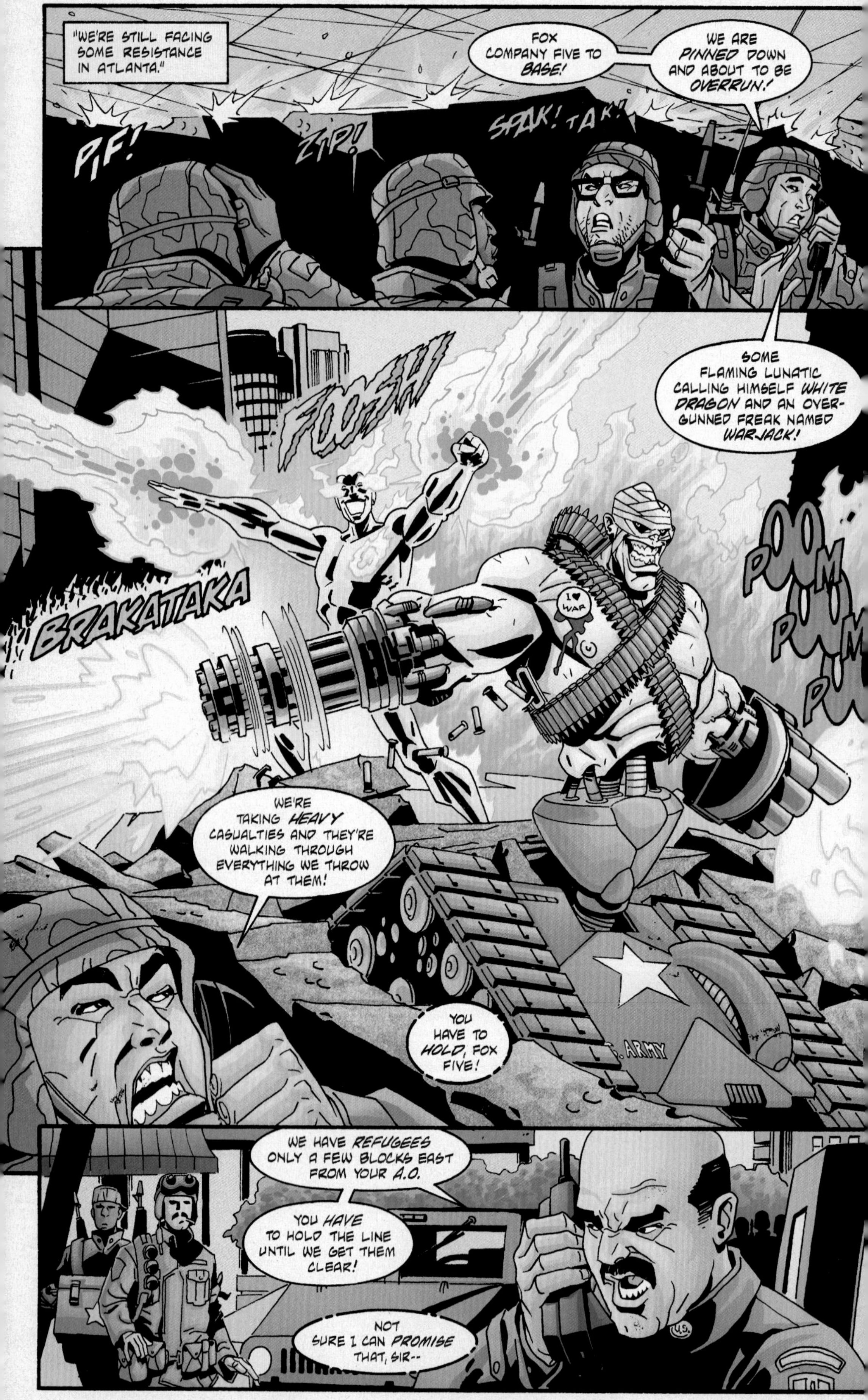
"WE'RE STILL FACING SOME RESISTANCE IN ATLANTA."
FOX COMPANY FIVE TO BASE!
WE ARE PINNED DOWN AND ABOUT TO BE OVERRUN!
PIF!
ZIP!
SPAK! TAK!
SOME FLAMING LUNATIC CALLING HIMSELF WHITE DRAGON AND AN OVER-GUNNED FREAK NAMED WARJACK!
FOOSH!
BRAKATAKA
POOM POOM POOM
I ♥ WAR
WE'RE TAKING HEAVY CASUALTIES AND THEY'RE WALKING THROUGH EVERYTHING WE THROW AT THEM!
YOU HAVE TO HOLD, FOX FIVE!
WE HAVE REFUGEES ONLY A FEW BLOCKS EAST FROM YOUR A.O.
YOU HAVE TO HOLD THE LINE UNTIL WE GET THEM CLEAR!
NOT SURE I CAN PROMISE THAT, SIR--

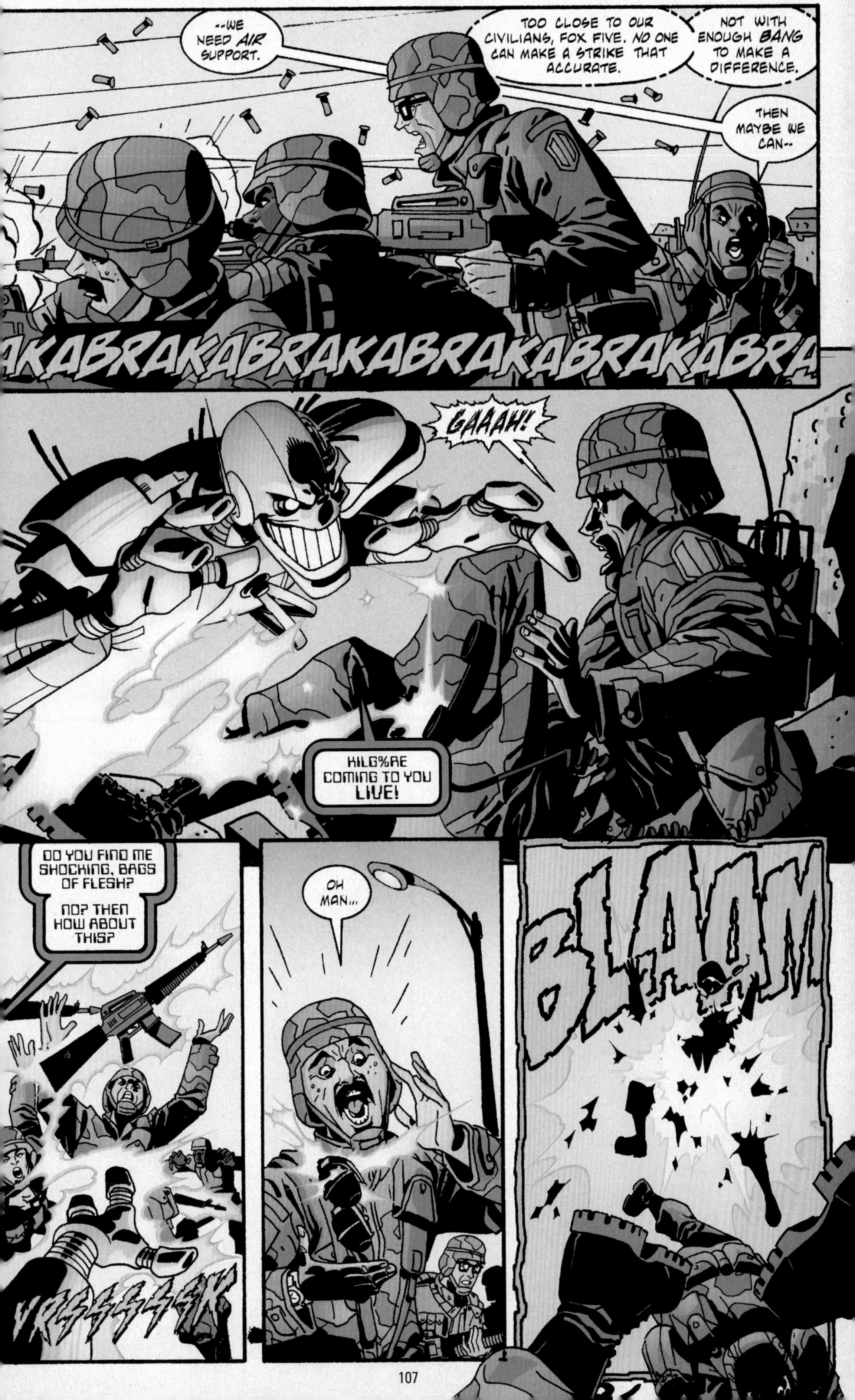

--WE NEED AIR SUPPORT.
TOO CLOSE TO OUR CIVILIANS, FOX FIVE. NO ONE CAN MAKE A STRIKE THAT ACCURATE.
NOT WITH ENOUGH BANG TO MAKE A DIFFERENCE.
THEN MAYBE WE CAN--
BRAKABRAKABRAKABRAKABRAKABRA
GAAAH!
KILG%RE COMING TO YOU LIVE!
DO YOU FIND ME SHOCKING, BAGS OF FLESH?
NO? THEN HOW ABOUT THIS?
VRSSSSSK
OH MAN...
BLAM

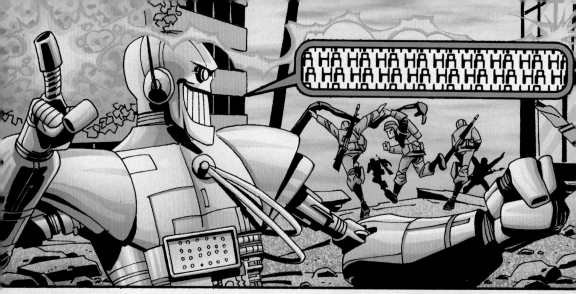

A HA HA HA HA HA HA HA HA HA HA HA HA HA HA HA HA HA HA HA HA HA HA

WHERE YOU GUYS GOING?

WE'RE *RETREATING*, SIR! I SUGGEST YOU DO THE *SAME!*

RETREAT?

NEVER *HEARD* THE WORD. NOT IN *MILITIA'S* DICTIONARY.

THOSE FREAKS *LAUGH* OFF GRENADES, SIR!

PING!

NOT *THIS* ONE, TROOP!

THIS IS A VERY *SPECIAL* GRENADE.

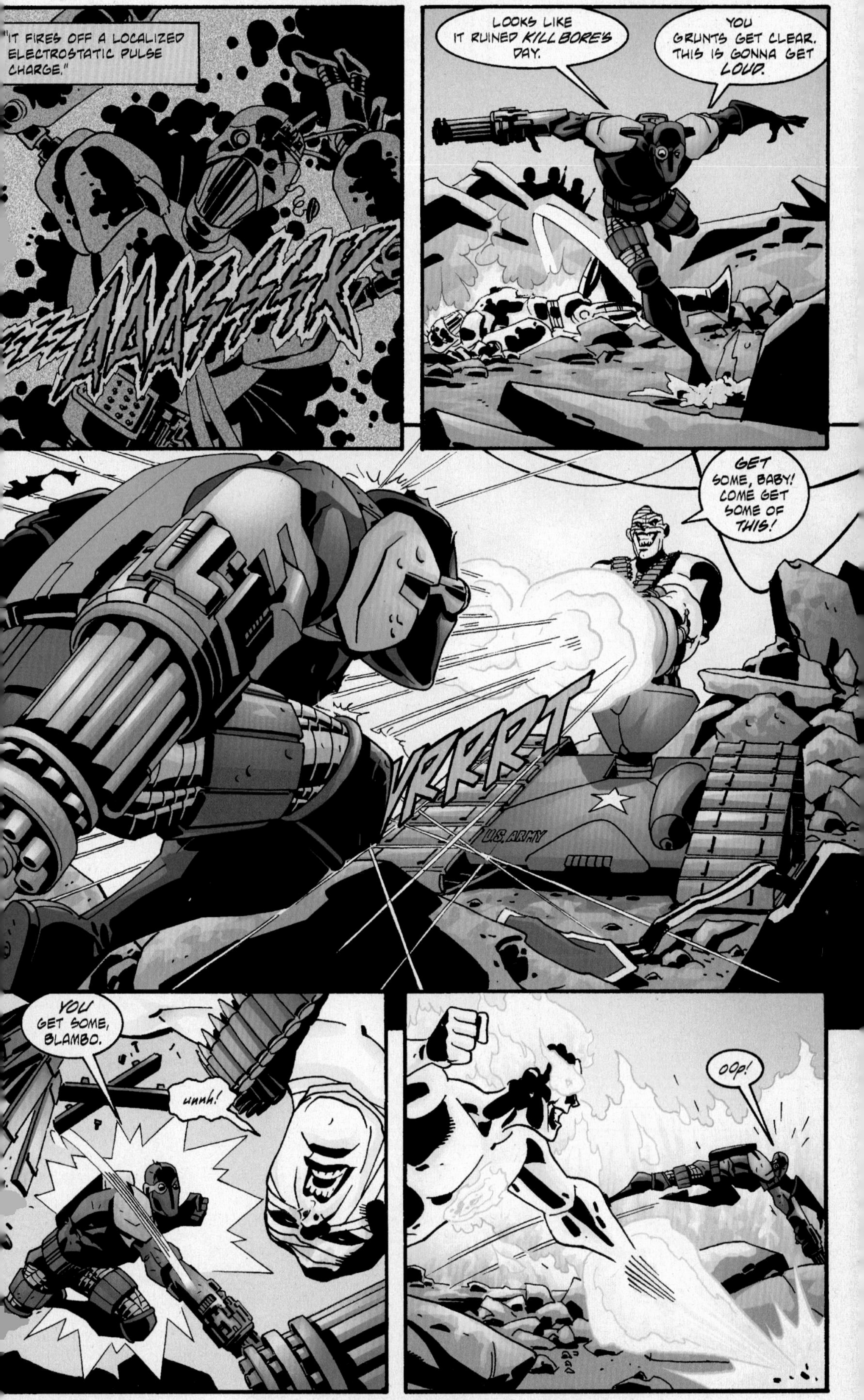
"IT FIRES OFF A LOCALIZED ELECTROSTATIC PULSE CHARGE."
AAASSSK
LOOKS LIKE IT RUINED KILLBORE'S DAY.
YOU GRUNTS GET CLEAR. THIS IS GONNA GET LOUD.
GET SOME, BABY! COME GET SOME OF THIS!
VRRRT
U.S. ARMY
YOU GET SOME, BLAMBO.
unnh!
OOp!

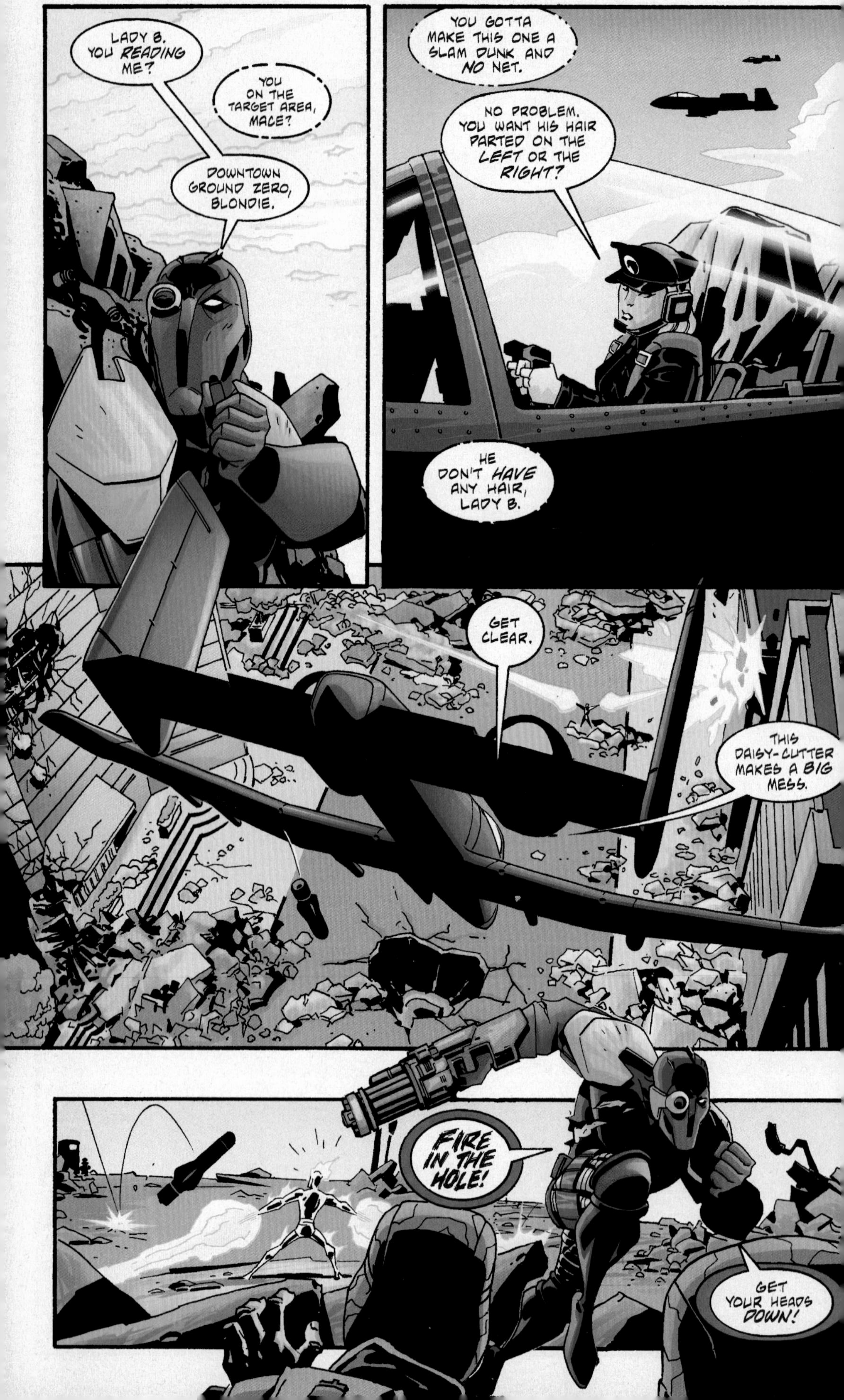
LADY B. YOU READING ME?
YOU ON THE TARGET AREA, MACE?
DOWNTOWN GROUND ZERO, BLONDIE.
YOU GOTTA MAKE THIS ONE A SLAM DUNK AND NO NET.
NO PROBLEM. YOU WANT HIS HAIR PARTED ON THE LEFT OR THE RIGHT?
HE DON'T HAVE ANY HAIR, LADY B.
GET CLEAR.
THIS DAISY-CUTTER MAKES A BIG MESS.
FIRE IN THE HOLE!
GET YOUR HEADS DOWN!

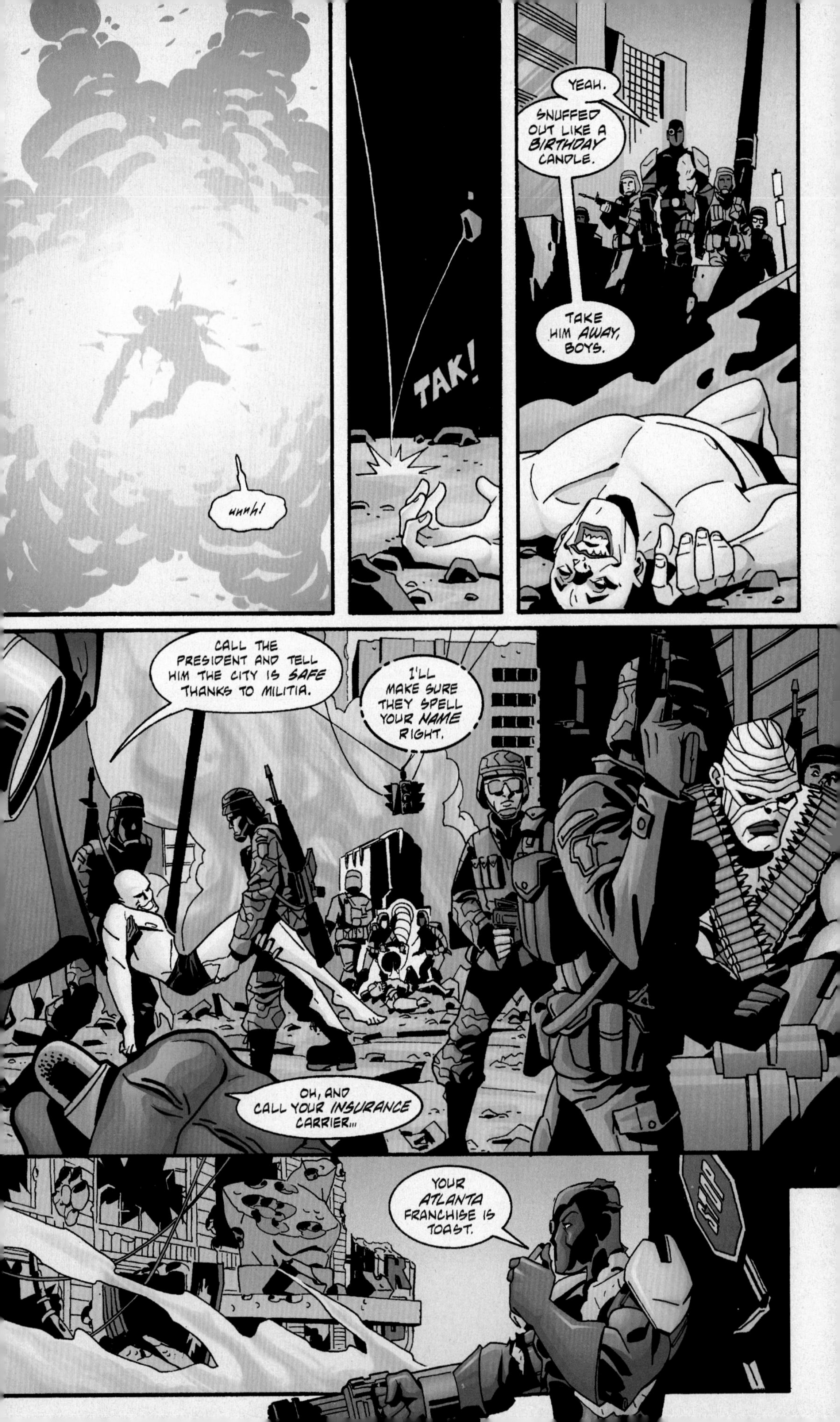
unnh!
TAK!
YEAH.
SNUFFED OUT LIKE A BIRTHDAY CANDLE.
TAKE HIM AWAY, BOYS.
CALL THE PRESIDENT AND TELL HIM THE CITY IS SAFE THANKS TO MILITIA.
I'LL MAKE SURE THEY SPELL YOUR NAME RIGHT.
OH, AND CALL YOUR INSURANCE CARRIER...
YOUR ATLANTA FRANCHISE IS TOAST.

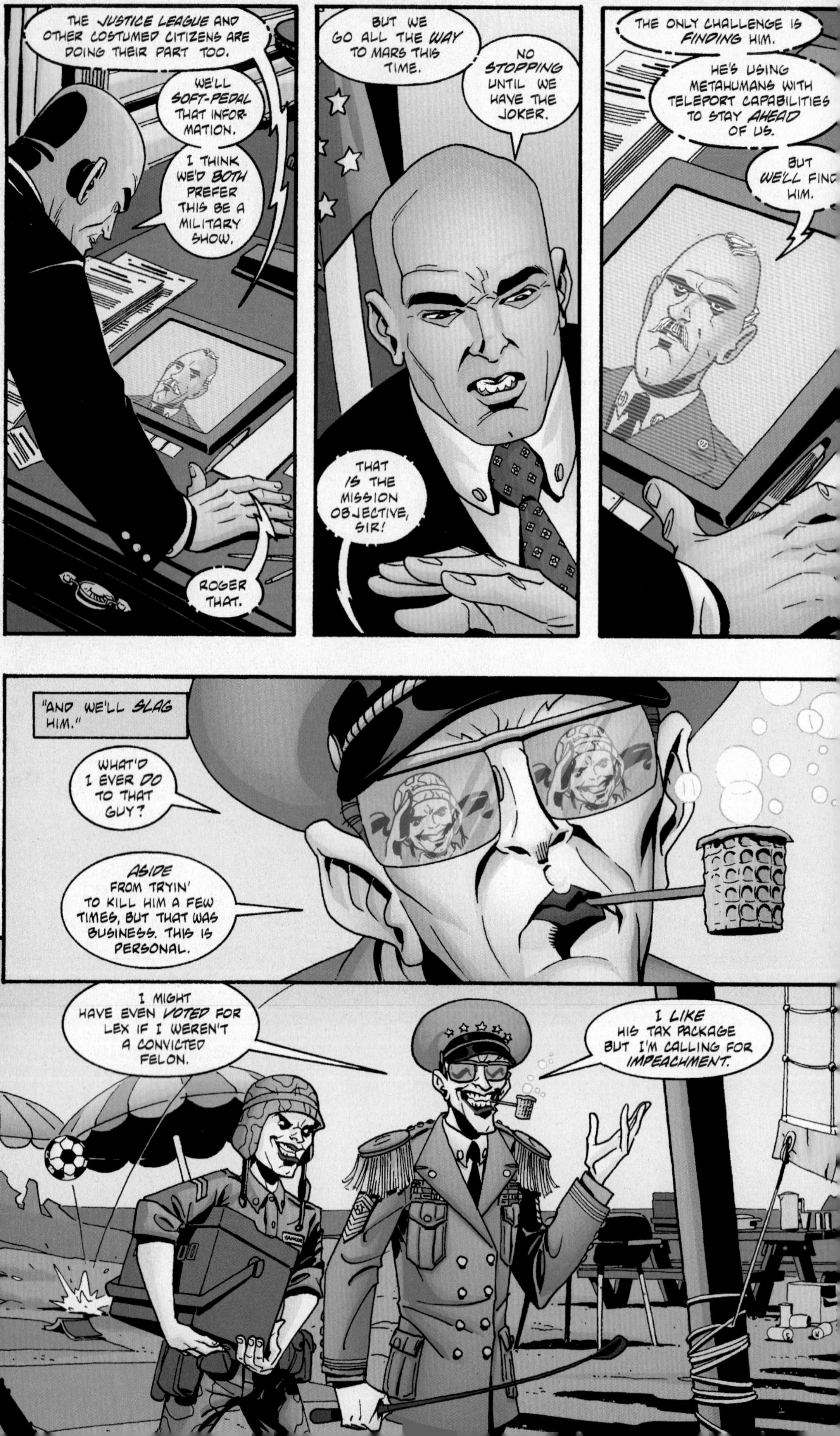
THE JUSTICE LEAGUE AND OTHER COSTUMED CITIZENS ARE DOING THEIR PART TOO.
WE'LL SOFT-PEDAL THAT INFORMATION.
I THINK WE'D BOTH PREFER THIS BE A MILITARY SHOW.
ROGER THAT.
BUT WE GO ALL THE WAY TO MARS THIS TIME.
NO STOPPING UNTIL WE HAVE THE JOKER.
THAT IS THE MISSION OBJECTIVE, SIR!
THE ONLY CHALLENGE IS FINDING HIM.
HE'S USING METAHUMANS WITH TELEPORT CAPABILITIES TO STAY AHEAD OF US.
BUT WE'LL FIND HIM.
"AND WE'LL SLAG HIM."
WHAT'D I EVER DO TO THAT GUY?
ASIDE FROM TRYIN' TO KILL HIM A FEW TIMES, BUT THAT WAS BUSINESS. THIS IS PERSONAL.
I MIGHT HAVE EVEN VOTED FOR LEX IF I WEREN'T A CONVICTED FELON.
I LIKE HIS TAX PACKAGE BUT I'M CALLING FOR IMPEACHMENT.

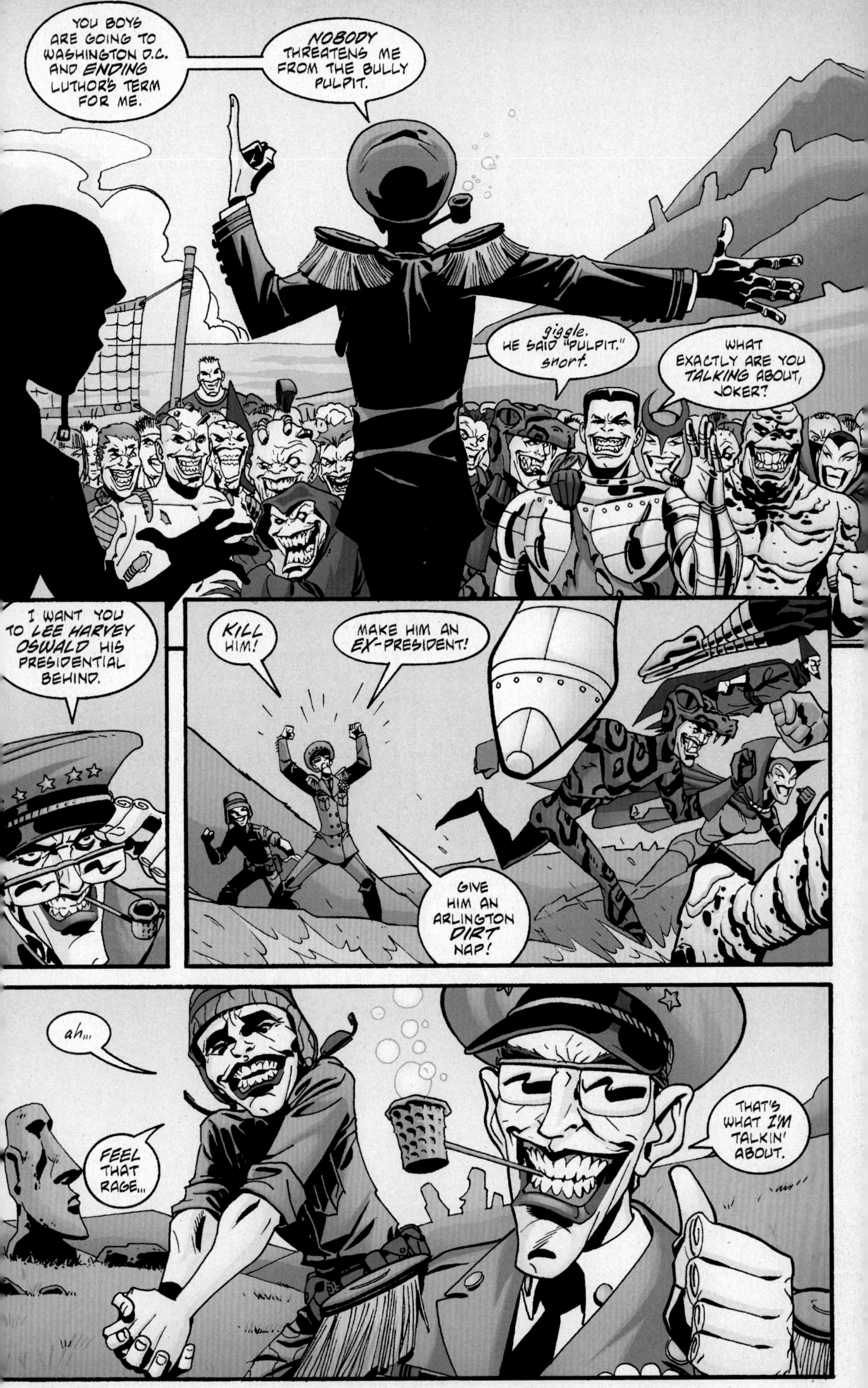
YOU BOYS ARE GOING TO WASHINGTON D.C. AND ENDING LUTHOR'S TERM FOR ME.
NOBODY THREATENS ME FROM THE BULLY PULPIT.
giggle. HE SAID "PULPIT." snort.
WHAT EXACTLY ARE YOU TALKING ABOUT, JOKER?
I WANT YOU TO LEE HARVEY OSWALD HIS PRESIDENTIAL BEHIND.
KILL HIM!
MAKE HIM AN EX-PRESIDENT!
GIVE HIM AN ARLINGTON DIRT NAP!
ah...
FEEL THAT RAGE...
THAT'S WHAT I'M TALKIN' ABOUT.

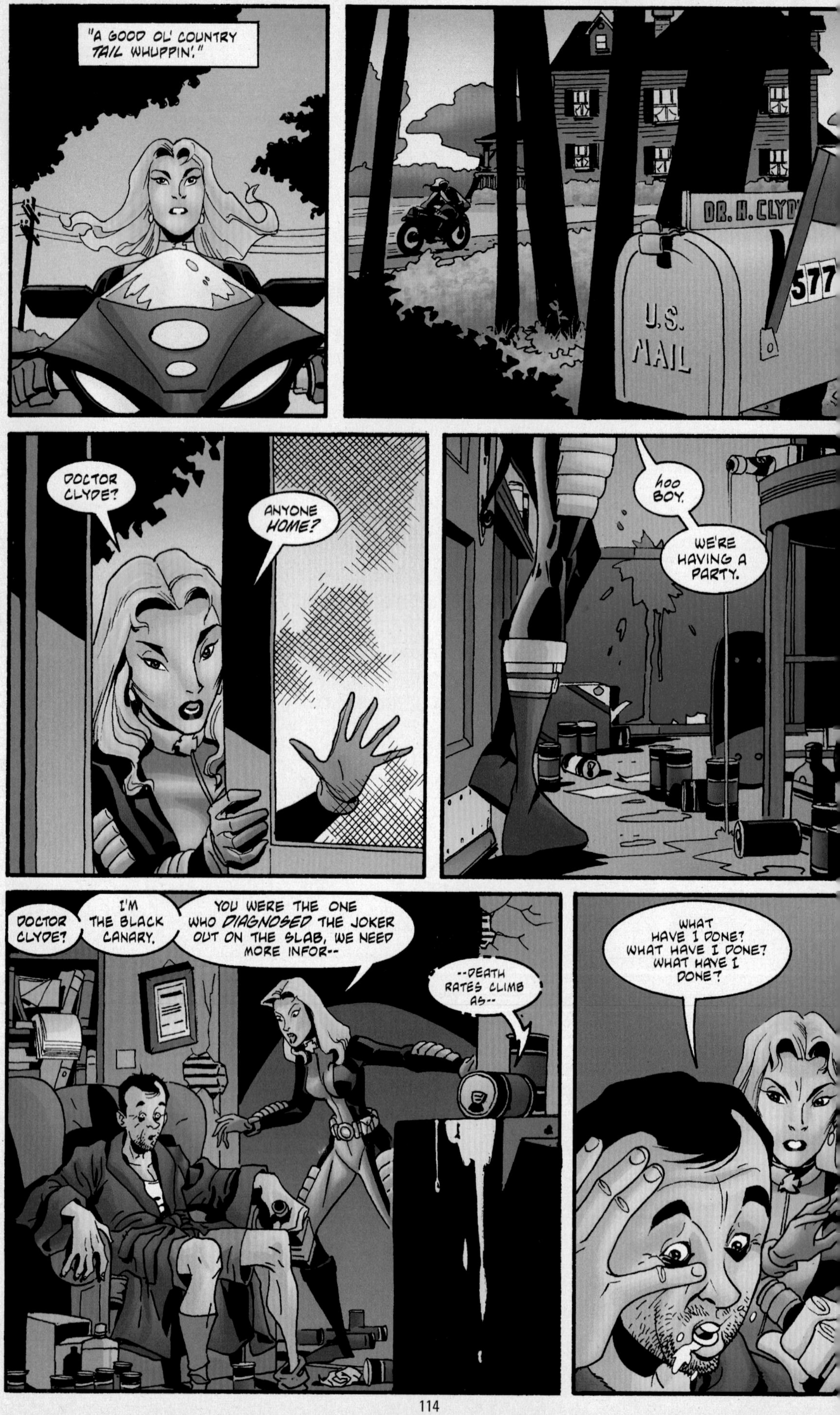
"A GOOD OL' COUNTRY TAIL WHUPPIN'."
DR. H. CLYD
577
U.S. MAIL
DOCTOR CLYDE?
ANYONE HOME?
hoo BOY.
WE'RE HAVING A PARTY.
DOCTOR CLYDE?
I'M THE BLACK CANARY.
YOU WERE THE ONE WHO DIAGNOSED THE JOKER OUT ON THE SLAB. WE NEED MORE INFOR--
--DEATH RATES CLIMB AS--
WHAT HAVE I DONE? WHAT HAVE I DONE? WHAT HAVE I DONE?

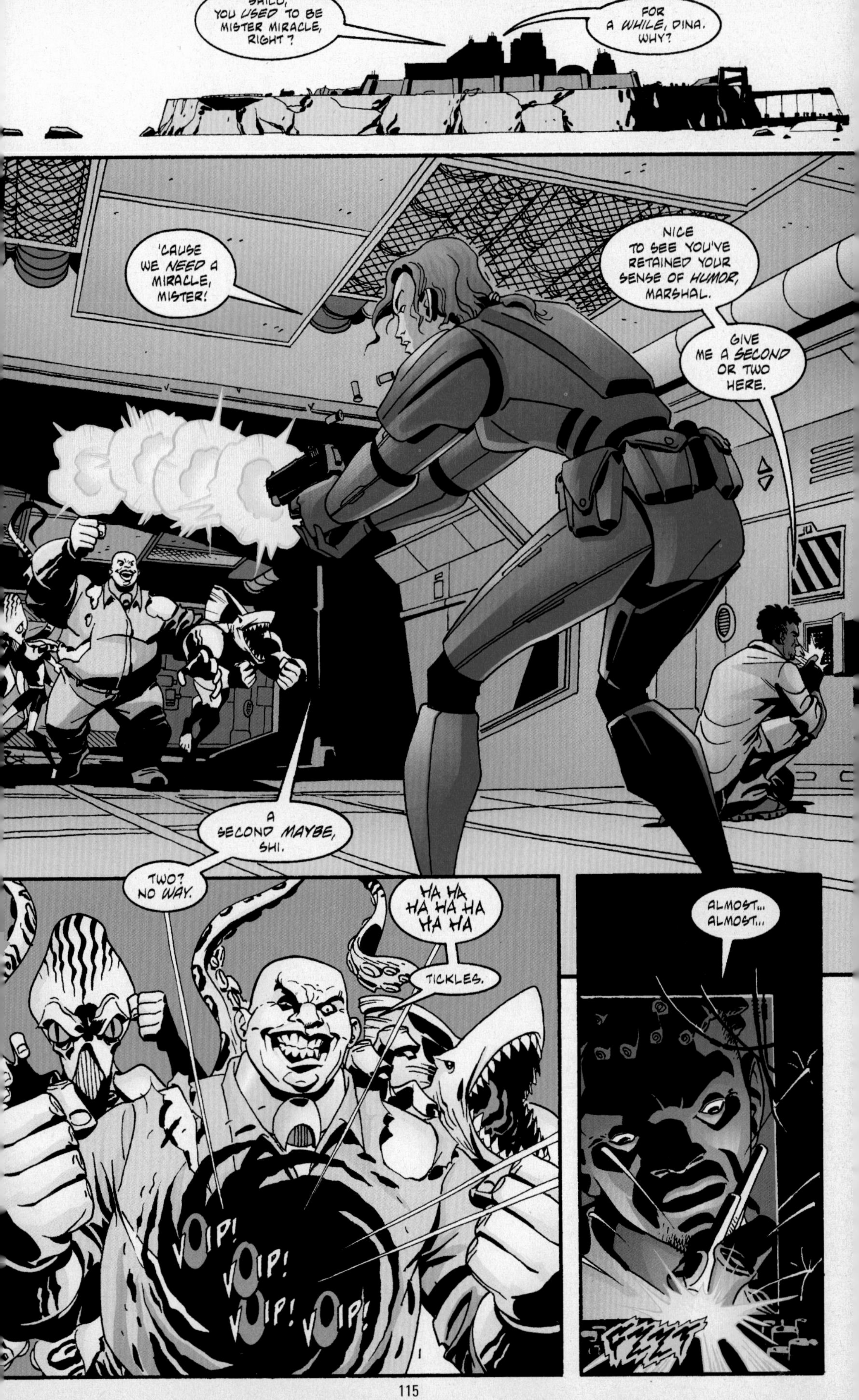
SHILO, YOU USED TO BE MISTER MIRACLE, RIGHT?
FOR A WHILE, DINA. WHY?
'CAUSE WE NEED A MIRACLE, MISTER!
NICE TO SEE YOU'VE RETAINED YOUR SENSE OF HUMOR, MARSHAL.
GIVE ME A SECOND OR TWO HERE.
A SECOND MAYBE, SHI.
TWO? NO WAY.
HA HA HA HA HA HA HA
TICKLES.
VOIP!
VOIP!
VOIP!
VOIP!
ALMOST... ALMOST...

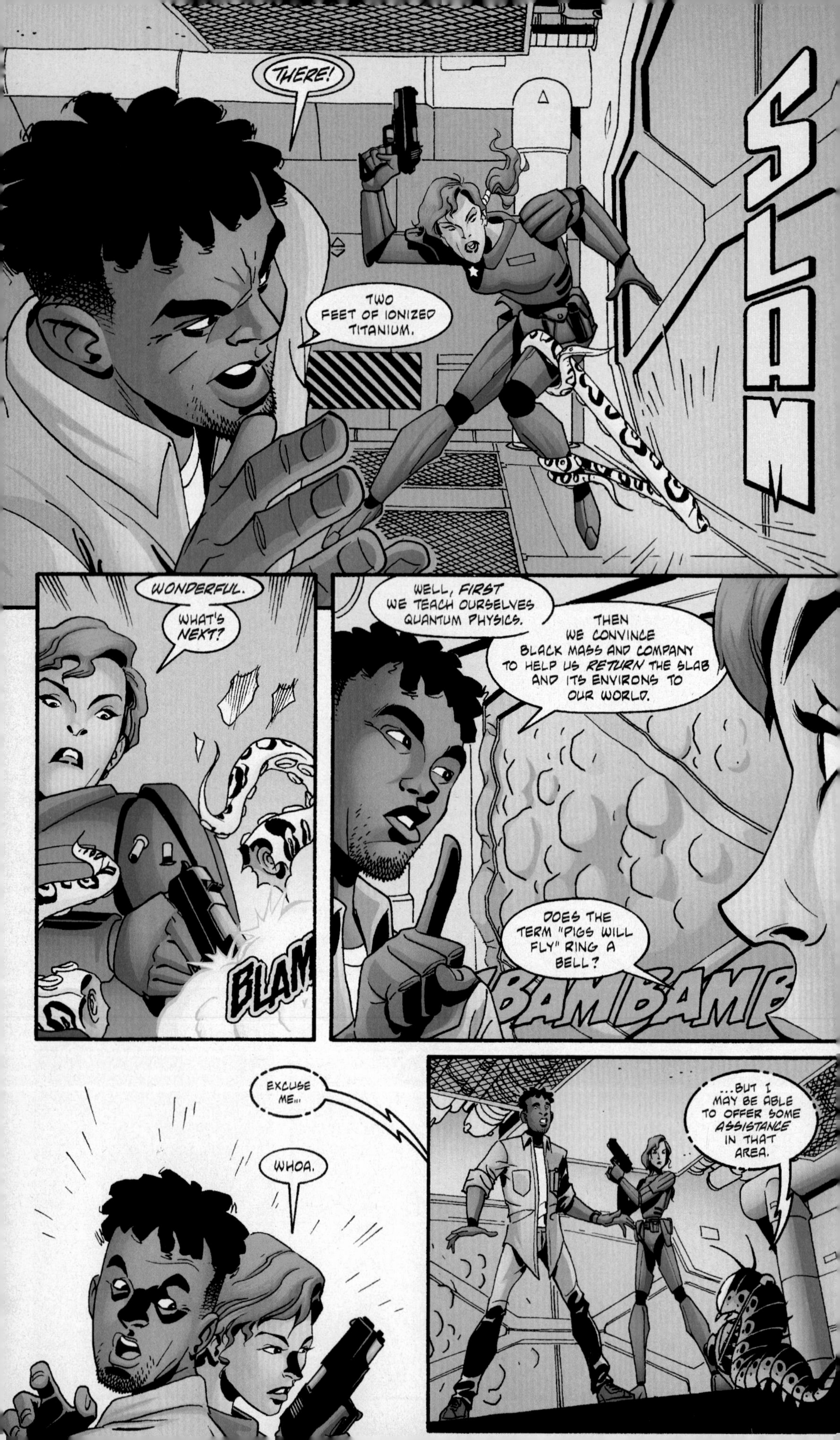
THERE!
TWO FEET OF IONIZED TITANIUM.
SLAM
WONDERFUL.
WHAT'S NEXT?
BLAM
WELL, FIRST WE TEACH OURSELVES QUANTUM PHYSICS.
THEN WE CONVINCE BLACK MASS AND COMPANY TO HELP US RETURN THE SLAB AND ITS ENVIRONS TO OUR WORLD.
DOES THE TERM "PIGS WILL FLY" RING A BELL?
BAMBAMB
EXCUSE ME...
WHOA.
...BUT I MAY BE ABLE TO OFFER SOME ASSISTANCE IN THAT AREA.

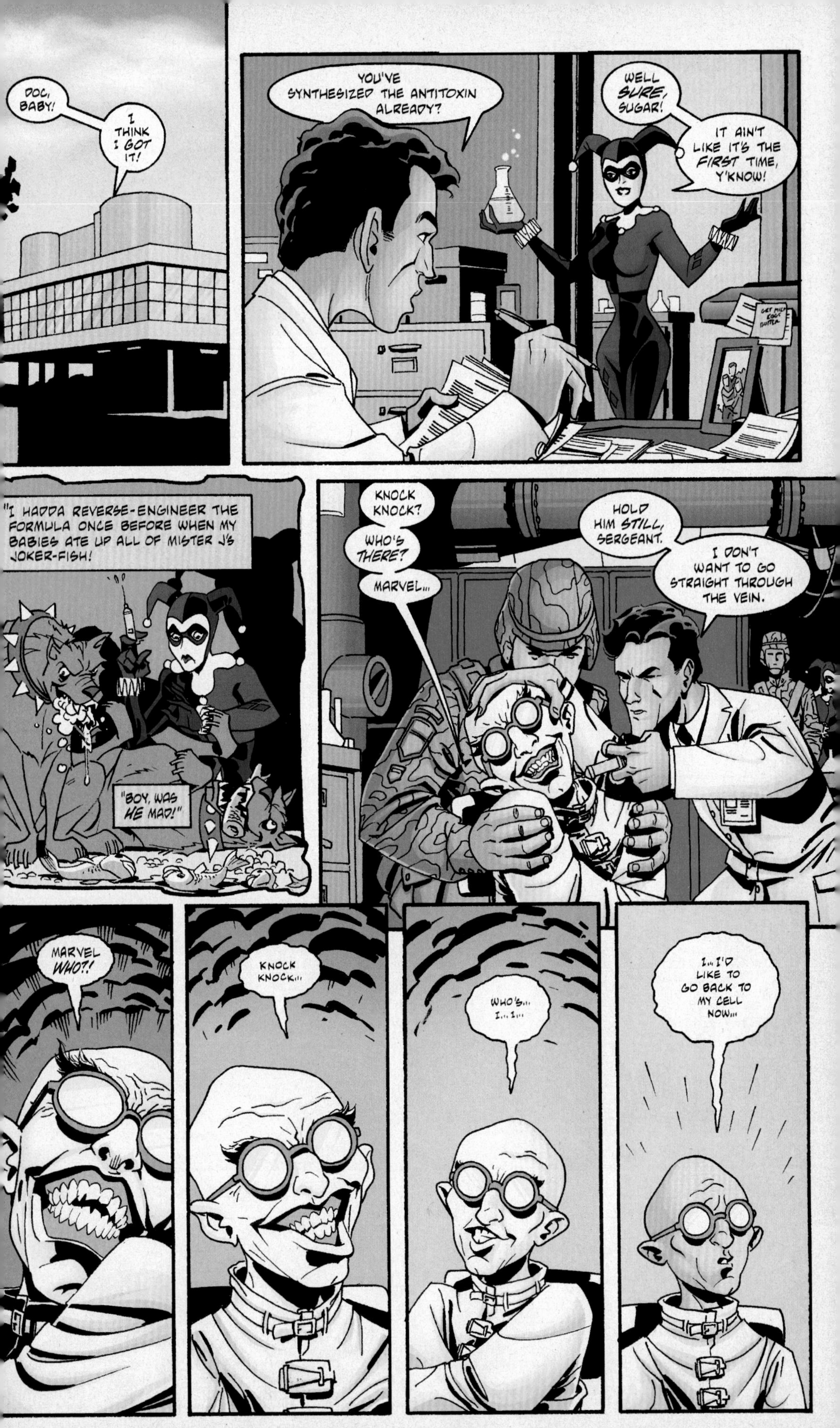
DOC, BABY!
I THINK I GOT IT!
YOU'VE SYNTHESIZED THE ANTITOXIN ALREADY?
WELL SURE, SUGAR!
IT AIN'T LIKE IT'S THE FIRST TIME, Y'KNOW!
"I HADDA REVERSE-ENGINEER THE FORMULA ONCE BEFORE WHEN MY BABIES ATE UP ALL OF MISTER J's JOKER-FISH!
"BOY, WAS HE MAD!"
KNOCK KNOCK?
WHO'S THERE?
MARVEL...
HOLD HIM STILL, SERGEANT.
I DON'T WANT TO GO STRAIGHT THROUGH THE VEIN.
MARVEL WHO?!
KNOCK KNOCK...
WHO'S... I... I...
I... I'D LIKE TO GO BACK TO MY CELL NOW...

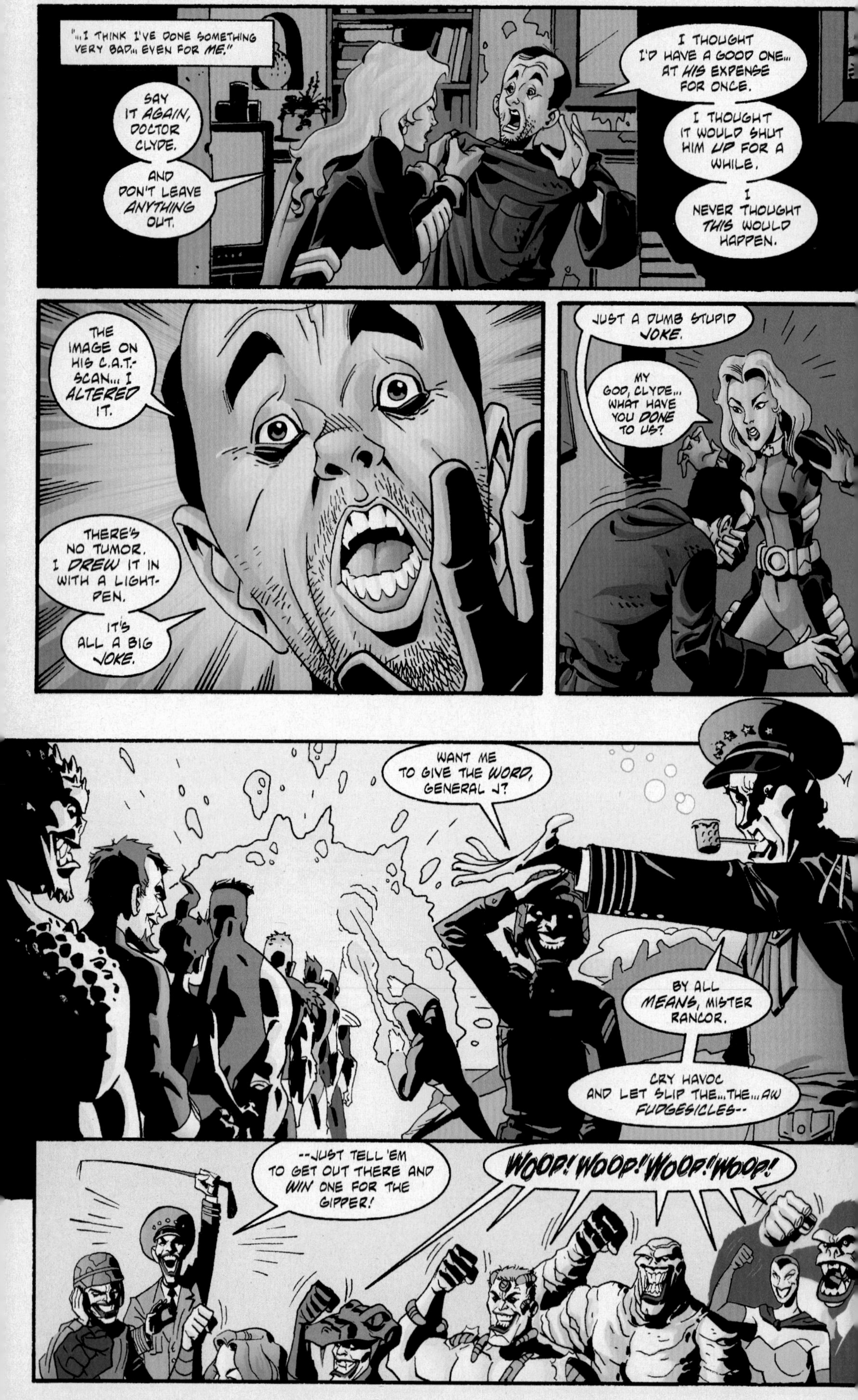
"...I THINK I'VE DONE SOMETHING VERY BAD... EVEN FOR ME."
SAY IT AGAIN, DOCTOR CLYDE.
AND DON'T LEAVE ANYTHING OUT.
I THOUGHT I'D HAVE A GOOD ONE... AT HIS EXPENSE FOR ONCE.
I THOUGHT IT WOULD SHUT HIM UP FOR A WHILE.
I NEVER THOUGHT THIS WOULD HAPPEN.
THE IMAGE ON HIS C.A.T.-SCAN... I ALTERED IT.
THERE'S NO TUMOR. I DREW IT IN WITH A LIGHT-PEN.
IT'S ALL A BIG JOKE.
JUST A DUMB STUPID JOKE.
MY GOD, CLYDE... WHAT HAVE YOU DONE TO US?
WANT ME TO GIVE THE WORD, GENERAL J?
BY ALL MEANS, MISTER RANCOR.
CRY HAVOC AND LET SLIP THE...THE...AW FUDGESICLES--
--JUST TELL 'EM TO GET OUT THERE AND WIN ONE FOR THE GIPPER!
WOOP! WOOP! WOOP! WOOP!

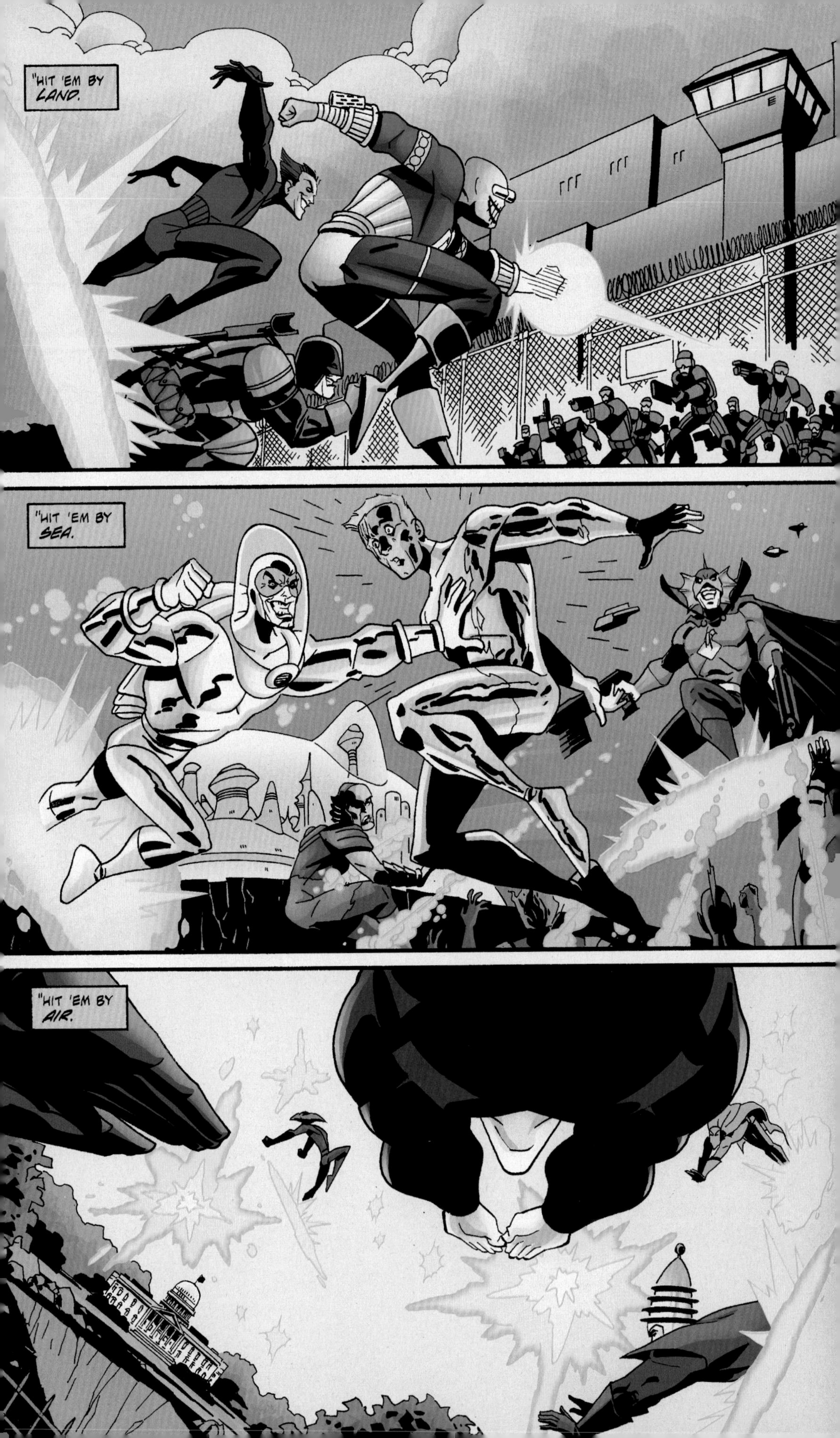
"HIT 'EM BY LAND.
"HIT 'EM BY SEA.
"HIT 'EM BY AIR.

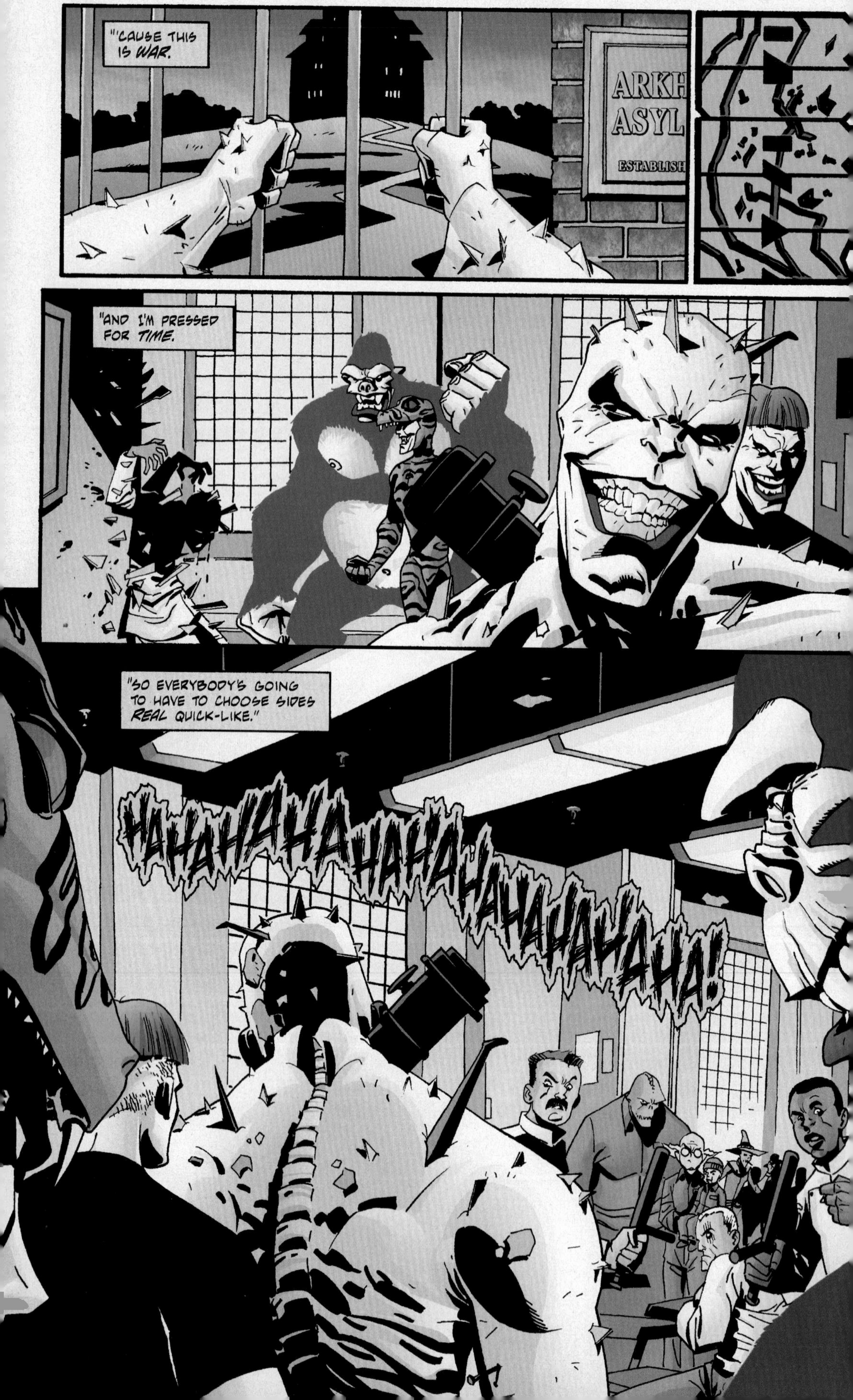
"'CAUSE THIS IS WAR.
ARKH
ASYL
ESTABLISH
"AND I'M PRESSED FOR TIME.
"SO EVERYBODY'S GOING TO HAVE TO CHOOSE SIDES REAL QUICK-LIKE."
HAHAHAHAHAHAHAHAHAHAHAHAHA!

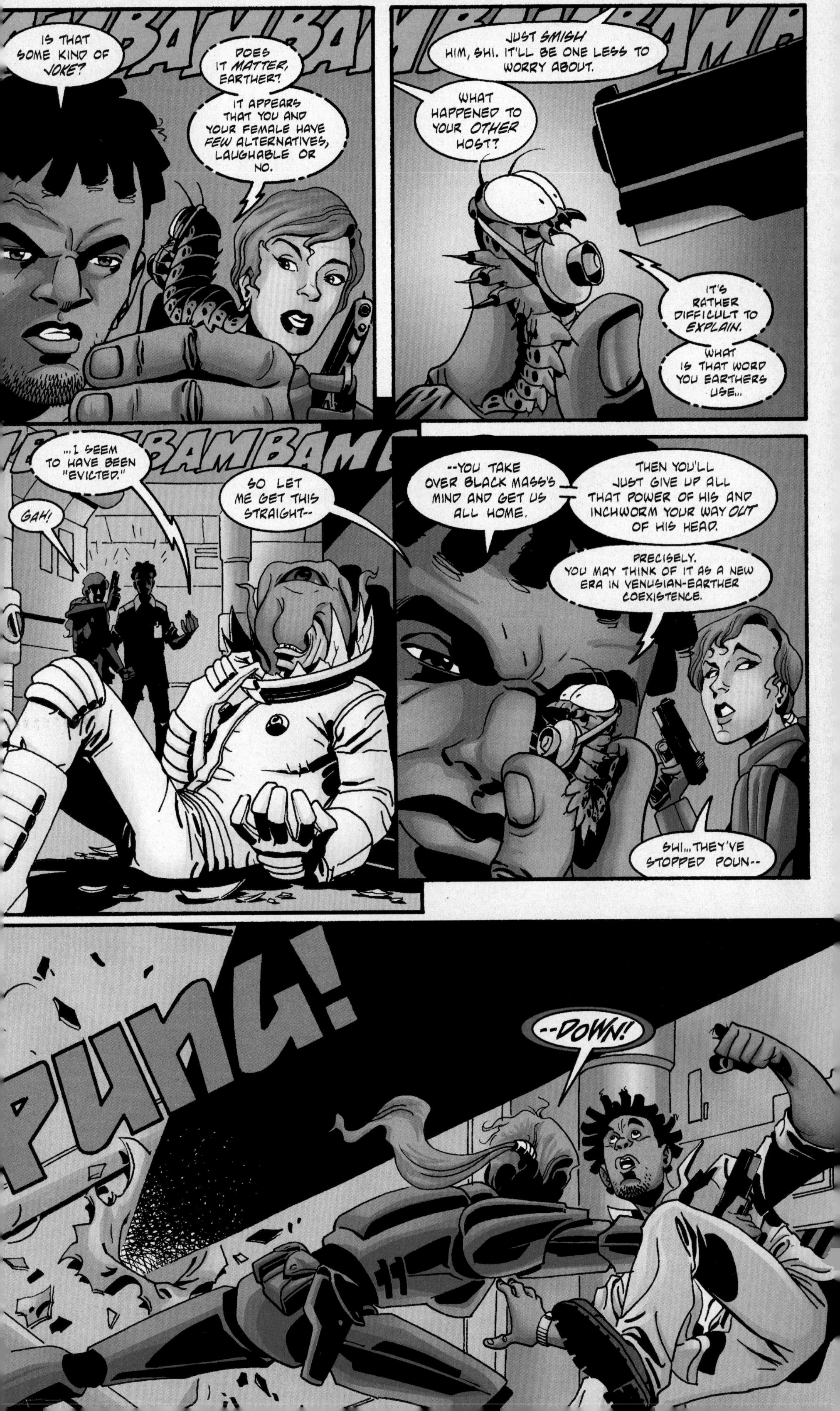
BAM BAM
IS THAT SOME KIND OF JOKE?
DOES IT MATTER, EARTHER?
IT APPEARS THAT YOU AND YOUR FEMALE HAVE FEW ALTERNATIVES, LAUGHABLE OR NO.
JUST SMISH HIM, SHI. IT'LL BE ONE LESS TO WORRY ABOUT.
WHAT HAPPENED TO YOUR OTHER HOST?
IT'S RATHER DIFFICULT TO EXPLAIN.
WHAT IS THAT WORD YOU EARTHERS USE...
BAM BAM BAM
...I SEEM TO HAVE BEEN "EVICTED."
GAH!
SO LET ME GET THIS STRAIGHT--
--YOU TAKE OVER BLACK MASS'S MIND AND GET US ALL HOME.
THEN YOU'LL JUST GIVE UP ALL THAT POWER OF HIS AND INCHWORM YOUR WAY OUT OF HIS HEAD.
PRECISELY. YOU MAY THINK OF IT AS A NEW ERA IN VENUSIAN-EARTHER COEXISTENCE.
SHI... THEY'VE STOPPED POUN--
PUNG!
--DOWN!

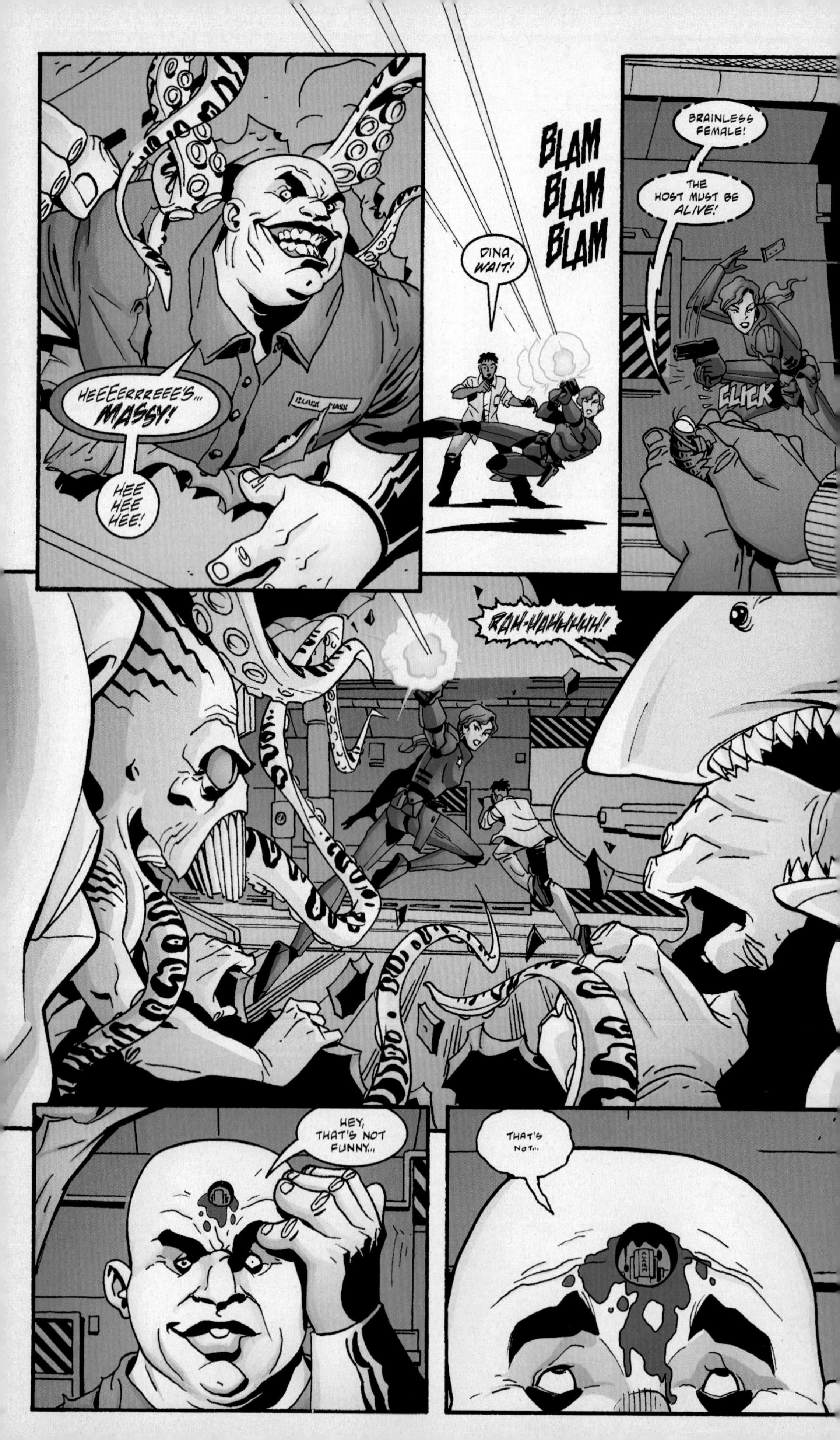
HEEEerrreee's... MASSY!
HEE HEE HEE!
BLACK MASS
BLAM BLAM BLAM
DINA, WAIT!
BRAINLESS FEMALE!
THE HOST MUST BE ALIVE!
CLICK
RAH-HAHHHHH!
HEY, THAT'S NOT FUNNY...
THAT'S NOT...

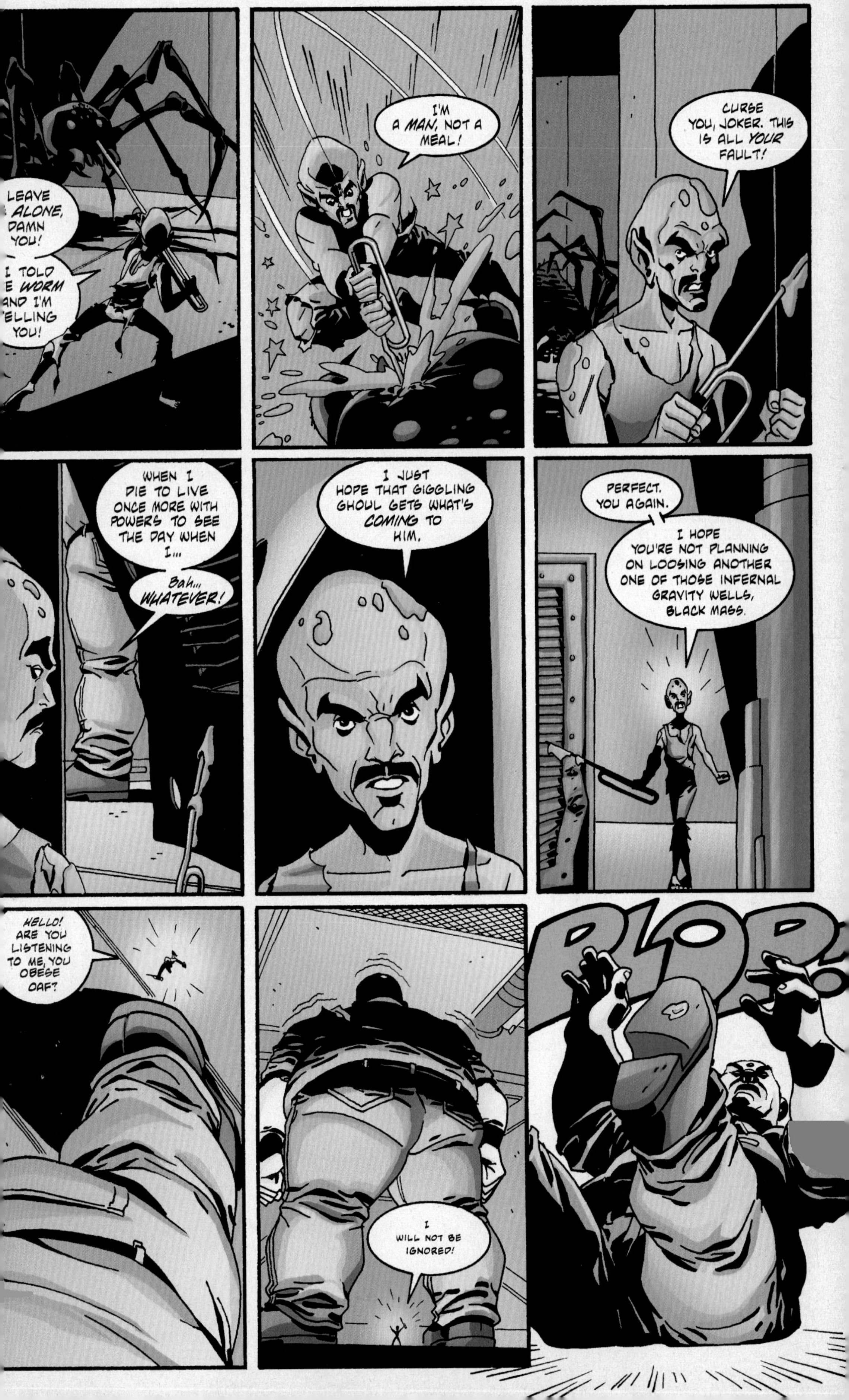
LEAVE
ALONE,
DAMN
YOU!
I TOLD
E WORM
AND I'M
TELLING
YOU!
I'M A MAN, NOT A MEAL!
CURSE YOU, JOKER. THIS IS ALL YOUR FAULT!
WHEN I DIE TO LIVE ONCE MORE WITH POWERS TO SEE THE DAY WHEN I...
Bah... WHATEVER!
I JUST HOPE THAT GIGGLING GHOUL GETS WHAT'S COMING TO HIM.
PERFECT. YOU AGAIN.
I HOPE YOU'RE NOT PLANNING ON LOOSING ANOTHER ONE OF THOSE INFERNAL GRAVITY WELLS, BLACK MASS.
HELLO! ARE YOU LISTENING TO ME, YOU OBESE OAF?
I WILL NOT BE IGNORED!
PLOP!

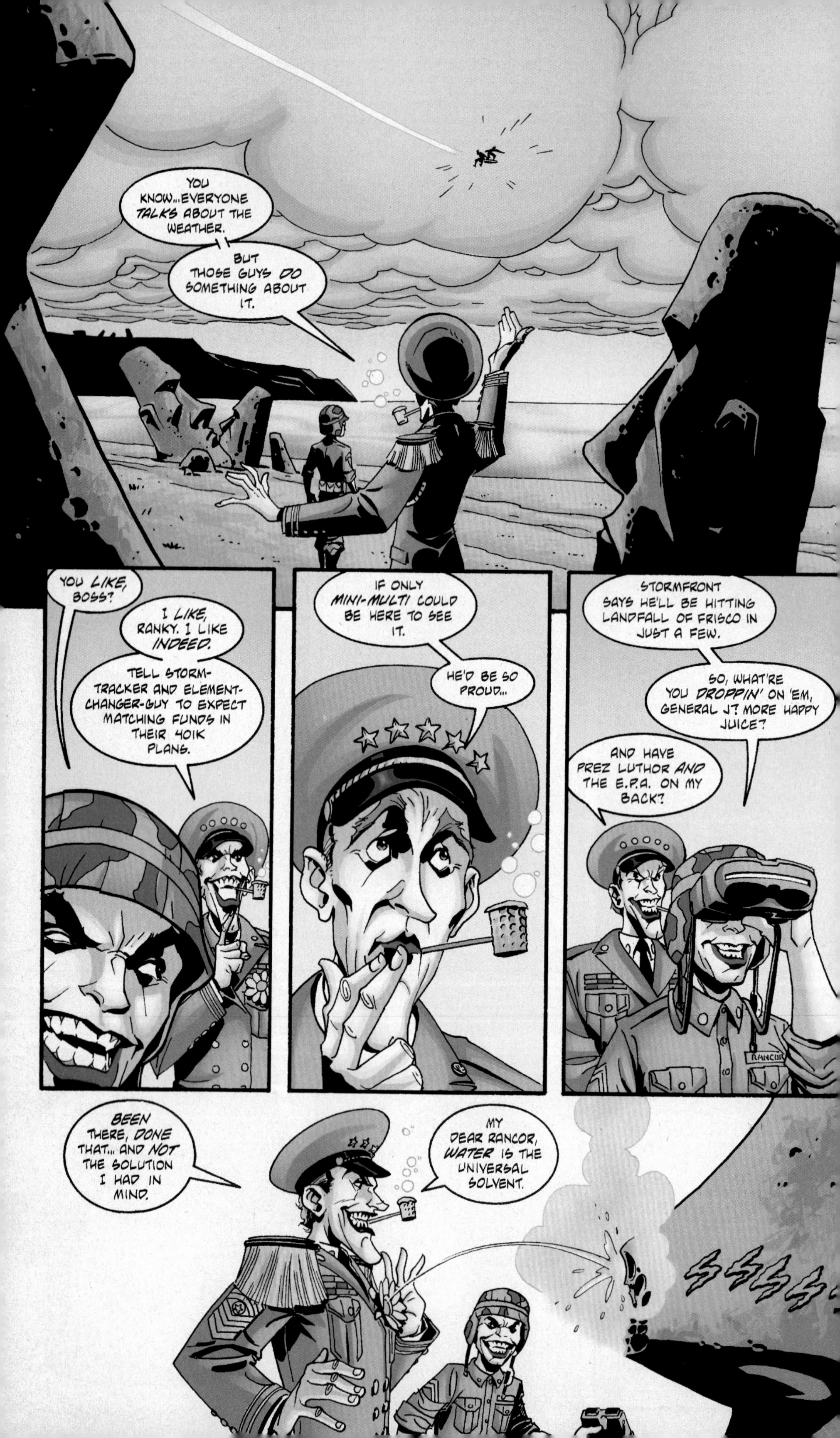
YOU KNOW... EVERYONE TALKS ABOUT THE WEATHER.
BUT THOSE GUYS DO SOMETHING ABOUT IT.
YOU LIKE, BOSS?
I LIKE, RANKY. I LIKE INDEED.
TELL STORM-TRACKER AND ELEMENT-CHANGER-GUY TO EXPECT MATCHING FUNDS IN THEIR 401K PLANS.
IF ONLY MINI-MULTI COULD BE HERE TO SEE IT.
HE'D BE SO PROUD...
STORMFRONT SAYS HE'LL BE HITTING LANDFALL OF FRISCO IN JUST A FEW.
SO, WHAT'RE YOU DROPPIN' ON 'EM, GENERAL J? MORE HAPPY JUICE?
AND HAVE PREZ LUTHOR AND THE E.P.A. ON MY BACK?
RANCOR
BEEN THERE, DONE THAT... AND NOT THE SOLUTION I HAD IN MIND.
MY DEAR RANCOR, WATER IS THE UNIVERSAL SOLVENT.
SSSSS

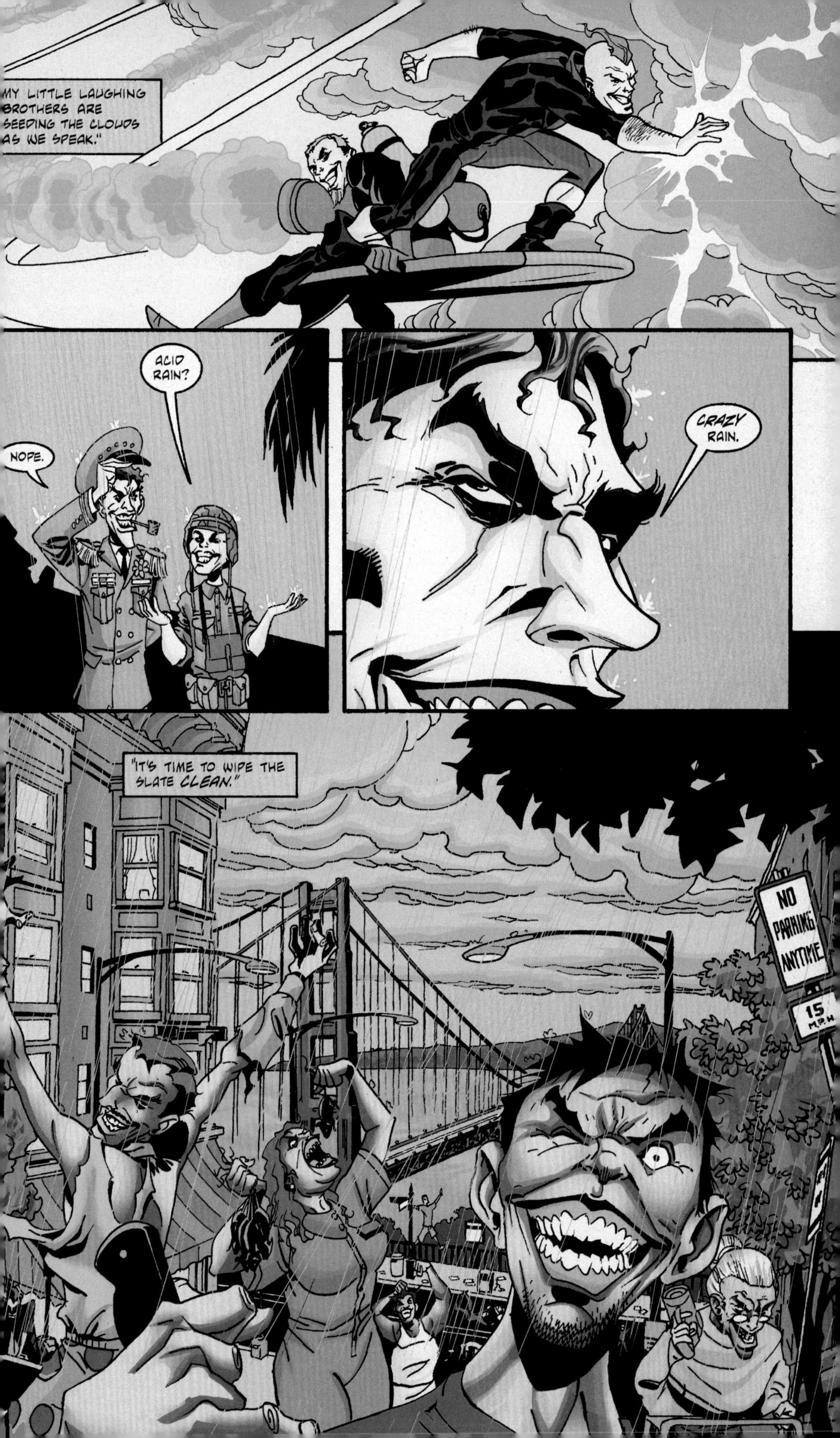
MY LITTLE LAUGHING BROTHERS ARE SEEDING THE CLOUDS AS WE SPEAK."
ACID RAIN?
NOPE.
CRAZY RAIN.
"IT'S TIME TO WIPE THE SLATE CLEAN."
NO PARKING ANYTIME
15 M.P.H.

# Joker: Last Laugh

## part five: mad, mad world

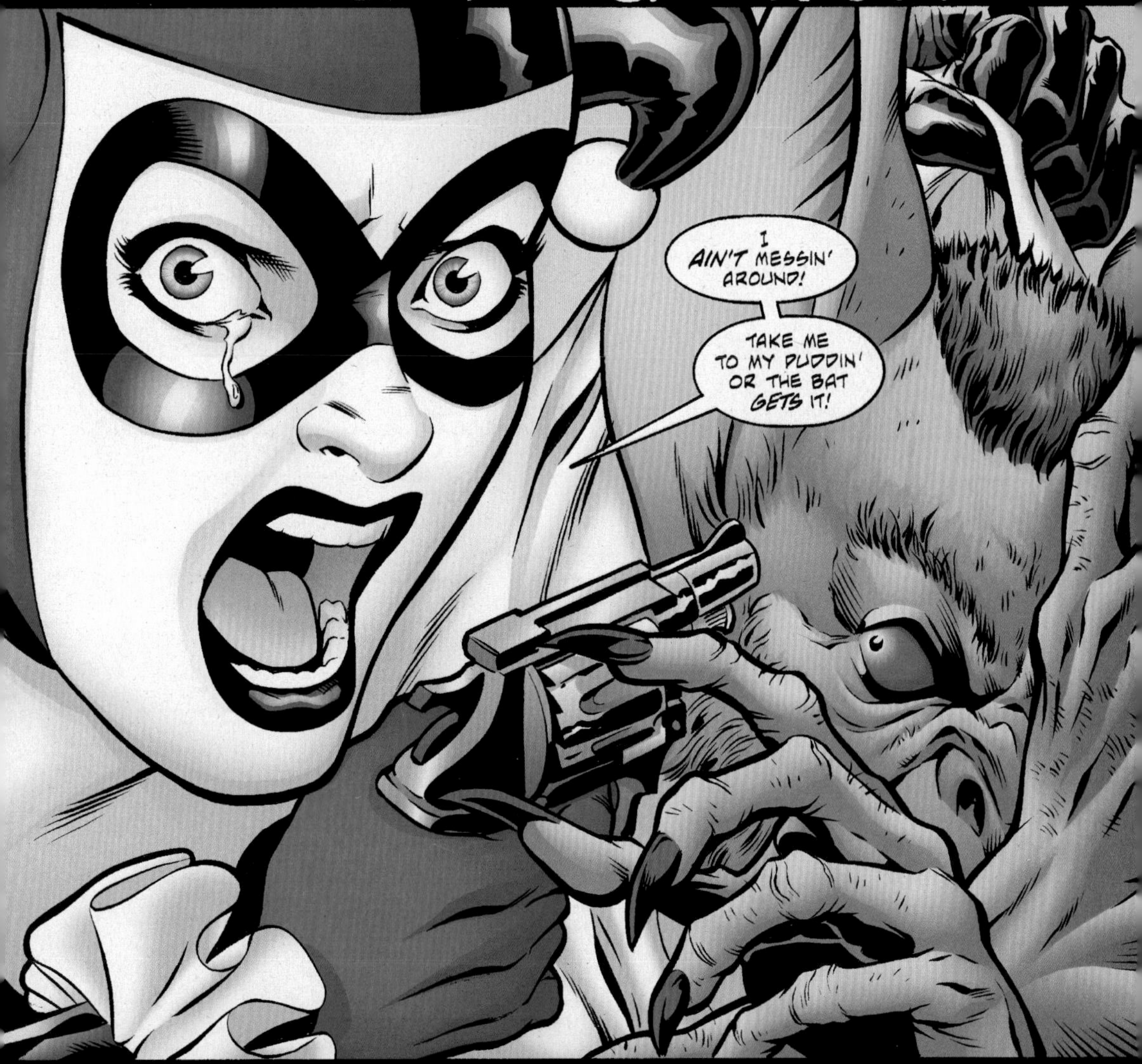
I AIN'T MESSIN' AROUND!
TAKE ME TO MY PUDDIN' OR THE BAT GETS IT!

written by Chuck Dixon & Scott Beatty

pencils & inks by Ron Randall

colors by Gina Going separations by Digital Chameleon

letters by Willie Schubert

assistant editor Nachie Castro editor Matt Idelson

---

Batman created by Bob Kane

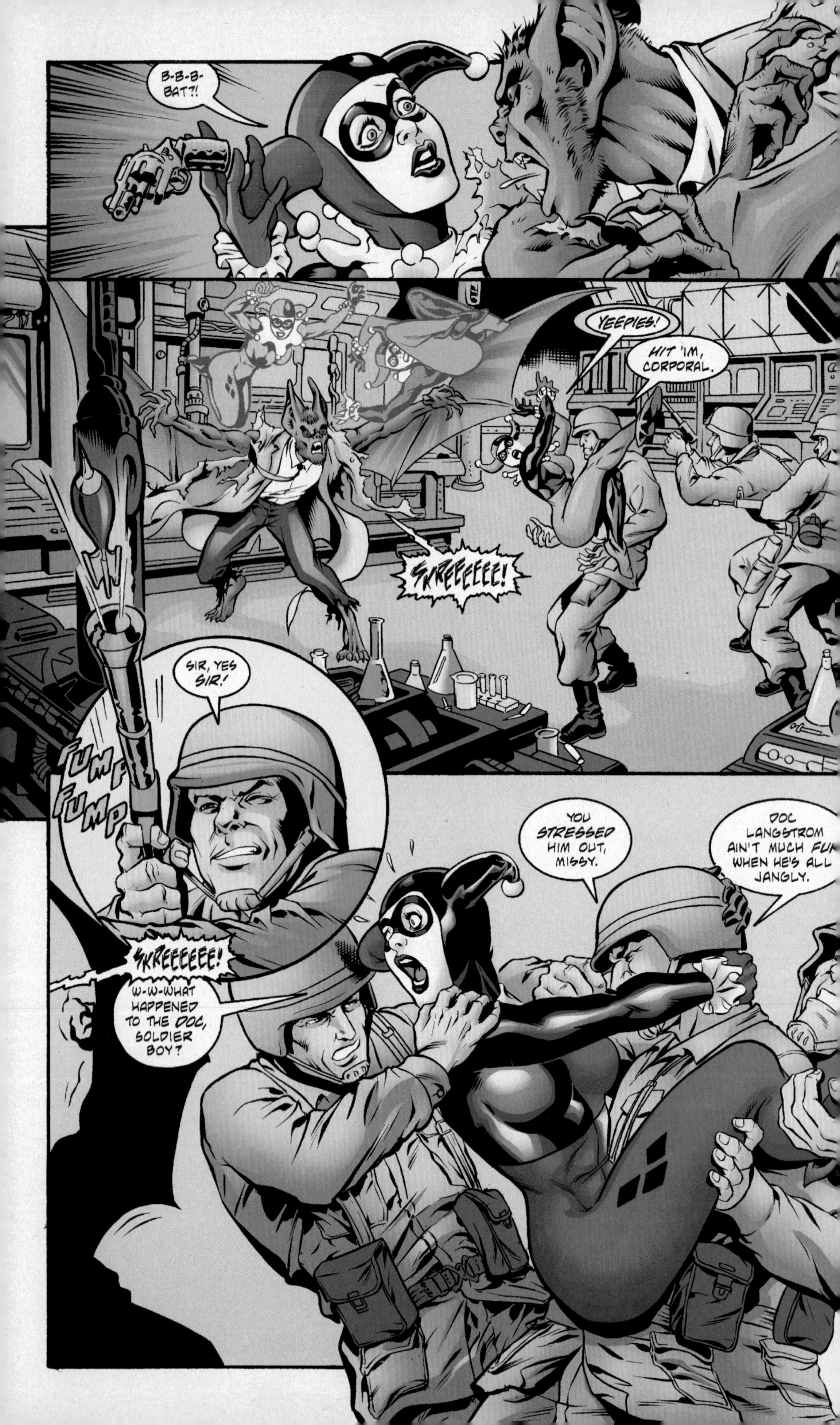
B-B-B-BAT?!
YEEPIES!
HIT 'IM, CORPORAL.
SKREEEEEEE!
SIR, YES SIR!
FUMP FUMP
SKREEEEEEE!
W-W-WHAT HAPPENED TO THE DOC, SOLDIER BOY?
YOU STRESSED HIM OUT, MISSY.
DOC LANGSTROM AIN'T MUCH FUN WHEN HE'S ALL JANGLY.

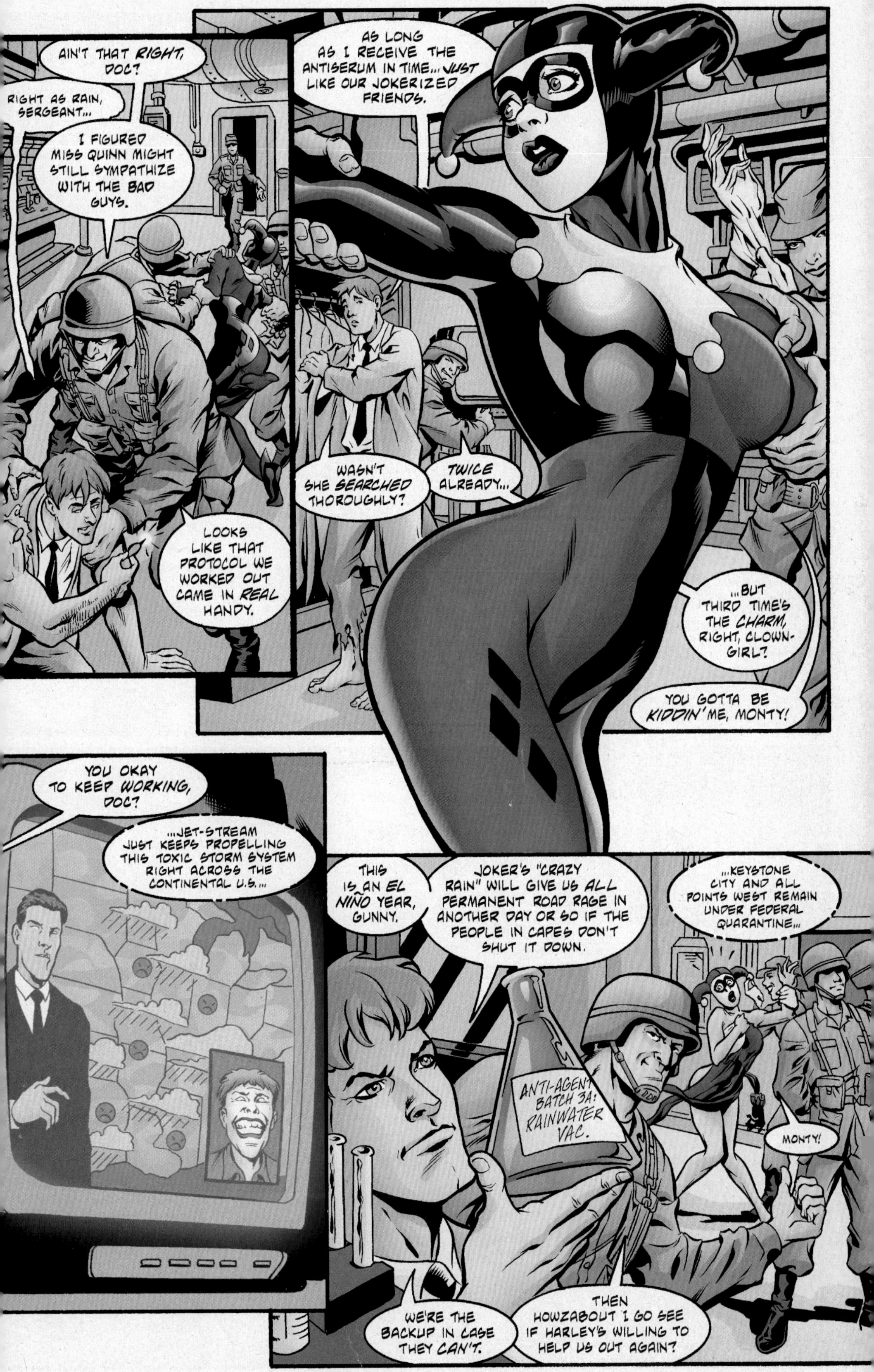
AIN'T THAT RIGHT, DOC?
RIGHT AS RAIN, SERGEANT...
I FIGURED MISS QUINN MIGHT STILL SYMPATHIZE WITH THE BAD GUYS.
LOOKS LIKE THAT PROTOCOL WE WORKED OUT CAME IN REAL HANDY.
AS LONG AS I RECEIVE THE ANTISERUM IN TIME... JUST LIKE OUR JOKERIZED FRIENDS.
WASN'T SHE SEARCHED THOROUGHLY?
TWICE ALREADY...
...BUT THIRD TIME'S THE CHARM, RIGHT, CLOWN-GIRL?
YOU GOTTA BE KIDDIN' ME, MONTY!
YOU OKAY TO KEEP WORKING, DOC?
...JET-STREAM JUST KEEPS PROPELLING THIS TOXIC STORM SYSTEM RIGHT ACROSS THE CONTINENTAL U.S....
THIS IS AN EL NIÑO YEAR, GUNNY.
JOKER'S "CRAZY RAIN" WILL GIVE US ALL PERMANENT ROAD RAGE IN ANOTHER DAY OR SO IF THE PEOPLE IN CAPES DON'T SHUT IT DOWN.
...KEYSTONE CITY AND ALL POINTS WEST REMAIN UNDER FEDERAL QUARANTINE...
ANTI-AGENT BATCH 3A: RAINWATER VAC.
MONTY!
WE'RE THE BACKUP IN CASE THEY CAN'T.
THEN HOWZABOUT I GO SEE IF HARLEY'S WILLING TO HELP US OUT AGAIN?

I'M IN POSITION. TELL ME AGAIN WHY YOU CALLED, ORACLE.
BECAUSE YOU'RE ALL THAT'S LEFT.
"I GOT A SOFT SPOT FOR GIRLS WITH GUNS."
WHO?!
IT'S ME, GAGY-CAKES!
SCARFY THE CLOWN!
HUNTRESS, WHAT'S HAPPENING?
GIVE US A KISS, GAT-DAME!
HUNTRESS!
HOLD ON!
PFFT

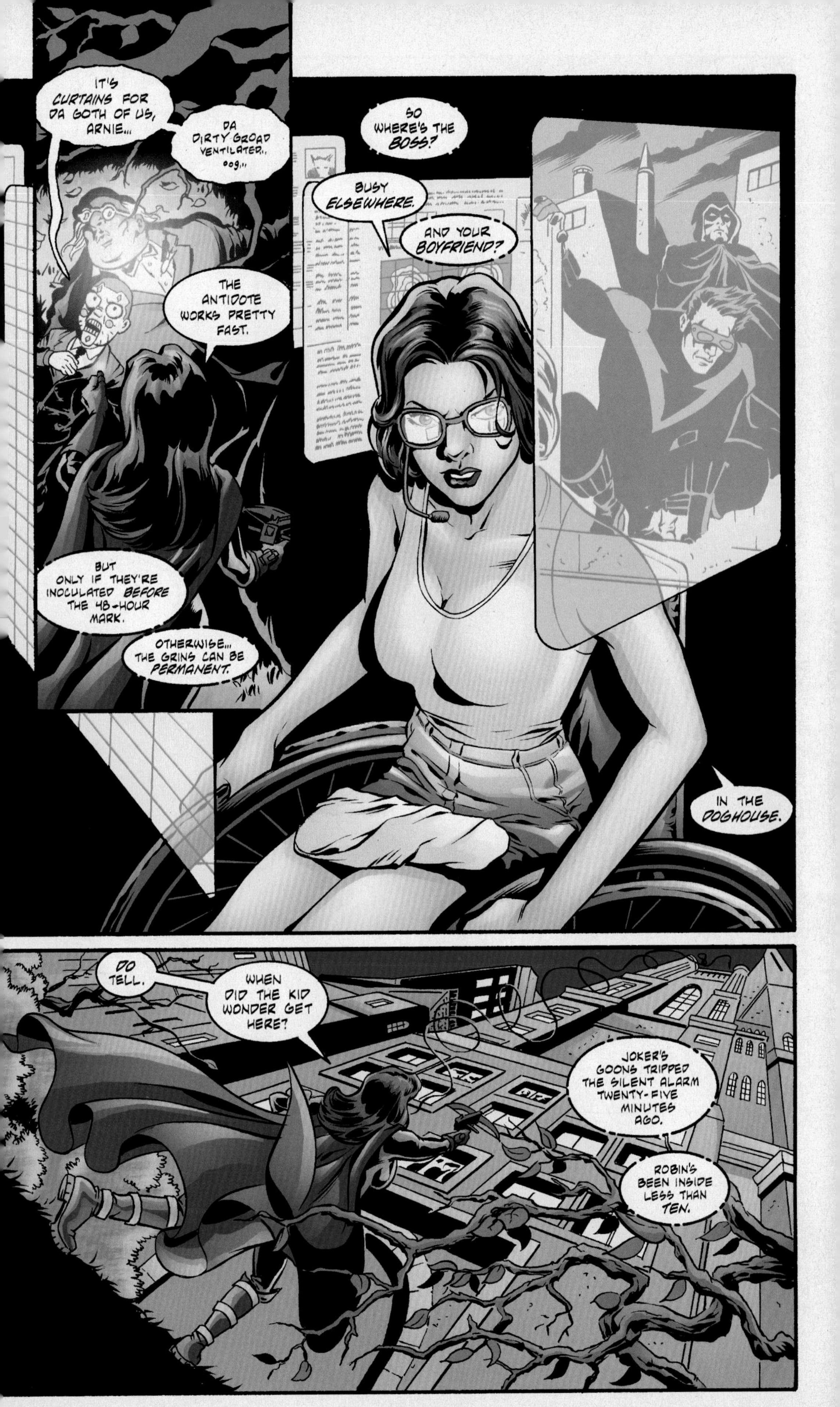

IT'S CURTAINS FOR DA GOTH OF US, ARNIE...
DA DIRTY GROAD VENTILATED.. OOG...
SO WHERE'S THE BOSS?
BUSY ELSEWHERE.
AND YOUR BOYFRIEND?
THE ANTIDOTE WORKS PRETTY FAST.
BUT ONLY IF THEY'RE INOCULATED BEFORE THE 48-HOUR MARK.
OTHERWISE... THE GRINS CAN BE PERMANENT.
IN THE DOGHOUSE.
DO TELL.
WHEN DID THE KID WONDER GET HERE?
JOKER'S GOONS TRIPPED THE SILENT ALARM TWENTY-FIVE MINUTES AGO.
ROBIN'S BEEN INSIDE LESS THAN TEN.

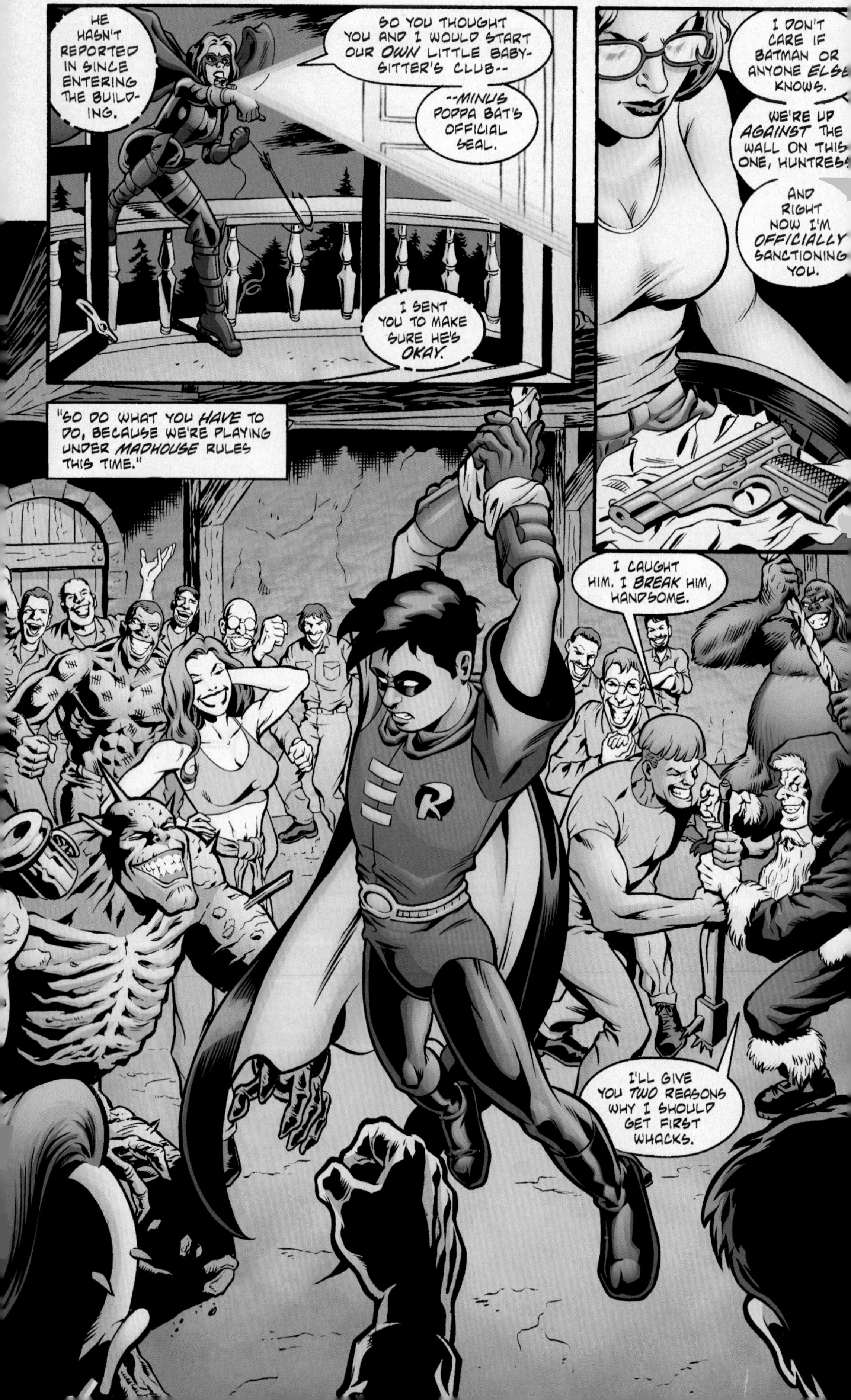
HE HASN'T REPORTED IN SINCE ENTERING THE BUILD-ING.
SO YOU THOUGHT YOU AND I WOULD START OUR OWN LITTLE BABY-SITTER'S CLUB--
--MINUS POPPA BAT'S OFFICIAL SEAL.
I SENT YOU TO MAKE SURE HE'S OKAY.
I DON'T CARE IF BATMAN OR ANYONE ELSE KNOWS.
WE'RE UP AGAINST THE WALL ON THIS ONE, HUNTRESS.
AND RIGHT NOW I'M OFFICIALLY SANCTIONING YOU.
"SO DO WHAT YOU HAVE TO DO, BECAUSE WE'RE PLAYING UNDER MADHOUSE RULES THIS TIME."
I CAUGHT HIM. I BREAK HIM, HANDSOME.
I'LL GIVE YOU TWO REASONS WHY I SHOULD GET FIRST WHACKS.

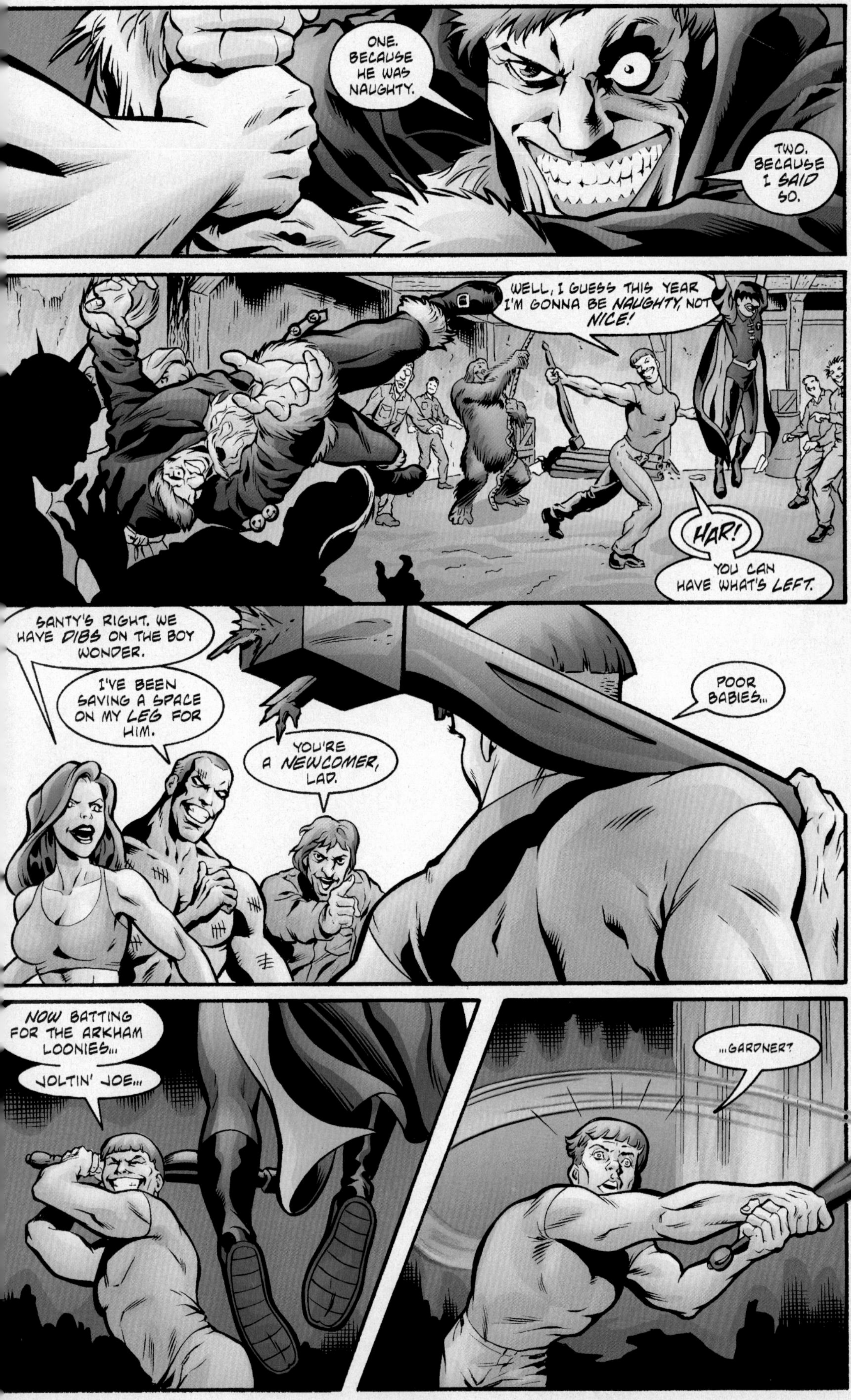
ONE. BECAUSE HE WAS NAUGHTY.
TWO. BECAUSE I SAID SO.
WELL, I GUESS THIS YEAR I'M GONNA BE NAUGHTY, NOT NICE!
HAR!
YOU CAN HAVE WHAT'S LEFT.
SANTY'S RIGHT. WE HAVE DIBS ON THE BOY WONDER.
I'VE BEEN SAVING A SPACE ON MY LEG FOR HIM.
YOU'RE A NEWCOMER, LAD.
POOR BABIES...
NOW BATTING FOR THE ARKHAM LOONIES...
JOLTIN' JOE...
...GARDNER?

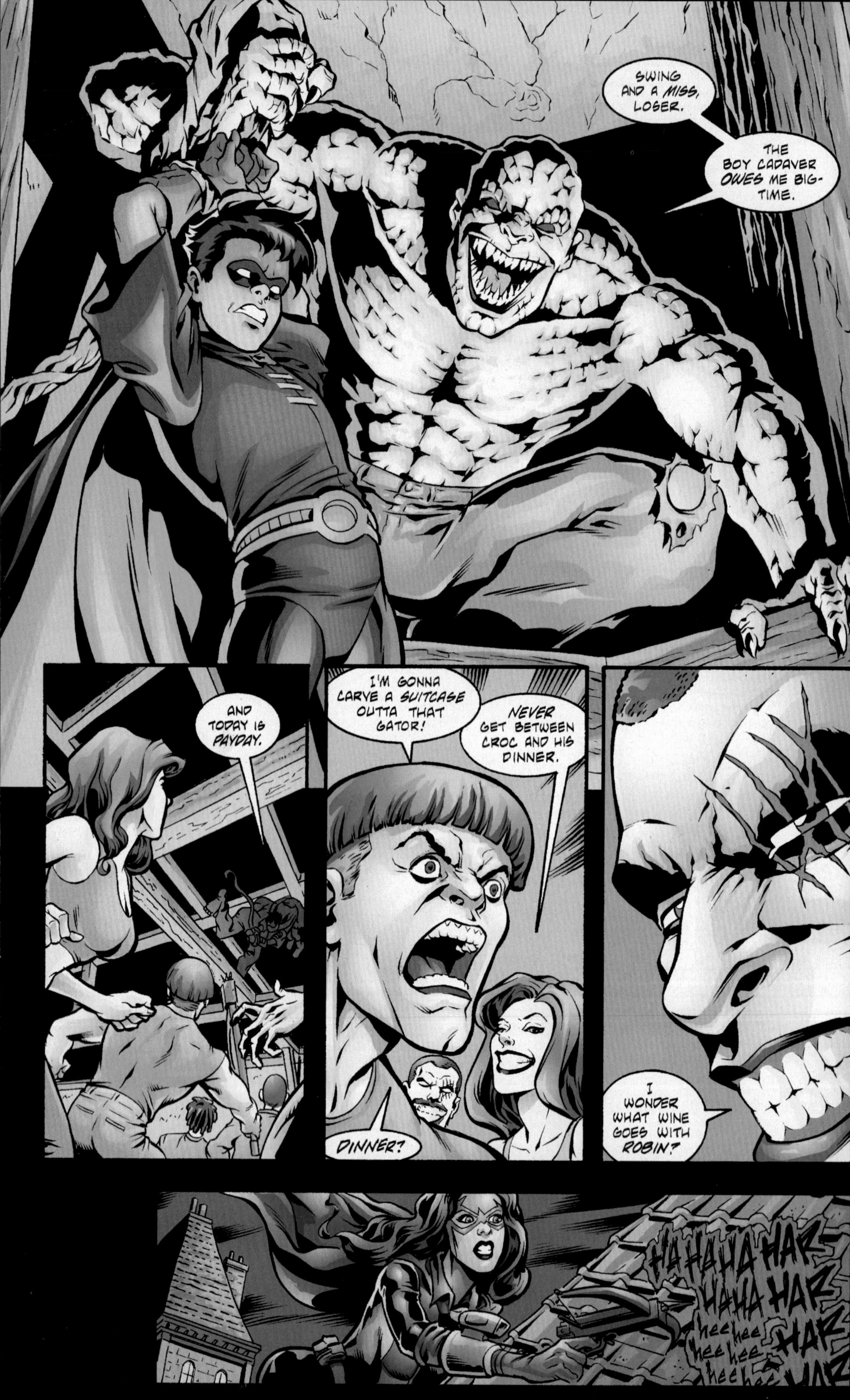

SWING AND A MISS, LOSER.
THE BOY CADAVER OWES ME BIG-TIME.
AND TODAY IS PAYDAY.
I'M GONNA CARVE A SUITCASE OUTTA THAT GATOR!
NEVER GET BETWEEN CROC AND HIS DINNER.
DINNER?
I WONDER WHAT WINE GOES WITH ROBIN?
HAHAHA HAR-
HAHA HAR
hee hee
hee hee
HAR

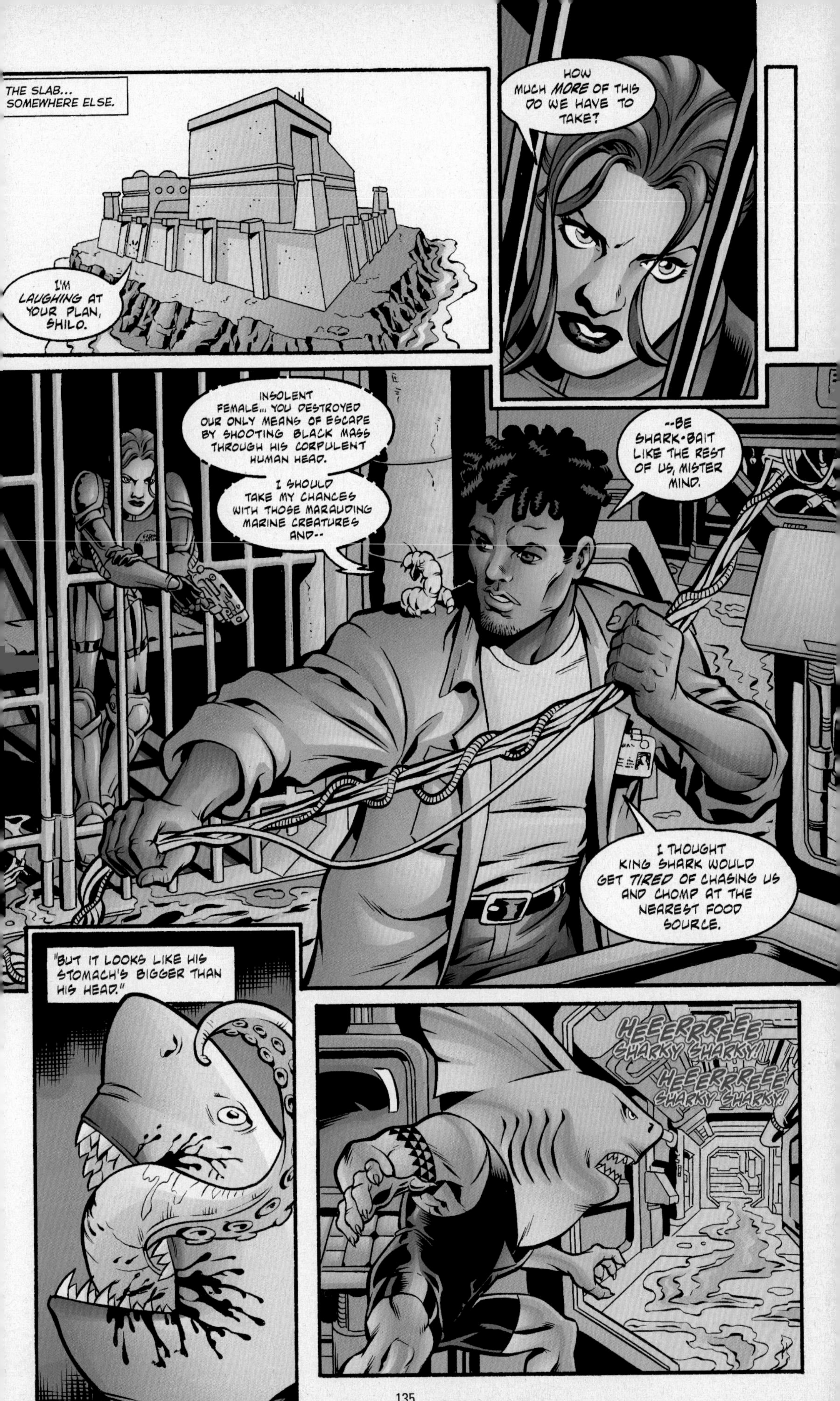
THE SLAB... SOMEWHERE ELSE.
I'M LAUGHING AT YOUR PLAN, SHILO.
HOW MUCH MORE OF THIS DO WE HAVE TO TAKE?
INSOLENT FEMALE... YOU DESTROYED OUR ONLY MEANS OF ESCAPE BY SHOOTING BLACK MASS THROUGH HIS CORPULENT HUMAN HEAD.
I SHOULD TAKE MY CHANCES WITH THOSE MARAUDING MARINE CREATURES AND--
--BE SHARK-BAIT LIKE THE REST OF US, MISTER MIND.
I THOUGHT KING SHARK WOULD GET TIRED OF CHASING US AND CHOMP AT THE NEAREST FOOD SOURCE.
"BUT IT LOOKS LIKE HIS STOMACH'S BIGGER THAN HIS HEAD."
HEEERRREEE SHARKY SHARKY!
HEEERRREEE SHARKY SHARKY!

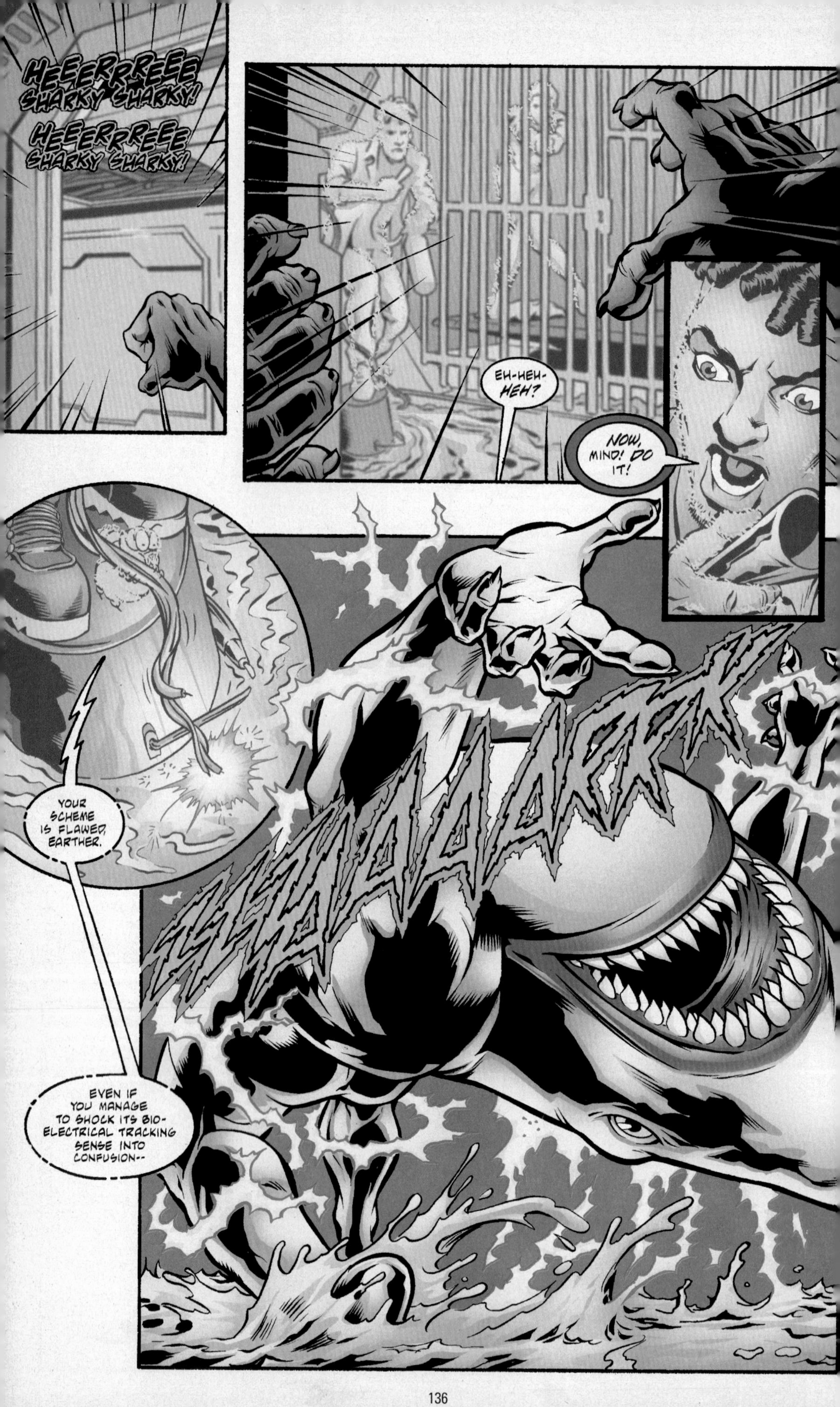
HEEERRREEE SHARKY SHARKY!
HEEERRREEE SHARKY SHARKY!
EH-HEH-HEH?
NOW, MIND! DO IT!
YOUR SCHEME IS FLAWED, EARTHER.
EVEN IF YOU MANAGE TO SHOCK ITS BIO-ELECTRICAL TRACKING SENSE INTO CONFUSION--

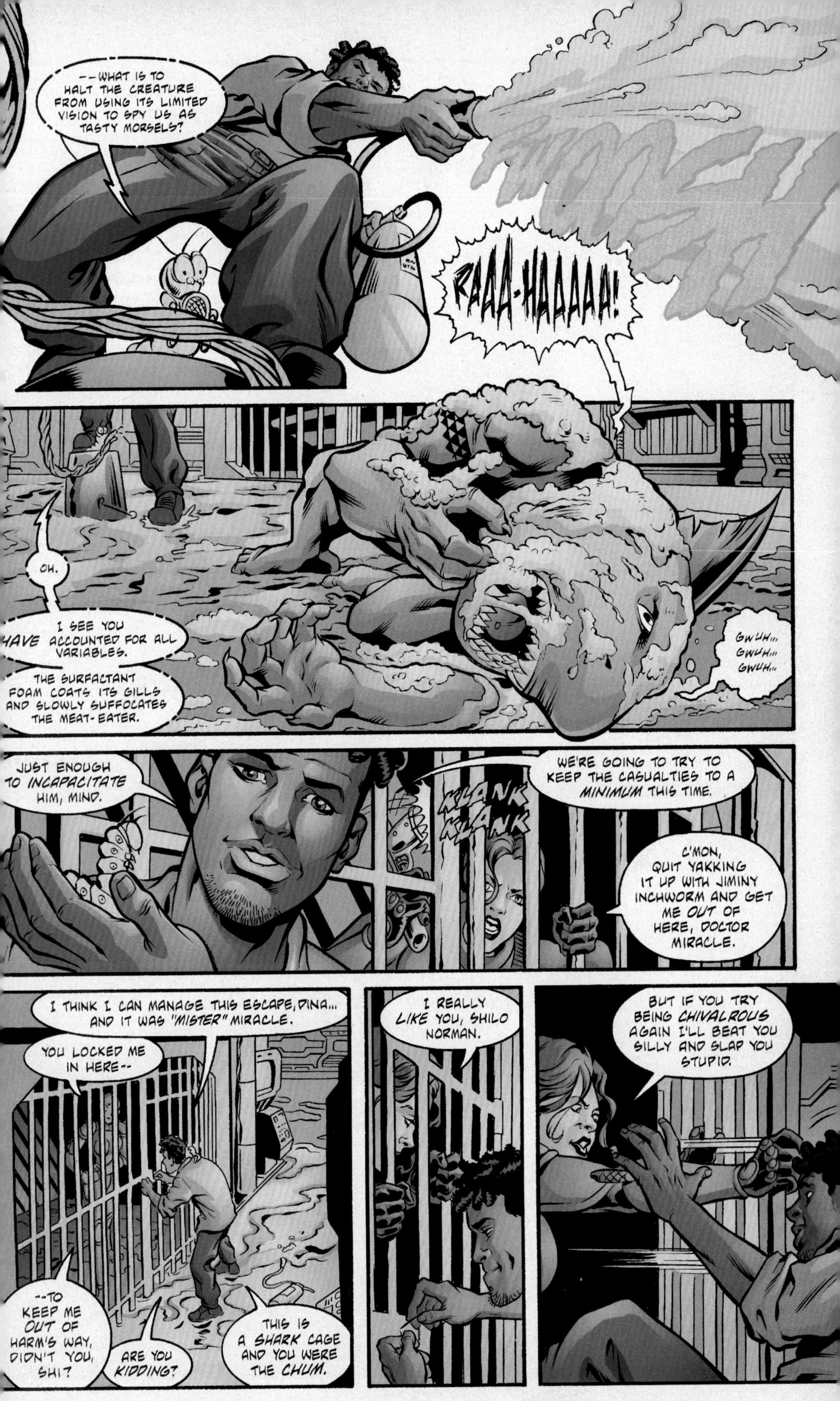
--WHAT IS TO HALT THE CREATURE FROM USING ITS LIMITED VISION TO SPY US AS TASTY MORSELS?
FWOOSH!
RAAA-HAAAAA!
OH.
I SEE YOU HAVE ACCOUNTED FOR ALL VARIABLES.
THE SURFACTANT FOAM COATS ITS GILLS AND SLOWLY SUFFOCATES THE MEAT-EATER.
GWUH... GWUH... GWUH...
JUST ENOUGH TO INCAPACITATE HIM, MIND.
WE'RE GOING TO TRY TO KEEP THE CASUALTIES TO A MINIMUM THIS TIME.
KLANK KLANK
C'MON, QUIT YAKKING IT UP WITH JIMINY INCHWORM AND GET ME OUT OF HERE, DOCTOR MIRACLE.
I THINK I CAN MANAGE THIS ESCAPE, DINA... AND IT WAS "MISTER" MIRACLE.
YOU LOCKED ME IN HERE--
--TO KEEP ME OUT OF HARM'S WAY, DIDN'T YOU, SHI?
ARE YOU KIDDING?
THIS IS A SHARK CAGE AND YOU WERE THE CHUM.
I REALLY LIKE YOU, SHILO NORMAN.
BUT IF YOU TRY BEING CHIVALROUS AGAIN I'LL BEAT YOU SILLY AND SLAP YOU STUPID.

ON MY WORLD, SHE WOULD BE A QUEEN.

OR SOMETHING.

AND WHAT IS YOUR NEXT COURSE OF ACTION, EARTHER?

FIRST WE DUMP SHARKY IN A HOLDING TANK--

--THEN WE FIGURE OUT HOW TO JUMP BACK TO NORMAL SPACE.

I DON'T SUPPOSE YOU KNOW ANYONE *ELSE* WHO CAN MANIPULATE BLACK HOLES.

PERHAPS...

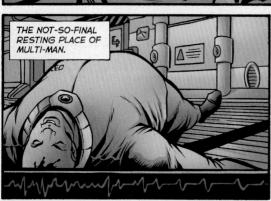

THE NOT-SO-FINAL RESTING PLACE OF MULTI-MAN.

...groan...

SPOIT!

"WHAT DO YOU *MEAN* HE'S NOT DYING?"

CURSE YOU, JOKER!

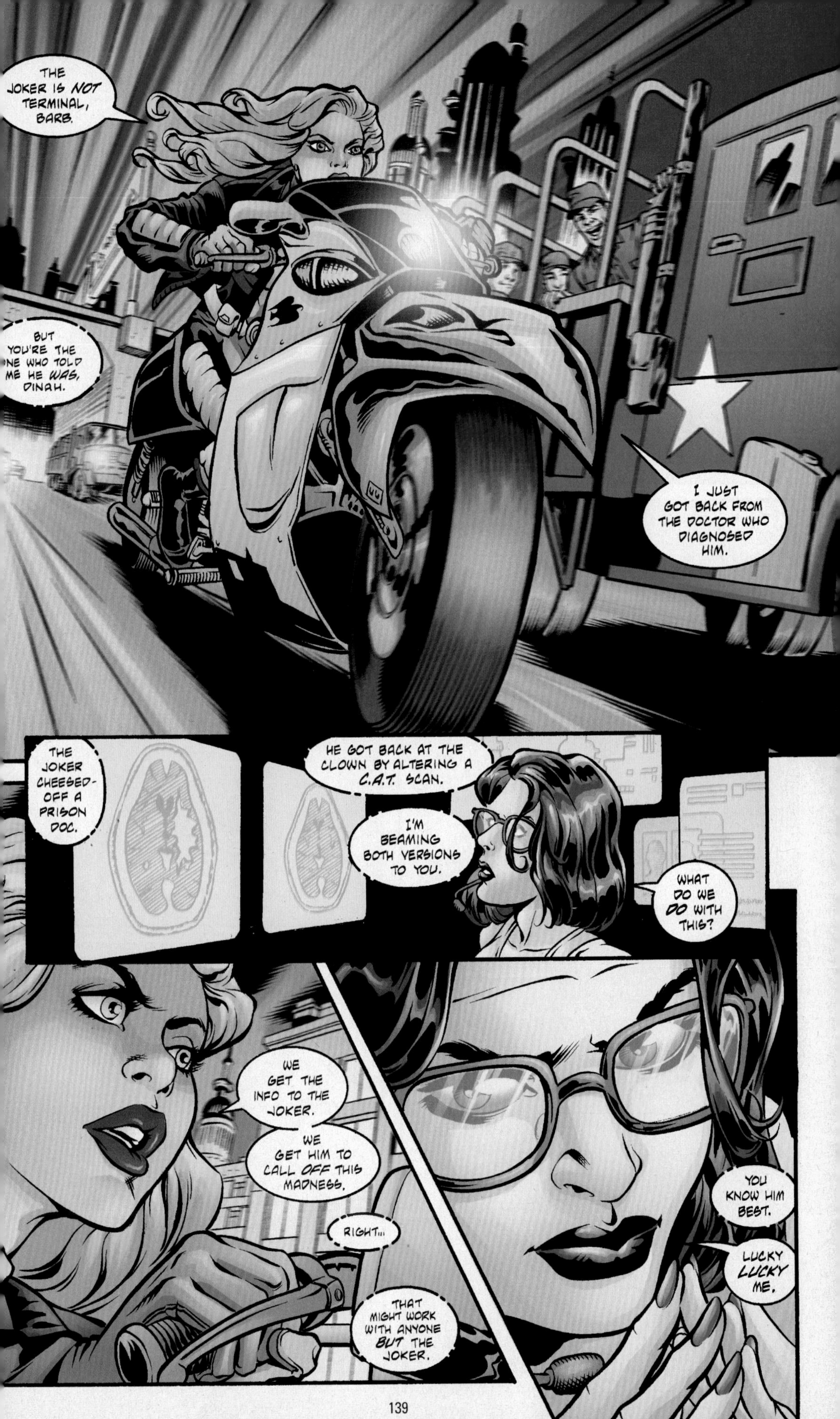
THE JOKER IS NOT TERMINAL, BARB.
BUT YOU'RE THE ONE WHO TOLD ME HE WAS, DINAH.
I JUST GOT BACK FROM THE DOCTOR WHO DIAGNOSED HIM.
THE JOKER CHEESED-OFF A PRISON DOC.
HE GOT BACK AT THE CLOWN BY ALTERING A C.A.T. SCAN.
I'M BEAMING BOTH VERSIONS TO YOU.
WHAT DO WE DO WITH THIS?
WE GET THE INFO TO THE JOKER.
WE GET HIM TO CALL OFF THIS MADNESS.
RIGHT...
THAT MIGHT WORK WITH ANYONE BUT THE JOKER.
YOU KNOW HIM BEST.
LUCKY LUCKY ME.

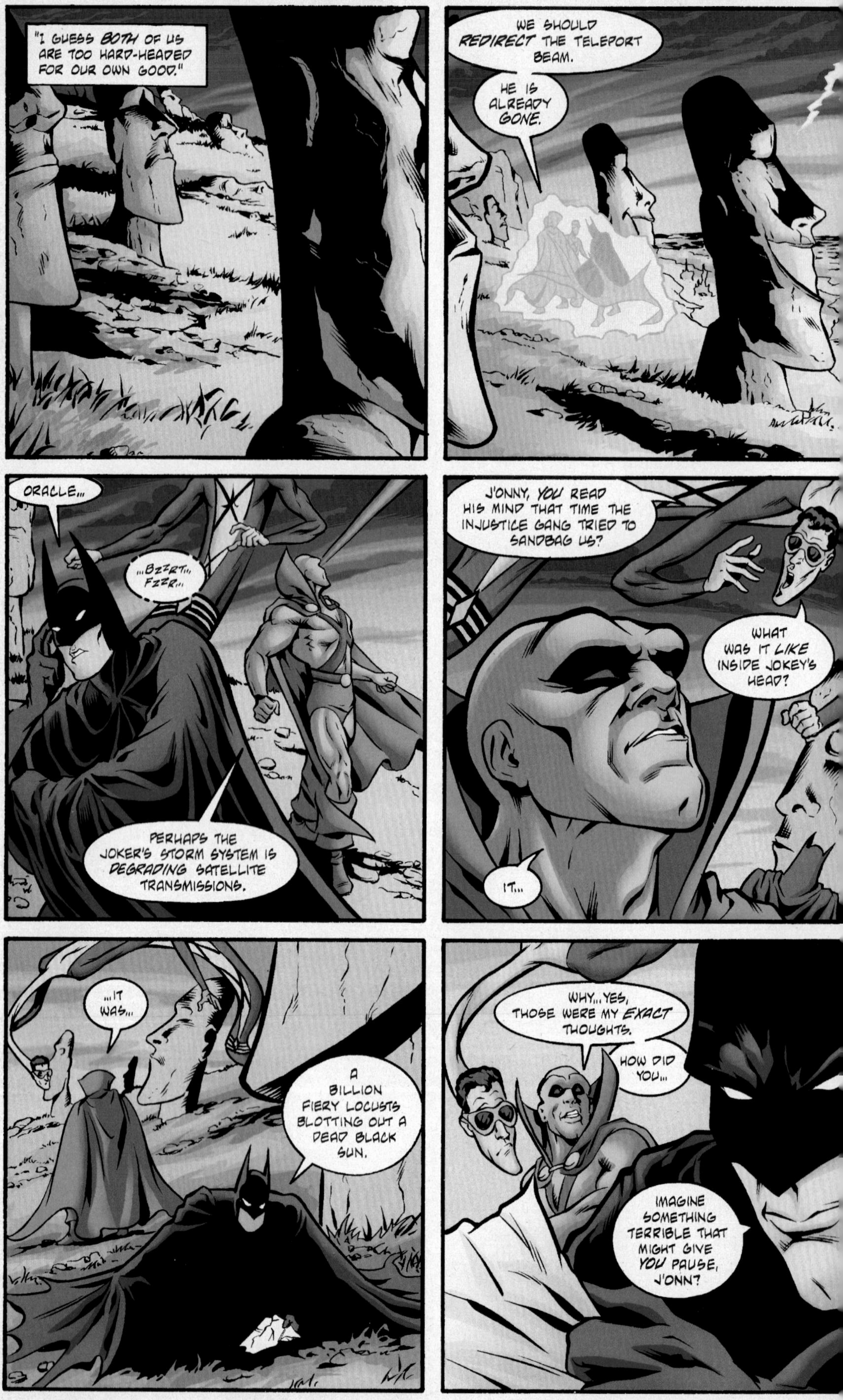
"I GUESS BOTH OF US ARE TOO HARD-HEADED FOR OUR OWN GOOD."
WE SHOULD REDIRECT THE TELEPORT BEAM.
HE IS ALREADY GONE.
ORACLE...
...BZZRT... FZZR...
PERHAPS THE JOKER'S STORM SYSTEM IS DEGRADING SATELLITE TRANSMISSIONS.
J'ONNY, YOU READ HIS MIND THAT TIME THE INJUSTICE GANG TRIED TO SANDBAG US?
WHAT WAS IT LIKE INSIDE JOKEY'S HEAD?
IT...
...IT WAS...
A BILLION FIERY LOCUSTS BLOTTING OUT A DEAD BLACK SUN.
WHY... YES, THOSE WERE MY EXACT THOUGHTS.
HOW DID YOU...
IMAGINE SOMETHING TERRIBLE THAT MIGHT GIVE YOU PAUSE, J'ONN?

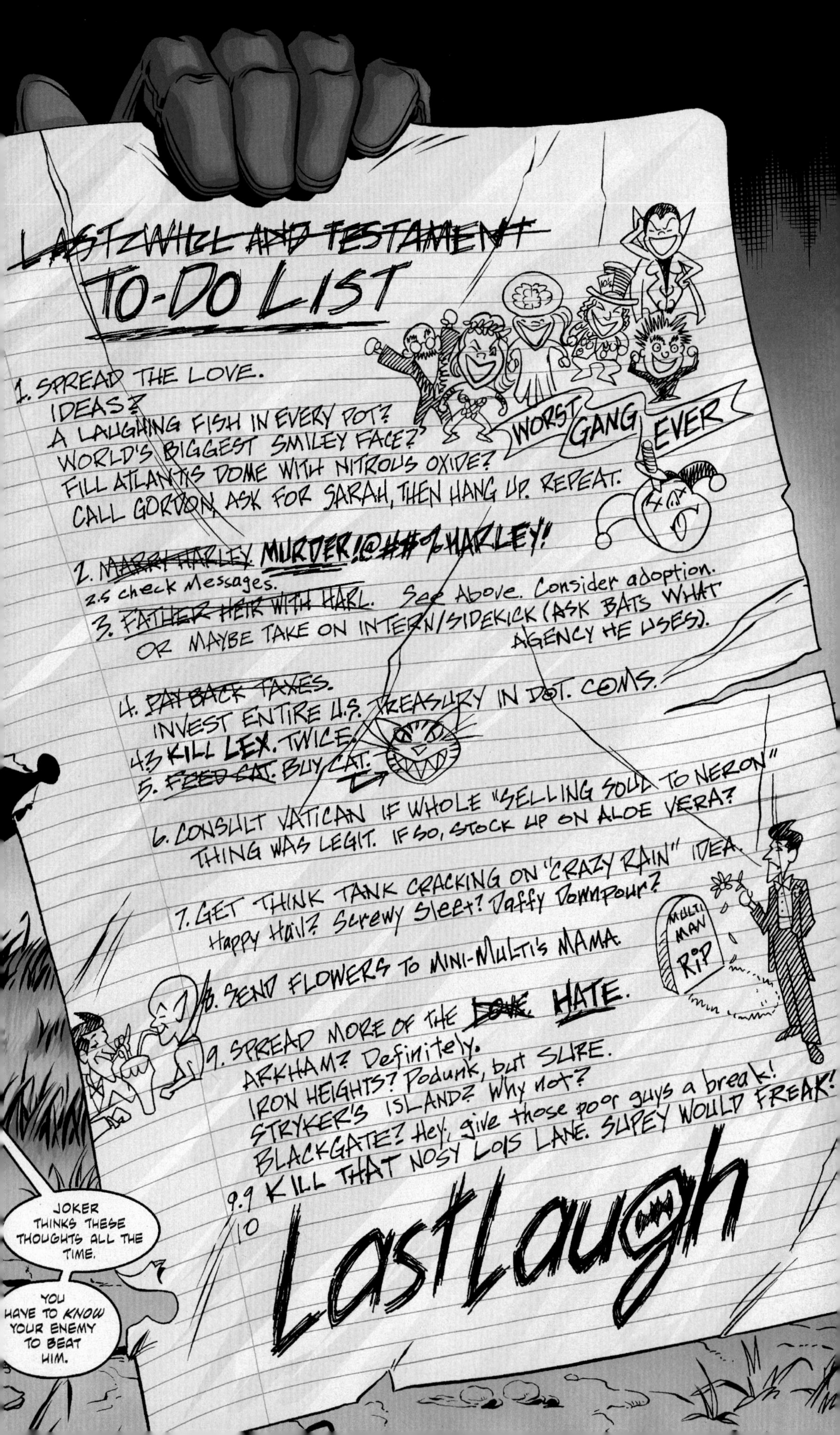
LAST WILL AND TESTAMENT
TO-DO LIST
1. SPREAD THE LOVE.
IDEAS?
A LAUGHING FISH IN EVERY POT?
WORLD'S BIGGEST SMILEY FACE?
FILL ATLANTIS DOME WITH NITROUS OXIDE?
CALL GORDON, ASK FOR SARAH, THEN HANG UP. REPEAT.
WORST GANG EVER
2. MARRY HARLEY. MURDER!@#% HARLEY!
2.5 check Messages.
3. FATHER HEIR WITH HARL. See Above. Consider adoption.
OR MAYBE TAKE ON INTERN/SIDEKICK (ASK BATS WHAT AGENCY HE USES).
4. PAY BACK TAXES.
INVEST ENTIRE U.S. TREASURY IN DOT. COMS.
4.3 KILL LEX. TWICE.
5. FEED CAT. BUY CAT.
6. CONSULT VATICAN IF WHOLE "SELLING SOUL TO NERON" THING WAS LEGIT. IF SO, STOCK UP ON ALOE VERA?
7. GET THINK TANK CRACKING ON "CRAZY RAIN" IDEA.
Happy Hail? Screwy Sleet? Daffy Downpour?
8. SEND FLOWERS TO MINI-MULTI'S MAMA.
MULTI MAN RIP
9. SPREAD MORE OF THE LOVE HATE.
ARKHAM? Definitely.
IRON HEIGHTS? Podunk, but SURE.
STRYKER'S ISLAND? Why not?
BLACKGATE? Hey, give those poor guys a break!
9.9 KILL THAT NOSY LOIS LANE. SUPEY WOULD FREAK!
10 Last Laugh
JOKER THINKS THESE THOUGHTS ALL THE TIME.
YOU HAVE TO KNOW YOUR ENEMY TO BEAT HIM.

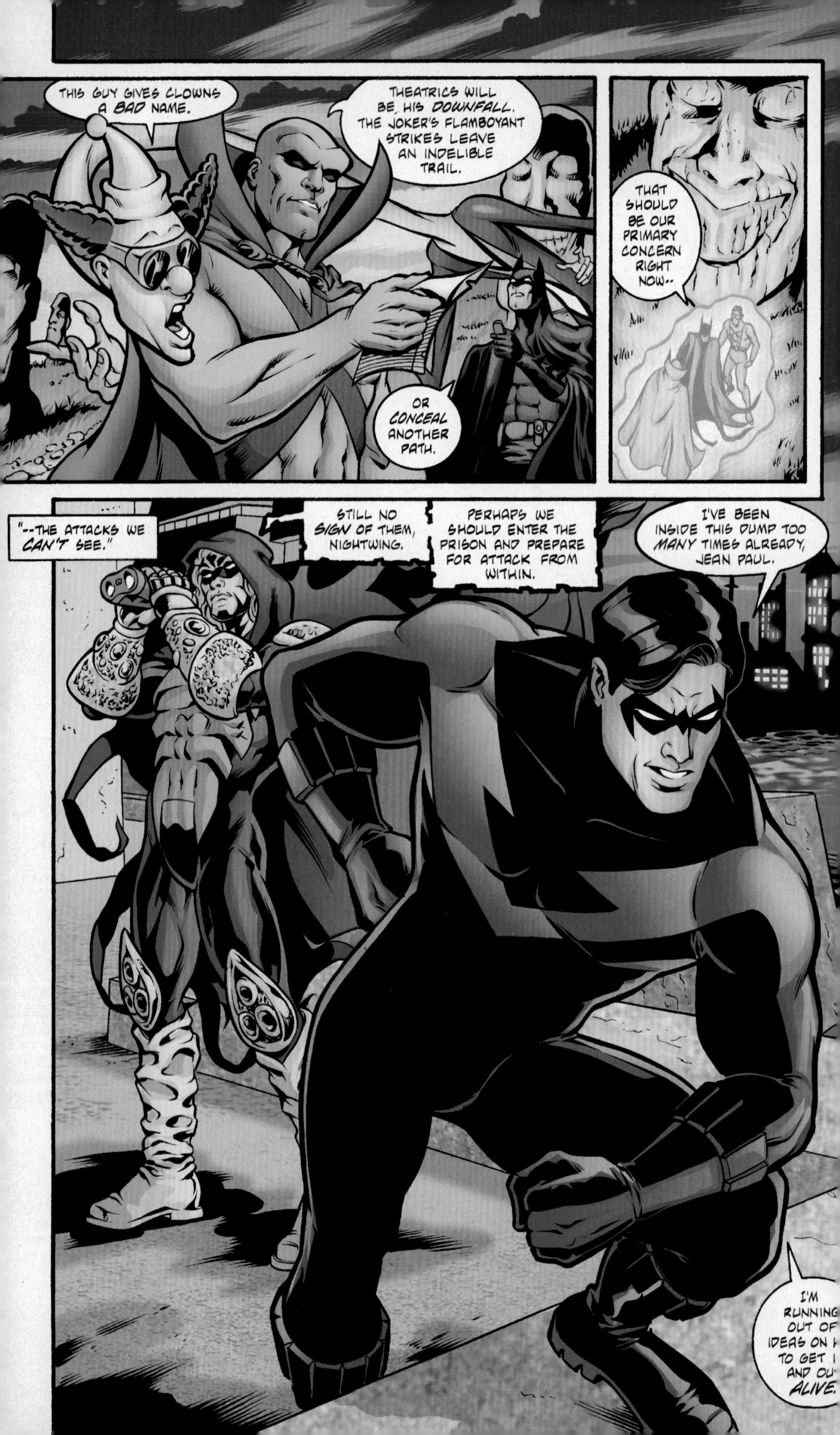
THIS GUY GIVES CLOWNS A BAD NAME.
THEATRICS WILL BE HIS DOWNFALL. THE JOKER'S FLAMBOYANT STRIKES LEAVE AN INDELIBLE TRAIL.
OR CONCEAL ANOTHER PATH.
THAT SHOULD BE OUR PRIMARY CONCERN RIGHT NOW..
"--THE ATTACKS WE CAN'T SEE."
STILL NO SIGN OF THEM, NIGHTWING.
PERHAPS WE SHOULD ENTER THE PRISON AND PREPARE FOR ATTACK FROM WITHIN.
I'VE BEEN INSIDE THIS DUMP TOO MANY TIMES ALREADY, JEAN PAUL.
I'M RUNNING OUT OF IDEAS ON H TO GET I AND OU ALIVE.

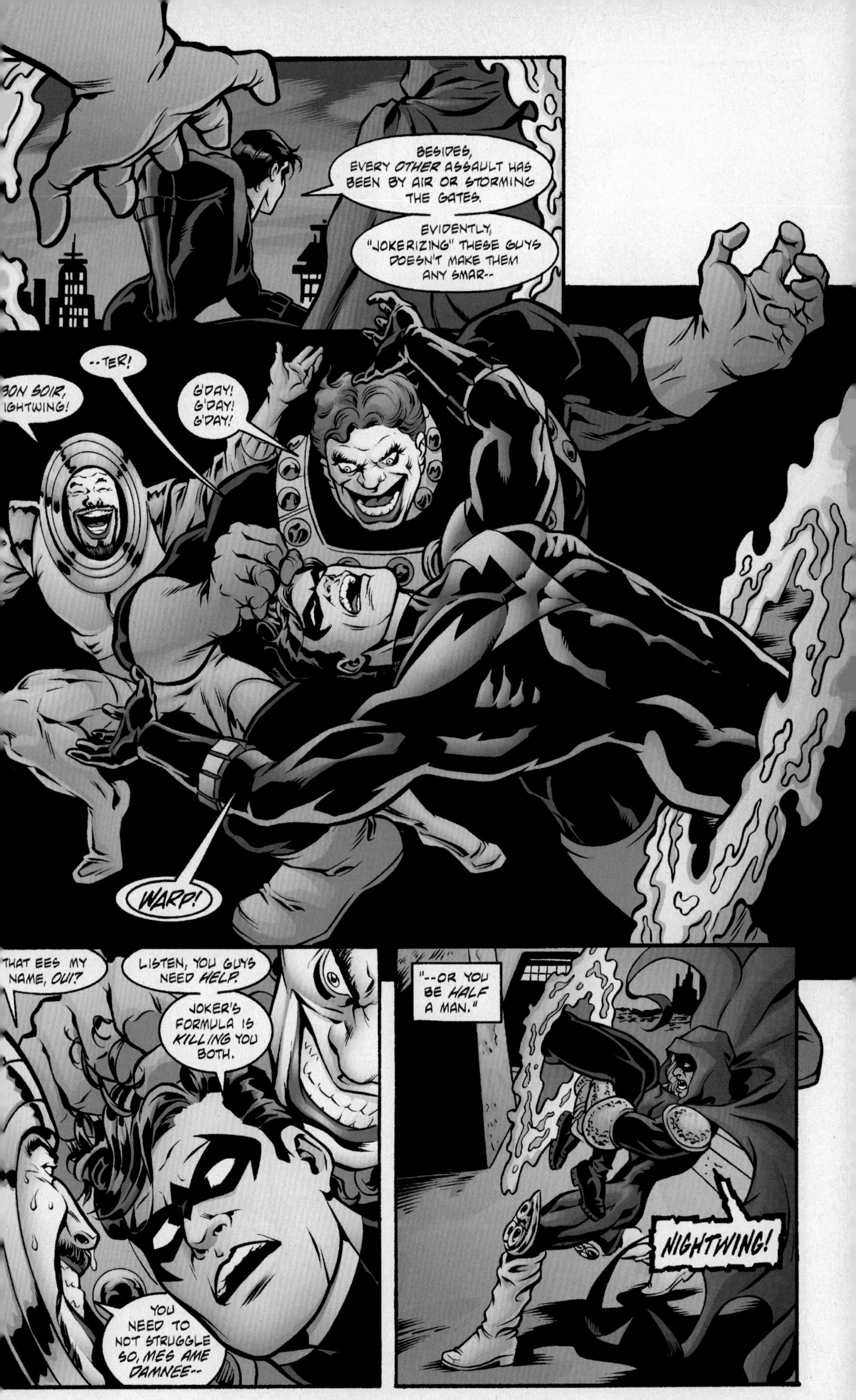

BESIDES, EVERY *OTHER* ASSAULT HAS BEEN BY AIR OR STORMING THE GATES.
EVIDENTLY, "JOKERIZING" THESE GUYS DOESN'T MAKE THEM ANY SMAR--
--TER!
BON SOIR, NIGHTWING!
G'DAY! G'DAY! G'DAY!
WARP!
THAT EES MY NAME, *OUI?*
LISTEN, YOU GUYS NEED *HELP.*
JOKER'S FORMULA IS *KILLING* YOU BOTH.
YOU NEED TO NOT STRUGGLE SO, *MES AME DAMNEE*--
"--OR YOU BE *HALF* A MAN."
NIGHTWING!

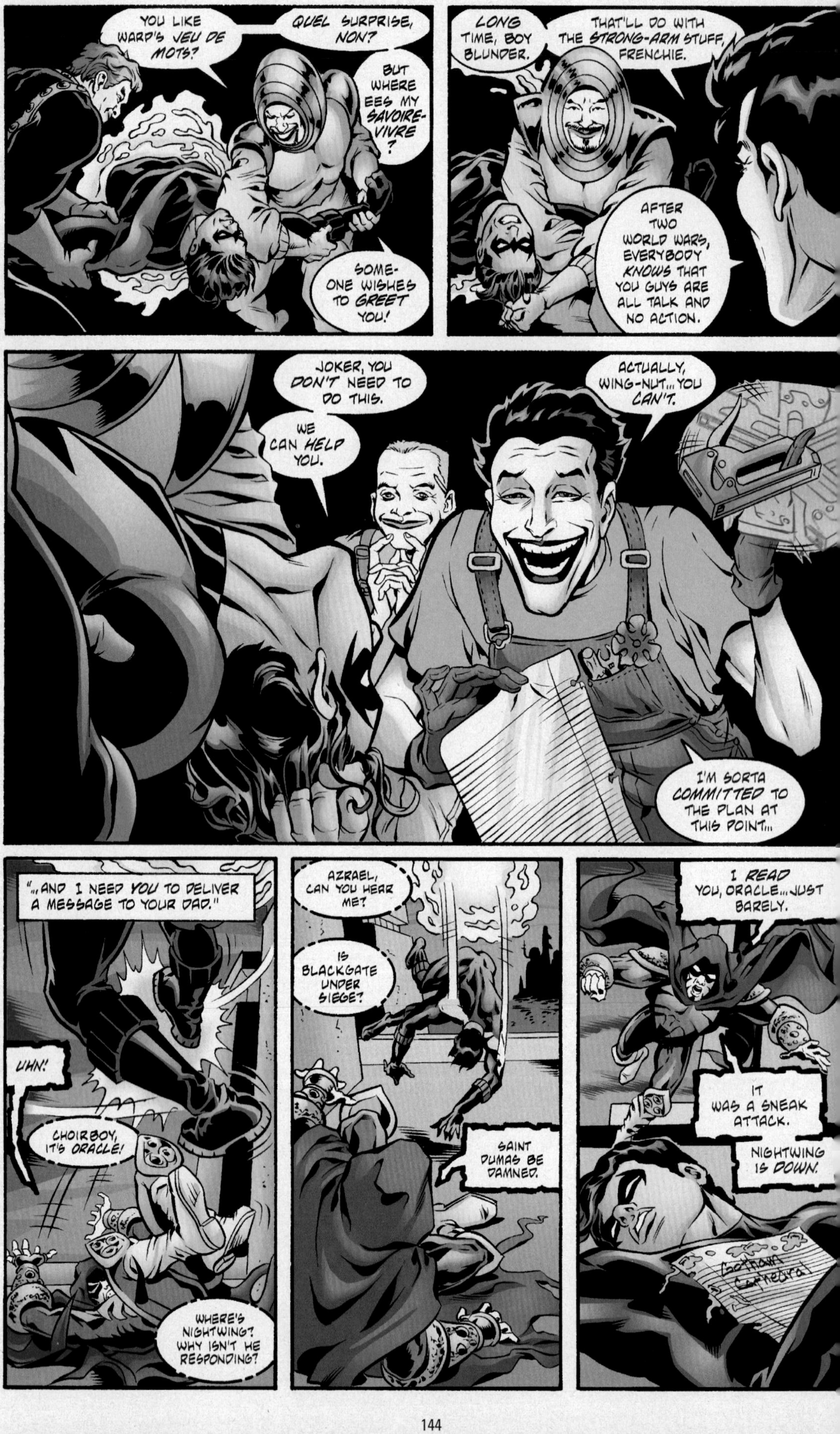
YOU LIKE WARP'S JEU DE MOTS?
QUEL SURPRISE, NON?
BUT WHERE EES MY SAVOIRE-VIVRE?
SOME-ONE WISHES TO GREET YOU!
LONG TIME, BOY BLUNDER.
THAT'LL DO WITH THE STRONG-ARM STUFF, FRENCHIE.
AFTER TWO WORLD WARS, EVERYBODY KNOWS THAT YOU GUYS ARE ALL TALK AND NO ACTION.
JOKER, YOU DON'T NEED TO DO THIS.
WE CAN HELP YOU.
ACTUALLY, WING-NUT... YOU CAN'T.
I'M SORTA COMMITTED TO THE PLAN AT THIS POINT...
"...AND I NEED YOU TO DELIVER A MESSAGE TO YOUR DAD."
UHN!
CHOIRBOY, IT'S ORACLE!
WHERE'S NIGHTWING? WHY ISN'T HE RESPONDING?
AZRAEL, CAN YOU HEAR ME?
IS BLACKGATE UNDER SIEGE?
SAINT DUMAS BE DAMNED.
I READ YOU, ORACLE... JUST BARELY.
IT WAS A SNEAK ATTACK.
NIGHTWING IS DOWN.
Gotham Cathedral

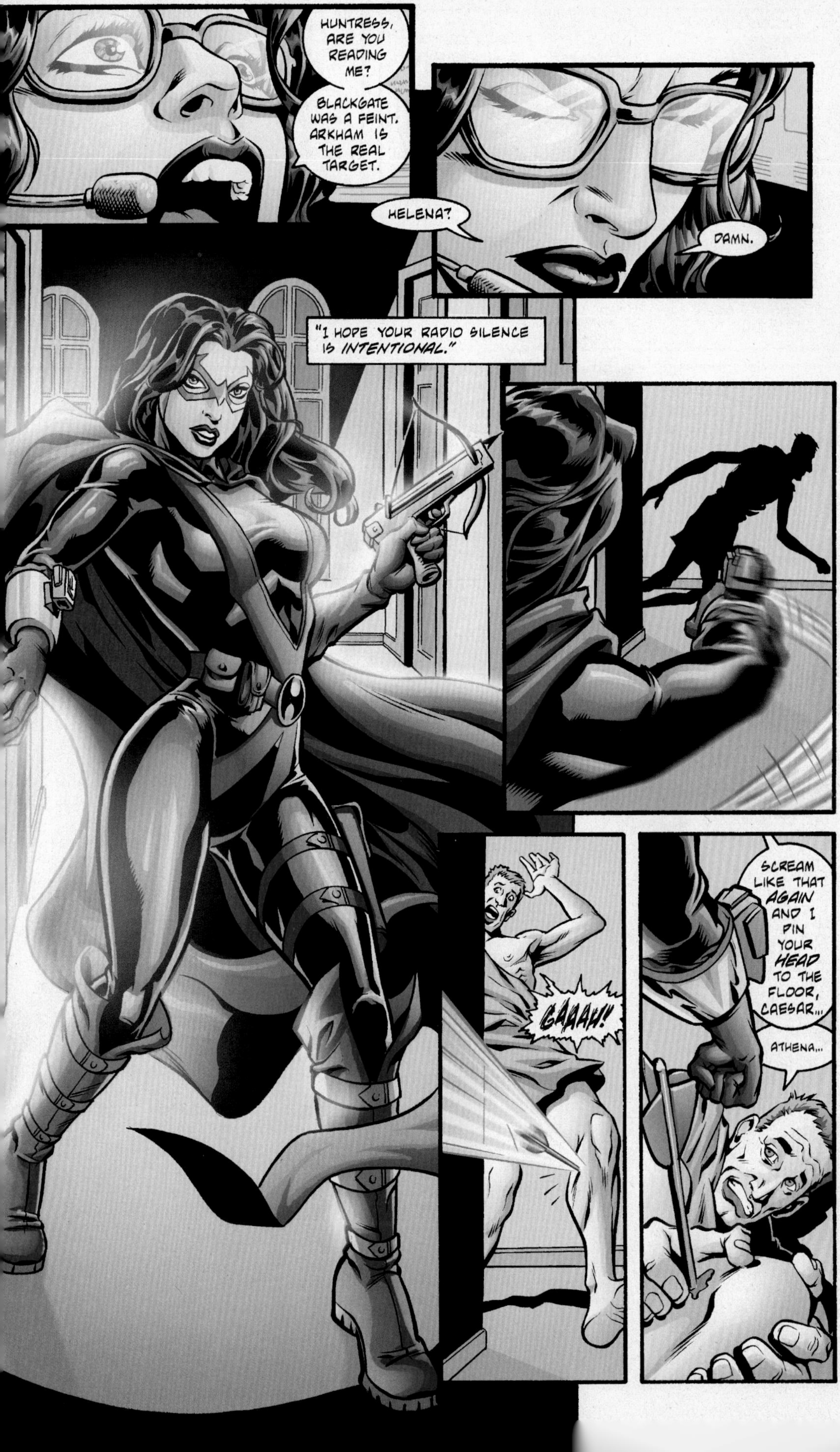
HUNTRESS, ARE YOU READING ME?
BLACKGATE WAS A FEINT. ARKHAM IS THE REAL TARGET.
HELENA?
DAMN.
"I HOPE YOUR RADIO SILENCE IS *INTENTIONAL.*"
GAAAH!
SCREAM LIKE THAT *AGAIN* AND I PIN YOUR *HEAD* TO THE FLOOR, CAESAR...
ATHENA...

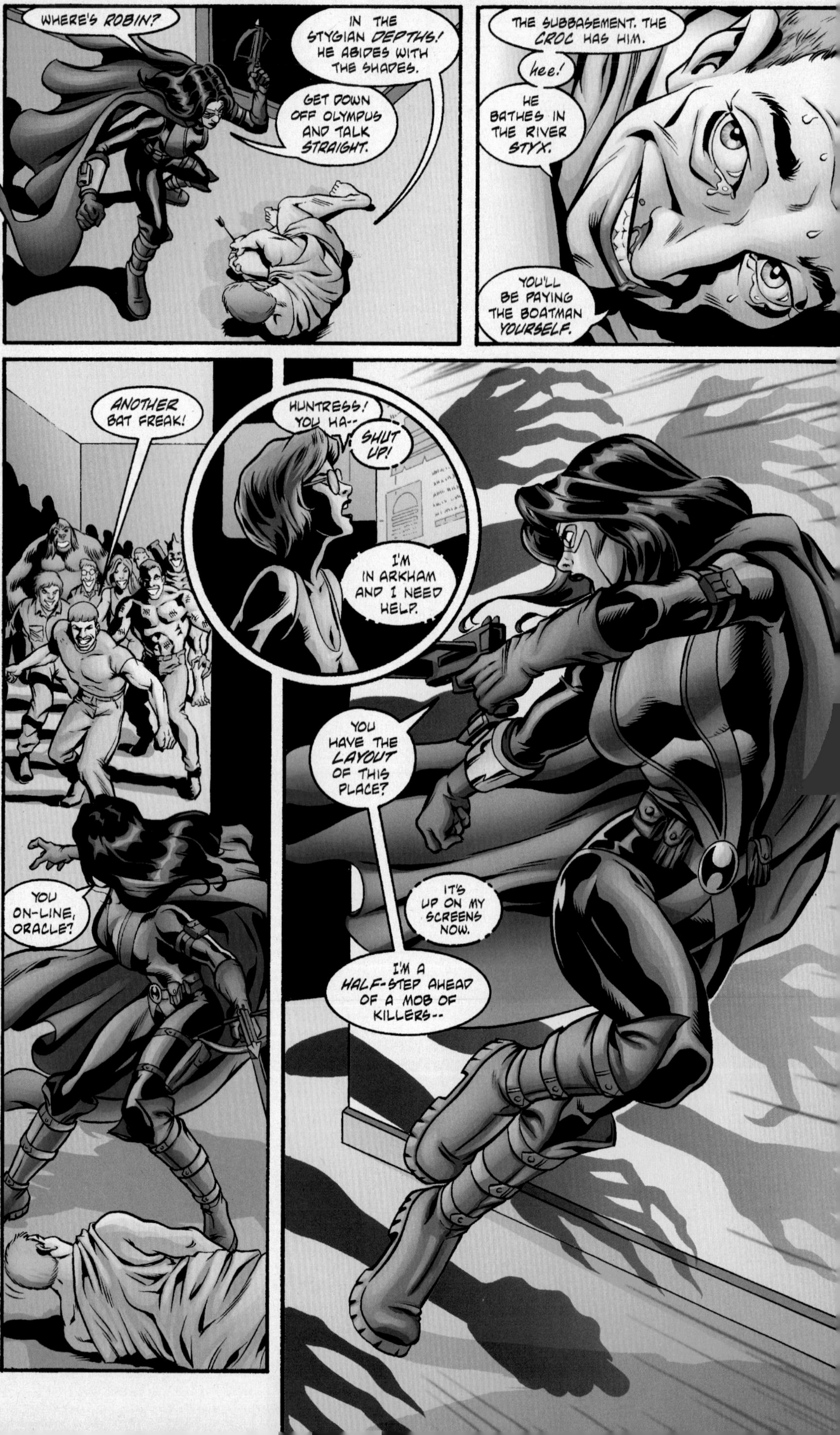
WHERE'S ROBIN?
IN THE STYGIAN DEPTHS! HE ABIDES WITH THE SHADES.
GET DOWN OFF OLYMPUS AND TALK STRAIGHT.
THE SUBBASEMENT. THE CROC HAS HIM.
hee!
HE BATHES IN THE RIVER STYX.
YOU'LL BE PAYING THE BOATMAN YOURSELF.
ANOTHER BAT FREAK!
YOU ON-LINE, ORACLE?
HUNTRESS! YOU HA--
SHUT UP!
I'M IN ARKHAM AND I NEED HELP.
YOU HAVE THE LAYOUT OF THIS PLACE?
IT'S UP ON MY SCREENS NOW.
I'M A HALF-STEP AHEAD OF A MOB OF KILLERS--

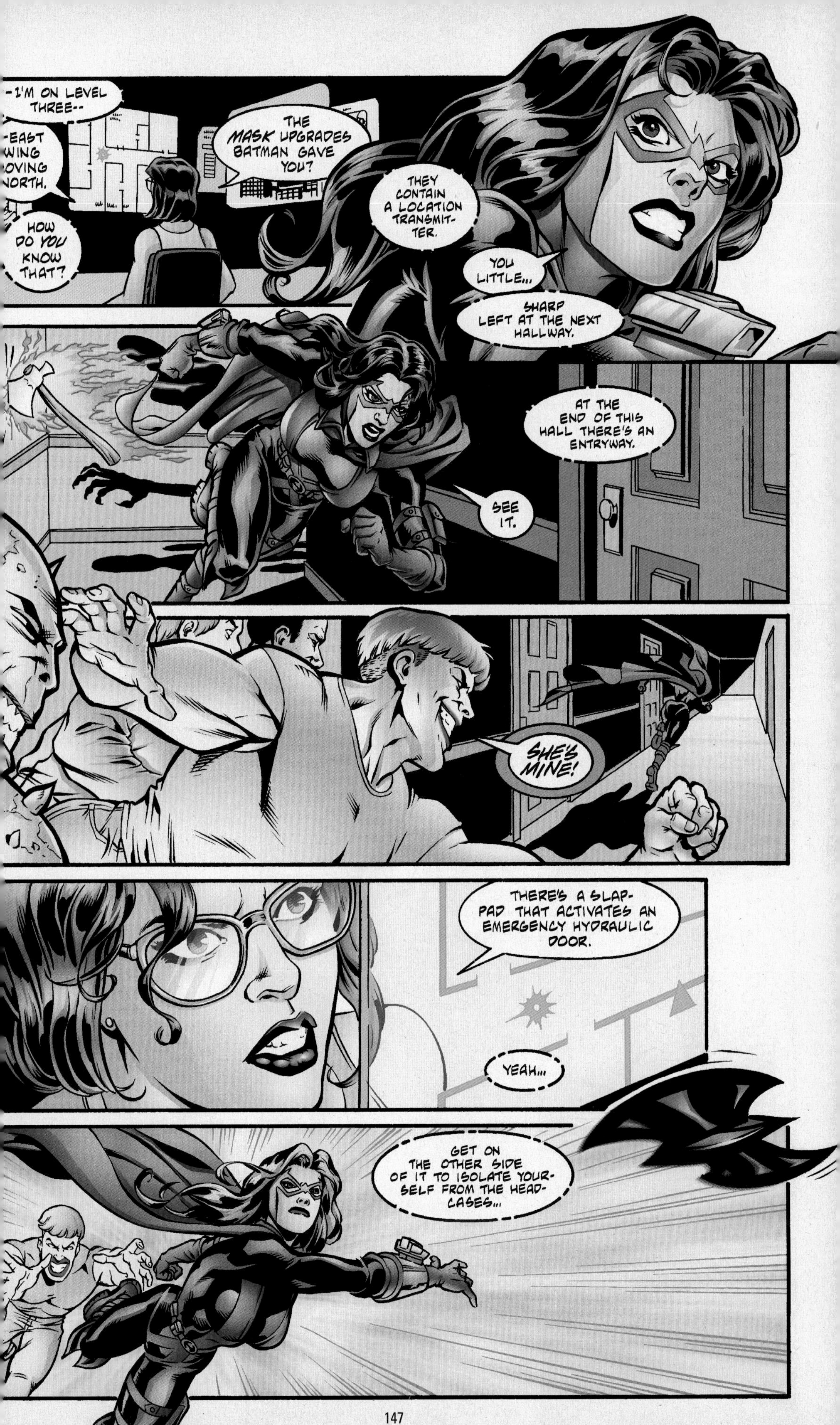

-I'M ON LEVEL THREE--
-EAST WING MOVING NORTH.
HOW DO YOU KNOW THAT?
THE MASK UPGRADES BATMAN GAVE YOU?
THEY CONTAIN A LOCATION TRANSMIT-TER.
YOU LITTLE...
SHARP LEFT AT THE NEXT HALLWAY.
AT THE END OF THIS HALL THERE'S AN ENTRYWAY.
SEE IT.
SHE'S MINE!
THERE'S A SLAP-PAD THAT ACTIVATES AN EMERGENCY HYDRAULIC DOOR.
YEAH...
GET ON THE OTHER SIDE OF IT TO ISOLATE YOUR-SELF FROM THE HEAD-CASES...

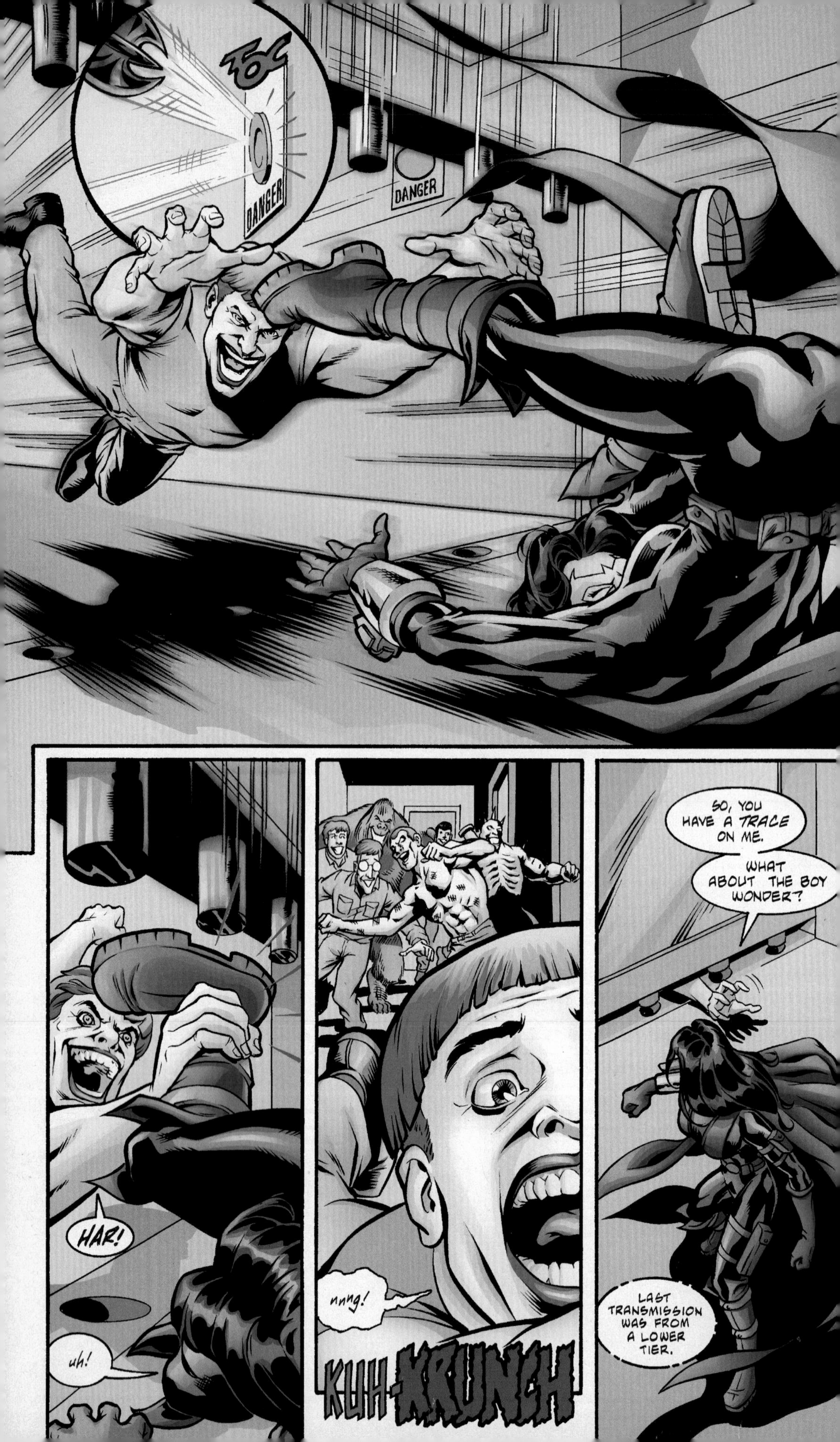

DANGER
DANGER
HAR!
uh!
nnng!
KUH-KRUNCH
SO, YOU HAVE A TRACE ON ME.
WHAT ABOUT THE BOY WONDER?
LAST TRANSMISSION WAS FROM A LOWER TIER.

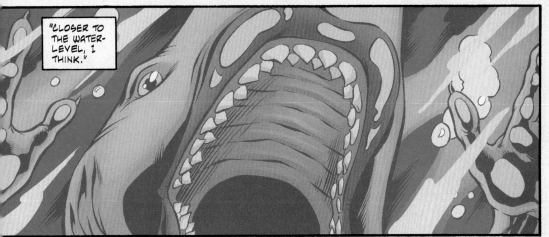

"CLOSER TO THE WATER-LEVEL, I THINK."

THAT'S WRONG IN SO MANY WAYS.

DINA!

I'M COMING! HOLD TIGHT...

...SHI?

uh... YOU TWO WANT SOME PRIVACY?

GIVE ME YOUR GUN.

WHAT?

HOW LONG WILL IT TAKE?

MINUTES, HOURS PERHAPS.

IT ALL DEPENDS ON MISTER PRAMBLE'S "STATE OF MIND" AS YOU EARTHERS SAY.

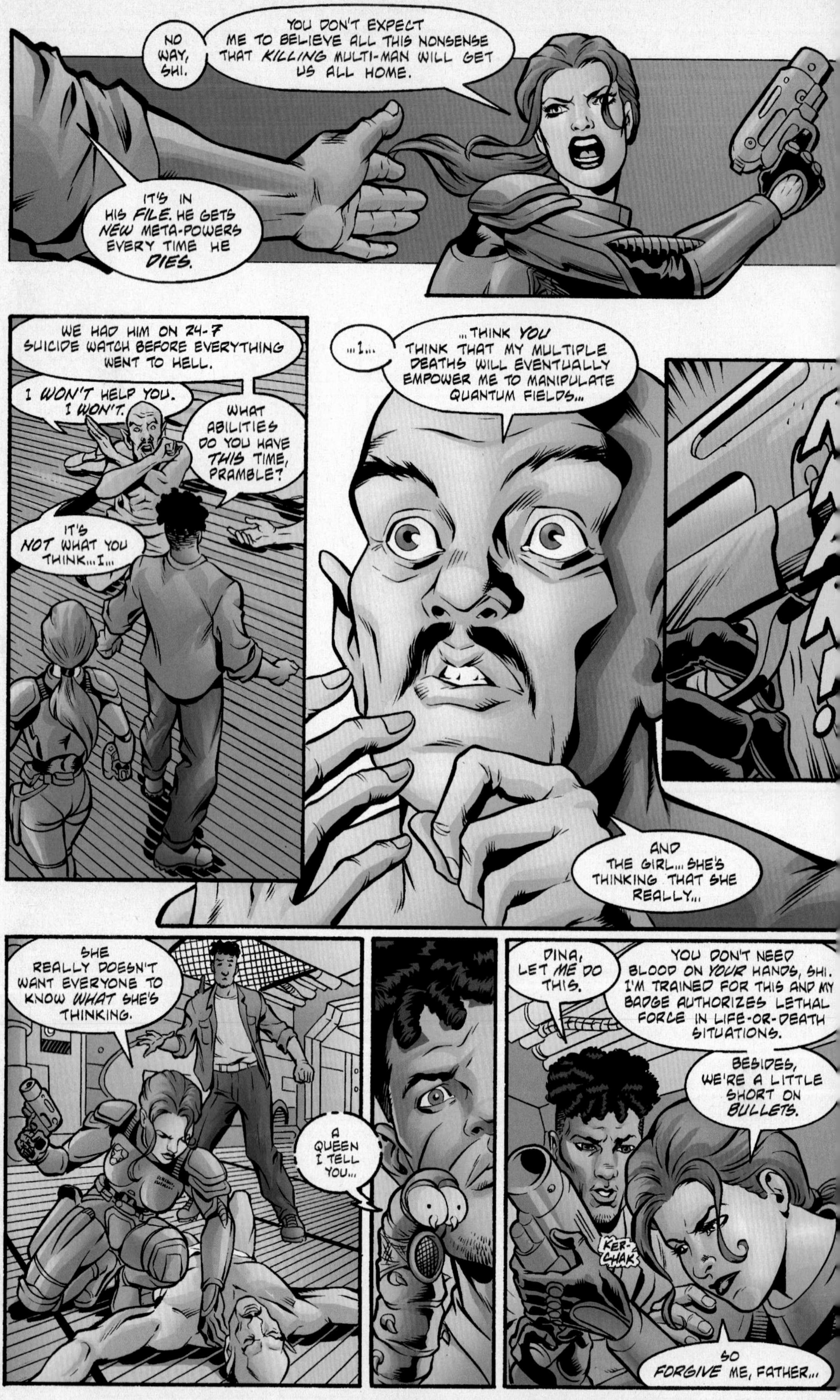

NO WAY, SHI.
YOU DON'T EXPECT ME TO BELIEVE ALL THIS NONSENSE THAT *KILLING* MULTI-MAN WILL GET US ALL HOME.
IT'S IN HIS *FILE*. HE GETS *NEW* META-POWERS EVERY TIME HE *DIES*.
WE HAD HIM ON 24-7 SUICIDE WATCH BEFORE EVERYTHING WENT TO HELL.
I *WON'T* HELP YOU. I *WON'T*.
WHAT ABILITIES DO YOU HAVE *THIS* TIME, PRAMBLE?
IT'S *NOT* WHAT YOU THINK... I...
...I...
...THINK *YOU* THINK THAT MY MULTIPLE DEATHS WILL EVENTUALLY EMPOWER ME TO MANIPULATE QUANTUM FIELDS...
AND THE GIRL... SHE'S THINKING THAT SHE REALLY...
SHE REALLY DOESN'T WANT EVERYONE TO KNOW *WHAT* SHE'S THINKING.
A QUEEN I TELL YOU...
DINA, LET *ME* DO THIS.
YOU DON'T NEED BLOOD ON *YOUR* HANDS, SHI. I'M TRAINED FOR THIS AND MY BADGE AUTHORIZES LETHAL FORCE IN LIFE-OR-DEATH SITUATIONS.
BESIDES, WE'RE A LITTLE SHORT ON *BULLETS*.
KER-CHAK
SO *FORGIVE* ME, FATHER...

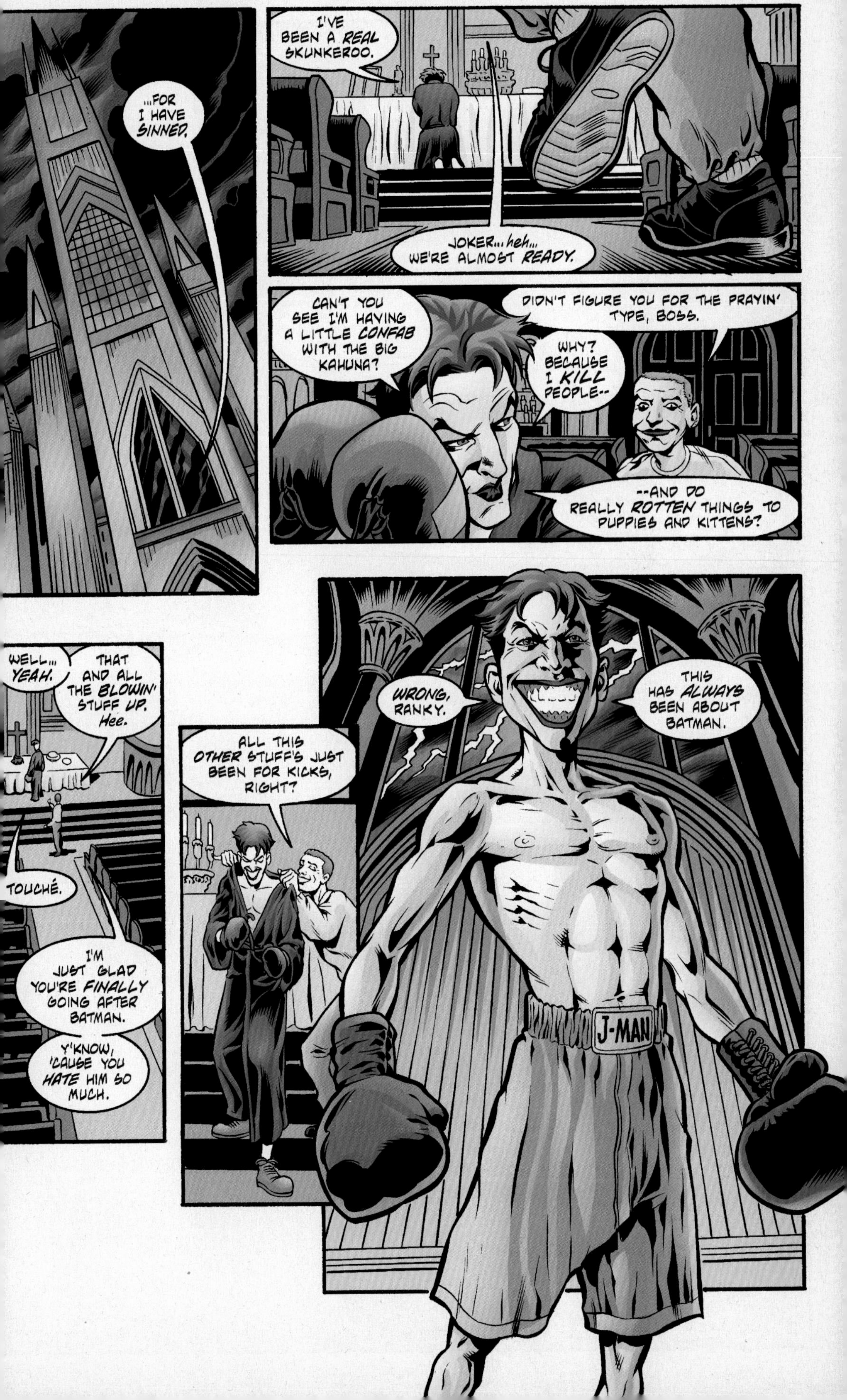
...FOR I HAVE SINNED.
I'VE BEEN A REAL SKUNKEROO.
JOKER... heh... WE'RE ALMOST READY.
DIDN'T FIGURE YOU FOR THE PRAYIN' TYPE, BOSS.
CAN'T YOU SEE I'M HAVING A LITTLE CONFAB WITH THE BIG KAHUNA?
WHY? BECAUSE I KILL PEOPLE--
--AND DO REALLY ROTTEN THINGS TO PUPPIES AND KITTENS?
WELL... YEAH.
THAT AND ALL THE BLOWIN' STUFF UP. Hee.
TOUCHÉ.
I'M JUST GLAD YOU'RE FINALLY GOING AFTER BATMAN.
Y'KNOW, 'CAUSE YOU HATE HIM SO MUCH.
ALL THIS OTHER STUFF'S JUST BEEN FOR KICKS, RIGHT?
WRONG, RANKY.
THIS HAS ALWAYS BEEN ABOUT BATMAN.
J-MAN

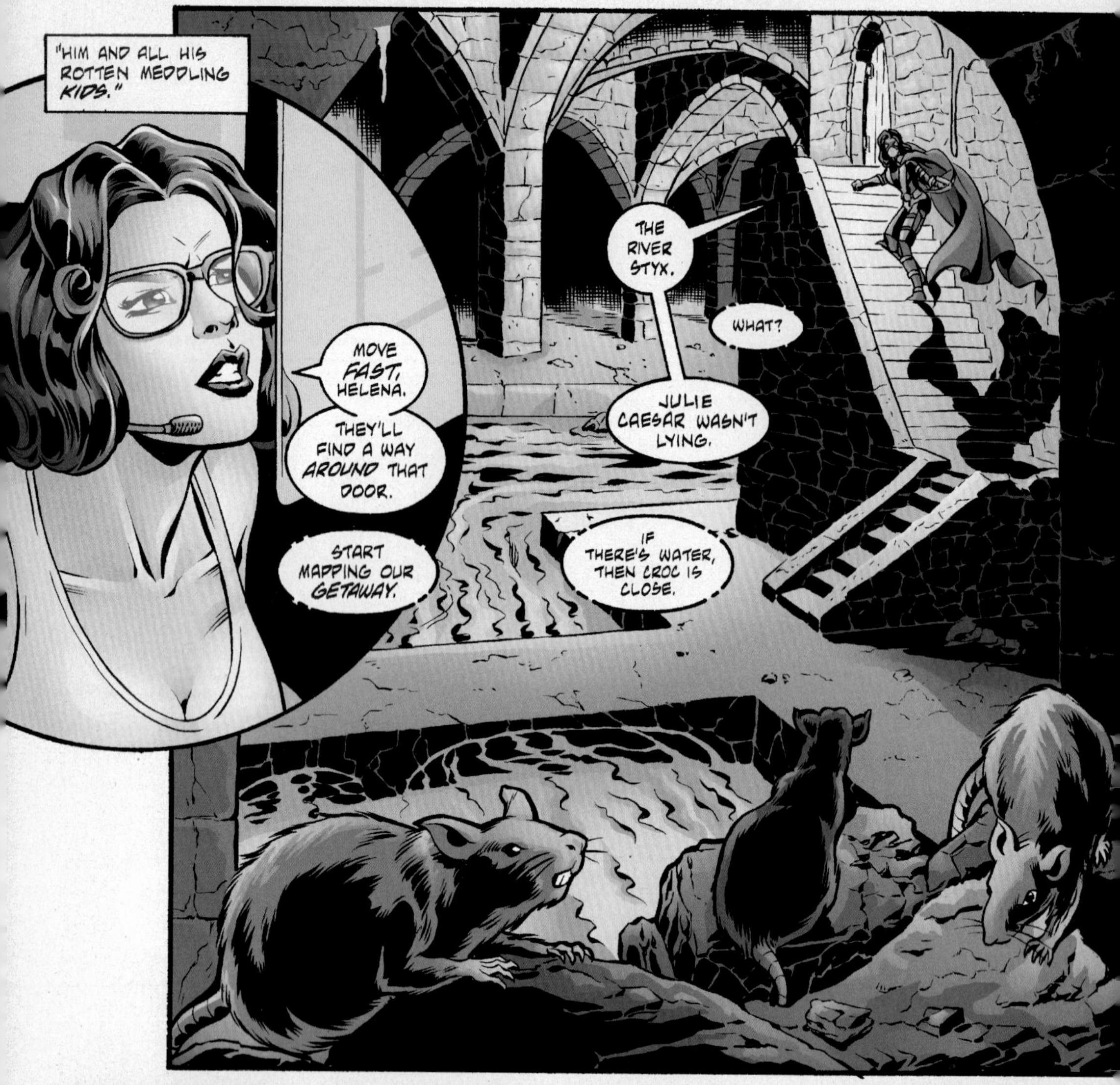
"HIM AND ALL HIS ROTTEN MEDDLING KIDS."
THE RIVER STYX.
WHAT?
JULIE CAESAR WASN'T LYING.
MOVE FAST, HELENA.
THEY'LL FIND A WAY AROUND THAT DOOR.
START MAPPING OUR GETAWAY.
IF THERE'S WATER, THEN CROC IS CLOSE.

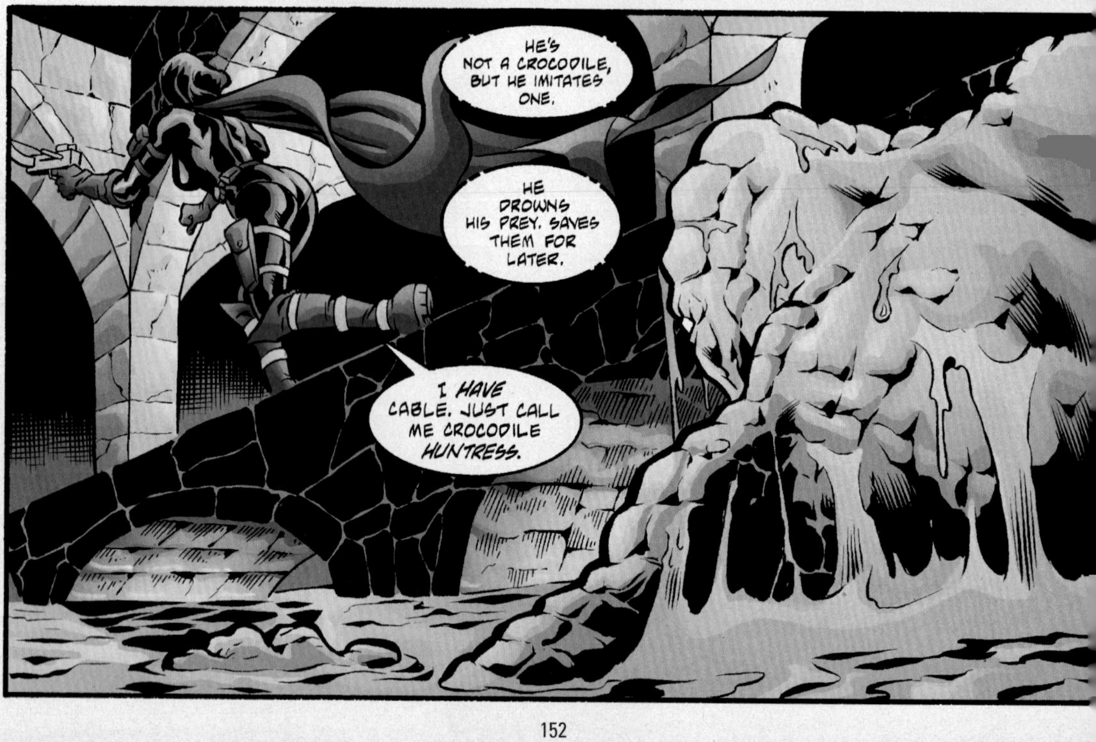
HE'S NOT A CROCODILE, BUT HE IMITATES ONE.
HE DROWNS HIS PREY. SAVES THEM FOR LATER.
I HAVE CABLE. JUST CALL ME CROCODILE HUNTRESS.

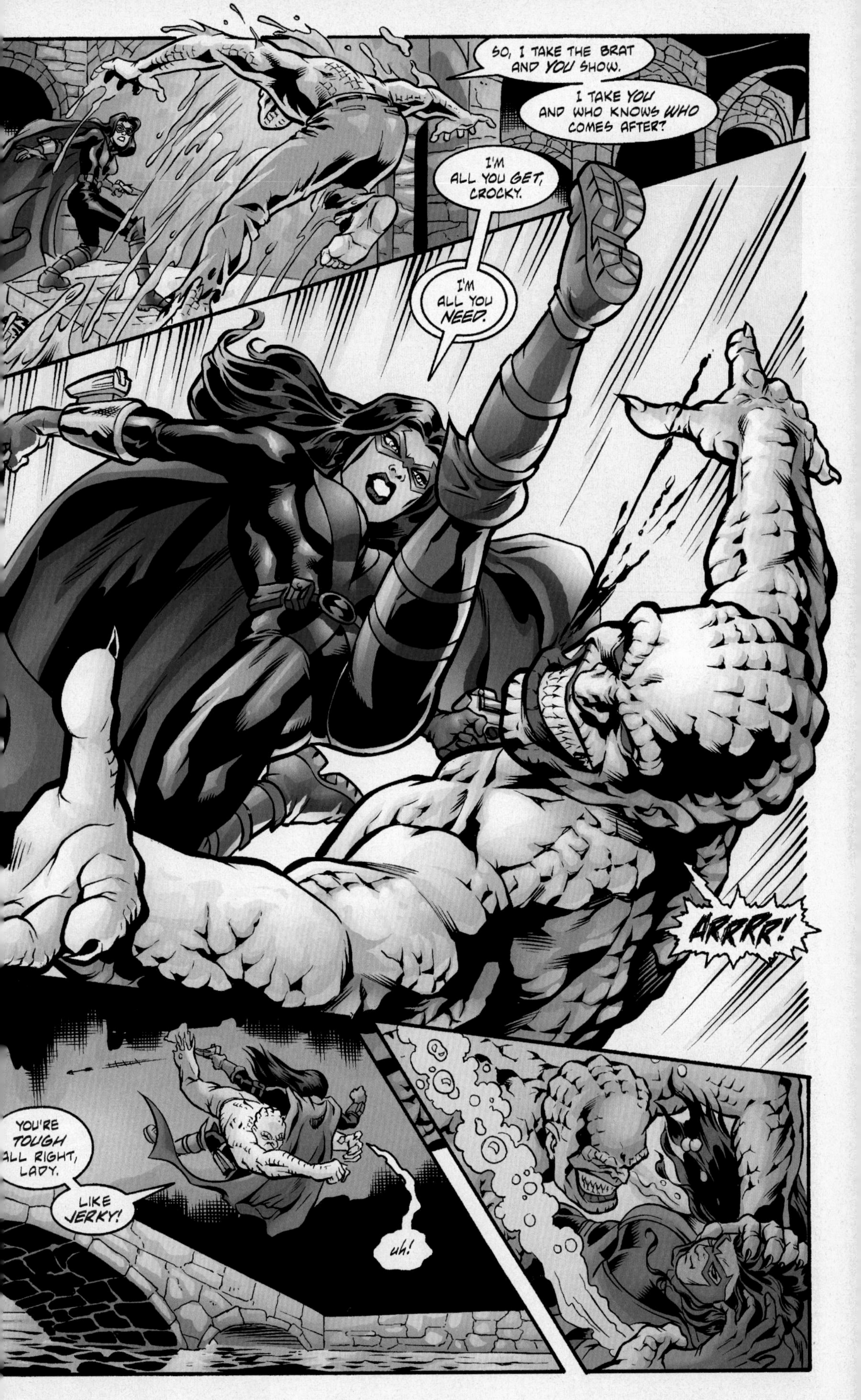
SO, I TAKE THE BRAT AND YOU SHOW.
I TAKE YOU AND WHO KNOWS WHO COMES AFTER?
I'M ALL YOU GET, CROCKY.
I'M ALL YOU NEED.
ARRRR!
YOU'RE TOUGH ALL RIGHT, LADY.
LIKE JERKY!
uh!

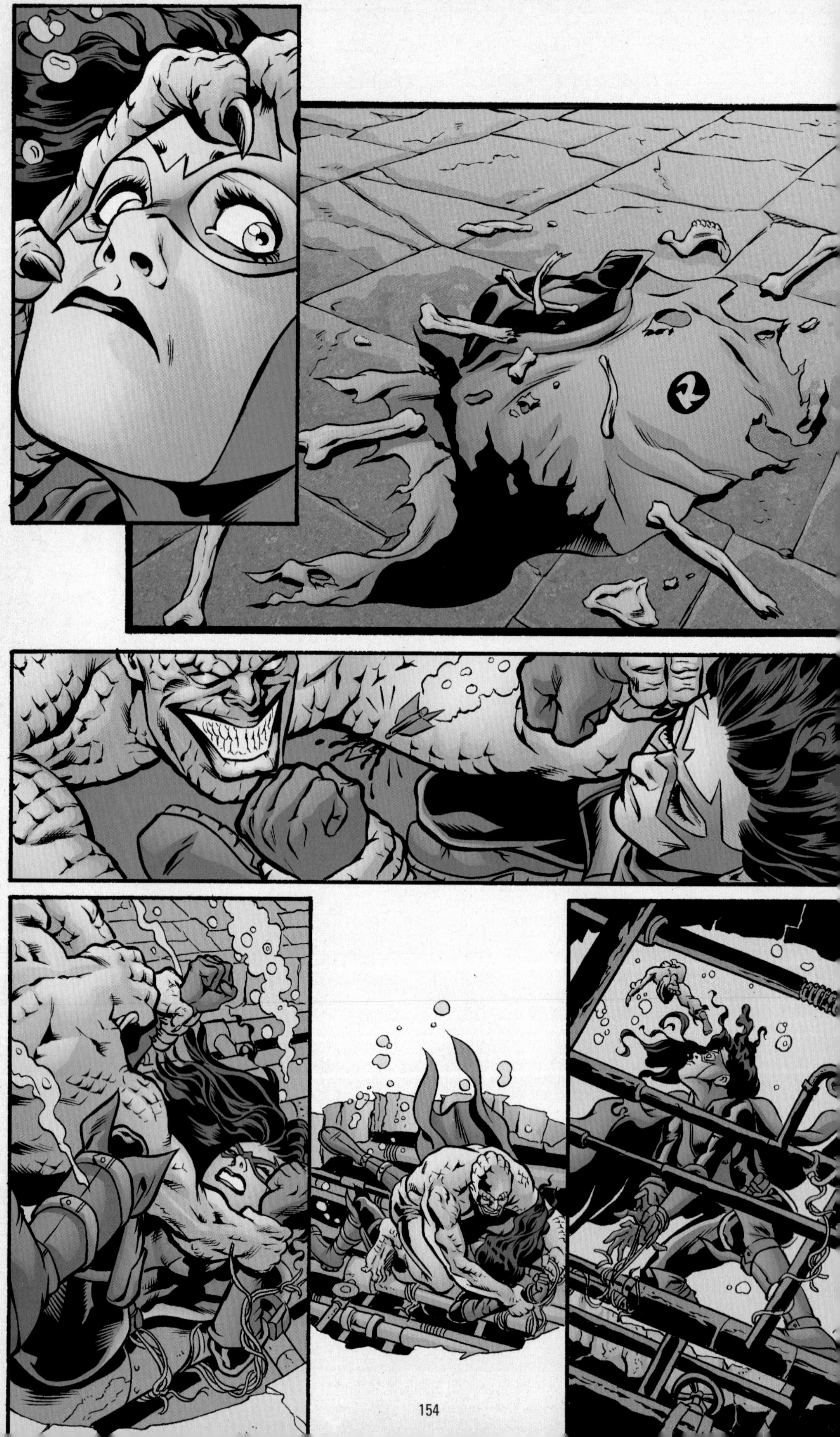

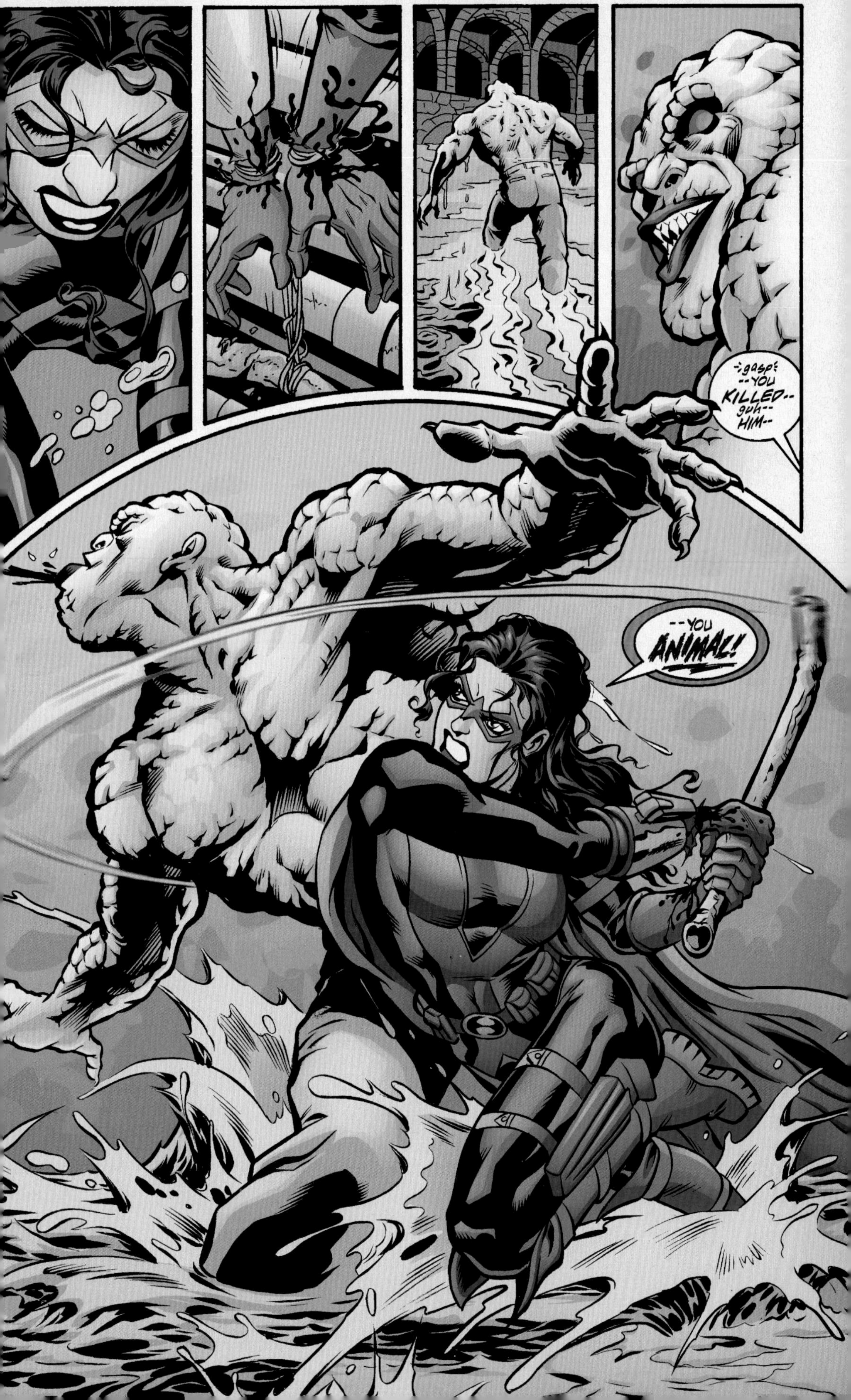

-:gasp:- --YOU KILLED-- guh-- HIM--
--YOU ANIMAL!

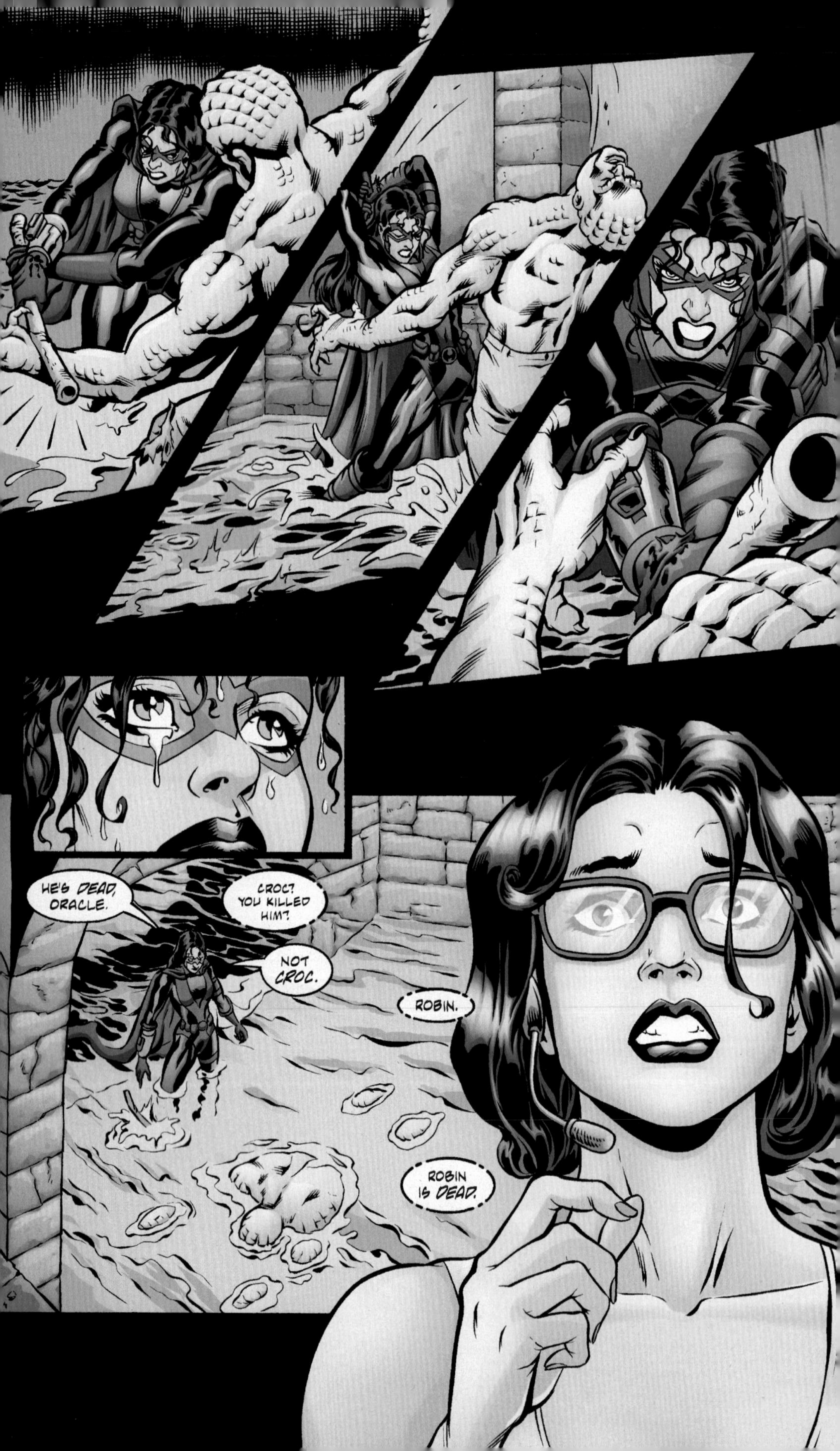
HE'S DEAD, ORACLE.
CROC? YOU KILLED HIM?
NOT CROC.
ROBIN.
ROBIN IS DEAD.

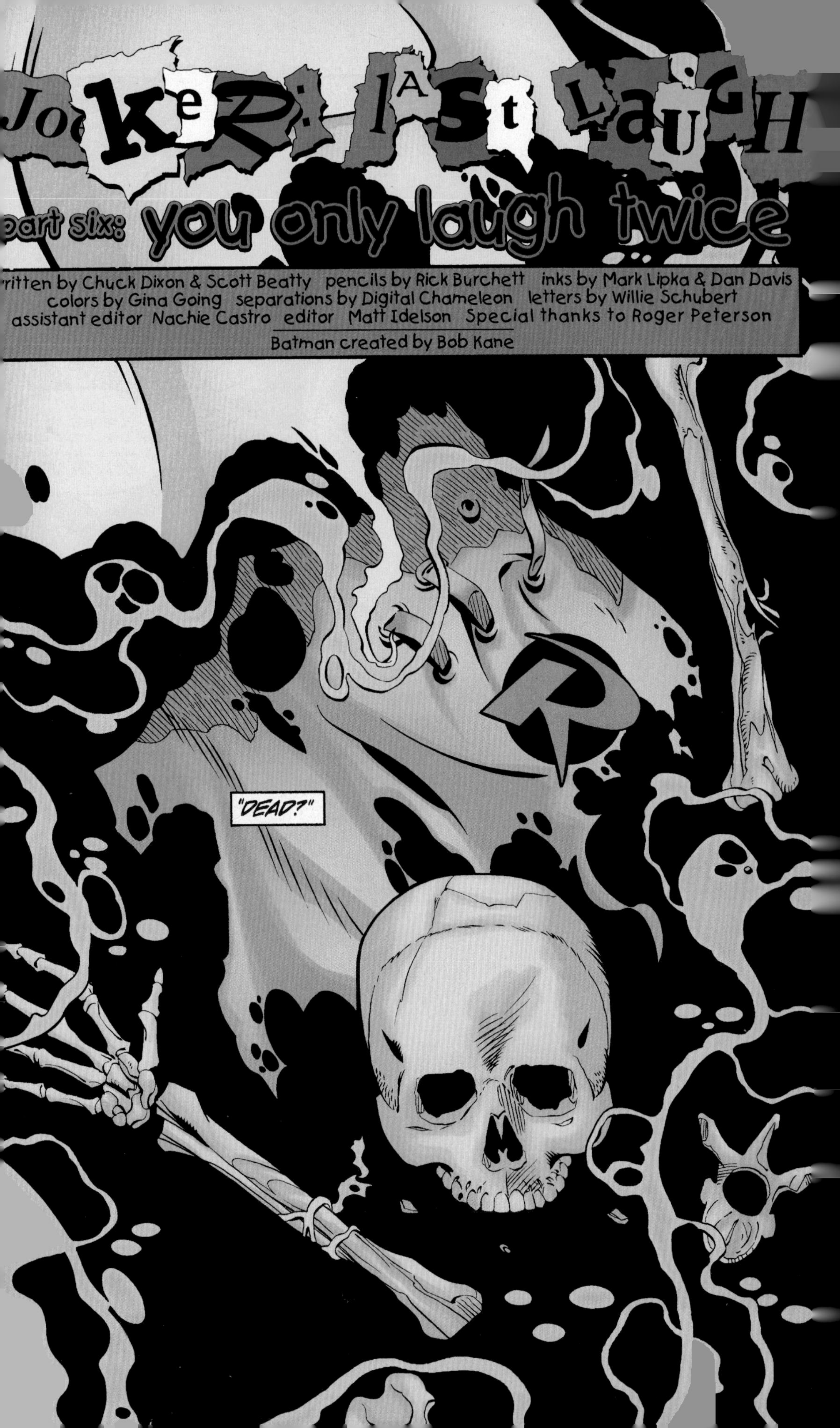

Joker: Last Laugh
part six: you only laugh twice
ritten by Chuck Dixon & Scott Beatty pencils by Rick Burchett inks by Mark Lipka & Dan Davis
colors by Gina Going separations by Digital Chameleon letters by Willie Schubert
assistant editor Nachie Castro editor Matt Idelson Special thanks to Roger Peterson
Batman created by Bob Kane
"DEAD?"

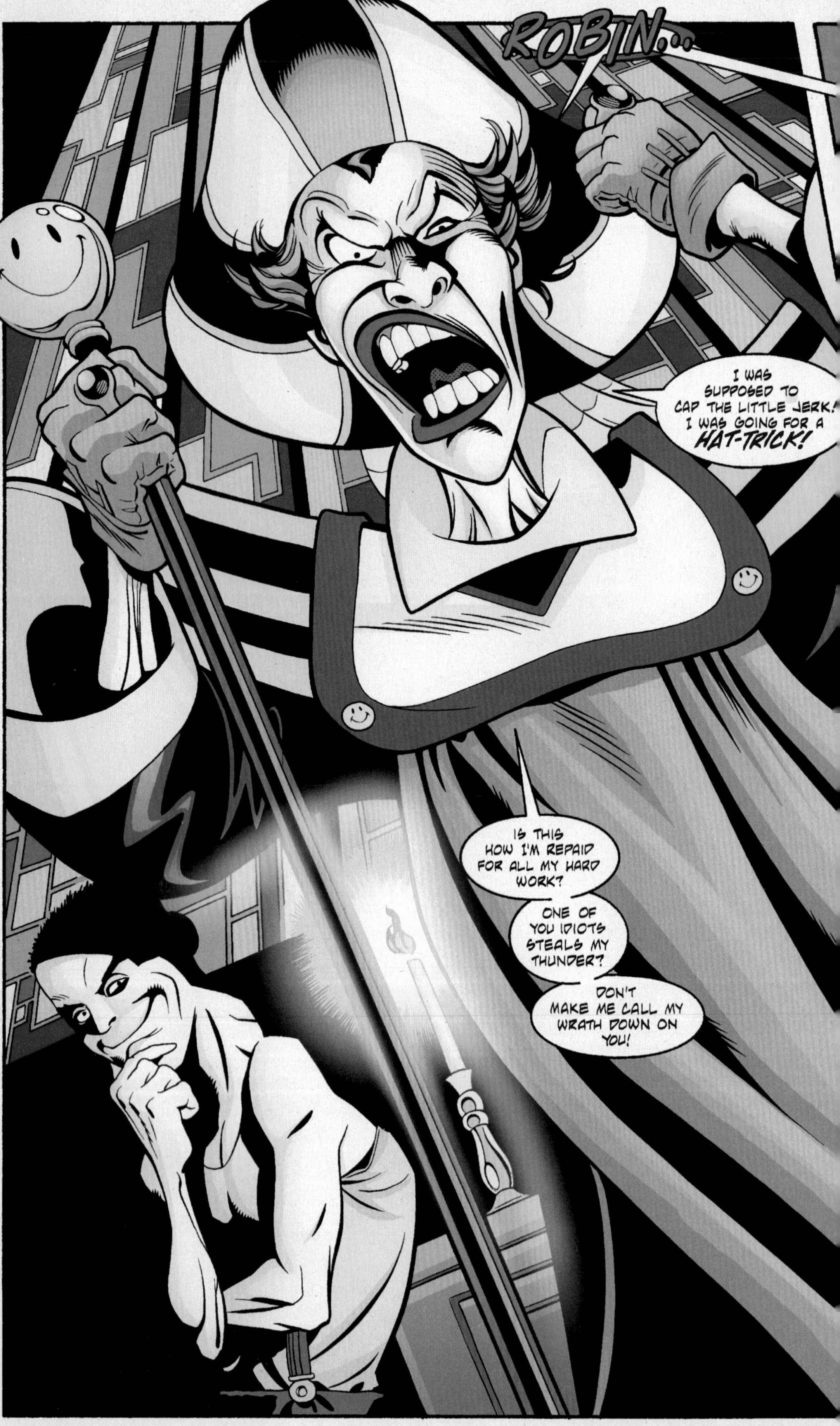
ROBIN...
I WAS SUPPOSED TO CAP THE LITTLE JERK! I WAS GOING FOR A HAT-TRICK!
IS THIS HOW I'M REPAID FOR ALL MY HARD WORK?
ONE OF YOU IDIOTS STEALS MY THUNDER?
DON'T MAKE ME CALL MY WRATH DOWN ON YOU!

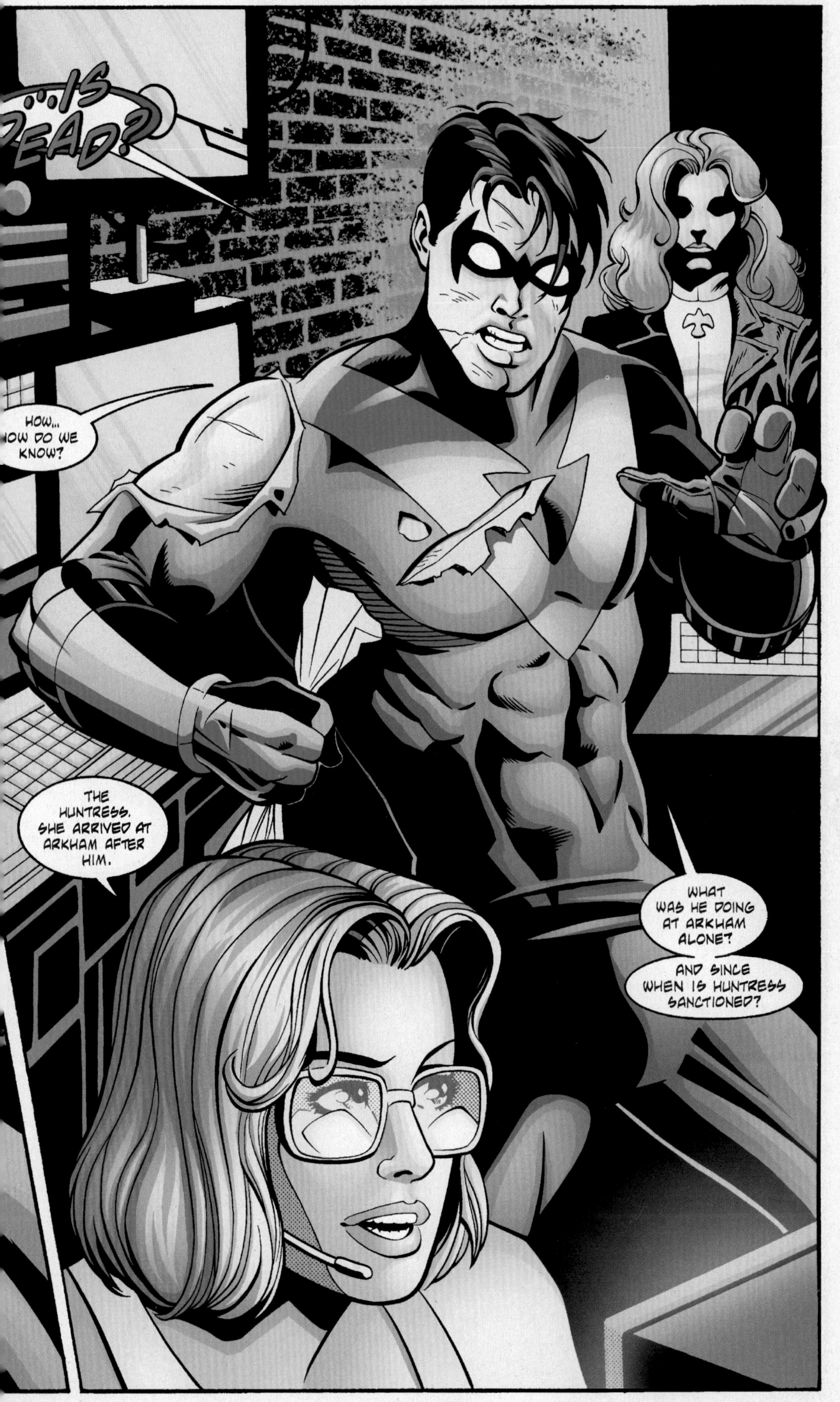
...IS ...DEAD?
HOW... HOW DO WE KNOW?
THE HUNTRESS. SHE ARRIVED AT ARKHAM AFTER HIM.
WHAT WAS HE DOING AT ARKHAM ALONE?
AND SINCE WHEN IS HUNTRESS SANCTIONED?

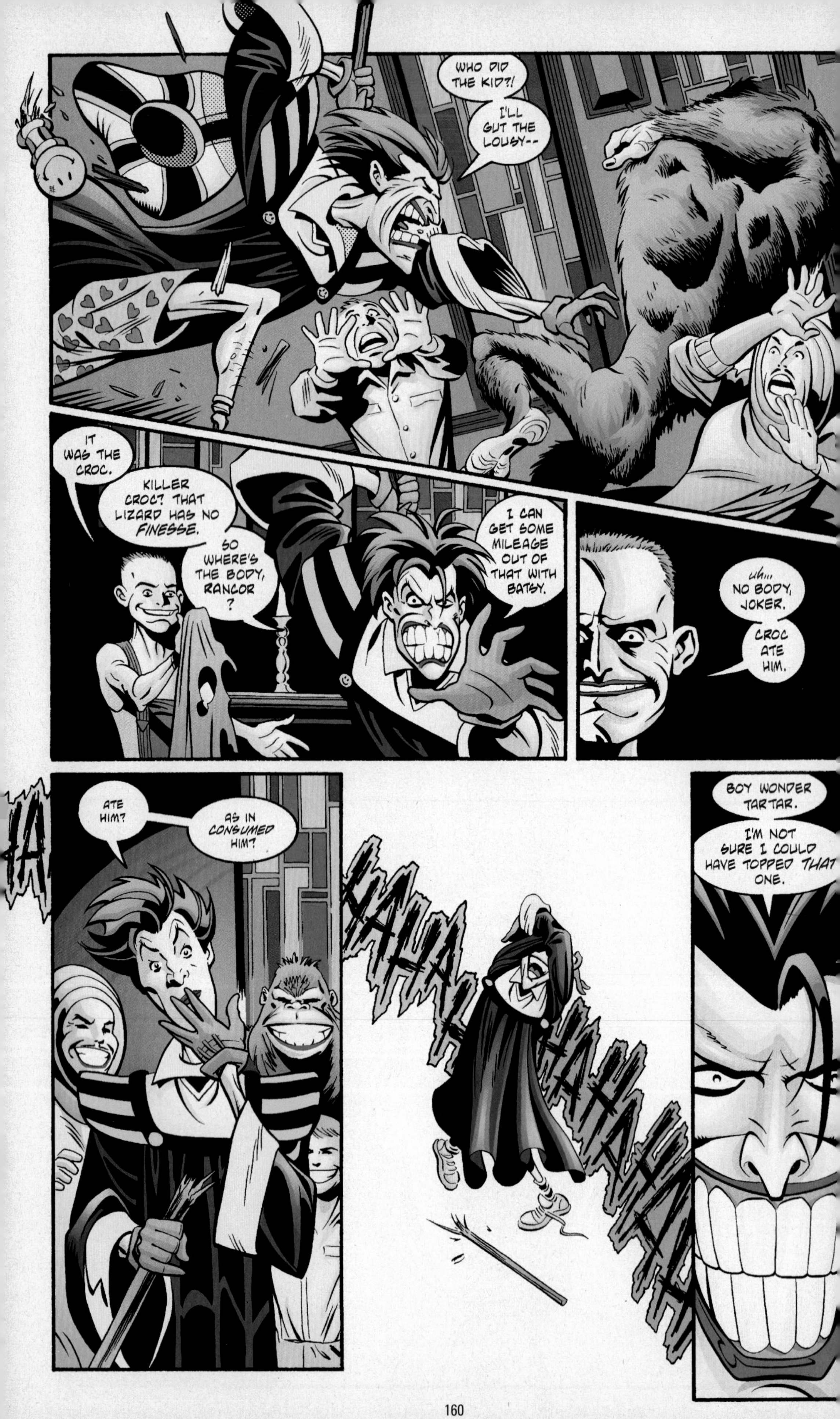
WHO DID THE KID?!
I'LL GUT THE LOUSY--
IT WAS THE CROC.
KILLER CROC? THAT LIZARD HAS NO FINESSE.
SO WHERE'S THE BODY, RANCOR?
I CAN GET SOME MILEAGE OUT OF THAT WITH BATSY.
uh... NO BODY, JOKER.
CROC ATE HIM.
ATE HIM?
AS IN CONSUMED HIM?
HAHAHAHAHAHAHAHAHAHAHAHA
BOY WONDER TARTAR.
I'M NOT SURE I COULD HAVE TOPPED THAT ONE.

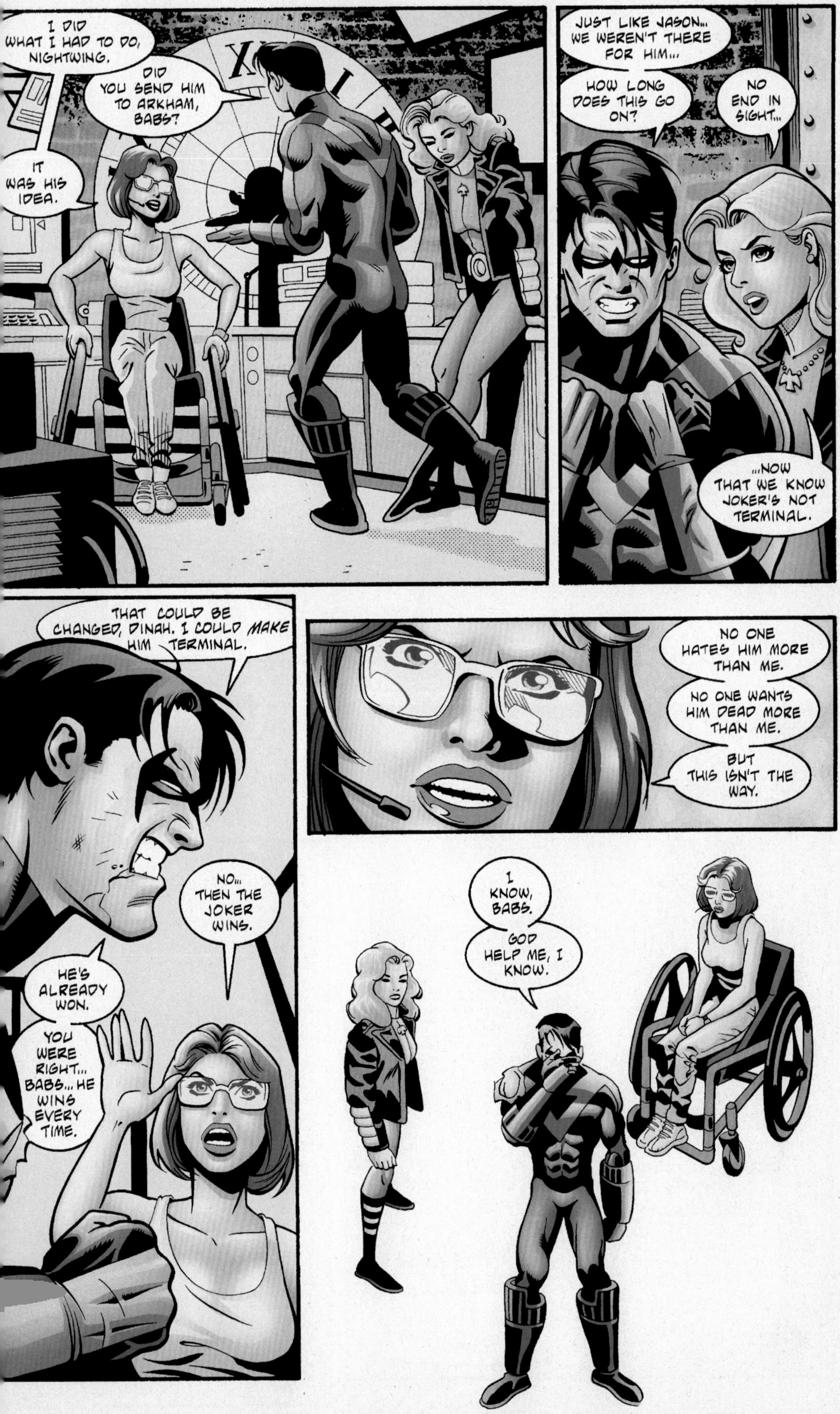
I DID WHAT I HAD TO DO, NIGHTWING.
DID YOU SEND HIM TO ARKHAM, BABS?
IT WAS HIS IDEA.
JUST LIKE JASON... WE WEREN'T THERE FOR HIM...
HOW LONG DOES THIS GO ON?
NO END IN SIGHT...
...NOW THAT WE KNOW JOKER'S NOT TERMINAL.
THAT COULD BE CHANGED, DINAH. I COULD MAKE HIM TERMINAL.
NO ONE HATES HIM MORE THAN ME.
NO ONE WANTS HIM DEAD MORE THAN ME.
BUT THIS ISN'T THE WAY.
NO... THEN THE JOKER WINS.
HE'S ALREADY WON.
YOU WERE RIGHT... BABS... HE WINS EVERY TIME.
I KNOW, BABS.
GOD HELP ME, I KNOW.

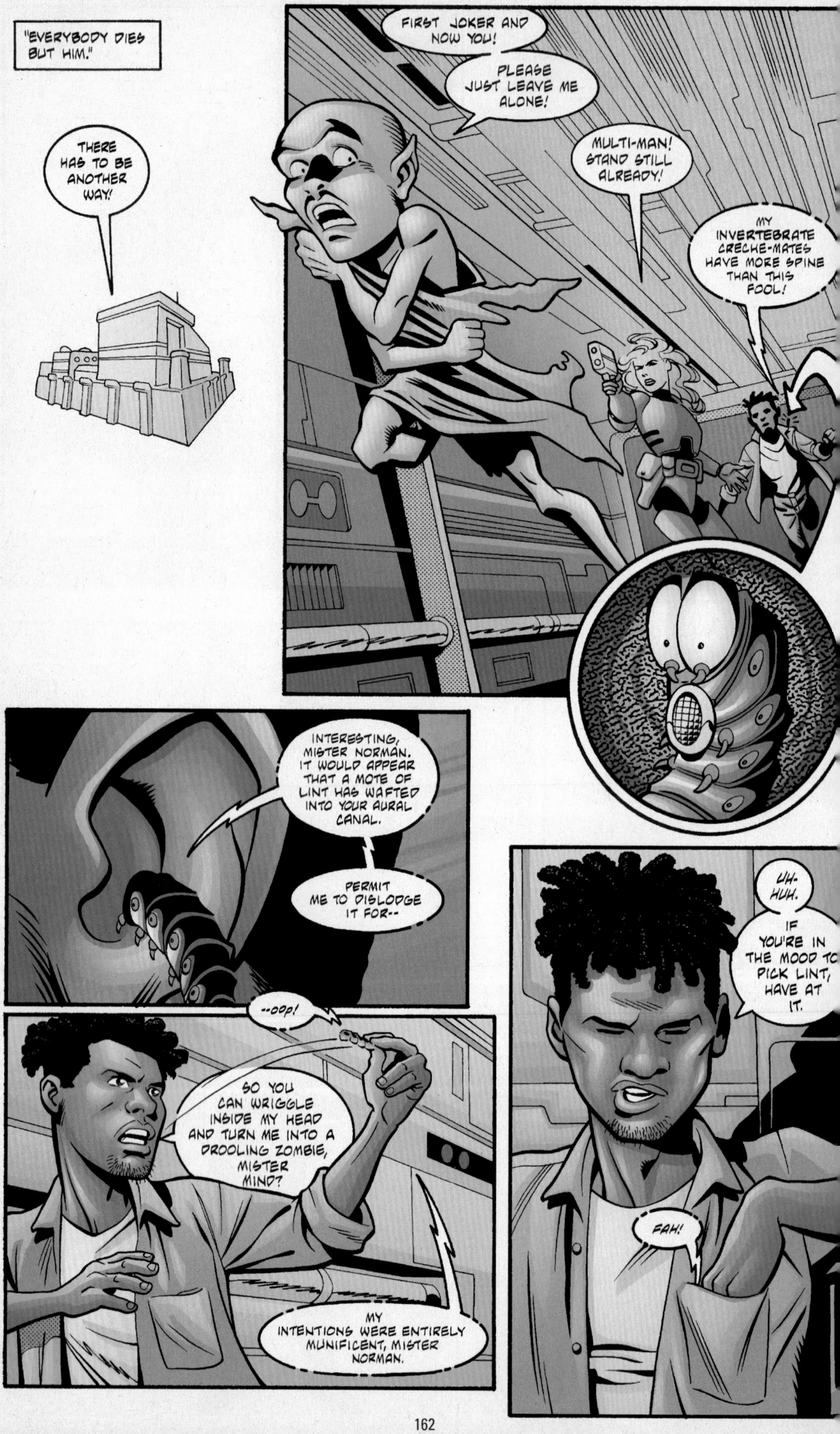
"EVERYBODY DIES BUT HIM."
THERE HAS TO BE ANOTHER WAY!
FIRST JOKER AND NOW YOU!
PLEASE JUST LEAVE ME ALONE!
MULTI-MAN! STAND STILL ALREADY!
MY INVERTEBRATE CRECHE-MATES HAVE MORE SPINE THAN THIS FOOL!
INTERESTING, MISTER NORMAN. IT WOULD APPEAR THAT A MOTE OF LINT HAS WAFTED INTO YOUR AURAL CANAL.
PERMIT ME TO DISLODGE IT FOR--
UH-HUH.
IF YOU'RE IN THE MOOD TO PICK LINT, HAVE AT IT.
--OOP!
SO YOU CAN WRIGGLE INSIDE MY HEAD AND TURN ME INTO A DROOLING ZOMBIE, MISTER MIND?
MY INTENTIONS WERE ENTIRELY MUNIFICENT, MISTER NORMAN.
FAH!

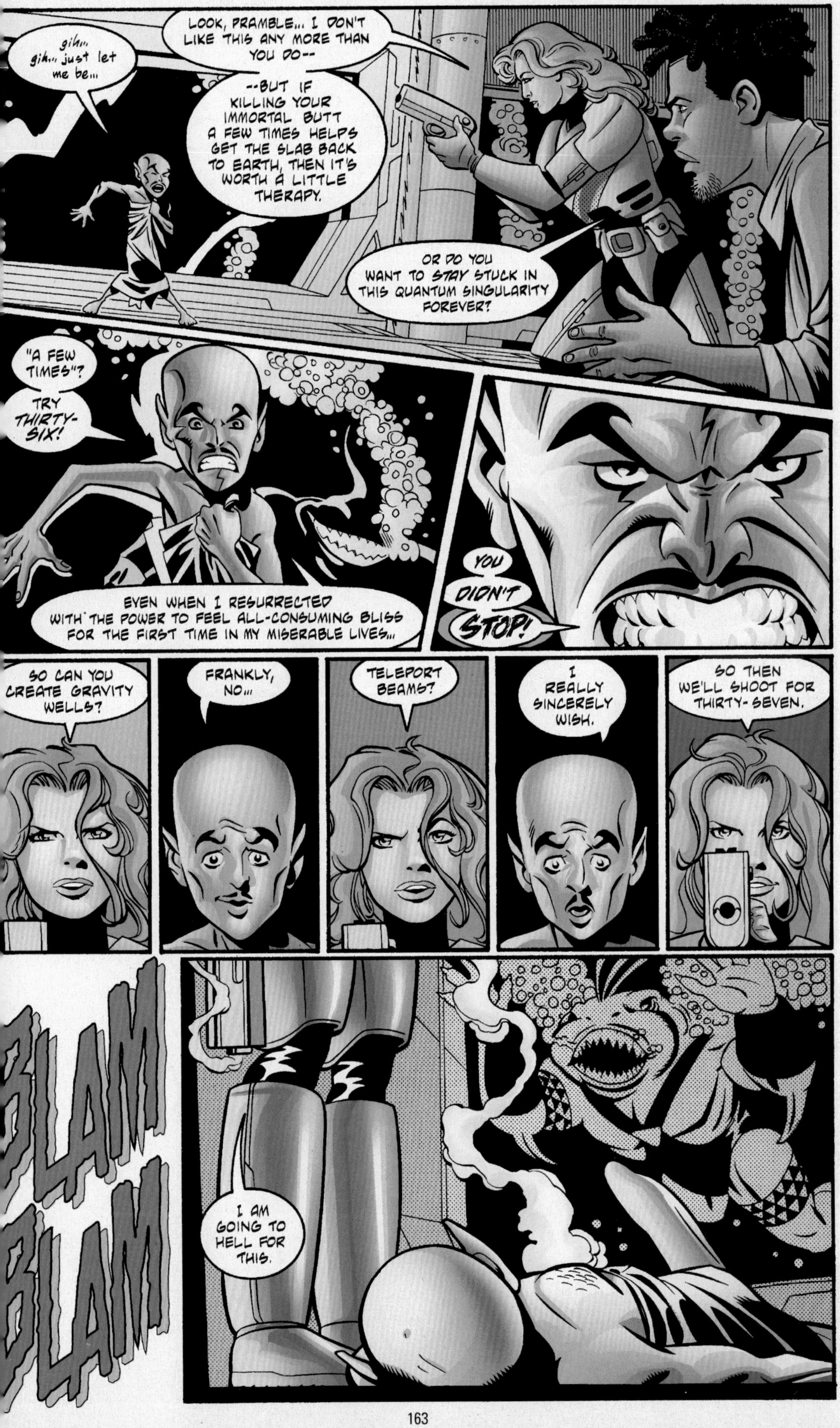
gih... gih... just let me be...
LOOK, PRAMBLE... I DON'T LIKE THIS ANY MORE THAN YOU DO--
--BUT IF KILLING YOUR IMMORTAL BUTT A FEW TIMES HELPS GET THE SLAB BACK TO EARTH, THEN IT'S WORTH A LITTLE THERAPY.
OR DO YOU WANT TO STAY STUCK IN THIS QUANTUM SINGULARITY FOREVER?
"A FEW TIMES"?
TRY THIRTY-SIX!
EVEN WHEN I RESURRECTED WITH THE POWER TO FEEL ALL-CONSUMING BLISS FOR THE FIRST TIME IN MY MISERABLE LIVES...
YOU
DIDN'T
STOP!
SO CAN YOU CREATE GRAVITY WELLS?
FRANKLY, NO...
TELEPORT BEAMS?
I REALLY SINCERELY WISH.
SO THEN WE'LL SHOOT FOR THIRTY-SEVEN.
BLAM
BLAM
I AM GOING TO HELL FOR THIS.

"IF WE'RE NOT THERE ALREADY."

NIGHTWING'S GONE, BARBARA.

DEET-DEET-DEET-DEET!

Gotham Cathedral

I TRIED TO STOP HIM...

...BUT HE SUCKER-PUNCHED ME AND TOOK MY BIKE.

HE DID APOLOGIZE THOUGH... STALWART TO A FAULT, YOUR GUY.

DEET-DEET-DEET-DEET

CANARY.

TELL ORACLE THAT ARKHAM IS SECURE.*

BATMAN...

I'M SO SORRY.

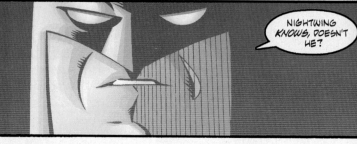

NIGHTWING KNOWS, DOESN'T HE?

JUST LIKE YOU SAID, J-MAN...

BEEP!

*SEE ROBIN #95.

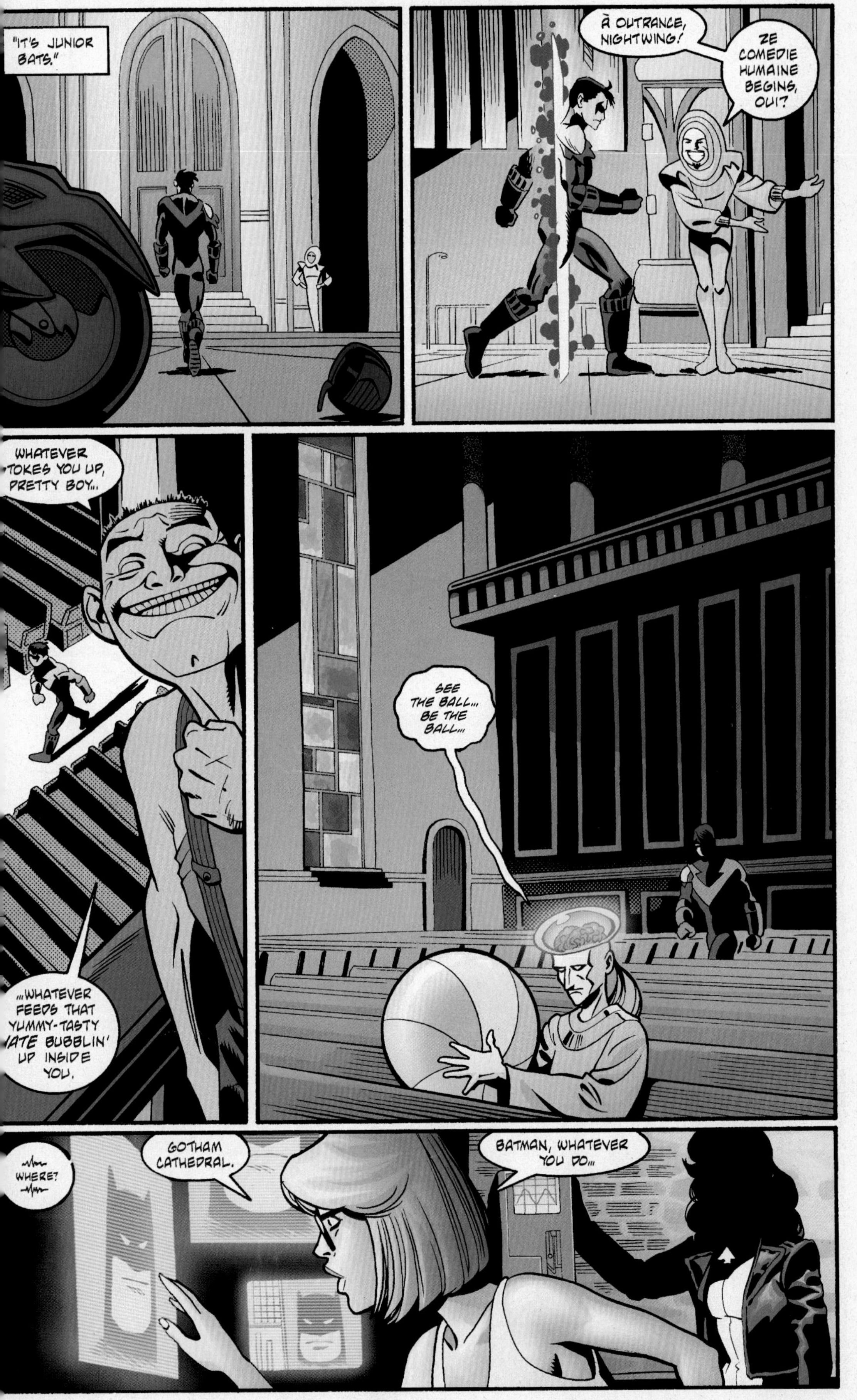
"IT'S JUNIOR BATS."
À OUTRANCE, NIGHTWING!
ZE COMEDIE HUMAINE BEGINS, OUI?
WHATEVER TOKES YOU UP, PRETTY BOY...
...WHATEVER FEEDS THAT YUMMY-TASTY HATE BUBBLIN' UP INSIDE YOU.
SEE THE BALL... BE THE BALL...
WHERE?
GOTHAM CATHEDRAL.
BATMAN, WHATEVER YOU DO...

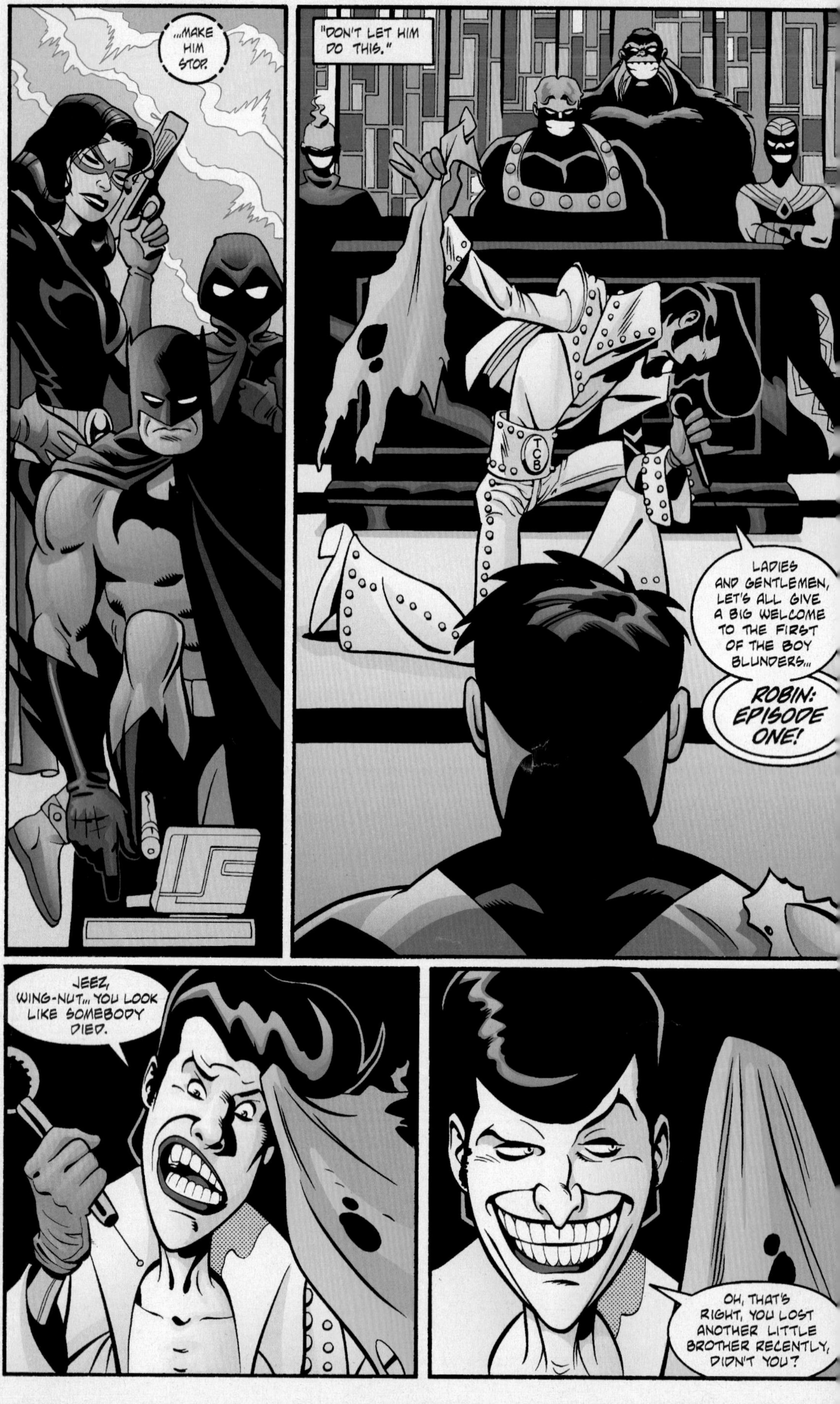
...MAKE HIM STOP.
"DON'T LET HIM DO THIS."
LADIES AND GENTLEMEN, LET'S ALL GIVE A BIG WELCOME TO THE FIRST OF THE BOY BLUNDERS...
ROBIN: EPISODE ONE!
JEEZ, WING-NUT... YOU LOOK LIKE SOMEBODY DIED.
OH, THAT'S RIGHT, YOU LOST ANOTHER LITTLE BROTHER RECENTLY, DIDN'T YOU?

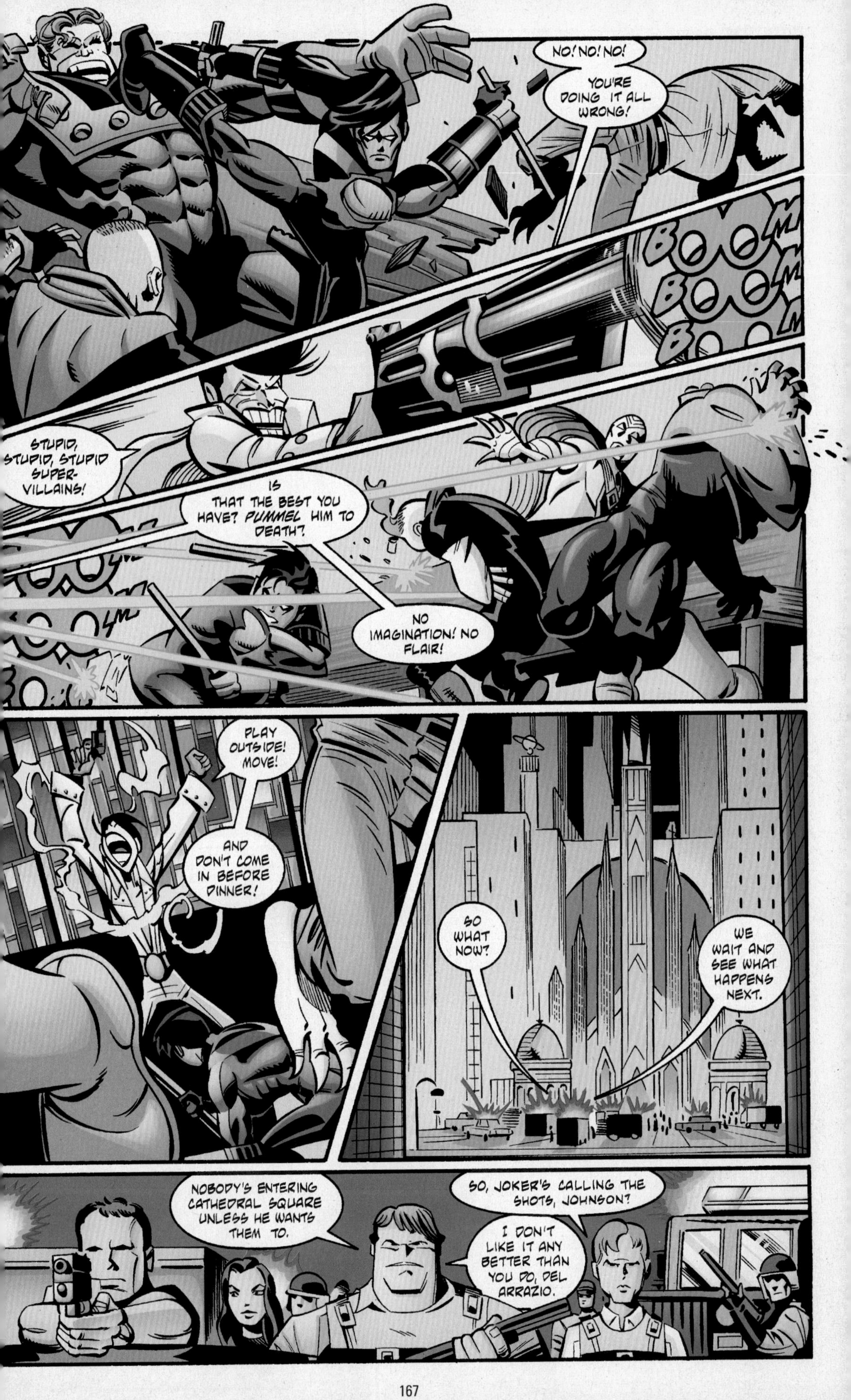
NO! NO! NO!
YOU'RE DOING IT ALL WRONG!
BOOOM BOOOM BOOOM
STUPID, STUPID, STUPID SUPER-VILLAINS!
IS THAT THE BEST YOU HAVE? PUMMEL HIM TO DEATH?
NO IMAGINATION! NO FLAIR!
PLAY OUTSIDE! MOVE!
AND DON'T COME IN BEFORE DINNER!
SO WHAT NOW?
WE WAIT AND SEE WHAT HAPPENS NEXT.
NOBODY'S ENTERING CATHEDRAL SQUARE UNLESS HE WANTS THEM TO.
SO, JOKER'S CALLING THE SHOTS, JOHNSON?
I DON'T LIKE IT ANY BETTER THAN YOU DO, DEL ARRAZIO.

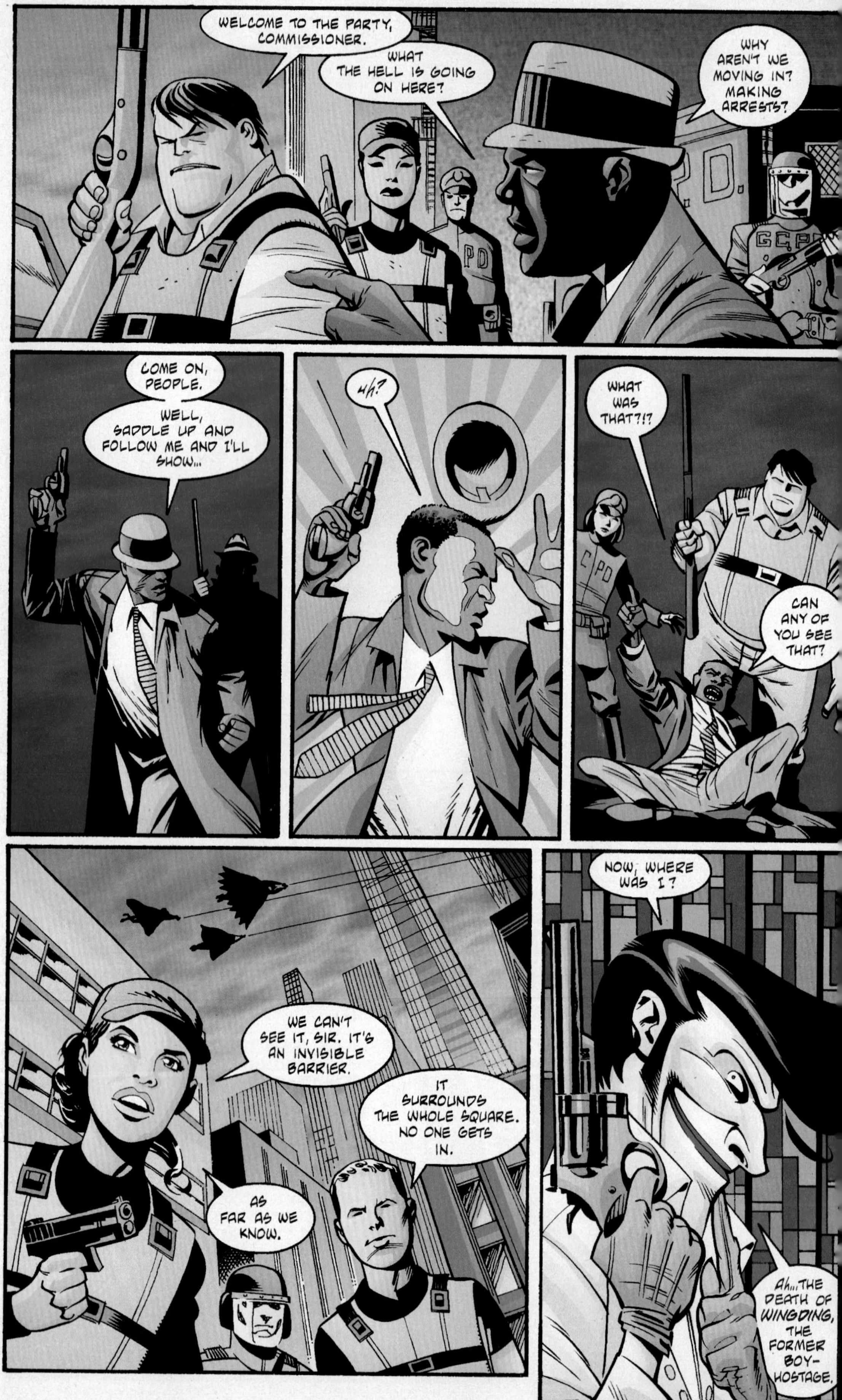
WELCOME TO THE PARTY, COMMISSIONER.
WHAT THE HELL IS GOING ON HERE?
WHY AREN'T WE MOVING IN? MAKING ARRESTS?
COME ON, PEOPLE.
WELL, SADDLE UP AND FOLLOW ME AND I'LL SHOW...
UH?
WHAT WAS THAT?!?
CAN ANY OF YOU SEE THAT?
WE CAN'T SEE IT, SIR. IT'S AN INVISIBLE BARRIER.
IT SURROUNDS THE WHOLE SQUARE. NO ONE GETS IN.
AS FAR AS WE KNOW.
NOW, WHERE WAS I?
AH...THE DEATH OF WINGDING, THE FORMER BOY-HOSTAGE.

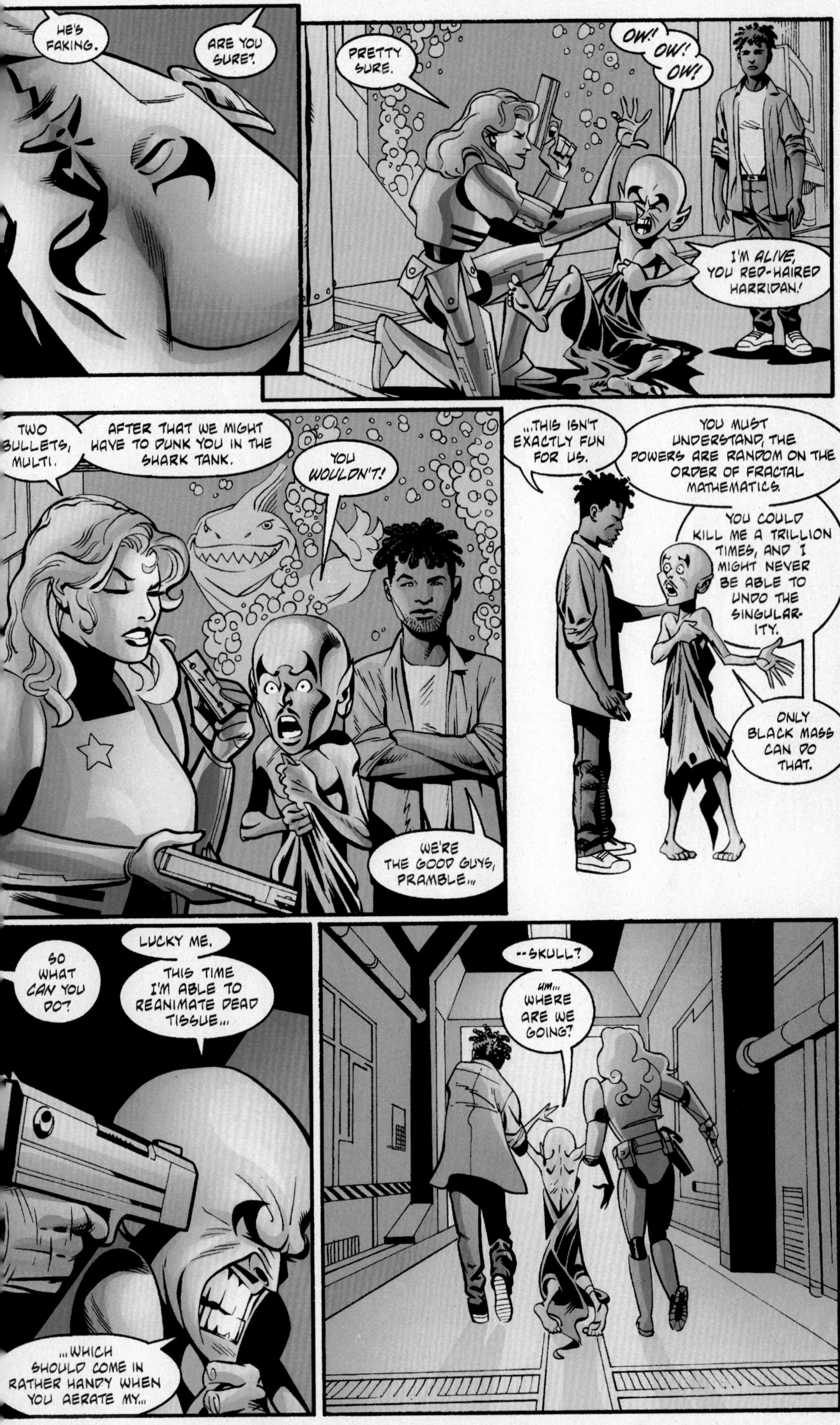
HE'S FAKING.
ARE YOU SURE?
PRETTY SURE.
OW! OW! OW!
I'M ALIVE, YOU RED-HAIRED HARRIDAN!
TWO BULLETS, MULTI.
AFTER THAT WE MIGHT HAVE TO DUNK YOU IN THE SHARK TANK.
YOU WOULDN'T!
WE'RE THE GOOD GUYS, PRAMBLE...
...THIS ISN'T EXACTLY FUN FOR US.
YOU MUST UNDERSTAND, THE POWERS ARE RANDOM ON THE ORDER OF FRACTAL MATHEMATICS.
YOU COULD KILL ME A TRILLION TIMES, AND I MIGHT NEVER BE ABLE TO UNDO THE SINGULAR-ITY.
ONLY BLACK MASS CAN DO THAT.
SO WHAT CAN YOU DO?
LUCKY ME.
THIS TIME I'M ABLE TO REANIMATE DEAD TISSUE...
...WHICH SHOULD COME IN RATHER HANDY WHEN YOU AERATE MY...
--SKULL?
UM... WHERE ARE WE GOING?

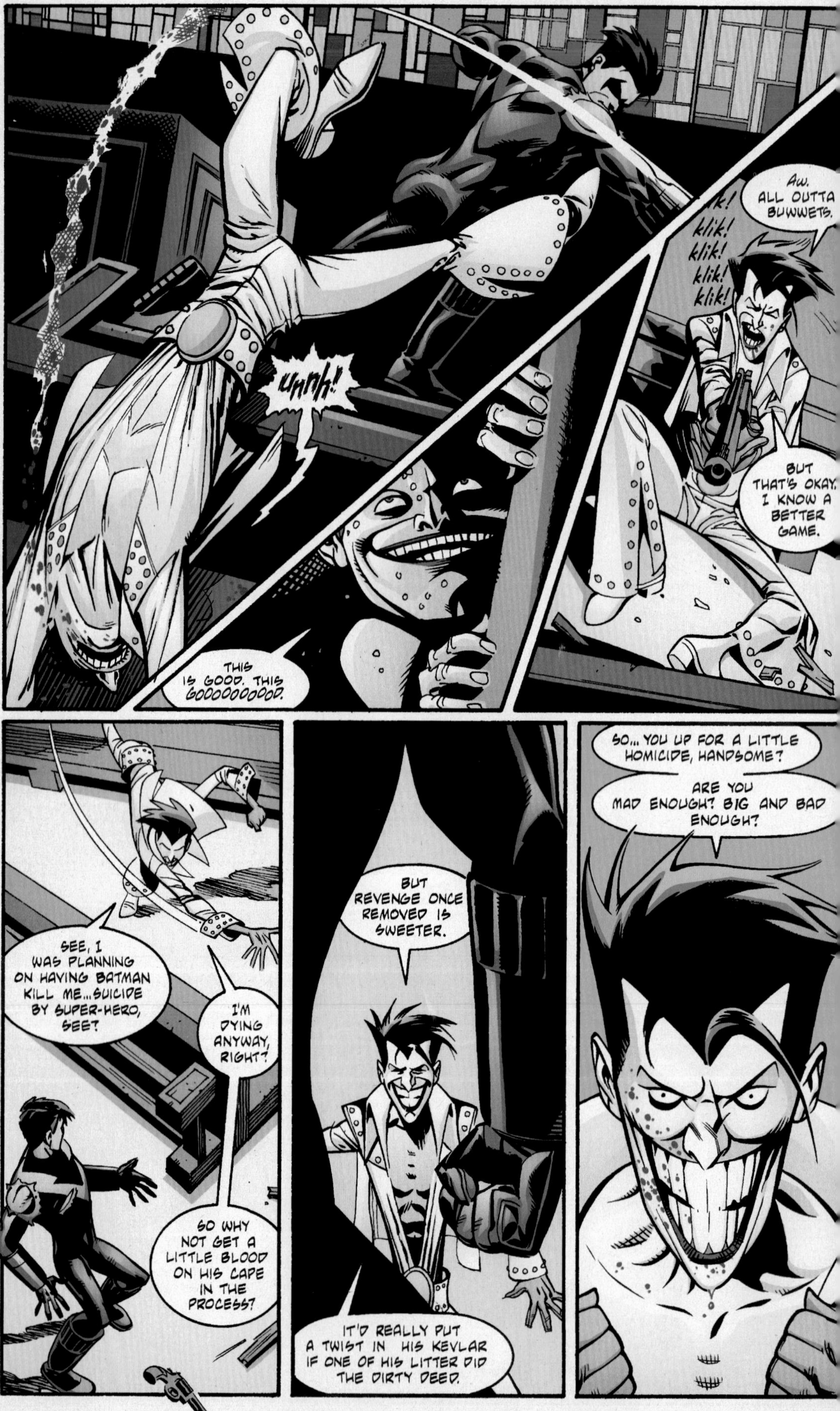
unnh!
...k! klik! klik! klik! klik!
Aw. ALL OUTTA BUWWETS.
BUT THAT'S OKAY. I KNOW A BETTER GAME.
THIS IS GOOD. THIS GOOOOOOOOOD.
SEE, I WAS PLANNING ON HAVING BATMAN KILL ME...SUICIDE BY SUPER-HERO, SEE?
I'M DYING ANYWAY, RIGHT?
SO WHY NOT GET A LITTLE BLOOD ON HIS CAPE IN THE PROCESS?
BUT REVENGE ONCE REMOVED IS SWEETER.
IT'D REALLY PUT A TWIST IN HIS KEVLAR IF ONE OF HIS LITTER DID THE DIRTY DEED.
SO... YOU UP FOR A LITTLE HOMICIDE, HANDSOME?
ARE YOU MAD ENOUGH? BIG AND BAD ENOUGH?

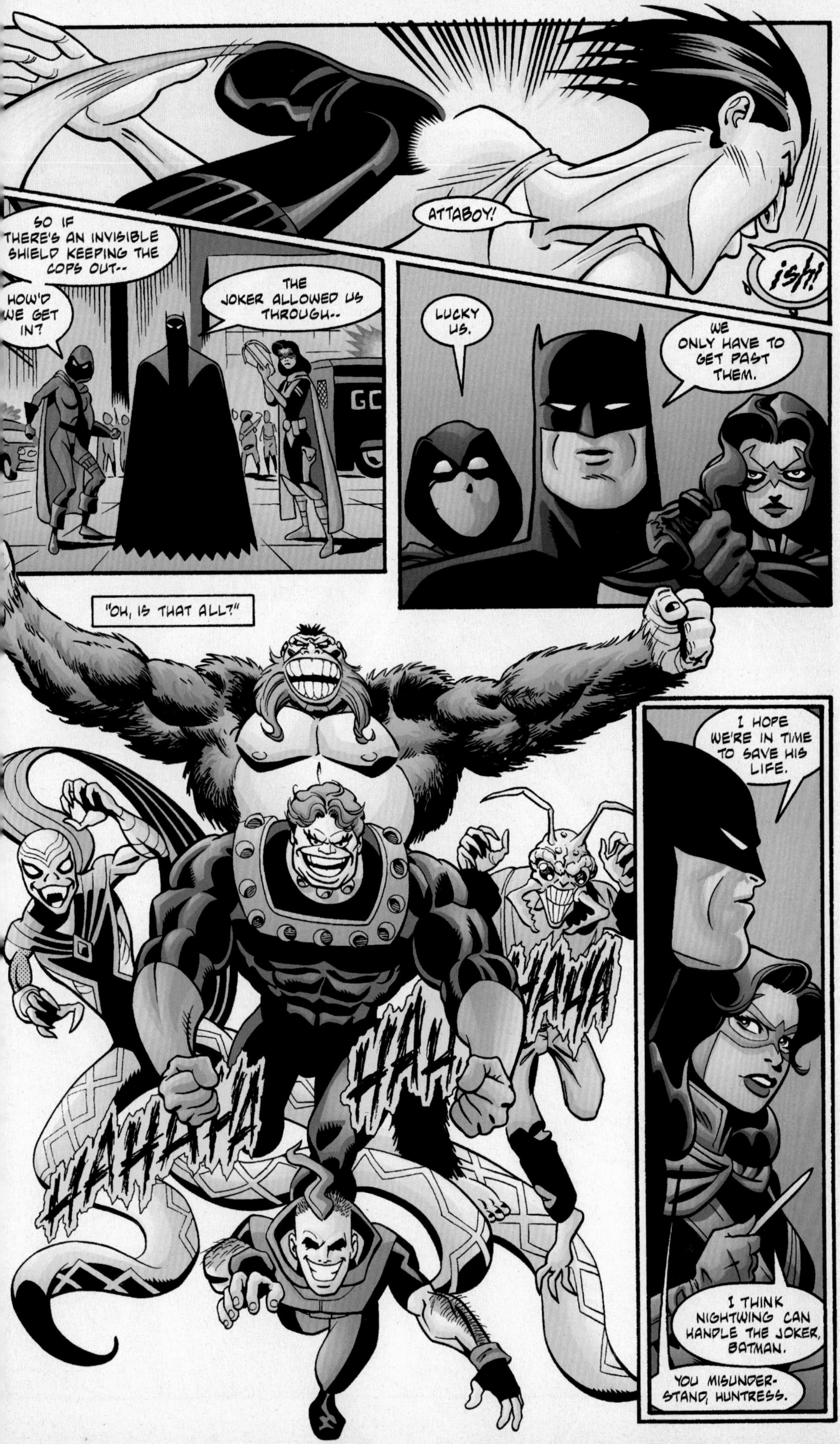

ATTABOY!
iSH!
SO IF THERE'S AN INVISIBLE SHIELD KEEPING THE COPS OUT--
HOW'D WE GET IN?
THE JOKER ALLOWED US THROUGH--
LUCKY US.
WE ONLY HAVE TO GET PAST THEM.
"OH, IS THAT ALL?"
I HOPE WE'RE IN TIME TO SAVE HIS LIFE.
HAHAHA HAH HAHA
I THINK NIGHTWING CAN HANDLE THE JOKER, BATMAN.
YOU MISUNDER-STAND, HUNTRESS.

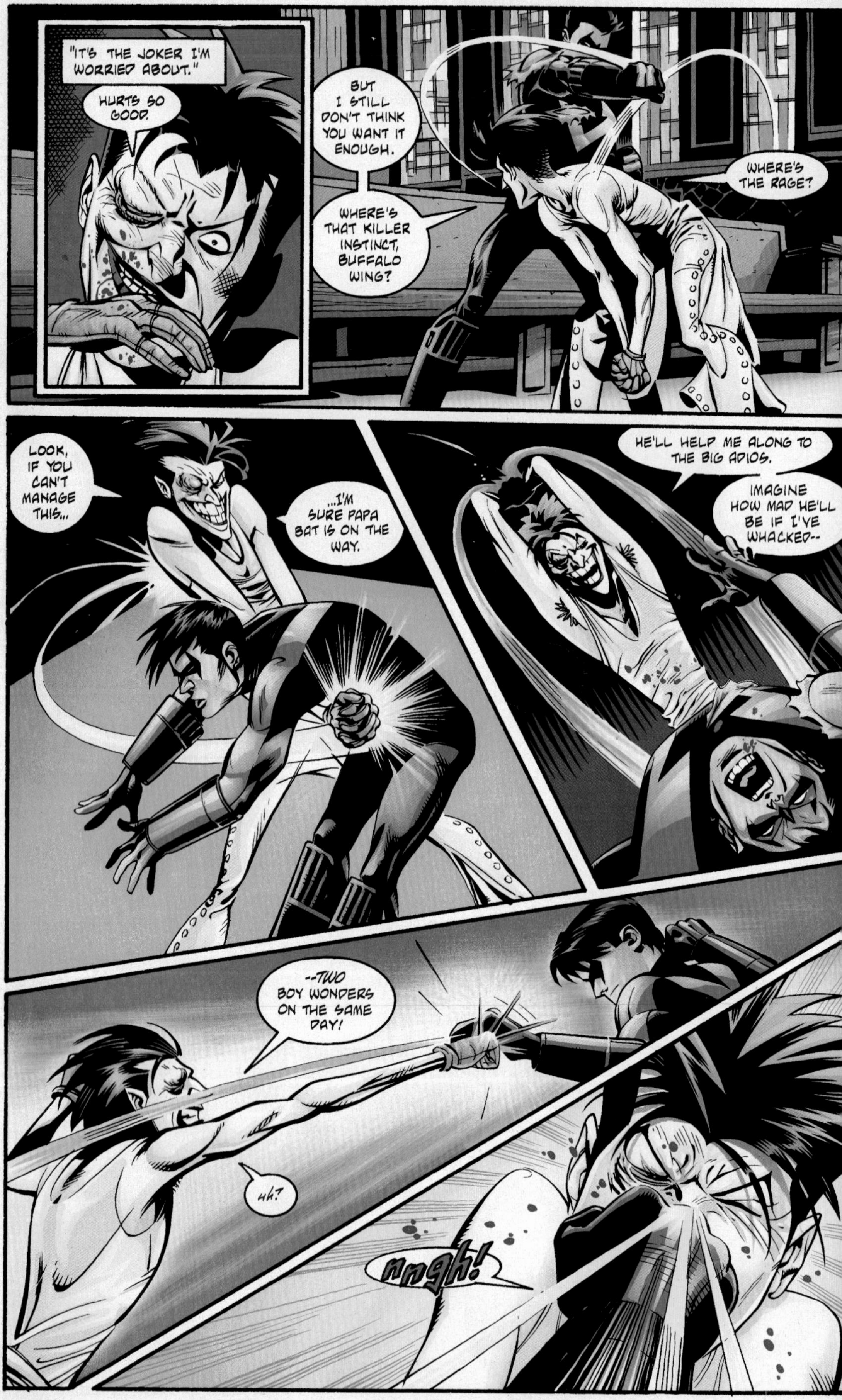
"IT'S THE JOKER I'M WORRIED ABOUT."
HURTS SO GOOD.
BUT I STILL DON'T THINK YOU WANT IT ENOUGH.
WHERE'S THAT KILLER INSTINCT, BUFFALO WING?
WHERE'S THE RAGE?
LOOK, IF YOU CAN'T MANAGE THIS...
...I'M SURE PAPA BAT IS ON THE WAY.
HE'LL HELP ME ALONG TO THE BIG ADIOS.
IMAGINE HOW MAD HE'LL BE IF I'VE WHACKED--
--TWO BOY WONDERS ON THE SAME DAY!
uh?
nngh!

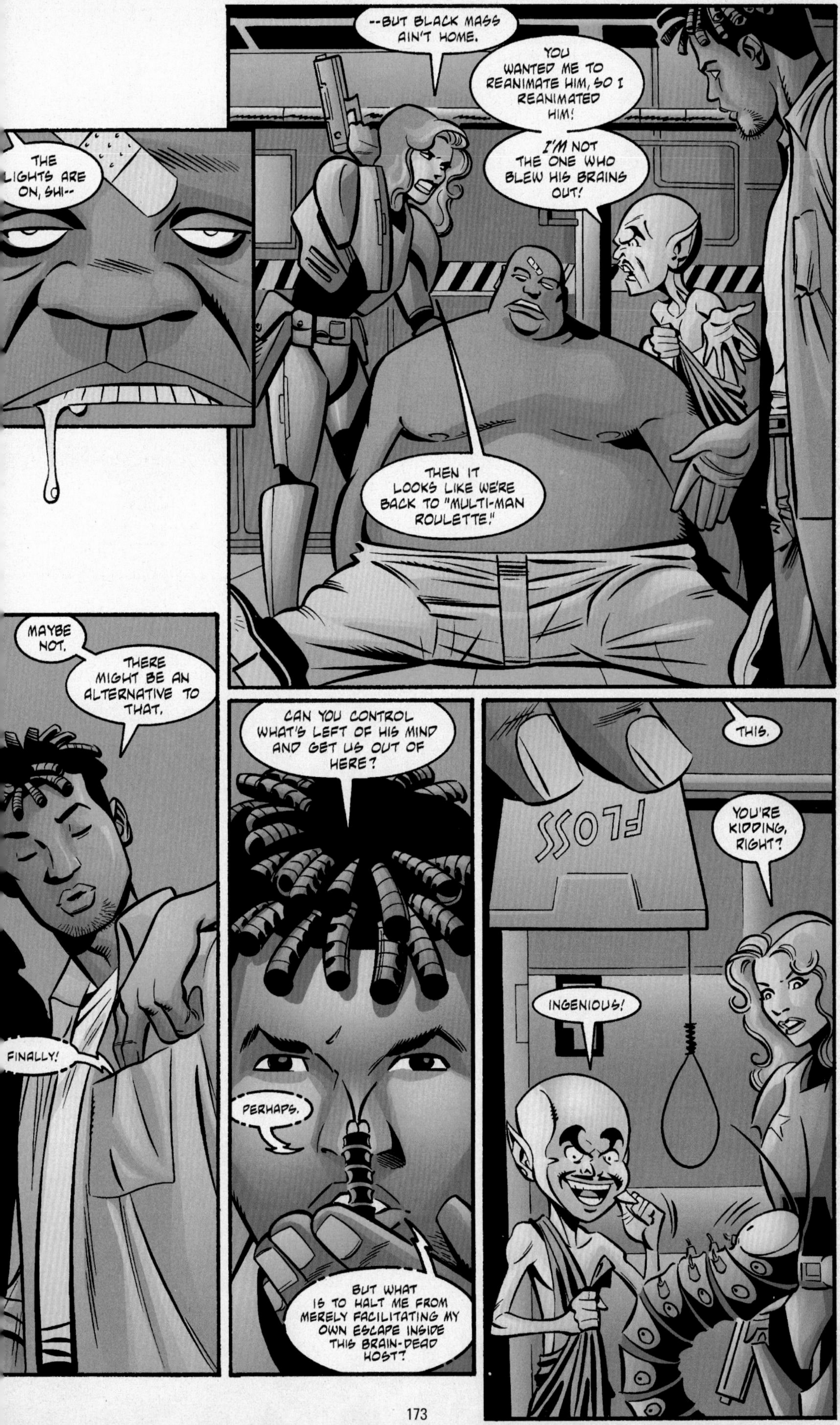
--BUT BLACK MASS AIN'T HOME.
YOU WANTED ME TO REANIMATE HIM, SO I REANIMATED HIM!
I'M NOT THE ONE WHO BLEW HIS BRAINS OUT!
THE LIGHTS ARE ON, SHI--
THEN IT LOOKS LIKE WE'RE BACK TO "MULTI-MAN ROULETTE."
MAYBE NOT.
THERE MIGHT BE AN ALTERNATIVE TO THAT.
FINALLY!
CAN YOU CONTROL WHAT'S LEFT OF HIS MIND AND GET US OUT OF HERE?
PERHAPS.
BUT WHAT IS TO HALT ME FROM MERELY FACILITATING MY OWN ESCAPE INSIDE THIS BRAIN-DEAD HOST?
THIS.
FLOSS
YOU'RE KIDDING, RIGHT?
INGENIOUS!

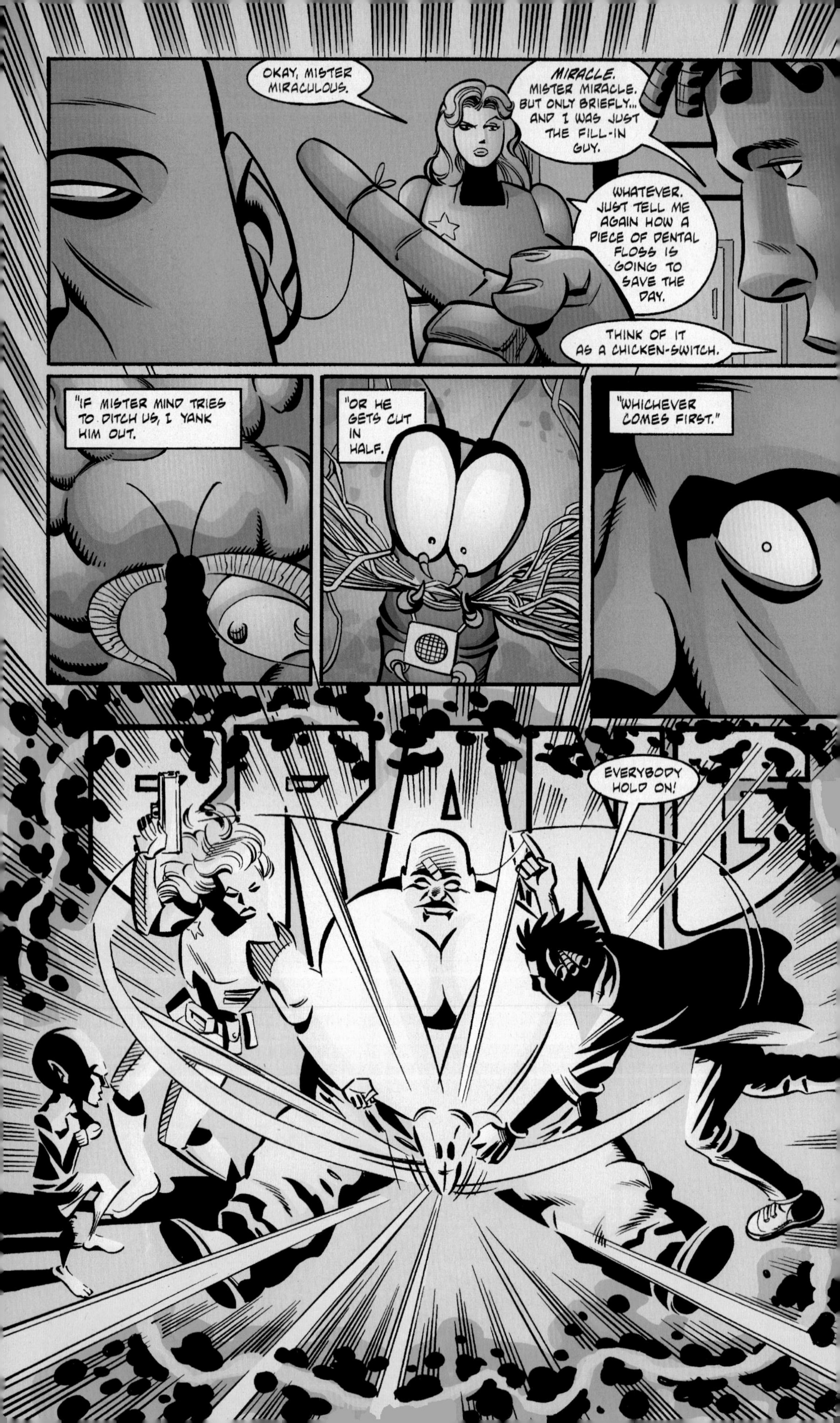
OKAY, MISTER MIRACULOUS.
MIRACLE. MISTER MIRACLE. BUT ONLY BRIEFLY... AND I WAS JUST THE FILL-IN GUY.
WHATEVER. JUST TELL ME AGAIN HOW A PIECE OF DENTAL FLOSS IS GOING TO SAVE THE DAY.
THINK OF IT AS A CHICKEN-SWITCH.
"IF MISTER MIND TRIES TO DITCH US, I YANK HIM OUT.
"OR HE GETS CUT IN HALF.
"WHICHEVER COMES FIRST."
EVERYBODY HOLD ON!

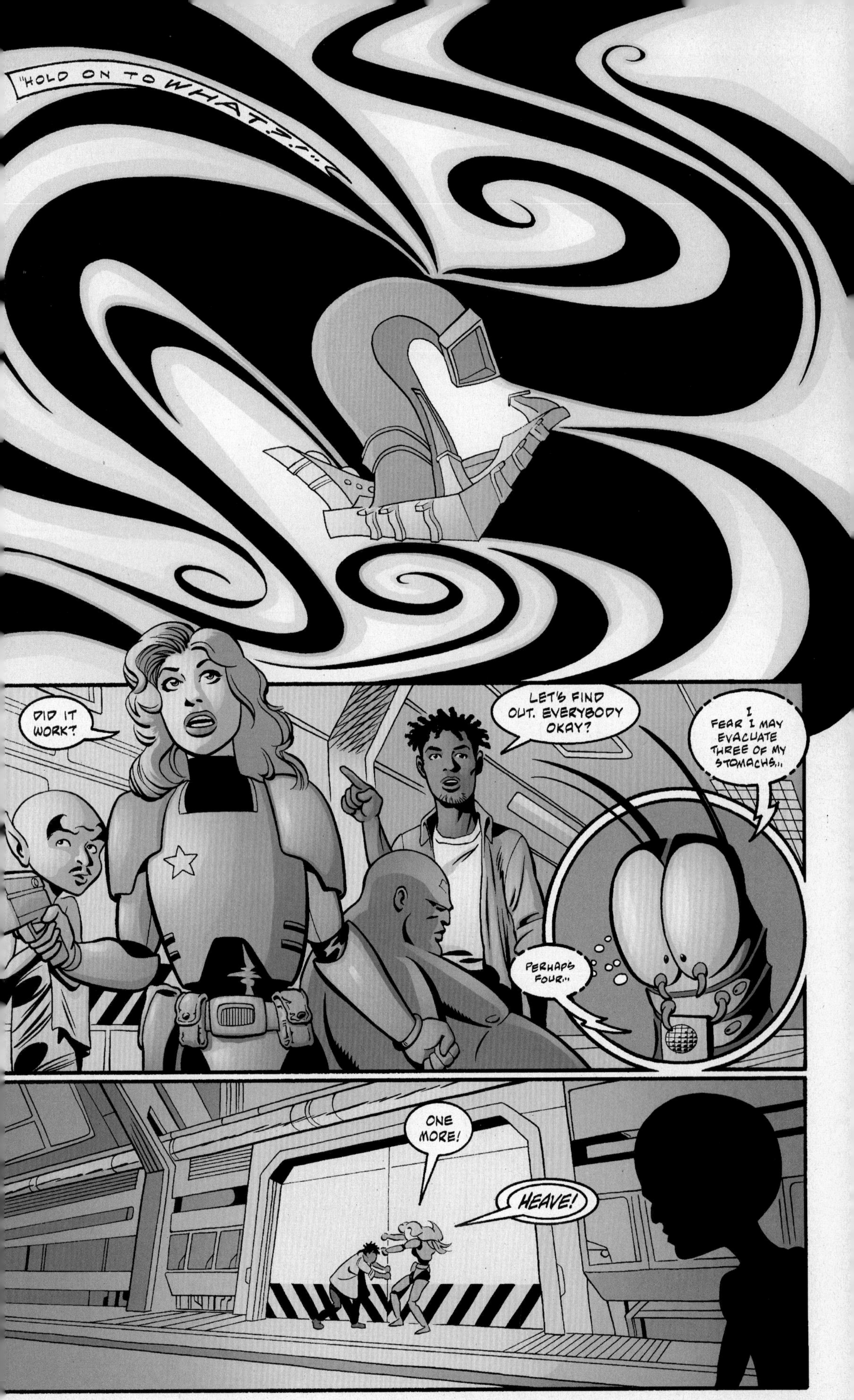
"HOLD ON TO WHAT?!..."
DID IT WORK?
LET'S FIND OUT. EVERYBODY OKAY?
I FEAR I MAY EVACUATE THREE OF MY STOMACHS...
PERHAPS FOUR...
ONE MORE!
HEAVE!

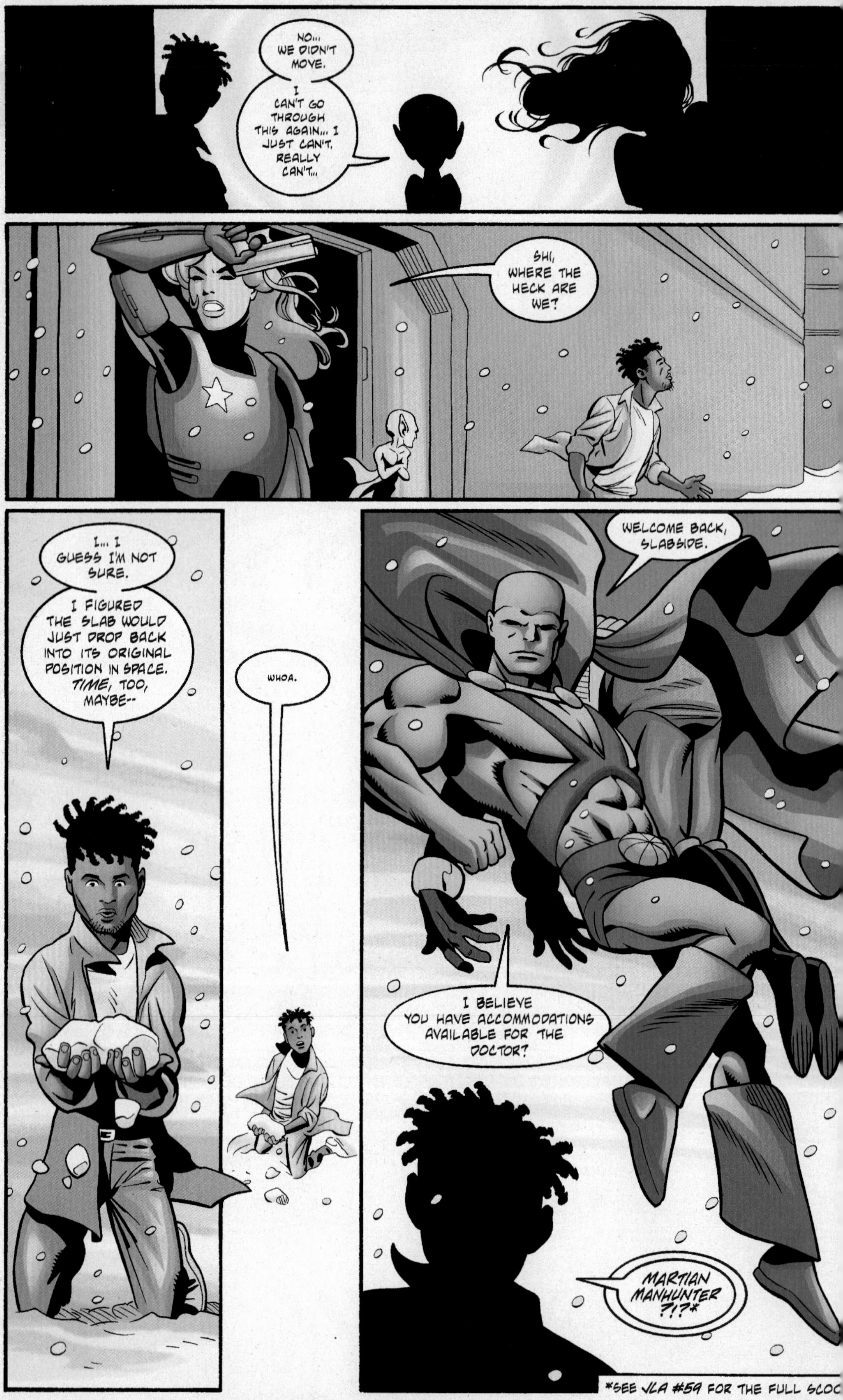
NO... WE DIDN'T MOVE.
I CAN'T GO THROUGH THIS AGAIN... I JUST CAN'T. REALLY CAN'T...
SHI, WHERE THE HECK ARE WE?
I... I GUESS I'M NOT SURE.
I FIGURED THE SLAB WOULD JUST DROP BACK INTO ITS ORIGINAL POSITION IN SPACE. TIME, TOO, MAYBE--
WHOA.
WELCOME BACK, SLABSIDE.
I BELIEVE YOU HAVE ACCOMMODATIONS AVAILABLE FOR THE DOCTOR?
MARTIAN MANHUNTER ?!?*
*SEE JLA #59 FOR THE FULL SCOO

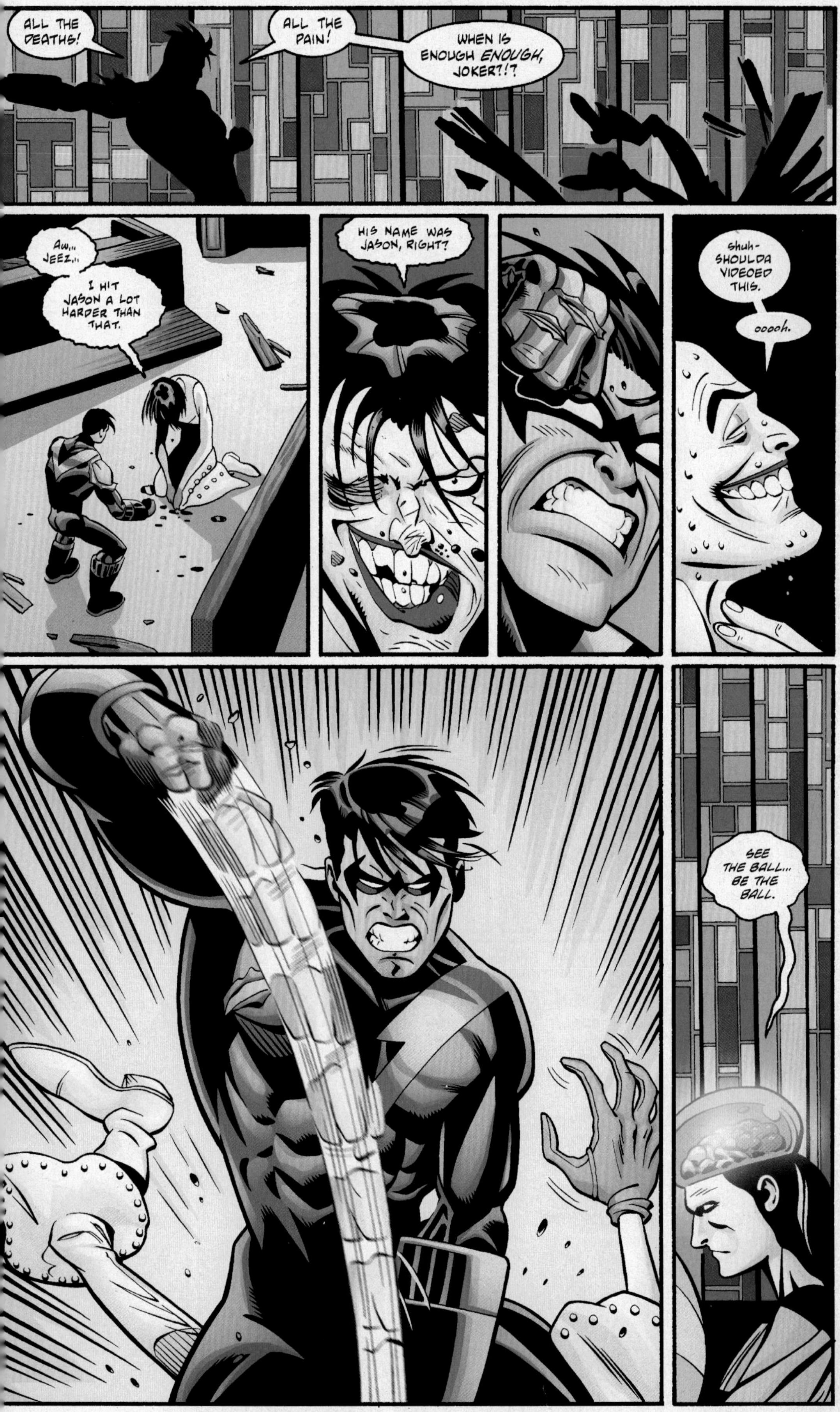

ALL THE DEATHS!
ALL THE PAIN!
WHEN IS ENOUGH ENOUGH, JOKER?!?
Aw... JEEZ...
I HIT JASON A LOT HARDER THAN THAT.
HIS NAME WAS JASON, RIGHT?
SHUH-SHOULDA VIDEOED THIS.
ooooh.
SEE THE BALL... BE THE BALL.

THAT TAKES THE SHIELD DOWN, I GUESS.

THE COPS CAN CLEAN UP THE REST, NIGHTWING.

NIGHTWING!

OH, MAN. TIME TO GO.

FUN'S OVER, WARPY!

D'ACCORD! LET US MAKE OURSELVES--

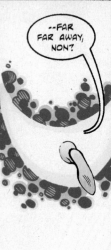

--FAR FAR AWAY, NON?

HE'S HAD ENOUGH, NIGHTWING.

ROBIN?

IT'S ME.

NO,,,

YOU'RE DEAD. IT'S A TRICK.

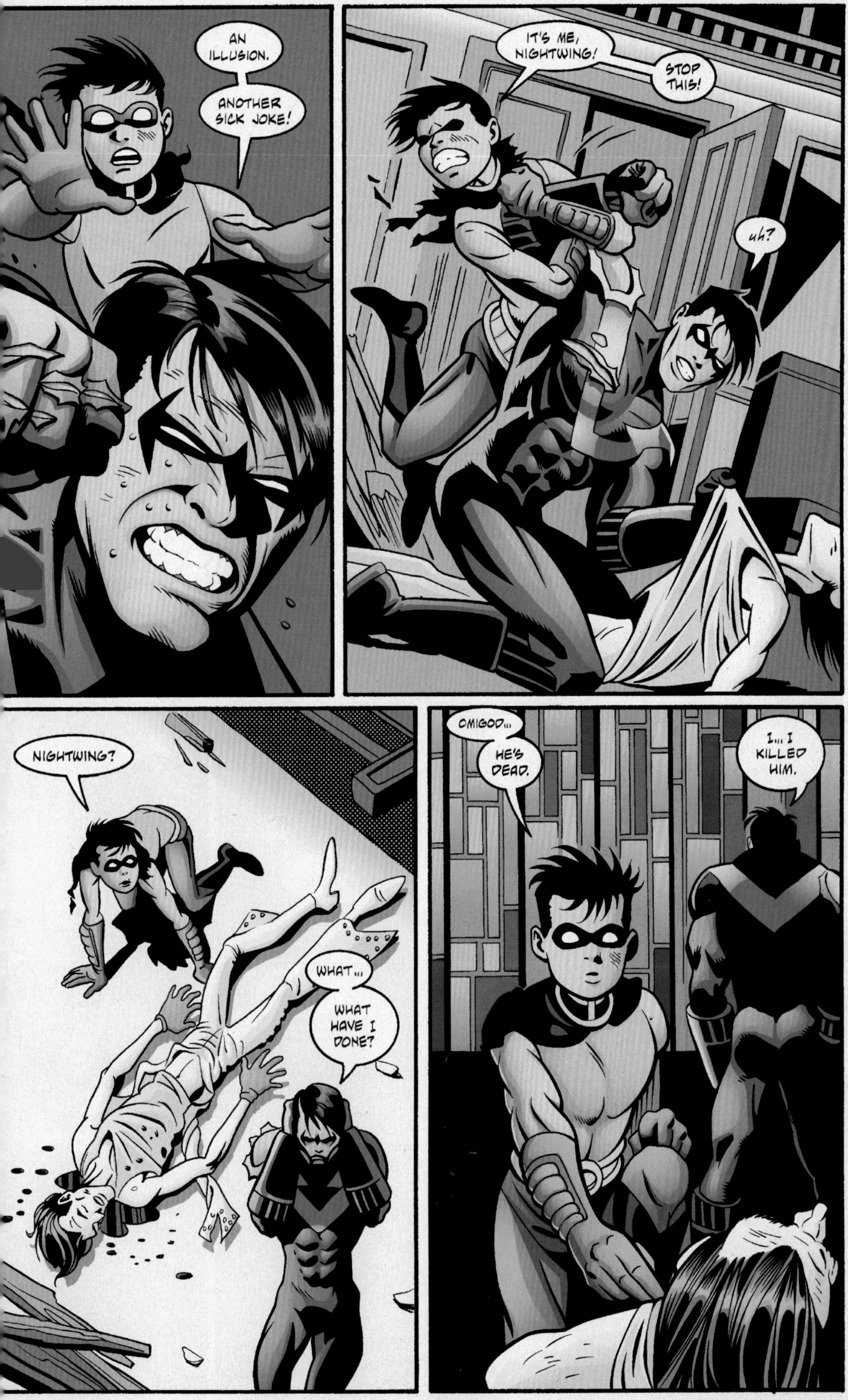

AN ILLUSION.
ANOTHER SICK JOKE!
IT'S ME, NIGHTWING!
STOP THIS!
uh?
NIGHTWING?
WHAT...
WHAT HAVE I DONE?
OMIGOD...
HE'S DEAD.
I... I KILLED HIM.

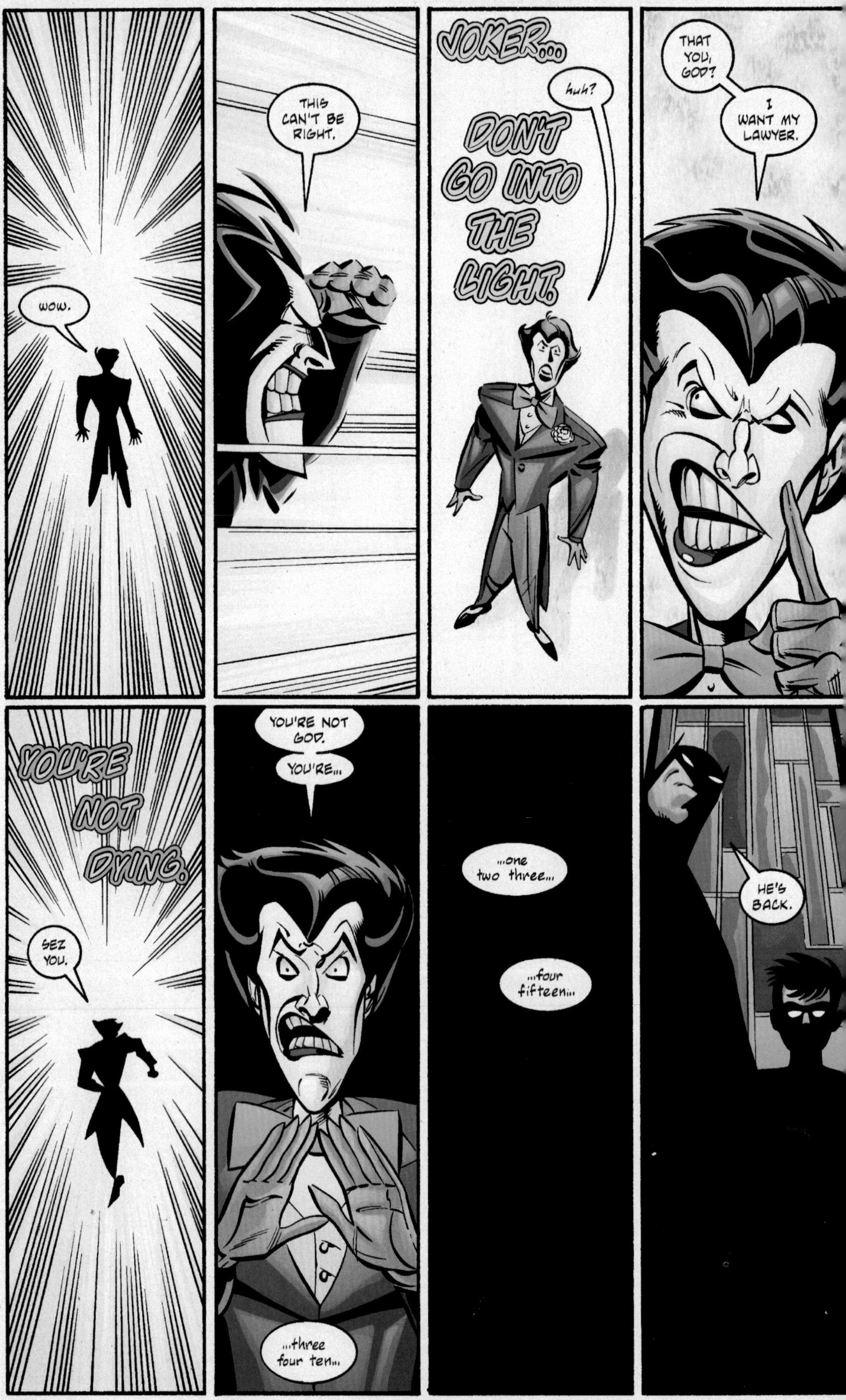
WOW.
THIS CAN'T BE RIGHT.
JOKER...
huh?
DON'T GO INTO THE LIGHT.
THAT YOU, GOD?
I WANT MY LAWYER.
YOU'RE NOT DYING.
SEZ YOU.
YOU'RE NOT GOD.
YOU'RE...
...three four ten...
...one two three...
...four fifteen...
HE'S BACK.

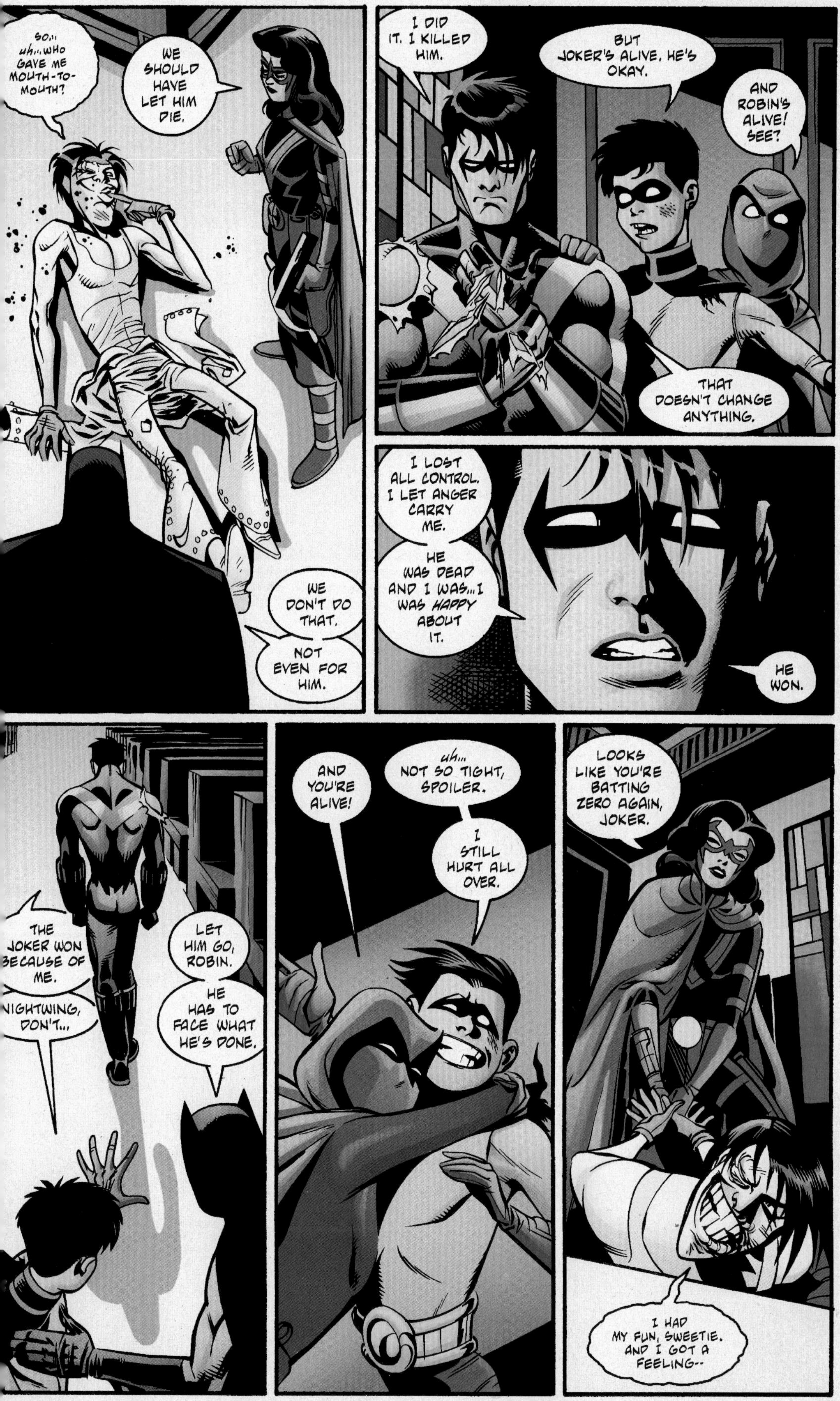
SO... uh... WHO GAVE ME MOUTH-TO-MOUTH?
WE SHOULD HAVE LET HIM DIE.
WE DON'T DO THAT.
NOT EVEN FOR HIM.
I DID IT. I KILLED HIM.
BUT JOKER'S ALIVE. HE'S OKAY.
AND ROBIN'S ALIVE! SEE?
THAT DOESN'T CHANGE ANYTHING.
I LOST ALL CONTROL. I LET ANGER CARRY ME.
HE WAS DEAD AND I WAS... I WAS HAPPY ABOUT IT.
HE WON.
THE JOKER WON BECAUSE OF ME.
NIGHTWING, DON'T...
LET HIM GO, ROBIN.
HE HAS TO FACE WHAT HE'S DONE.
AND YOU'RE ALIVE!
uh... NOT SO TIGHT, SPOILER.
I STILL HURT ALL OVER.
LOOKS LIKE YOU'RE BATTING ZERO AGAIN, JOKER.
I HAD MY FUN, SWEETIE. AND I GOT A FEELING--

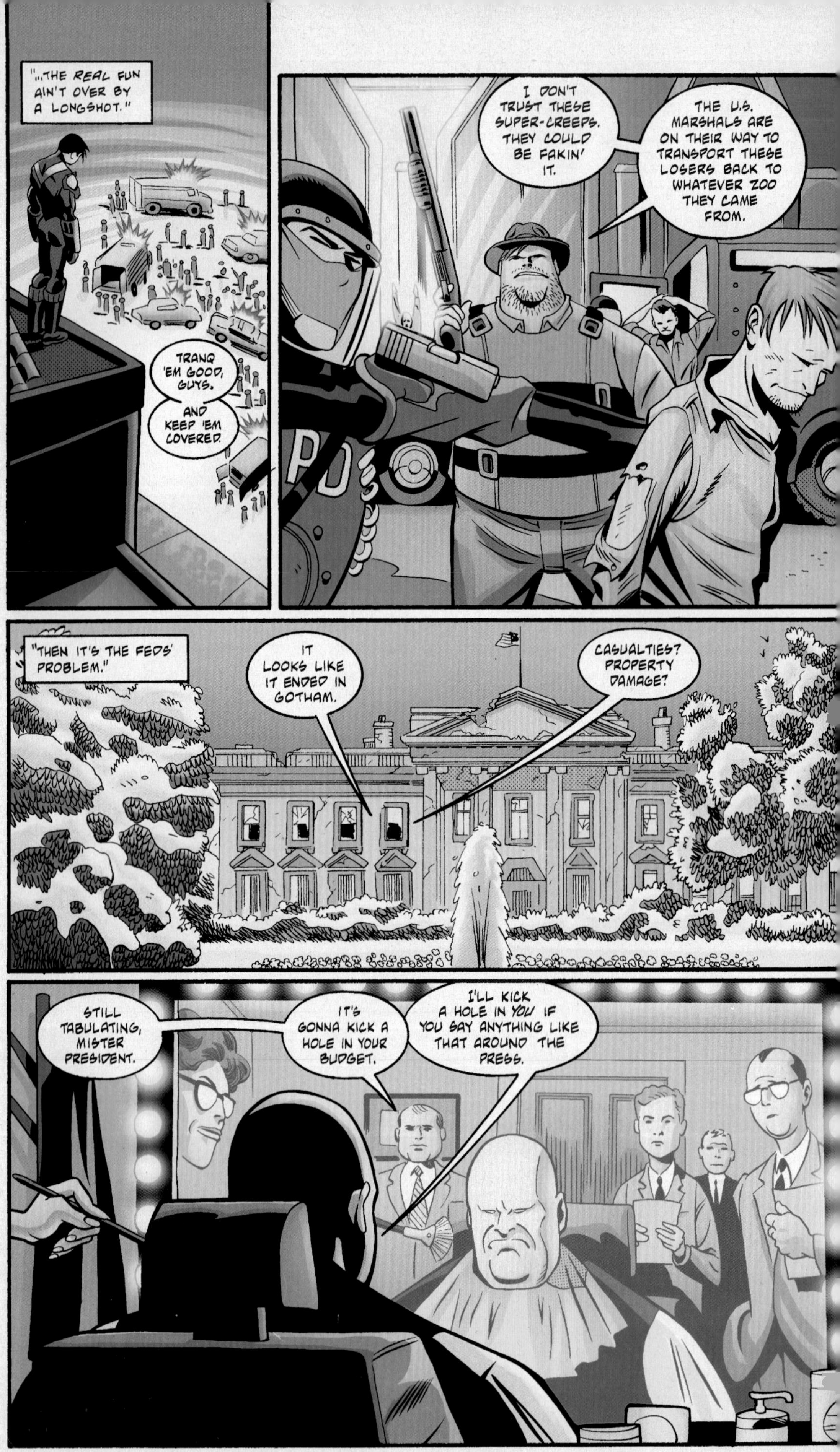
"...THE REAL FUN AIN'T OVER BY A LONGSHOT."
TRANQ 'EM GOOD, GUYS.
AND KEEP 'EM COVERED.
I DON'T TRUST THESE SUPER-CREEPS. THEY COULD BE FAKIN' IT.
THE U.S. MARSHALS ARE ON THEIR WAY TO TRANSPORT THESE LOSERS BACK TO WHATEVER ZOO THEY CAME FROM.
"THEN IT'S THE FEDS' PROBLEM."
IT LOOKS LIKE IT ENDED IN GOTHAM.
CASUALTIES? PROPERTY DAMAGE?
STILL TABULATING, MISTER PRESIDENT.
IT'S GONNA KICK A HOLE IN YOUR BUDGET.
I'LL KICK A HOLE IN YOU IF YOU SAY ANYTHING LIKE THAT AROUND THE PRESS.

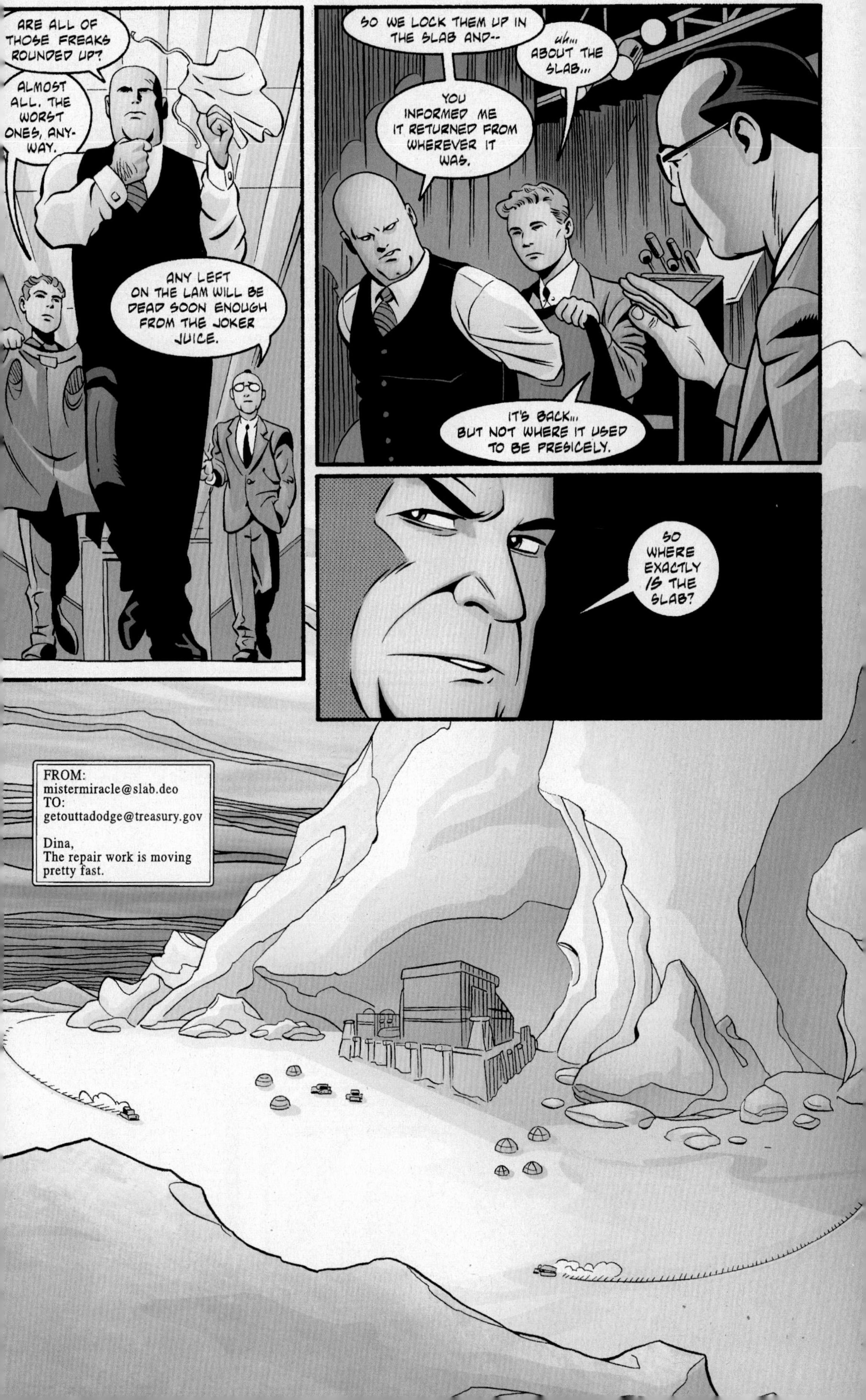
ARE ALL OF THOSE FREAKS ROUNDED UP?
ALMOST ALL. THE WORST ONES, ANYWAY.
ANY LEFT ON THE LAM WILL BE DEAD SOON ENOUGH FROM THE JOKER JUICE.
SO WE LOCK THEM UP IN THE SLAB AND--
YOU INFORMED ME IT RETURNED FROM WHEREVER IT WAS.
uh... ABOUT THE SLAB...
IT'S BACK... BUT NOT WHERE IT USED TO BE PRESICELY.
SO WHERE EXACTLY IS THE SLAB?
FROM:
mistermiracle@slab.deo
TO:
getouttadodge@treasury.gov
Dina,
The repair work is moving pretty fast.

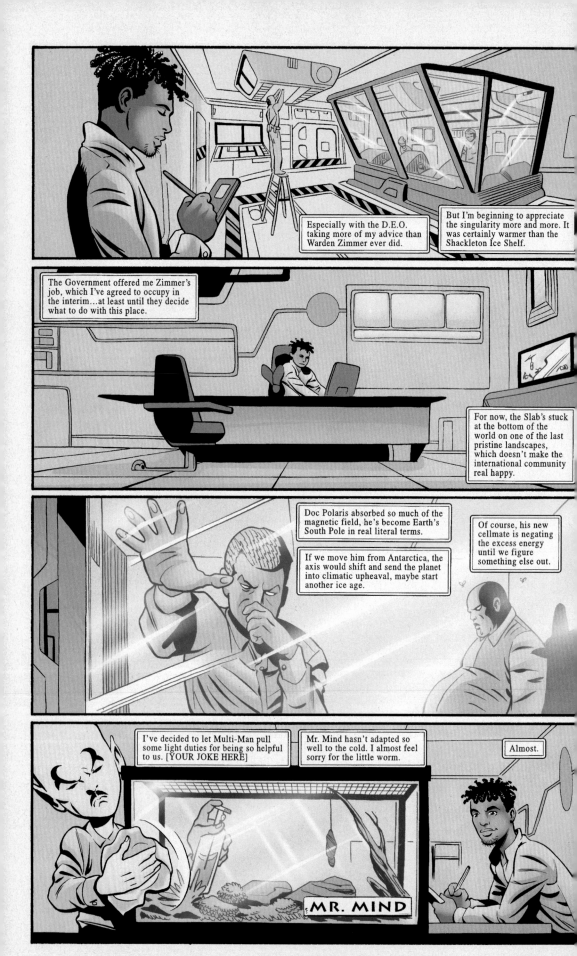

Especially with the D.E.O. taking more of my advice than Warden Zimmer ever did.

But I'm beginning to appreciate the singularity more and more. It was certainly warmer than the Shackleton Ice Shelf.

The Government offered me Zimmer's job, which I've agreed to occupy in the interim...at least until they decide what to do with this place.

For now, the Slab's stuck at the bottom of the world on one of the last pristine landscapes, which doesn't make the international community real happy.

Doc Polaris absorbed so much of the magnetic field, he's become Earth's South Pole in real literal terms.

If we move him from Antarctica, the axis would shift and send the planet into climatic upheaval, maybe start another ice age.

Of course, his new cellmate is negating the excess energy until we figure something else out.

I've decided to let Multi-Man pull some light duties for being so helpful to us. [YOUR JOKE HERE]

Mr. Mind hasn't adapted so well to the cold. I almost feel sorry for the little worm.

Almost.

MR. MIND

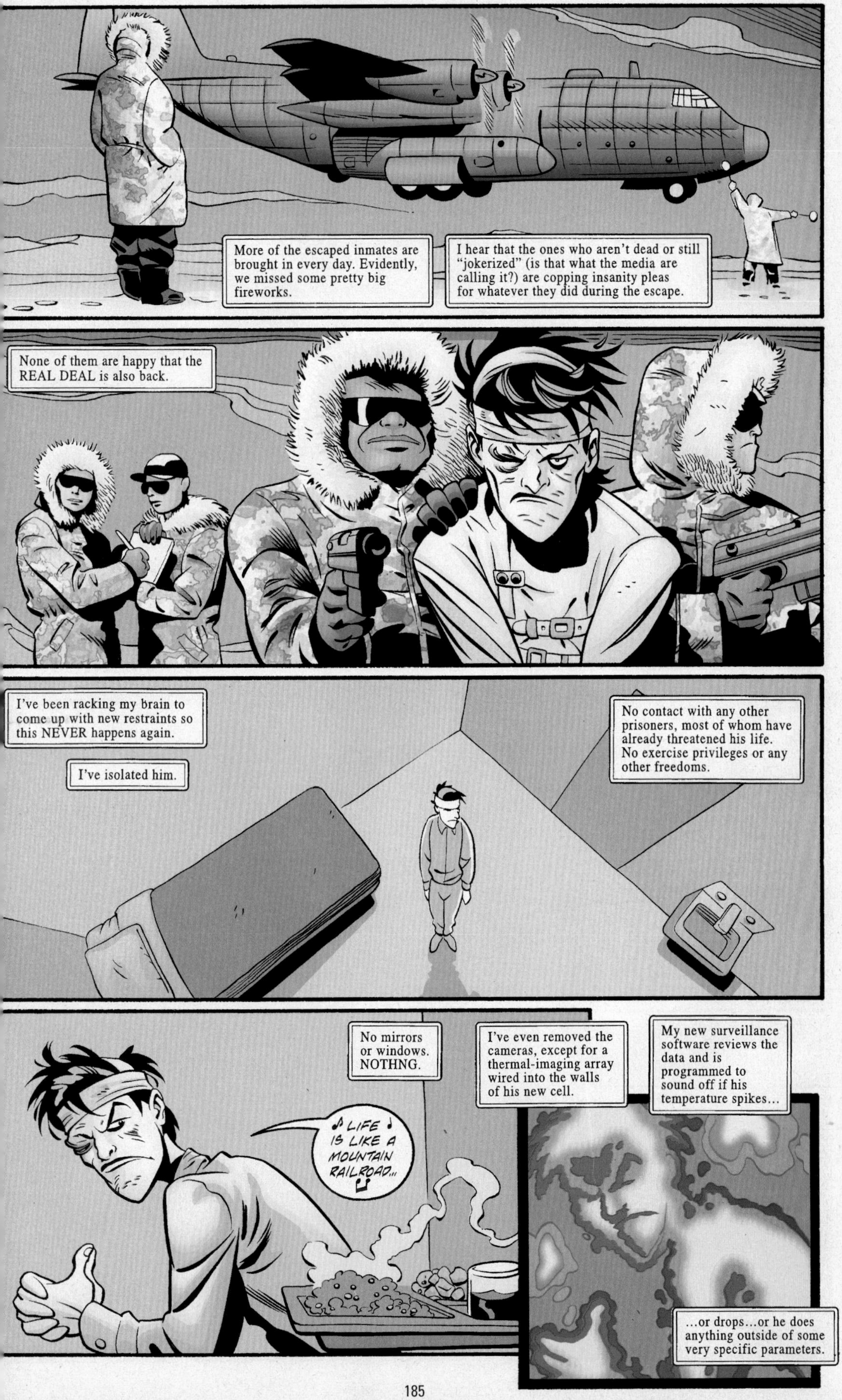
More of the escaped inmates are brought in every day. Evidently, we missed some pretty big fireworks.
I hear that the ones who aren't dead or still "jokerized" (is that what the media are calling it?) are copping insanity pleas for whatever they did during the escape.
None of them are happy that the REAL DEAL is also back.
I've been racking my brain to come up with new restraints so this NEVER happens again.
I've isolated him.
No contact with any other prisoners, most of whom have already threatened his life. No exercise privileges or any other freedoms.
No mirrors or windows. NOTHNG.
I've even removed the cameras, except for a thermal-imaging array wired into the walls of his new cell.
LIFE IS LIKE A MOUNTAIN RAILROAD...
My new surveillance software reviews the data and is programmed to sound off if his temperature spikes...
...or drops...or he does anything outside of some very specific parameters.

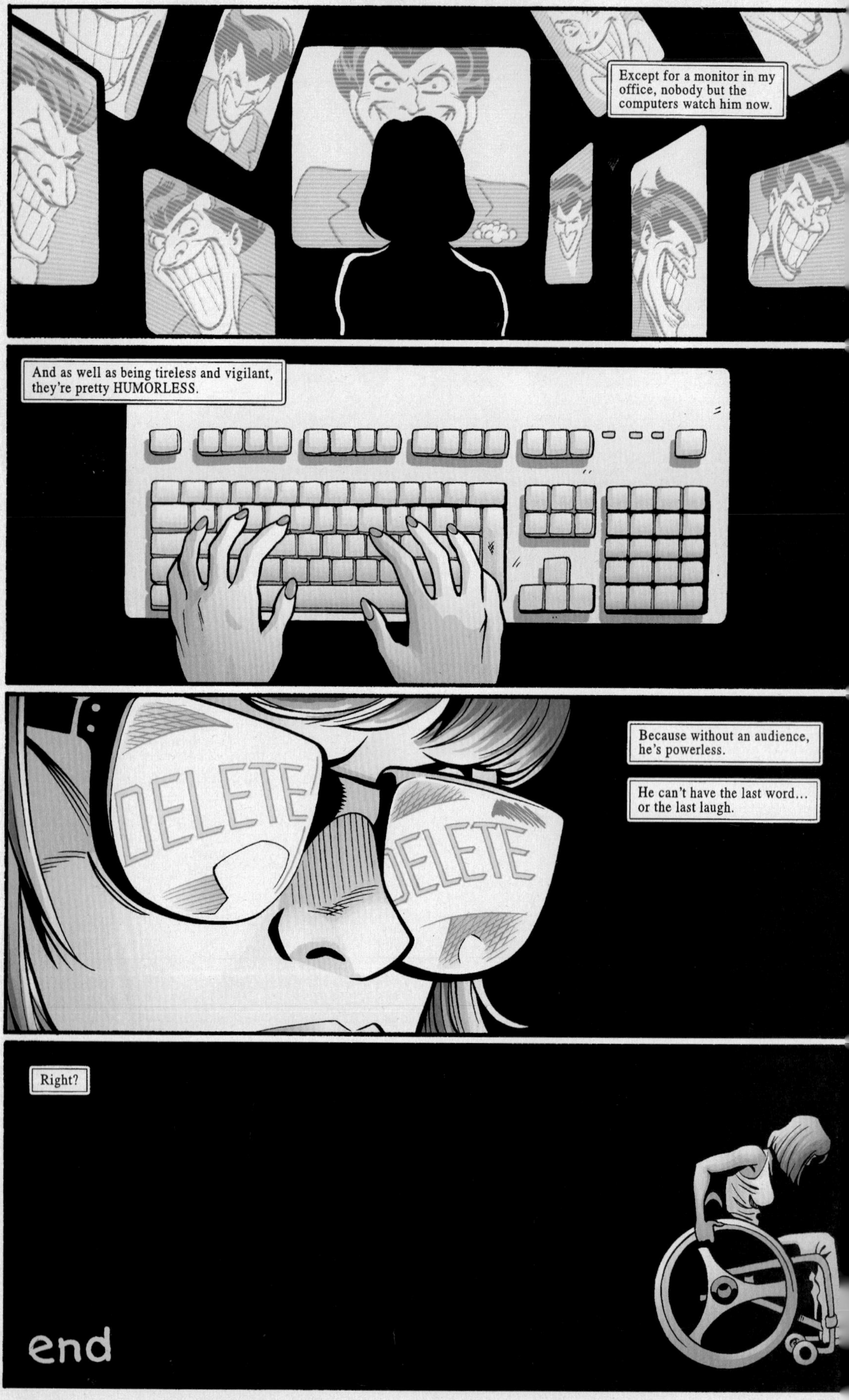
Except for a monitor in my office, nobody but the computers watch him now.
And as well as being tireless and vigilant, they're pretty HUMORLESS.
DELETE
DELETE
Because without an audience, he's powerless.
He can't have the last word... or the last laugh.
Right?
end

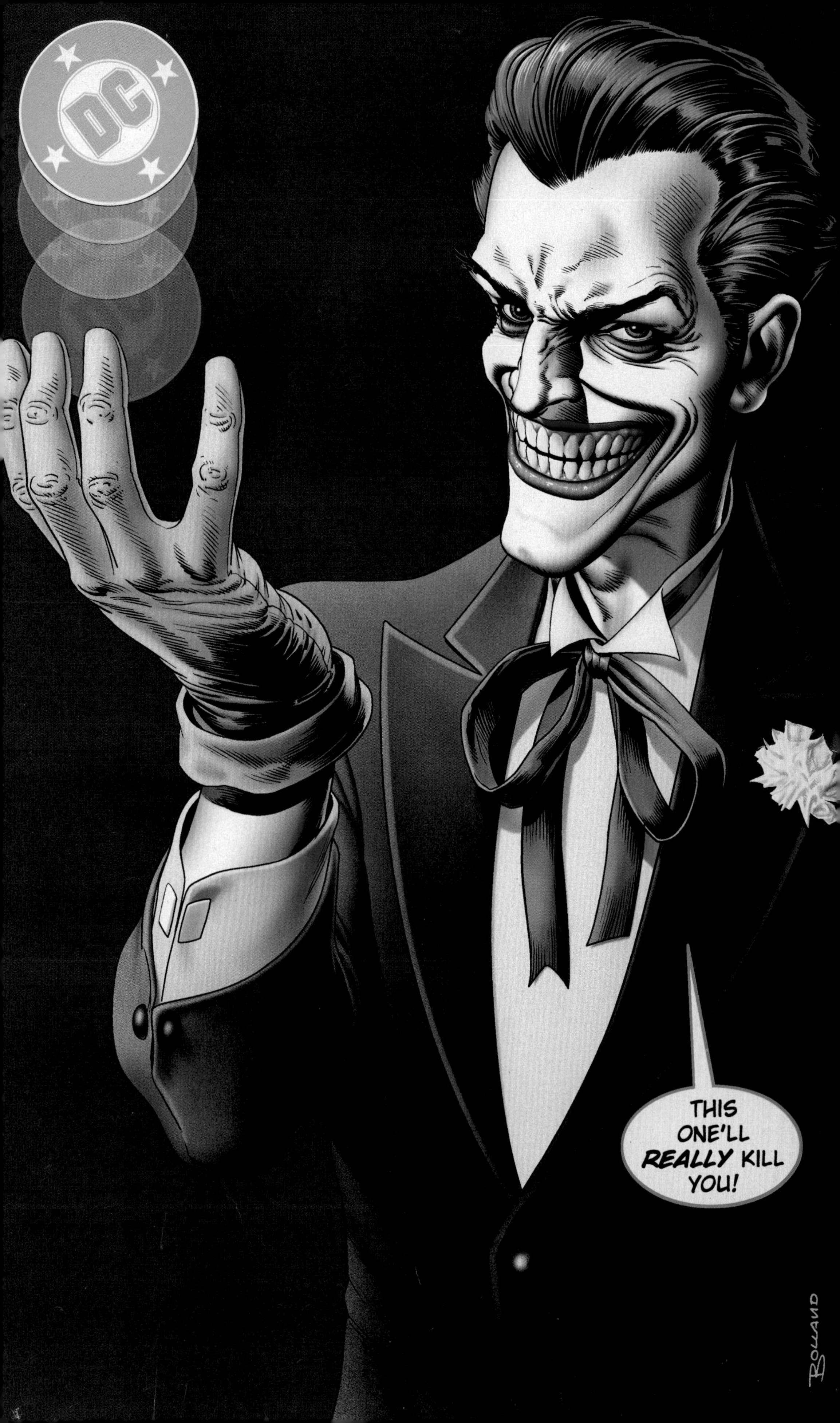
DC
THIS ONE'LL *REALLY* KILL YOU!
BOLLAND

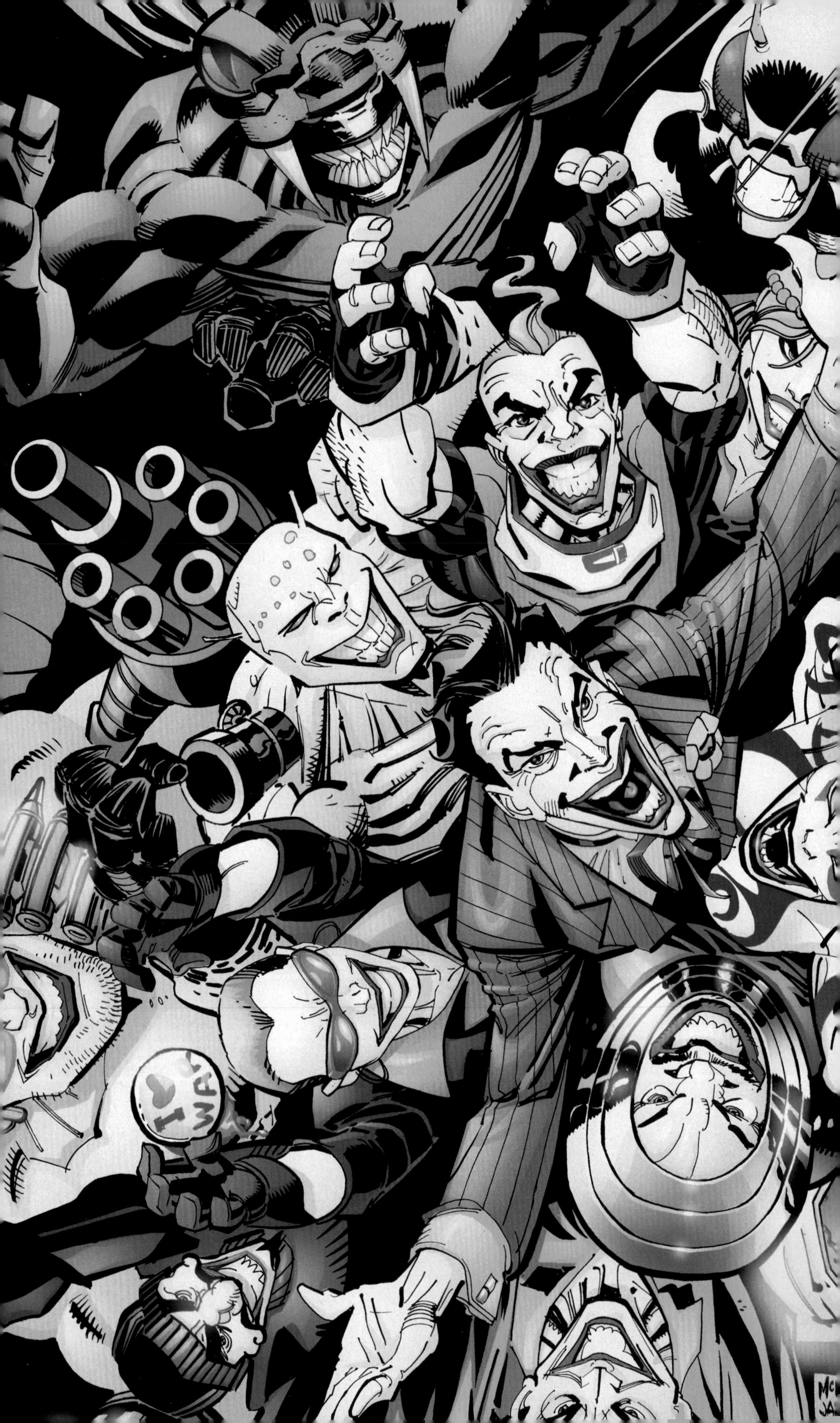

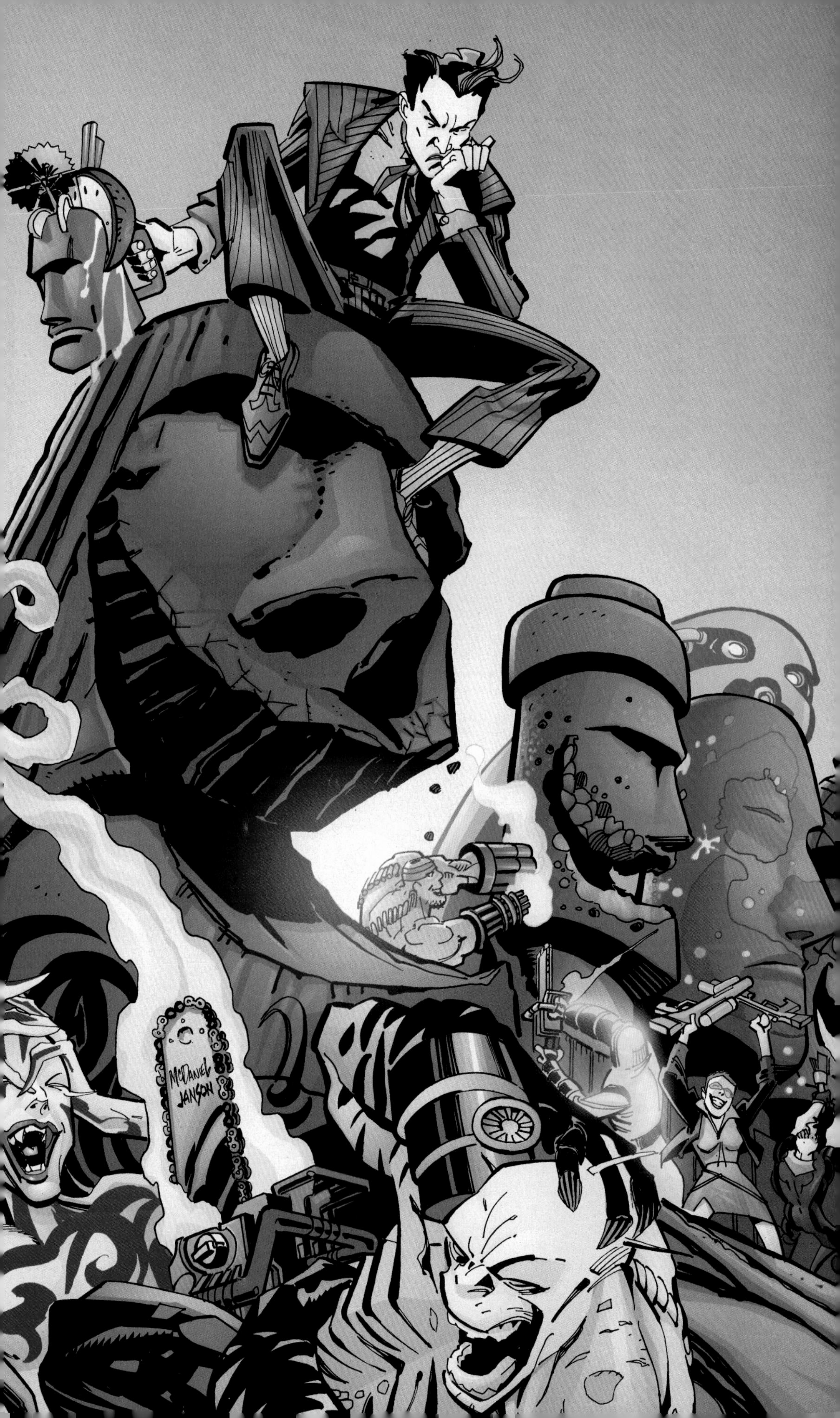
McDANIEL
JANSON

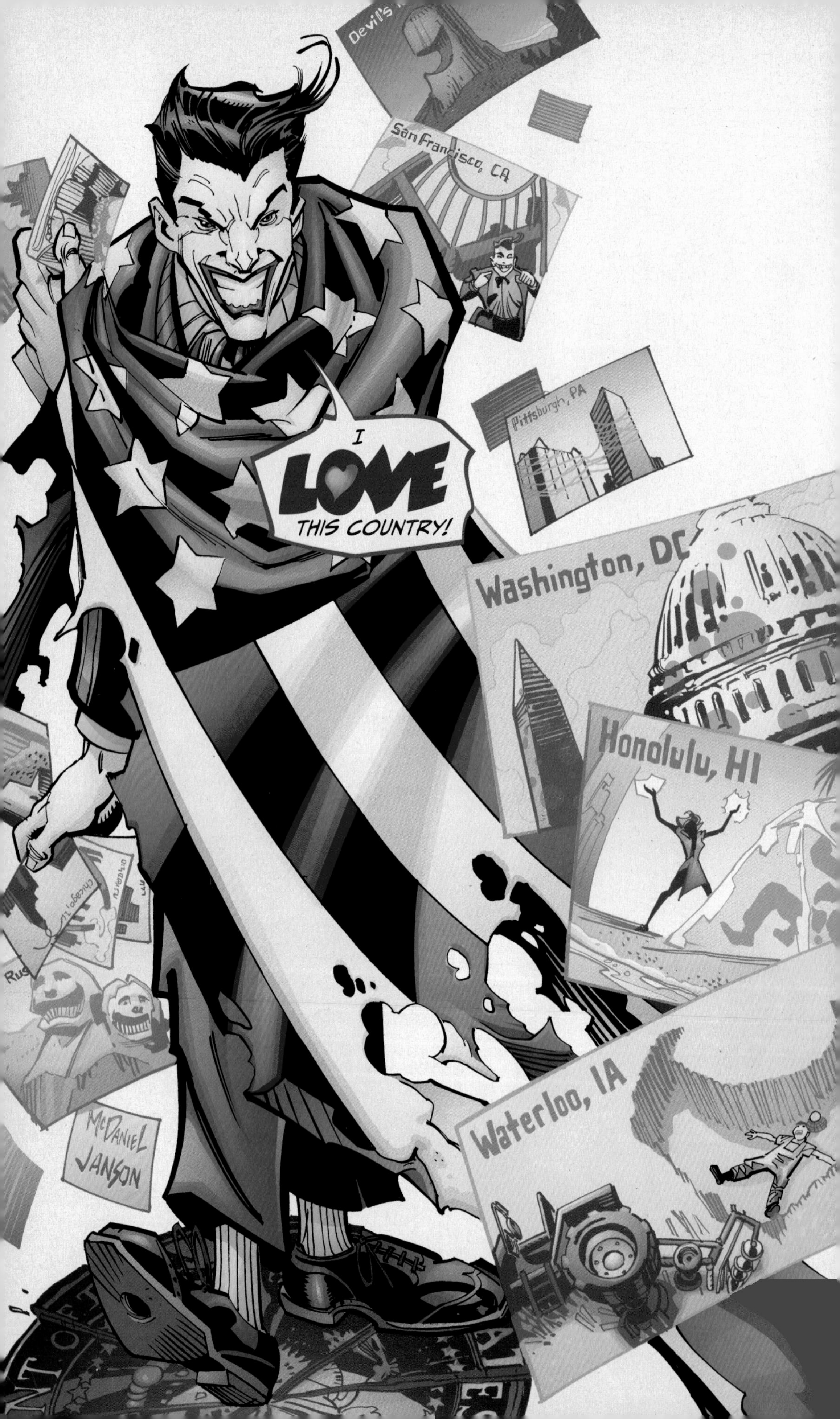
I LOVE THIS COUNTRY!
Devil's
San Francisco, CA
Pittsburgh, PA
Washington, DC
Honolulu, HI
Waterloo, IA
McDaniel Janson

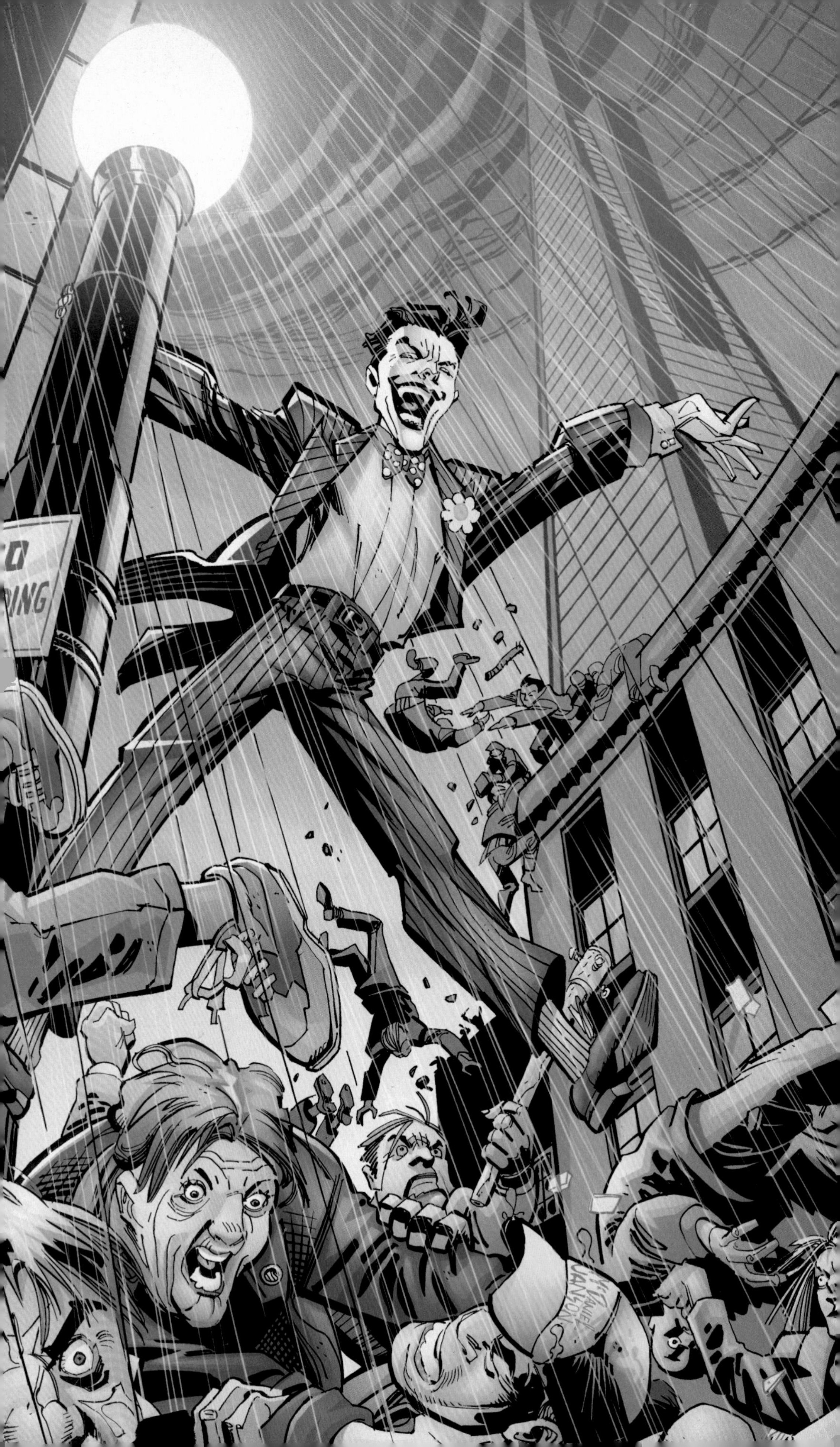

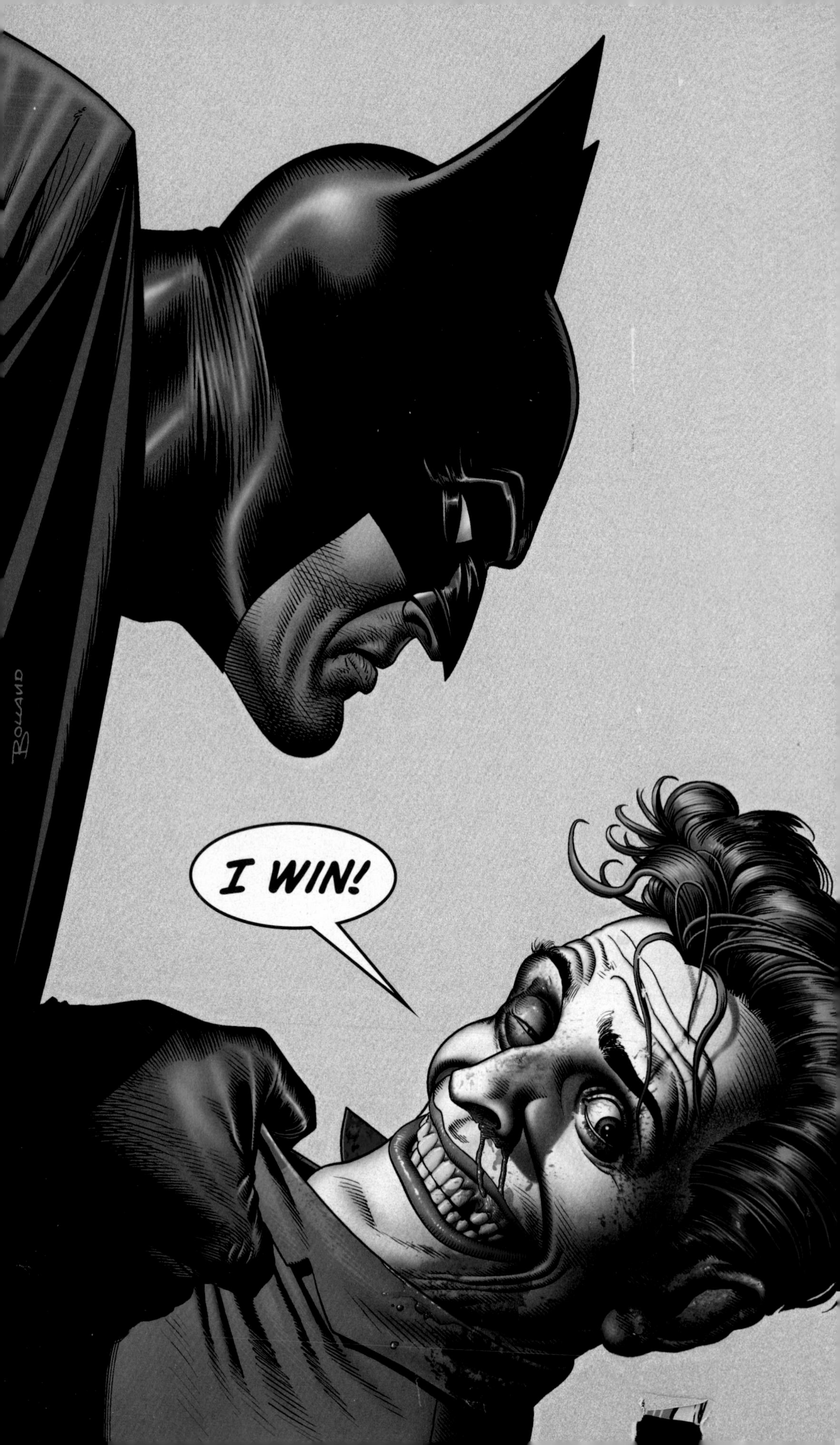
I WIN!
BOLLAND